Nature Sports

This book represents the first international collection that challenges current thinking and research in the emerging field of nature sports. Owing to its inherent connections with fields such as business, leisure, health, tourism and education, this emerging field has attracted perspectives from a wide range of theoretical viewpoints – much of which are discussed within this collection.

In simple terms, nature sports refer to a group of sporting activities that predominantly take place in natural and rural areas. Participation can be both competitive and recreational, with the primary aim to work in relation to nature, where participants seek harmony rather than the quest to conquer it. Within this book, experts from around the globe consider the very essence of nature sport(s), including numerous practical examples of it in action, offering invaluable insights to those both familiar and new to the field. Driven by an increase in non-traditional sports, coupled with growing concerns about the environment, nature sports have experienced significant expansion and interest in both participation and academic debate.

This book is a valuable resource for students and academics in fields such as alternative sports, alternative sport subcultures, sport philosophy, sport and social issues, ethics and phenomenology. It is also a fascinating read for outdoor educators and practitioners. The chapters in this book were originally published as special issues in *Annals of Leisure Research*.

Ricardo Melo is a Professor and Researcher specializing in nature sports and sport tourism, and their contributions to local sustainable development in the environmental, economic and sociocultural dimensions. Currently, he is also interested in learning communities, ecopedagogy, and the connection between leisure and education, especially education that takes place in nature.

Derek Van Rheenen is a Critical Studies Scholar who uses sport to interrogate historical patterns of alienation, discrimination and inequity in schools and broader society. Adopting a critical pedagogy, his scholarship envisions sport as a potential platform for social and environmental justice. Much of his work focuses on the ways in which the intersection of nature sports and sustainability may foster a more just and healthy planet for future generations.

Sean Gammon has been writing and researching in sport tourism for over twenty years – focussing on the experience(s) of the sport tourist and exploring the breadth and significance of sports heritage in generating tourism. He also continues to contribute to the field of leisure studies, where he is currently researching the health-giving properties of leisure states of mind.

Nature Sports

Concepts and Practice

Edited by
**Ricardo Melo, Derek Van Rheenen
and Sean Gammon**

Routledge
Taylor & Francis Group

LONDON AND NEW YORK

First published 2024
by Routledge
4 Park Square, Milton Park, Abingdon, Oxon OX14 4RN

and by Routledge
605 Third Avenue, New York, NY 10158

Routledge is an imprint of the Taylor & Francis Group, an informa business

Preface © 2024 Ricardo Melo, Derek Van Rheenen and Sean Gammon
Chapters 1–14 © 2024 Australia and New Zealand Association of Leisure Studies

British Library Cataloguing in Publication Data
A catalogue record for this book is available from the British Library

ISBN13: 978-1-032-55853-0 (hbk)
ISBN13: 978-1-032-55854-7 (pbk)
ISBN13: 978-1-003-43258-6 (ebk)

DOI: 10.4324/9781003432586

Typeset in Myriad Pro
by Newgen Publishing UK

Publisher's Note
The publisher accepts responsibility for any inconsistencies that may have arisen during the conversion of this book from journal articles to book chapters, namely the inclusion of journal terminology.

Disclaimer
Every effort has been made to contact copyright holders for their permission to reprint material in this book. The publishers would be grateful to hear from any copyright holder who is not here acknowledged and will undertake to rectify any errors or omissions in future editions of this book.

Contents

Citation Information

The chapters in this book were originally published in the journal *Annals of Leisure Research*, volume 23, issue 1 and 2 (2020). When citing this material, please use the original page numbering for each article, as follows:

For any permission-related enquiries please visit:
www.tandfonline.com/page/help/permissions

Notes on Contributors

José Álvarez-García, Department of Financial Economics and Accounting, University of Extremadura, Spain.

Andrew W. Bailey, Department of Health and Human Performance, University of Tennessee- Chattanooga, USA.

Jack Black, Academy of Sport and Physical Activity, Sheffield Hallam University, UK.

Douglas Booth, School of Physical Education, University of Otago, New Zealand.

James Brown, Practitioner in the field of Sustainable Surf Tourism.

Eric Brymer, Carnegie School of Sport, Leeds Beckett University, UK.

Ralf Buckley, School of Environment and Science, Griffith University, Australia.

Raffaella Ferrero Camoletto, Department of Cultures, Politics and Society, University of Turin, Italy.

Jim Cherrington, Academy of Sport and Physical Activity, Sheffield Hallam University, UK.

Andrew Church, Research and Enterprise, University of Bedfordshire, UK.

Loel Collins, Moray House School of Education and Sport Institute for Sport, University of Edinburgh, UK.

María de la Cruz Del Río-Rama, Department of Business Organization and Marketing, University of Vigo, Ourense, Spain.

Amador Durán-Sánchez, Faculty of Business, Finance and Tourism, University of Extremadura, Spain.

Sean Gammon, Lancashire School of Business and Enterprise, University of Lancashire, UK.

Eric Hungenberg, Department of Health and Human Performance, University of Tennessee- Chattanooga, USA.

John H. Kerr, University of British Columbia, UK.

Katherine King, Department of Sport & Events Management Staff, Bournemouth University, UK.

Leon Mach, School for Field Studies, Bocas del Toro, Panama.

Susan Houge Mackenzie, Department of Tourism, University of Otago, New Zealand.

Davide Marcelli, Department of Cultures, Politics and Society, University of Turin, Italy.

Ricardo Melo, Polytechnic Institute of Coimbra, Coimbra Education School, Portugal.

Jess Ponting, Center for Surf Research, San Diego State University, USA.

Kai Reinhart, Department of Sport Education and Sports History, University of Münster, Germany.

Jessica Savage, School for Cross-faculty Studies, University of Warwick, UK.

Nicholas Tiller, Faculty of Health and Wellbeing, Sheffield Hallam University, UK.

Derek Van Rheenen, Berkeley School of Education, University of California, USA.

Preface

Ricardo Melo, Derek Van Rheenen and Sean Gammon

The idea of producing a special issue about nature sports dates back to 2016. The three editors of this book first met in 2014 at the second annual International Research Network in Sport Tourism (IRNIST) Conference organized in Coimbra, Portugal. Professor Ricardo Melo hosted and coordinated the conference and invited Professors Derek Van Rheenen and Sean Gammon to be keynote speakers at the event. We laughed a lot together in addition to learning from fellow scholars in the emerging field of sport tourism. Based on the good times shared, the three of us decided we should work on a project together. Ricardo proposed the idea of developing an edited volume on nature sports.

Ricardo's academic work and research at the time had been focused on the topic. He had finished his PhD about nature sports and local sustainable development in May 2014. But his academic journey studying nature sports started in the beginning of the 21st century, when he pursued a bachelor's degree on this topic, the first sports degree in Portugal with that area of specialization. The course of study was very practical, aiming to prepare future nature sports practitioners to best manage the expanding supply and demand of these type of sports. The degree focused on various nature sport practices, such as mountain biking (MTB), orienteering, rock climbing, hiking, mountaineering, caving, snowboarding, canyoning, diving, kayaking, windsurfing, sailing, paragliding, among other nature sports. Because he was an academic pioneer in the emerging subfield of nature sports, he was invited in 2007 to teach subjects related to these sports within several bachelor's and master's students, mostly in the newly developed Sports and Leisure and Tourism Program at Coimbra Education School – Polytechnic Institute of Coimbra (ESEC–IPC). More than 20 years later, Ricardo remains a nature sports enthusiast, participating in MTB and trail running events, hiking, mountaineering, rock climbing and snowboarding. He is also an Adjunct Professor at ESEC–IPC.

Derek Van Rheenen, a critical studies scholar and accomplished athlete situates sport within the larger political-economic and ideological structures of modern society, defines sport as political struggle. Cutting across all of his research projects is a passion for cultural critique and a corresponding commitment to social change. Based on the urgency promoted by climate change and other environmental crises today, he promotes a hopeful vision in his writings – a politics of possibility and a mandate for moral and political action. One area of focus is at the intersection of nature sports and global sustainability.

Sean Gammon, an expert in sport tourism and leisure studies, has researched extensively in sport tourist encounters including those who actively participate in sport, those who spectate and those who visit sport related attractions. In addition to his work in sport tourism, he continues to contribute to the field of leisure studies, exploring the relationship between positive leisure experiences and subjective well-being.

After our initial decision to collaborate on the topic of nature sports, we began to discuss several options, including publishing a book or a special issue in an academic journal. All of us agreed that the kind of works that we wanted to publish better fits as a special issue in a reputable journal. We agreed we would first publish a special issue, outlining the current state of knowledge into the emerging field and industry. We started the journey by contacting Neil Carr, editor of *Annals of Leisure Research* to determine whether the topic of nature sports for a special issue would be of interest for the journal and its readership. Following his enthusiastic consent, we launched a call for papers. We invited early pioneers and emerging experts in the field to contribute to this special issue. The call for papers generated significant interest from around the world, as we received over 40 submissions for consideration. Based on these novel contributions, we reviewed and edited a two-part series published in 2020 (*Annals of Leisure Research*, volume 23, issue 1 and 2). The special issue was well received, often cited as a foundational volume in the emerging area of inquiry. Three years later, we find ourselves collaborating once again, editing the current book.

Aims of the book

The book, based on our previous special issue, seeks to explore this fertile area of study, encourage dialogue and contribute further to the study of nature sports as a global phenomenon. Contributions address the environmental, economic and socio-cultural dimensions of nature sports. Nature sports are one the fastest growing sports segments and have become a significant focus of the leisure and tourism industries globally. Nature sports have been studied in relationship to the environment, health, education and tourism (Buckley, 2018; Melo and Gomes, 2016; Melo, Van Rheenen and Gammon, 2020a). In spite of such socio-cultural and economic significance, these activities have been largely neglected in the literature and several problems have emerged concerning studies into these activities. One of the first problems has to do with terminology and definition. This is due, in part, because there exists an array of distinct terms with a range of theoretical assumptions describing these practices (e.g., adventure sports, outdoor recreation, etc.). Some works have been conducted attempting to clarify these terminological and conceptual problems, but there has been little to no consensus as to a uniform definition.

Why the term nature sports?

Nature sports emerged as a unifying concept from a collection of terms – action sports, adventure sports, alternative sports, Californian sports, extreme sports, gravity sports, lifestyle sports, nature challenge activities, new sports, outdoor sports, panic sports, risk sports or whiz sports, among others – which encompass a large group of sports activities that have the potential to challenge participants in an innovative way (Melo and Gomes, 2017a; Melo, Van Rheenen and Gammon, 2020a). Collectively, these terms remind us that sport is highly ambiguous, socially constructed and contested, while consistently evolving into new forms and configurations (Booth, 2020; Van Rheenen, 2019).

These sporting activities reflect the social and cultural changes of late capitalism that have taken place since the end of the 20th century, which have triggered a significant transformation within the wider sport system and society at large (Melo, Van Rheenen and Gammon, 2020a; Melo, 2013). Although each of the nature sports has its specificity, its own history and unique identities and patterns of development, there are similarities in their ethos, ideologies, as well as in the consumer industries they help propagate the products that sustain their cultures (Melo, Van Rheenen and Gammon, 2020a; Wheaton, 2004). Nature sports represent a countercultural phenomenon (Collins and Brymer, 2020; Melo, 2017), highlighting the socio-cultural ways in which these new sporting practices have developed in contrast to traditional sport and its dominant values (Melo and Gomes, 2017a; Van Rheenen and Melo, 2021; Wheaton, 2004).

Nature sports comprise a set of sports activities developed and experienced in natural or rural spaces (Melo, Van Rheenen and Gammon, 2020a), involving the dynamic interaction between practitioners and the biophysical environment of spaces – mountains, forests, rivers, oceans, ice, snow, caves, rocky cliffs, etc. – as well as the dynamic forces they create – gravity, waves, thermal currents, rough water, wind, rain, sun, etc. (Booth, 2020; Rinehart, 2017). These activities are carried out in a variety of natural contexts, including in the air (paragliding and hang-gliding, etc.), in rivers, seas or oceans (canoeing, surfing, sailing, windsurfing, etc.), on land (MTB, climbing, trekking, etc.) or even below the earth's surface, such as speleology and deep sea diving.

Nature sports contain a set of characteristics that distinguish them from other types of sports (Melo, Van Rheenen and Gammon, 2020a). These activities are primarily experienced outdoors, in natural environments or in rural areas, although the rise of artificial sites to replicate these activities closer to urban areas has led to interesting conversations around the fluid nature of 'nature' (Bessy and Naria, 2005; Camoletto and Marcelli, 2020). Despite these philosophical inquiries, the connection of these activities to the environment has led to logical discussion into the potential for these practices to promote sustainability efforts, such as protection, preservation and even regeneration.

Nature sports include a sense of adventure and an inherent level of risk, whether real or perceived (Breivik, 2010; Lyng, 2005; Melo, 2017). They have a spontaneous and playful quality, with participation predominantly experienced in informal contexts, often without government bodies or clubs or other forms of external regulation (Melo and Gomes, 2017b; Wheaton, 2016). They are generally autonomous activities, even if some nature sports are practiced collectively, such as canoeing, or those that create sporting subcultures, such as surfing. They are generally non-aggressive activities, which have little to no human body contact (Wheaton, 2013, 2016), involving interaction with a natural or material resource, where participants gain the opportunity to strive, employ and develop their skills in relation to the elements of nature (Krein, 2014).

Although competition is not a fundamental element of nature sports, it does not mean that these activities or events are less intense or dramatic than traditional sports, as they produce their own challenges and emotions, as well as their own forms of unpredictability, tension, suspense and excitement (Booth, 2020). Additionally, some nature sports activities are highly competitive, as evidenced by their inclusion in the modern Olympic Games, such as sailing, windsurfing, mountain biking, surfing and climbing, and in the Winter Olympic Games, such as skiing and snowboarding (Melo, Van Rheenen and Gammon, 2020b). Nonetheless, the underlying logic or structure of nature sports often differ from traditional sports practices (Melo, Van Rheenen and Gammon, 2020a). As such, this unique group of physical activities offers an alternative to traditional ways of seeing, doing and understanding sport (Melo, Van Rheenen and Gammon, 2020a; Van Rheenen and Melo, 2021; Wheaton, 2004).

Scope and purpose of the book

Written by international experts in nature sports, the chapters included in the book are geared towards academic researchers and students, interested in nature sports, sports economics, management and sustainable development, as well as policymakers and professionals tasked with organizing nature sports activities. This book brings together 26 authors from a range of countries, including Europe (Germany, Italy, Portugal, Spain, United Kingdom), the Americas (Canada, Costa Rica, Panama, USA) and Oceania (Australia, New Zealand), illustrating both commonalities and differences in participants' experiences and outcomes.

References

Bessy, O., and O. Naria. 2005. "Les enjeux des loisirs et du tourisme sportif de nature dans le dévelopement durable de la Réunion." In *Management et marketing du sport: du local au global*, edited by P. Boucher and C. Sobry, 307–339. Paris: Éditions Septentrion.

Booth, D. 2020. "Nature Sports: Ontology, Embodied Being, Politics." *Annals of Leisure Research*. doi:10.1080/11745398.2018.1524306.

Breivik, G. 2010. "Trends in Adventure Sports in a Postmodern Society." *Sport in Society* 13 (2): 260–273.

Buckley, R. 2018. "Nature Sports, Health and Ageing: The Value of Euphoria." *Annals of Leisure Research*. doi:10.1080/11745398.2018.1483734.

Camoletto, R., and D. Marcelli. 2020. "Keeping it Natural? Challenging Indoorization in Italian Rock Climbing." *Annals of Leisure Research*. doi:10.1080/11745398.2018.1561307.

Collins, L., and E. Eric Brymer. 2020. "Understanding Nature Sports: A Participant Centred Perspective and Its Implications for the Design and Facilitating of Learning and Performance." *Annals of Leisure Research*. doi:10.1080/11745398.2018.1525302.

Krein, K. 2014. "Nature Sports." *Journal of the Philosophy of Sport* 41 (2): 193–208.

Lyng, S., ed. 2005. *Edgework: The Sociology of Risk-Taking*. New York: Routledge.

Melo, R. 2013. "Desportos de Natureza e Desenvolvimento Local Sustentável: Análise dos Praticantese das Organizações Promotoras dos Desportos de Natureza." Unpublished doctoral diss., University of Coimbra, Coimbra.

Melo, R. 2017. "Understanding Nature Sports Participation: A Literature Review." In *Sport Tourism: New Challenges in a Globalized World*, Coordinates by R. Melo and C. Sobry, 241–275. Newcastle upon Tyne: Cambridge Scholars Publishing.

Melo, R., and R. Gomes. 2016. "Nature Sports and Sustainable Local Development: Practitioners and Organizations Managers' Perspectives in Portugal." In *Sport Tourism and Local Sustainable Development*, edited by C. Sobry, 75–100. Lille: L'Harmattan.

Melo, R., and R. Gomes. 2017a. "A Sociocultural Approach to Understanding the Development of Nature Sports." In *Sport Tourism: New Challenges in a Globalized World,* Coordinates by R. Meloand and C. Sobry, 60–90. Newcastle upon Tyne: Cambridge Scholars Publishing.

Melo, R., and R. Gomes. 2017b. "Nature Sports Participation: Understanding Demand, Practice Profile, Motivations and Constraints." *European Journal of Tourism Research* 16: 108–135.

Melo, R., D. Van Rheenen and S. Gammon. 2020a. "Part I: Nature Sports: A Unifying Concept." *Annals of Leisure Research*, 23, nº 1: 1–18.

Melo, R., D. Van Rheenen and S. Gammon. 2020b. "Part II: Nature Sports: Current Trends and the Path Ahead." *Annals of Leisure Research*, 23, nº 2: 133–142.

Rinehart, R. 2017. "Alternative, Extreme (and Avant-Garde) Sport." In *The Routledge History of American Sport*, edited by L. Borish, D. Wiggins and G. Gems, 414–428. Abingdon: Routledge.

Van Rheenen, D. (2019). "Reproducing Race Logic in Higher Education: Exploitation, Athletic Privilege and Institutional Resentment." In *'Race', 'Racism' and 'Race Logic' in Youth Sport, Physical Activity and Health: Global Perspectives*, edited by S. Dgakas, L. Azzarito and K. Hylton, 87–99. Routledge Critical Perspectives on Equality and Social Justice in Sport and Leisure. New York, NY: Routledge.

Van Rheenen, D., and R. Melo. 2021. "Nature Sports: Prospects for Sustainability." *Sustainability*, 13, nº 16, 8732.

Wheaton, B. 2004. "Introduction: Mapping the Lifestyle Sport-scape." In *Understanding Lifestyle Sports: Consumption, Identity and Difference*, edited by B. Wheaton, 1–28. London: Routledge.

Wheaton, B. 2013. *The Cultural Politics of Lifestyle Sports*. London: Routledge.

Wheaton, B. 2016. "Lifestyle Sport." In *Sport and Society: A Student Introduction*, org. B. Houlihan and D. Malcolm, 109–133. London: Sage Publishing.

Part I

Nature Sports: Concepts and Scopes

Nature sports: a unifying concept

Ricardo Melo, Derek Van Rheenen and Sean Gammon

Introduction

Nature sports serve as the contextual reference for this special issue. These sports, also labelled action sports, adventure sports, alternative sports, Californian sports, extreme sports, gravity sports, lifestyle sports, nature challenge activities, new sports, outdoor sports, panic sports, risk sports or whiz sports, among others (Bourdieu 1979; Pociello 1981; Midol and Broyer 1995; Rinehart and Sydnor 2003; Wheaton 2004, 2013, 2016; Booth and Thorpe 2007; Davidson and Stebbins 2011; Melo and Gomes 2017a; Rinehart 2017; Durán-Sánchez, Álvarez-Garcia, and Del Río-Rama 2019), comprise a group of physical activities that have the potential to challenge participants in a novel way and provide an alternative to the traditional ways of seeing, doing and understanding sport (Wheaton 2004).

Despite their semantic differences, these terms represent distinctive ways of looking at this countercultural phenomenon (Collins and Brymer 2018; Melo and Gomes 2017a). As such, these terms have tended to highlight the socio-cultural characteristics of these sports that have emerged in contrast to traditional sports and their dominant values (Bourdieu 1979; Rinehart and Sydnor 2003; Wheaton 2004; Booth and Thorpe 2007; Breivik 2010; Melo and Gomes 2017a).

In this regard, modern sports are popular culture practices defined by political and ideological struggle (Bourdieu 1978; Van Rheenen 2014). That is, while dominant forms of sporting practices often reproduce dominant cultural ideologies, such as the reigning race, class and gender relations at a particular moment and place in time (Carrington and MacDonald 2009; Van Rheenen 2013), these cultural practices are also contested, providing the potential for resistance and counter-hegemonic expression (Fairclough 2001; Andrews 2006; Reinhart 2019; Whannel 2009).

Nature sports activities emerged in recent decades, especially after the flourishing of a new sport paradigm that had its origin in North America in the 1960s and 1970s (Bourdieu 1979; Pociello 1981; Wheaton 2016). These practices emerged in line with the new values and social demands that developed within the praxis of active leisure time (Betrán and Betrán 1995), significantly reshaping the field of modern sport. These transformations are reflected in the system of practices, where their evolutions can be identified globally (Durán-Sánchez, Álvarez-Garcia, and Del Río-Rama 2019; Pociello 1981) and that, in some way, explain the evolution of the concept of sport itself.

Nature sports involve either the creation of new activities such as windsurfing, mountain biking and hang-gliding or the adaptation of older residual cultural forms, such as the (re)emergence of surfing culture in California in the 1960s, or sport climbing in rock climbing (Camoletto and Marcelli 2019; Wheaton 2004). The emergence of these new sporting modalities in Europe took place through a dual and dynamic process. On the one hand, through the importation of new sports such as surfing, windsurfing and free flying, by the members of the great and new petty bourgeoisie (Bourdieu 1979; Pociello 1981). On the other hand, by the creation of new modalities through a process of internal differentiation of stabilized practices (Pociello 1981), such as skiing and canoeing, which have given rise to new modalities such as off-piste skiing or freestyle canoeing, respectively (Melo 2013).

These novel modalities tend to emphasize the risk factors – real or perceived – that are inherent in these sports (Breivik 2010), as well as the characteristics associated with the lifestyles of their practitioners (Wheaton 2004). However, as Collins and Brymer (2018) discuss the risk-focused perspective might assume that participants are only interested in thrills and excitement, ignoring the opportunities that these activities have for enhancing health, well-being and more meaningful connections to nature. In particular, as Houge Makenzie and Brymer (2018) argue a growing body of literature supports the proposition that a positive psychology framework can expand current conceptualisations of nature sport participation beyond thrill or sensation seeking.

Nature sports have experienced worldwide growth in the last several decades. The diffusion of these unique sporting practices globally has generated a desire to better understand this historical phenomenon. In particular, efforts at defining and conceptualizing this diverse set of physical activities has led scholars and practitioners to frame the boundaries and contours of this emerging field of enquiry. The following section highlights some of these key conceptual themes.

Key conceptualizations and characteristics of nature sports

What are nature sports? 'Nature sports' is an expression that has emerged in recent years as a sports field that is related to the leisure and tourism industries, but also with environment, health and education. Nature sports comprise a group of sporting activities that are developed and experienced in natural or rural areas, ranging from formal to informal practices, and which may contribute to sustainable local development (Melo and Gomes 2017a), although some question the assumed linkages between nature sports participation and a genuine ethic of care for the environment (Booth 2018). These practices are performed in a variety of natural contexts including in the air (paragliding and hang-gliding, etc.), on land (mountain biking, rock-climbing, trekking, etc.) and in water (kayaking, sailing, surfing, windsurfing, etc.).

According to Bessy and Mouton (2004), the nature sports designation only arose in the late twentieth century, and was associated with the emergence of new sports venues in nature and the increased number of participants taking part in a set of social and structural practices. Nature sports reflect the social and cultural changes of late capitalism that have taken place in the last decades, which have had repercussions in the economic, technological and hyper-mediated environment.

These changes have triggered a deep transformation within the system of sports practices (Melo 2013). Although each nature sport 'has its own specificity; its own history, (politics of) identities and development patterns, there are commonalities in their ethos, ideologies as well as the consumer industries that produce the commodities that underpin their cultures' (Wheaton 2004, 11). In this sense, nature sports is a complex concept which presents a set of specific characteristics that will be emphasized throughout the articles of this two part special issue. These themes and characteristics have also been found in the wider literature, as exemplified and embodied within specific sports and contexts:

Nature based activities – Nature sports are developed outdoors in natural (with or without environmental protection) or rural areas. These natural spaces constitute the base for the practice of nature sports activities even if, to facilitate their practice, these spaces are modified through the placement of equipment and/or the construction of infrastructure or facilities to support these activities (Melo 2013).

In this context, nature can be defined for the purpose of this definition as any natural setting perceived by practitioners as at most only minimally modified by human beings (Stebbins 2019). Examples of these spaces are the sea, rivers and other watercourses, canyons, mountains, snowfields, cliffs, rock faces, forests, caves, the sky, etc. Nature sports involve a dynamic interaction between participants and these natural features (Krein 2014), as well as the dynamic forces that create them – waves, gravity, thermal currents, wind, rain, sun (Booth 2018; Rinehart 2017). Contact with nature is also seen as the main reason for practice (Melo and Gomes 2017a), as a form of avoidance and escape from an everyday life that is routine, mundane and controlled, providing new sensations, emotions and other states of consciousness, and enabling experiences of which individuals do not have regular access to, especially in urban environments (Melo 2013).

Excluded from the scope of what we have termed nature sports activities here are those practices developed in urban (e.g. skateboarding), artificialized (e.g. bungee jumping) or indoor (e.g. indoor rock climbing) spaces, and also motorized sports (e.g. motocross), hunting and fishing, garden visits, and golf (Bessy and Naria 2005; Melo 2013). However, as Camoletto and Marcelli (2019) demonstrate the dichotomy between indoor and outdoor spaces within a sport such as climbing has become less rigid over time, recognizing 'nature' as a frame of reference rather than a fixed context and rigid analytical construct.

Sustainable activities – Nature is also related with sustainability and, in this regard, nature sports correspond to a set of activities, products, and services directly connected to nature, associating its practice with the new trend towards ecological consumption (Melo 2013). Nature sports have tended to become more sustainable, soft and discrete activities, representing a relationship of complementarity with nature (Joaquim 1997). These activities correspond to a clear manifestation of and a trend for eco-consumption (Gomes 2009), a green version of the adventure activities (Breivik 2010), following an ideological trend of the post-modern taste for the ecological (Betrán and Betrán 1995).

This dimension of participation in nature sports suggests that these practices are a recent historical phenomenon and a trend structurally anchored in contemporary ways of life (Bessy and Naria 2005). In this regard, Chazaud (2004) and Pociello (1981) point to the tendency of naturalization or greening of sports practices. Brymer and Gray (2009), in their empirical work on the representation of nature, also report that there is an ecocentric relationship between these sports and nature, a relationship that is described by participants in these activities as omnipresent and ubiquitous, a source of innate power.

On the other hand, Gomes (2009) points out that eco-activities, such as eco-tourism, eco-leisure and eco-sports, represent the imaginary construction of a return to a wild nature, to a lost paradise, and a new search for the local roots of a given locale. Nature sports evoke the search for an identity rooted in an idealized territory or place (Melo 2013). The search for the perfect wave by surfers, the majestic place for flight by paragliders, or an unspoiled and exotic path for people who practice trekking is often connected to a kind of spiritual symbolism or quest, based simultaneously on a wandering and contemplative attitude (Gomes 2009; Melo 2013).

Adventure and risk activities – The search for new experiences, sensations of adventure, and the challenge to abilities associated with the risk factor (real or perceived) are, in addition to connections to nature, the most accentuated reasons for practicing nature sports (Melo and Gomes 2017b). The 'voluntary risk taking' (Lyng 2005) emerges as a form of compensation or adaptation to the imperatives of (post)modern society (Breivik 2010; Melo 2017) and, in this sense, nature sports activities appear as an ideal way of respecting these imperatives.

However, adventure and risk are presented in the field of nature sports practice in a paradoxical way. On the one hand, the challenge to test bodily limits has been observed in these practices. Ultra-marathons offer one such example, where participants travel more than 200 kilometers, over the course of more than 24 consecutive hours (Cherrington, Black, and Tiller 2018). The attempt to achieve new feats and new records (e.g. faster ascension of higher and higher mountains), practiced by experienced adventurers, acknowledges real risks and dangers. On the other hand, the market has witnessed the emergence of a set of commercialized activities that emphasize a high level of perceived risk, when in fact the risk is relatively small or non-existent (Melo 2013). Marketing efforts intentionally promote these activities for inexperienced individuals, who believe these activities pose a great challenge to their capabilities (Dolnicar and Dickson 2004; Palmer 2004; Melo 2013). In this regard, nature sports participants embrace and even fetishize notions of risk and danger (Lewis 2004; Wheaton 2004).

Hedonistic and non-competitive activities – Nature sports activities reveal a demand for other types of sports sociabilities, promoting comradarie, human connectedness and greater conviviality (Pociello 1981). Results of several studies (e.g. Melo 2013; Wheaton 2013) have revealed the hedonistic tendency of society, coupled with a greater demand for independent and informal activities that require less organizational commitment. Conversely there has been a decreased demand for organized activities that require a greater commitment (e.g. sport clubs).

Despite some nature sports activities which remain competitive in scope, even aspiring to Olympic modalities, such as sailing, windsurfing, mountain biking (cross-country) and more recently surfing and rock-climbing, the structure of nature sports activities often varies from traditional or dominant sporting practices. These activities involve interacting with a natural or material feature, rather than with other human beings, and participants gain the opportunity to strive, employ, and develop their skills in relationship to nature (Krein 2014). They are non-aggressive activities that involve no human bodily contact (Bourdieu 1979; Wheaton 2013). In this regard, nature sports participants' behaviours, preferences and the benefits accrued differ from other sport participants.

Although nature sports participants seek health and fitness benefits, they have a different set of motivations that change the emotional state involved in the nature sports hactivities experience, quickly changing from a state of tension to one of calm (Butts 2001). This allows a sense of spirituality and transcendence (Watson 2007) that facilitates 'flow', 'thrill', the 'sublime' (Booth 2018; Stranger 2011), 'rush' (Buckley 2012), 'slow time' (Wittmann 2011; Arstila 2012; Buckley 2014), 'euphoria' (Buckley 2018), and 'hedonic' and 'eudaimonic' outcomes (Houge Mackenzie and Brymer 2018) rather than competition (Krein 2014).

Autonomous and individualistic activities – Nature sports are predominantly individualistic activities in form and attitude (Wheaton 2013), even if some nature sports are practiced collectively, such as kayaking, or create the formation of sporting sub-cultures, such as in surfing. Nature sports have a spontaneous nature, 'with participation predominantly taking place in informal settings, often without governing bodies or clubs or other forms of external regulation' (Wheaton 2016, 117).

In this regard, nature sports symbolize a sense of spatial, temporal and institutional autonomy (Melo 2013). Space autonomy refers to the freedom that practitioners seek to practice their respective activities in different locations and to gain new spaces for practice. The spaces correspond, in most circumstances, to open terrain, such as the sea, air, river or mountain, and are unbound (in a normalized and regularized way) by human action. Spatial boundaries are usually imposed by geographical accident (e.g. confluence between the sea and beach sand, or between sky and land), by physical ability (e.g. to reach the peak of a mountain or to ride a mountain bike course) or practitioners' technique (e.g. to climb a difficult path or to surf a larger or more dangerous wave). It is a phenomenon that Pociello (1981) has previously designated as the deterritorialization of nature sports practices.

Temporal autonomy refers to the possibility of a practice based on the individual's self-interest and decision-making, independently of others, during his or her free time, whether during the week or weekend, whether in the morning or afternoon. In spite of this autonomy, time remains, in contemporary society, one of the most critical factors in participant decision-making, as it is the main constraint for the practice of nature sports (Melo and Gomes 2017b).

Finally, institutional autonomy describes the possibility of participants' self-organization of these practices, including the size and make-up of social groups associated with these activities (Melo 2013; Wheaton 2013). Institutional autonomy also refers to the possibility of choosing between different sports activities, and socio-organizational contexts, ranging from the most informal to the most organized options (Melo 2013).

Active participation activities – Nature sports correspond mostly to a participatory ideology that contributes to an active lifestyle. These activities are predominantly about participation rather than spectating (Wheaton 2013), which implies a 'commitment in time, and/ or money and a style of life and forms of collective expression, attitudes and social identity that develops in and around the activity' (11).

Nature sports relationships

The importance of nature sports is also evidenced by the growing attention given to other sectors, including, leisure, tourism, the environment, health and education. In this regard, the following part of this editorial will explore the relationships between nature sports and these various sectors.

Nature sports and leisure

Leisure has generally been associated with terms such as relaxation, recuperation, triviality, frivolity, and freedom from obligation (Green and Jones 2005). These authors have argued that 'the term "leisure" is, in contemporary society, now so broad ranging that it has little analytical usefulness as a concept with which to explain non-obligatory activities' (Green and Jones 2005, 165), such as nature sports. However, for many individuals, participation in nature sports activities such as kayaking, mountain biking, mountain climbing, rock climbing, surfing, and snowboarding, among others (Bartram 2001; Kane and Zink 2004; Stebbins 2005; Dilley and Scraton 2010; Davidson and Stebbins 2011; Getz and McConnell 2011; Portugal et al. 2017), include involvement and progression in the form of a career, commitment and significant personal effort to acquire skills or knowledge, a sense of belonging and the acquisition of an ethos of a defined culture, the need to persevere in learning, the expectation of receiving benefits resulting from participating, and an identity that results from participating in the selected activities (Melo 2017).

This is what Stebbins (1992) has previously defined as serious leisure,

> the systematic pursuit of an amateur, a hobbyist, or a volunteer activity that participants find so substantial and interesting that, in the typical case, they launch themselves on a career centred on acquiring and expressing its special skills, knowledge, and experience. (3)

From our perspective, nature sports can be classifiable in all four types of serious pursuits: amateur, hobbyist, career volunteer and occupational devotee. It should be noted, however, that Stebbins (2019) focuses on a lack of inter-human competition within what he refers to as nature challenge activities (NCAs) and categorizes them as a sub-type of 'activity participation hobby' rather than as a 'hobbyist sport.'

Certainly some participation in nature sports activities can be considered casual rather than serious leisure, since effort and challenge are minimal and they occur in contexts where individuals only participate once or twice in a nature sports activity, either to have an introductory experience and/or to be able to say they have done it (Davidson and Stebbins 2011; Melo 2017).

It is also possible to undertake pre-planned projects in nature sports activities (Davidson and Stebbins 2011; Melo 2017). For example, nature sports participants can enrol in 'a surf trip during a week that would have been planned in advance by booking ahead the accommodation, transport and other appropriate services, and putting aside the money and time needed to do it' (Melo 2017, 236). This is directly related to tourism and the development of a specific type of tourism connected to nature sports.

Nature sports and tourism

Natural contexts (e.g. the environment) and nature sports are major components of tourism (Hall and Page 2006; Gammon 2015). The relationship between nature sports and place(s) is evident from the fact that a significant number of these sports are dependent on specific types of environments. These environments generally exist in places located at a distance from participants' home, meaning that travel and tourism are required (Higham and Hinch 2009; Melo and Gomes 2016a, 2016b).

Indeed, the growing demand for travel related to sport has created the need for a new tourism segment, referred to as sport or sports tourism (Gammon and Robinson 2003; Weed and Bull 2004; Melo and Sobry 2017; Van Rheenen et al. 2017). Active participation in nature sports is directly associated with active sport tourism, one of three major components of sport tourism (Gibson 1998). Active nature sport tourism can be divided into five types of travel: (i) independent travel where nature sports participants take part in informal nature sports activities such as climbing, hang-gliding, surfing or snorkelling; (ii) organized travel where participants hire the services of a touristic company or agency to engage in specific nature sport tourism activities, such as white water rafting; (iii) travel to participate in nature sports competitions such as trail running events; (iv) travel to develop skills in a particular practice and/or prepare for sports competitions, such as surfing camps and (v) travel where tourists take advantage of nature sports facilities at a holiday destination, though nature sport is not the primary purpose of the trip, such as participating in kayaking, trekking, and mountain biking.

As Gammon and Robinson (2003) have argued, these types of active sport tourism travel refer to different motivations for the trip, ranging from primary (sport participation as the main motive for travel), to secondary and even tertiary motives (trips that follow other main motivations, such as the sun and sea).

Figures indicate that the nature-based tourism market, which includes soft (e.g. trekking) and hard nature sports (e.g. rafting, kayaking and hiking), is often presented as the fastest growing segment within the tourism industry, with an increase of between 10% and 30% per year (Mehmetoglu 2007; Balmford et al. 2009). Further, it is estimated that 10–20% of all global international travel, directly or indirectly, is related to the enjoyment of, and interaction with, nature (Centre for Responsible Travel 2015).

The relationship between nature sports and tourism has drawn considerable attention to the potential and real environmental, economic and socio-cultural impacts of these activities, both positive and negative. These impacts can be observed in surfing (Mach et al. 2018) and climbing (Bailey and Hungenberg 2018), as well as in other nature sports activities (Melo and Gomes 2016a, 2017c). In addition to these contributions, numerous leisure and tourism scholars have discussed these tripartite impacts in terms of the triple bottom line (Elkington 1997; Getz 2009; Dwyer 2015; Van Rheenen 2017), seeking to enhance positive outcomes while mitigating the negative impacts. Nature sports have a particular focus on these activities relative to the environment.

Nature sports and the environment

The development of nature sports has corresponded socially and historically with the articulation of environmental policies. Nature sports and other outdoor recreation activities developed in the USA in part because of the national policies regarding the preservation of land in the second half of the nineteenth century, conservation and management of natural spaces in the late nineteenth century, and in particular through the creation of the national park system in the beginning of the twentieth century (Jensen and Guthrie 2006). The creation of the park system in the USA, followed by similar initiatives throughout the world, allowed the combination of wildlife protection with the practice of nature sports and other recreational opportunities (Bell 2008).

Recognizing the need for local and global strategies to address environmental concerns, the Brundtland Report – Our Common Future (WCED 1987), followed by the United Nations Conference on Environment and Development held in 1992 in Rio de Janeiro, in 1995 in Copenhagen, and in 2002 in Johannesburg, placed the concept of sustainable development on the world political agenda. Sustainable development is linked to three fundamental dimensions: economic development, social cohesion and protection of the environment, which are interconnected but also interdependent (Melo 2013). Nature sports are directly related with this concept of sustainability, as has been previously discussed within this editorial.

Despite the potential negative environmental impacts that may occur as a by-product of these activities, such as noise and visual pollution, soil erosion, water and air pollution, natural landscape destruction, fauna and flora destruction, and the deterioration of monuments and historic sites, nature sports promise the possibility of environmental conservation and protection when developed and managed in a sustainable and intentional manner (Melo and Gomes 2016a). The various sites and facilities developed for these activities (trails, tracks, routes, take-off and landing areas, mooring buoys, submerged paths, shops, parking, etc.) have contributed to sound conservation management practices, thus reducing the exploitative use of the natural environment, allowing nature sports participants to enjoy nature without harming it (Melo 2013).

As a first step, nature sports promote the active and sensitive discovery and appreciation of heritage sites. As a second step, these activities ensure an appropriation and defence of the latter, since participants who immerse themselves in nature (at least potentially) become aware of the beauty and grandeur of these places, creating the possibility for the construction of an eco-citizenship (Melo 2013). For example, Brymer, Downey, and Gray (2009) suggest that 'feeling connected to nature leads to a desire to care for the natural world and contributes to more environmentally sustainable practices' (193). In this regard, nature sports participants develop an intimate and reciprocal relationship with the natural world (Brymer and Gray 2010).

Nature sports guides and service providers have an important role in the promotion of sustainability, acting as environmental interpreters, role models and activists (Weiler and Davis 1993; Pereira and Mykletun 2012; Melo and Leite 2018).

Space and land management, as discussed in King and Church (2019), remain important areas for the conservation of the environment, where nature sports and conservation combine to create a symbiotic relationship based on sustainability. Ideally, a positive economic impact can help maintain ecosystem protection, while a healthy ecosystem provides the venue for sustainable market supply, even growth (Boley and Green 2016). Beyond these management strategies for environmental protection and conservation, another significant social benefit of nature sports participation is the potential positive impact on health.

Nature sports and health

The connection between nature sports and health has been highlighted by several authors (Frumkin et al. 2017; Buckley, Brough, and Westaway 2018; Kerr and Houge Mackenzie

2018; Hough Mackenzie and Brymer 2018). Buckley (2018) argues that contact with nature through the practice of nature sports contributes to physical, psychological and social health and well-being. Europarc Federation (2018) has stated that there is increasing evidence that access to the natural environment, including practicing nature sports activities, can help guard against, treat and manage key health issues such as depression, coronary heart disease and stroke, type 2 diabetes, obesity, and dementia. Other key benefits have also been highlighted, such as therapeutic and restorative qualities which enhance recovery, reduce social isolation, and lead to greater community cohesion and opportunities to establish lifelong healthy behaviours (Europarc Federation 2018).

Evidence from several reviews (Buckley and Brough 2017a, 2017b) has demonstrated that poor mental health imposes a range of social and economic costs on the economies of developed nations, in aggregate equivalent to around 10% of their GDP, but that these costs can be decreased or alleviated through increased exposure to nature, and by the practice of nature sports (Buckley 2018).

In this regard, several policy initiatives at the national, regional and/or local level have been established, connecting the natural environment and health (Europarc Federation 2018). For example, Scotland is making significant progress in the green health agenda and is seen as a front-runner within the UK and Europe in this important healthcare area (Europarc Federation 2018). Actions to encourage more use of Scotland's outdoors as 'Our Natural Health Service' are being strongly linked to public health and physical activity agendas within the Scottish Government and its health sector. Evidence indicates that green exercise can contribute to tackling physical inactivity, mental health challenges and health inequalities (Pretty et al. 2007; Hough Mackenzie and Brymer 2018; Europarc Federation 2018).

Finland provides another case in point, where the benefits of nature for human health and wellbeing are seen as an increasingly important topic in society. Cross-governmental cooperation and development between various sectors of the state administration and specialists from sports, outdoor and nature sectors have increased substantially over the last few years and, under the umbrella of Parks & Wildlife Finland (P&WF), the 'Healthy Parks, Healthy People Finland 2025' programme has been developed. The goal of this programme is to improve the social, physical and mental well-being of the Finnish population through the utilization of green space and contact with nature. The aim is to inspire people to become physically active and to spend more time in the natural environment during their leisure time (Europarc Federation 2018).

Nature sports and education

The educational link with nature (and nature sports activities) has a long tradition. This pedagogical tradition is rooted in the formative process that began during the sixteenth-seventeenth centuries (Melo and Gomes 2017a). Since that period, but especially since the beginning of the twentieth century, many people and organizations have engaged in nature (sports) activities by attributing educational benefits to them (Funollet 1989; Cubero 2008; Melo and Gomes 2017a). Examples are the naturalist movement in France, founded by Georges Hébert in the beginning of the twentieth century; the Scout Movement, which emerged in England in 1907 as an initiative of Robert Baden Powell, and; Outward Bound, originally created in England by Kurt Hahn, during World

War Two (Melo and Gomes 2017a). This last programme was imported later into the United States by Joshua Miner and is considered as a precursor of the outdoor adventure education concept, which includes trekking, mountaineering, climbing, orienteering, kayaking, and many other nature sports activities (Watters 1986; Berry and Hodgson 2011).

Outdoor adventure education programmes founded on nature sports activities include a

> variety of teaching and learning activities and experiences usually involving a close interaction with a natural setting and containing elements of real or perceived danger or risk in which the outcome, although uncertain, can be influenced by the actions of the participants and circumstances. (Ewert and Sibthorp 2014, 12)

This kind of education conducted in natural and wilderness settings, involves ecologic relationships, physical skills to meet situational challenges, and interpersonal growth (Gilbertson et al. 2006). These learning experiences encourage direct, active, and meaningful social engagement with real-life, long-term consequences (Prouty 2007).

There has been sustained growth and interest in nature and adventure-based learning in recent years. The purposeful use of adventure and nature has now reached the point where there is a significant degree of interest in studying the subject at academic and professional levels. This is reflected in the large number of opportunities to study adventure and nature-related disciplines at post-sixteen, undergraduate and postgraduate levels in the UK, the USA, Australia, Canada, New Zealand and elsewhere (Hodgson and Berry 2011). This educational movement, using nature sports activities for intentional learning experiences, has evolved beyond narrowly defined sport and technical-based training, especially risk, danger, and disaster management. The movement now encompasses a broader, theoretically grounded understanding of what is necessary to plan and deliver educational experiences that aim to recognize and validate participant-centric approaches and outcomes that move beyond a singular focus on safety (Hodgson and Berry 2011; Collins and Brymer 2018).

Concluding remarks: nature sports as sports activities

Based on the foregoing discussion within this editorial, it may seem unnecessary, even rhetorical, to pose the following two questions: (i) can and should we consider a diverse set of physical activities that occur in relation to nature or the environment, such as mountaineering, surfing, and free-flight, among others, to be 'sports'?; (ii) does this diverse set of activities constitute a particular and novel form of modern sports today, a unifying form of practice we can and should designate as 'nature sports'? We believe the answer to both of these guiding questions is resoundingly affirmative.

As noted in our introduction, sport is highly ambiguous, socially constructed and contested, and continually emerging into new forms and configurations. Sport, as a social and cultural phenomenon, influences and is influenced by the socio-cultural context in which it has developed – sharing, showing, playing and setting the values of that very context (Melo 2017). Sport both becomes and accompanies the changes and developments of society, maintaining a systemic isomorphism relationship (Martin and Martin 2001).

The concept that is included in the European Sports Charter and which emerged in the postmodern period, presents sports as '[...] all forms of physical activity which, through casual or organised participation, aim at expressing or improving physical fitness and mental well-being, forming social relationships or obtaining results in competition at all levels' (Council of Europe 1992, 3). This definition implies a broader notion of sport, encompassing a wider range of activities not included in previous definitions that besides the competitive side, makes sports a space of satisfaction of the new social needs, of escaping the routine, of looking for evasion, of adventure and of risk (Melo 2009). This definition is consistent with the ideas proposed by many authors, who argue that a broader definition of sport allows for increased significance in the relationship between sport and other areas of social life (e.g. Standeven and De Knop 1999; Melo and Gomes 2017a), offering myriad meanings attributed to new forms, including those that are associated with leisure, tourism, health, education, the environment and nature.

Nature sports activities meet precisely this new conception of sport, as they favour the development of novel and emerging sports projects, allowing participants to experience and perform varied practices, from the structured to the more informal, while favouring self-organized forms which are at least currently the most popular among nature sports participants (Bessy and Mouton 2004; Melo 2013; Melo and Gomes 2016b).

In accordance with Krein's (2014) proposition, competition against others is not an essential component of nature sports. Instead, natural features play at least one of the primary roles that human competitors utilize in traditional or standard sports (Krein 2014). As Booth (2018) describes nature sports participants interact with surfaces, textures and fluids of physical geographical features as well as the dynamic forces that create them. It is a reframing of the ontological assumptions grounded in dominant definitions of sport regarding both competition and nature, whereby social connections with the environment need not be antagonistic and one based on controlling and conquering nature.

Considering these factors, and contrary to traditional and dominant definitions of sport, we contend that nature sports must be included within the sport concept, culturally and analytically situated within its own unique body of literature. The following contributions within the first part of this special issue explore the dynamic, embodied intersection of nature and human beings engaged in a diverse collection of sporting activities.

We wish to thank the authors for their innovative and probing scholarship, as their contributions offer conceptual heft to this emerging field of research. The authors have challenged fellow scholars to question existing theoretical assumptions and heuristic biases within the field and to broaden our perspectives to be more inclusive, expansive, intentionally relational and participant-centred. In particular, these contributions have underscored the need to reconceptualise nature within the nature sport literature as a set of fluid positions and orientations through which embodied experiences inscribe and produce meaning and purpose.

Volume one contributions

The first part of this special issue, then, focuses on the current state of the nature sport literature, seeking to expand our conceptual understanding of this diverse array of activities. The authors in this collection examine existing analytical concepts and categories, challenging several theoretical assumptions, such as the separation of nature from culture and a heuristic bias on risk taking and risk management in nature sports.

In his critical commentary, Robert A. Stebbins seeks to unpack some of the terminological and conceptual challenges confronting scholars at the nature-sport nexus. The author defines nature challenge activities (NCAs) as leisure activities pursued in one or more of six elements of nature, including air, water, land, plants, animals and ice or snow. Stebbins distinguishes these activities from sport, which he defines as inter-human, competitive, physical activity with a recognized set of rules.

In the first article of this part of the special issue, Douglas Booth criticizes traditional and dominant definitions of sport as social constructions that render the natural environment passive and malleable for human meaning and use. He argues that social constructionism has obscured 'the sensuous experiences of embodiment.' As such, the author envisions nature sport as a potential vehicle for embodied and political enquiry, a transformative ontology in which nature and culture embrace and converge to form 'co-constitutive' relationships.

This dynamic relationship between human beings and nature expressed within these sporting practices is further complicated by the relocalisation of nature sports to artificial spaces, such as wave parks or indoor climbing walls and facilities. Utilizing interviews and participant observation in the second paper of this part of the special issue, Raffaella Ferrero Camoletto and Davide Marcelli explore the impact of indoorisation on the construction of authenticity among participants, questioning what constitutes a 'real climber?' While these authors argue that the dichotomy between indoor and outdoor practices has declined since artificial climbing walls were first introduced in the 1960's, their study investigates how climbers give meaning to the relative 'naturalness' of their practice. The process of indoorisation has prompted the development of new forms of climbing, increasingly spectacularised with shocking colours and unique shapes, where nature is now defined as 'a convertible and adjusted scenery.' As a result, nature becomes a frame of reference for articulated distinctions and hierarchies among climbers.

In 'Practice in Nature: State of the Art of Research,' Amador Durán-Sánchez, José Álvarez-Garcia and María de la Cruz del Río-Rama conduct a descriptive and exploratory literature review that reveals disparate terminology across multiple academic disciplines with conflicting theoretical assumptions. While the vast majority of authors come from North America, Western Europe and Oceania, the most common terms found in the key word search for publications within this literature review were 'extreme' and 'risk' sports, highlighting an emphasis on danger, overcoming fear and conquering nature. Yet emerging scholarship, including contributions to this part of the special issue, contest traditional definitions and models that fail to capture a wide range of research outcomes, myriad motivations and lived experiences of nature sport participants.

For example, in the next contribution to this special issue, Susan Houge Mackenzie and Eric Brymer suggest that a positive psychology or well-being framework can expand current conceptualisations of nature sports. Rather than focusing on performance metrics and deficit models of risk seeking, the authors argue that adventurous nature sport activities facilitate both hedonic (pleasure, positive emotions and the avoidance of pain) and eudaimonic (well-being, self-realization and purpose/meaning) outcomes. Meta-analyses of adventure education and adventure therapy studies have found evidence of improved self-awareness, acceptance and resilience, as well as autonomous decision-making among participants. Nature sport activities have been successfully utilized to reduce emotional and behavioural symptoms, such as anger and anxiety, and

foster chemical dependence recovery, particularly among younger programme participants. According to these authors, these successes may be due to how adventurous
nature sports help forge intimate and meaningful connections to others (social relatedness) and to nature, fundamental dimensions of human health and well-being.

While Houge Mackenzie and Brymer highlight the positive impact of nature sports on
youth, Ralf Buckley suggests that these activities can make substantial contributions to the
physical, psychological and social health (e.g. a cascade effect) of aging participants. Using
an auto-ethnographic approach, the author analyses ageing trajectories within ten adventurous nature sports, finding that exercise and euphoria temporarily override chronic pain
and psychological stress associated with aging. Buckley argues that older participants pay
closer attention to their natural surroundings and savour these experiences more intensely
than younger participants. In addition to the improved quality of life for older participants
engaged in lifelong nature sports, the author points out the positive economic impact on
national healthcare as an important public policy issue today despite the lack of literature
on the subject.

In the final contribution to this first part of the special issue, Loel Collins and Eric Brymer
articulate a participant centred approach for the design and facilitation of learning and
participant experience within nature sports activities. The authors demonstrate that risk
management and disaster prevention have been emphasized above all else in the
content and training of adventure recreation providers while participation experiences
have been largely ignored. In support of findings made by other contributors in this
part of the special issue, Collins and Brymer argue that learning design must move
beyond a risk-centric approach to one that recognizes individual differences and situational demands while intentionally promoting the relationship between learners and
the environment. This novel approach of intentional collaboration and reflection among
a community of practice will enhance the personal and social benefits of nature sports,
firmly placing the participant at the centre of the learning process.

In the second part of this special issue, we continue to explore participant benefits and
outcomes through selected case studies while also addressing concerns of environmental
impact and the need for an integrated approach to resource management and stakeholder engagement within the growing nature sport industry. The second issue will highlight nature sports as a global phenomenon, a diversified market and sensory experience
for a shifting demographic of participants.

This shifting demographic reflects a new profile of participation, far more inclusive and
expansive than previously conceived. Like nature itself, these sporting activities have
become an open and inviting terrain, a growth market for the many rather than the
few – for boys as well as girls, men and women, young and the ageing, as well as opportunities for participants with varying degrees of ability. Increased demand and diversification challenges both public and private entities to balance potential economic growth
with environmental and social sustainability. With growth we see opportunity but also
the need for responsibility. This two-part special issue contextualizes the rise of nature
sports within a global climate requiring ethical attention and intention.

Disclosure statement

No potential conflict of interest was reported by the authors.

References

Andrews, D. L. 2006. *Sport–Commerce–Culture: Essays on Sport in Late Capitalist America.* Vol. 11. New York: Peter Lang.

Arstila, V. 2012. "Time Slows Down During Accidents." *Frontiers in Psychology* 3: 196.

Bailey, A. W., and E. Hungenberg. 2018. "Managing the Rock-climbing Economy: A Case from Chattanooga." *Annals of Leisure Research.* doi:10.1080/11745398.2018.1488146.

Balmford, A., J. Beresford, J. Green, R. Naidoo, M. Walpole, and A. Manica. 2009. "A Global Perspective on Trends in Nature-based Tourism." *PLoS Biology* 7 (6): e1000144.

Bartram, S. 2001. "Serious Leisure Careers among Whitewater Kayakers: A Feminist Perspective." *World Leisure Journal* 43 (2): 4–11.

Bell, S. 2008. *Design for Outdoor Recreation.* New York: Taylor & Francis.

Berry, M., and C. Hodgson, eds. 2011. *Adventure Education: An Introduction.* London: Routledge.

Bessy, O., and M. Mouton. 2004. "Du plein air au sport de nature. Nouvelles pratiques, nouveaux enjeux. Cahier Espaces: Sports de nature." *Évolutions de l'offre et de la demande* 81: 13–29.

Bessy, O., and O. Naria. 2005. "Les enjeux des loisirs et du tourisme sportif de nature dans le développement durable de la Réunion." In *Management et marketing du sport: du local au global,* edited by P. Boucher and C. Sobry, 307–339. Paris: Éditions Septentrion.

Betrán, J., and A. Betrán. 1995. "La crisis de la modernidad y el advenimiento de la posmodernidad: el deporte y las prácticas físicas alternativas en el tiempo de ocio activo." *Apunts: Educación Física y Deportes* 41: 10–29.

Boley, B. B., and G. T. Green. 2016. "Ecotourism and Natural Resource Conservation: The 'Potential' for a Sustainable Symbiotic Relationship." *Journal of Ecotourism* 15 (1): 36–50.

Booth, D. 2018. "Nature Sports: Ontology, Embodied Being, Politics." *Annals of Leisure Research.* doi:10.1080/11745398.2018.1524306.

Booth, D., and H. Thorpe. 2007. *Berkshire Encyclopedia of Extreme Sport.* Great Barrington: Berkshire Reference Works.

Bourdieu, P. 1978. "Sport and Social Class." *Social Science Information* 17: 819–840.

Bourdieu, P. 1979. *La Distinction: Critique sociale du jugement.* Paris: Editions de Minuit.

Breivik, G. 2010. "Trends in Adventure Sports in a Postmodern Society." *Sport in Society* 13 (2): 260–273.

Brymer, E., G. Downey, and T. Gray. 2009. "Extreme Sports as a Precursor to Environmental Sustainability." *Journal of Sport & Tourism* 14 (2–3): 193–204.

Brymer, E., and T. Gray. 2009. "Dancing with Nature: Rhythm and Harmony in Extreme Sport Participation." *Journal of Adventure Education & Outdoor Learning* 9 (2): 135–149.

Brymer, E., and T. Gray. 2010. "Developing an Intimate 'Relationship' with Nature through Extreme Sports Participation." *Leisure/Loisir* 34 (4): 361–374.

Buckley, R. 2012. "Rush as a Key Motivation in Skilled Adventure Tourism: Resolving the Risk Recreation Paradox." *Tourism Management* 33: 961–970.

Buckley, R. C. 2014. "Slow Time Perception Can be Learned." *Frontiers in Psychology* 5: 209.

Buckley, R. 2018. "Nature Sports, Health and Ageing: The Value of Euphoria." *Annals of Leisure Research.* doi:10.1080/11745398.2018.1483734.

Buckley, R. C., and P. Brough. 2017a. "Nature, Eco and Adventure Therapies for Mental Health and Chronic Disease." *Frontiers in Public Health* 5: 220.

Buckley, R. C., and P. Brough. 2017b. "Economic Value of Parks via Human Mental Health: An Analytical Framework." *Frontiers in Ecology and Evolution* 5: 1247.

Buckley, R. C., P. Brough, and D. Westaway. 2018. "Bringing Outdoor Therapies into Mainstream Mental Health." *Frontiers in Public Health* 6: 119.

Butts, S. 2001. "Good to the Last Drop: Understanding Surfers' Motivations." *Sociology of Sport Online* 4 (1). http://www.physed.otago.ac.nz/sosol/v4i1/v4i1butt.htm.

Camoletto, R., and D. Marcelli. 2019. "Keeping it Natural? Challenging indoorization in Italian Rock Climbing." *Annals of Leisure Research.* doi:10.1080/11745398.2018.1561307.

Carrington, B., and I. MacDonald. 2009. *Marxism, Cultural Studies and Sport.* New York: Routledge.

Centre for Responsible Travel. 2015. The Case for Responsible Travel: Trends & Statistics 2015. Accessed May 5, 2015. https://ecotourism.app.box.com/s/rxiyp65744sqilmrybfk8mys3qvjbe9g.

Chazaud, P. 2004. *Management du tourisme et des loisirs sportifs de pleine nature*. Voiron: Editions PUS.

Cherrington, J., J. Black, and N. Tiller. 2018. "Running away from the Taskscape: Ultramarathon as 'Dark Ecology'." *Annals of Leisure Research*. doi:10.1080/11745398.2018.1491800.

Collins, L., and E. Eric Brymer. 2018. "Understanding Nature Sports: A Participant Centred Perspective and Its Implications for the Design and Facilitating of Learning and Performance." *Annals of Leisure Research*. doi:10.1080/11745398.2018.1525302.

Council of Europe. 1992. *European Sports Charter*. Rhodes: Council of Europe.

Cubero, H. 2008. *El pensamiento y la biografía del profesorado de Actividad Física en el Medio Natural: un estudio multicaso en la formación universitaria orientado a la comprensión de modelos formativos*. Valladolid: Universidad de Valladolid. Tesis doctoral inédita.

Davidson, L., and R. Stebbins. 2011. *Serious Leisure and Nature: Sustainable Consumption in the Outdoors*. Houndmills, Basingstoke: Palgrave Macmillan.

Dilley, R., and S. Scraton. 2010. "Women, Climbing and Serious Leisure." *Leisure Studies* 29 (2): 125–141.

Dolnicar, S., and T. Dickson. 2004. "No Risk, No Fun - The Role of Perceived Risk in Adventure Tourism." Proceedings of the 13th International Research Conference of the Council of Australian University Tourism and Hospitality.

Durán-Sánchez, A., J. Álvarez-García, and M. Del Río-Rama. 2019. "Nature Sports: State of the Art of Research." *Annals of Leisure Research*. doi:10.1080/11745398.2019.1584535.

Dwyer, L. 2015. "Triple Bottom Line Reporting as a Basis for Sustainable Tourism: Opportunities and Challenges." *Acta Turistica* 27 (1): 33–62.

Elkington, J. 1997. *Cannibals with Forks. The Triple Bottom Line of 21st Century*. Oxford: Capstone.

Europarc Federation. 2018. *Health & Well-being Benefits from Parks & Protected Areas*. Regensburg: Europarc Federation.

Ewert, A., and J. Sibthorp. 2014. *Outdoor Adventure Education: Foundations, Theory, and Research*. Champaign, IL: Human Kinetics.

Fairclough, N. 2001. *Language and Power*. New Jersey: Pearson Education.

Frumkin, H., G. N. Bratman, S. J. Breslow, B. Cochran, P. H. Kahn, J. J. Lawler, P. S. Levin, et al. 2017. "Nature Contact and Human Health: A Research Agenda." *Environmental Health Perspectives* 125: 075001.

Funollet, F. 1989. "Las actividades en la naturaleza. Origen y perspectivas de futuro." *Apunts: Educación Física y Deportes* 18: 4–11.

Gammon, S. 2015. "Sport Tourism. Finding its Place?" In *Landscapes of Leisure. Space, Place and Identity*, edited by S. Gammon and R. Elkington, 110–122. London & New York: Palgrave Macmillan.

Gammon, S., and T. Robinson. 2003. "Sport and Tourism: A Conceptual Framework." *Journal of Sport & Tourism* 8 (1): 21–26.

Getz, D. 2009. "Policy for Sustainable and Responsible Festivals and Events: Institutionalization of a New Paradigm." *Journal of Policy Research in Tourism, Leisure and Events* 1 (1): 61–78.

Getz, D., and A. McConnell. 2011. "Serious Sport Tourism and Event Travel Careers." *Journal of Sport Management* 25: 326–338.

Gibson, H. 1998. "Active Sport Tourism: Who Participates?" *Leisure Studies* 17 (2): 155–170.

Gilbertson, K., T. Bates, T. Mclaughlin, and A. Ewert. 2006. *Outdoor Education: Methods and Strategies*. Champaign, IL: Human Kinetics.

Gomes, R. 2009. "El ocio y el deporte en la época del turismo global." *Apunts: Educación Física y Deportes* 97: 37–46.

Green, C., and I. Jones. 2005. "Serious Leisure, Social Identity and Sport Tourism." *Sport in Society: Cultures, Commerce, Media, Politics* 8 (2): 164–181.

Hall, C., and S. Page. 2006. *The Geography of Tourism and Recreation. Environment, Place and Space*. 3rd ed. London: Routledge.

Higham, J., and T. Hinch. 2009. *Sport and Tourism: Globalization, Mobility and Identity*. Oxford: Elsevier.

Hodgson, C., and M. Berry. 2011. "Introduction." In *Adventure Education: An Introduction*, edited by M. Berry and C. Hodgson, 1–4. London: Routledge.

Houge Mackenzie, S., and E. Brymer. 2018. "Conceptualizing Adventurous Nature Sport: A Positive Psychology Perspective." *Annals of Leisure Research*. doi:10.1080/11745398.2018.1483733.

Jensen, C., and S. Guthrie. 2006. *Outdoor Recreation in America*. 6th ed. Champaign: Human Kinetics.

Joaquim, G. 1997. "Da Identidade à Sustentabilidade ou a Emergência do «Turismo Responsável»." *Sociologia Problemas e Práticas* 23: 71–100.

Kane, M., and R. Zink. 2004. "Package Adventure Tours: Markers in Serious Leisure Career." *Leisure Studies* 23 (4): 329–345.

Kerr, J. H., and S. Houge Mackenzie. 2018. "'I Don't Want to Die. That's Not Why I Do It At All': Multifaceted Motivation, Psychological Health, and Personal Development in BASE Jumping." *Annals of Leisure Research*. doi:10.1080/11745398.2018.1483732.

King, K., and A. Church. 2019. "Beyond Transgression: Mountain Biking, Young People and Managing Green Spaces." *Annals of Leisure Research*. doi:10.1080/11745398.2019.1571928.

Krein, K. 2014. "Nature Sports." *Journal of the Philosophy of Sport* 41 (2): 193–208.

Lewis, N. 2004. "Sustainable Adventure: Embodied Experiences and Ecological Practices within British Climbing." In *Understanding Lifestyle Sports – Consumption, Identity and Difference*, edited by B. Wheaton, 70–93. London: Routledge.

Lyng, S., ed. 2005. *Edgework: The Sociology of Risk-Taking*. New York: Routledge.

Mach, L., J. Ponting, J. Brown, and J. Savage. 2018. "Riding Waves of Intra-seasonal Demand in Surf Tourism: Analysing the Nexus of Seasonality and 21st Century Surf Forecasting Technology." *Annals of Leisure Research*. doi:10.1080/11745398.2018.1491801.

Martin, R., and J. Martin. 2001. "Culturas Deportivas y Valores Sociales: Una Aproximación a la Dimensión Social del Deporte." *Apunts: Educación Física y Deportes* 64: 33–45.

Mehmetoglu, M. 2007. "Typologising Nature Based Tourists by Activity-theoretical and Practical Implications." *Tourism Management* 28: 651–660.

Melo, R. 2009. "Desportos de Natureza: reflexões sobre a sua definição conceptual." *Exedra* 2: 33–56.

Melo, R. 2013. "Desportos de Natureza e Desenvolvimento Local Sustentável: Análise dos praticantes e das Organizações Promotoras dos Desportos de Natureza." Unpublished doctoral diss., University of Coimbra, Coimbra.

Melo, R. 2017. "Understanding Nature Sports Participation: A Literature Review." In *Sport Tourism: New Challenges in a Globalized World*, Coordinates by R. Melo and C. Sobry, 241–275. Newcastle upon Tyne: Cambridge Scholars Publishing.

Melo, R., and R. Gomes. 2016a. "Nature Sports and Sustainable Local Development: Practitioners and Organizations Managers' Perspectives in Portugal." In *Sport Tourism and Local Sustainable Development*, edited by C. Sobry, 75–100. Lille: L'Harmattan.

Melo, R., and R. Gomes. 2016b. "Understanding Nature Sports Organizations in Portugal." *The Open Sports Sciences Journal* 9: 13–25.

Melo, R., and R. Gomes. 2017a. "A Sociocultural Approach to Understanding the Development of Nature Sports." In *Sport Tourism: New Challenges in a Globalized World*, Coordinates by R. Melo and C. Sobry, 60–90. Newcastle upon Tyne: Cambridge Scholars Publishing.

Melo, R., and R. Gomes. 2017b. "Nature Sports Participation: Understanding Demand, Practice Profile, Motivations and Constraints." *European Journal of Tourism Research* 16: 108–135.

Melo, R., and R. Gomes. 2017c. "Profiling the Typologies of Nature Sports Organizations in Portugal." In *Sport Management as an Emerging Economy Activity*, edited by M. Peris-Ortiz, J. Álvarez-García, and M. C. del Rio-Rama, 235–255. Cham: Springer.

Melo, R., and D. Leite. 2018. "The Professional Culture of the Portuguese Nature Sports Technicians." In *Proceedings of the STC'18*, edited by C. Sobry. Sport Tourism Conference – Sport Tourism and Local Sustainable Development.

Melo, R., and C. Sobry, Coordinates. 2017. *Sport Tourism: New Challenges in a Globalized World*. Newcastle upon Tyne: Cambridge Scholars Publishing.

Midol, N., and G. Broyer. 1995. "Toward an Anthropological Analysis of New Sport Cultures: The Case of Whiz Sports in France." *Sociology of Sport Journal* 12: 204–212.

Palmer, C. 2004. "Death, Danger and the Selling of Risk in Adventure Sports." In *Understanding Lifestyle Sports - Consumption, Identity and Difference*, edited by B. Wheaton, 55–69. London: Routledge.

Pereira, E., and R. Mykletun. 2012. "Guides as Contributors to Sustainable Tourism? A Case Study from the Amazon." *Scandinavian Journal of Hospitality and Tourism* 12 (1): 74–94.

Pociello, C. 1981. "La force, l'énergie, la grâce et les réflexes. Le jeu complexe des dispositions culturelles et sportives." In *Sports et société*, edited by C. Pociello, 171–237. Paris: Editions Vigot.

Portugal, A., F. Campos, F. Martins, and R. Melo. 2017. "Understanding the Relation between Serious Surfing, Surfing Profile, Surf Travel Behaviour and Destination Attributes Preferences." *European Journal of Tourism Research* 16: 57–73.

Pretty, J., J. Peacock, R. Hine, M. Sellens, N. South, and M. Griffin. 2007. "Green Exercise in the UK Countryside: Effects on Health and Psychological Well-Being, and Implications for Policy." *Journal of Environmental Planning and Management* 50 (2): 211–231.

Prouty, D. 2007. "Introduction to Adventure Education." In *Adventure Education: Theory and Applications*, edited by D. Prouty, J. Panicucci, and R. Collinson, 3–17. Champaign, IL: Human Kinetics.

Reinhart, K. 2019. "Climbing in Saxon Switzerland (GDR) – A Path to Freedom in a Socialist Dictatorship." *Annals of Leisure Research.* doi:10.1080/11745398.2019.1577745.

Rinehart, R. 2017. "Alternative, Extreme (and Avant-Garde) Sport." In *The Routledge History of American Sport*, edited by L. Borish, D. Wiggins, and G. Gems, 414–428. Abingdon: Routledge.

Rinehart, R., and S. Sydnor. 2003. *To the Extreme – Alternative Sports, Inside and Out.* Albany: State University of New York Press.

Standeven, J., and P. De Knop. 1999. *Sport Tourism.* Champaign: Human Kinetics.

Stebbins, R. 1992. *Amateurs, Professionals, and Serious Leisure.* Montreal: McGill- Queen's University Press.

Stebbins, R. 2005. *Challenging Mountain Nature: Risk, Motive and Lifestyle in Three Hobbyist Sports.* Calgary, AB: Detselig.

Stebbins, R. 2019. "Sport and Nature: A Comment on Their Relationship." *Annals of Leisure Research.* doi:10.1080/11745398.2019.1672569

Stranger, M. 2011. *Surfing Life: Surface, Substructure and the Commodification of the Sublime.* Surrey: Ashgate Publishing.

Van Rheenen, D. 2013. "Exploitation in College Sports: Race, Revenue and Educational Reward." *International Review for the Sociology of Sport* 48 (5): 550–571. Reprinted in *Sport and Leisure Management.* Edited by M. Weed. NZ: Canterbury Christ Church University, December 2013.

Van Rheenen, D. 2014. "A Skunk at the Garden Party: The Sochi Olympics, State-sponsored Homophobia and Prospects for Human Rights through Mega Sporting Events." *Journal of Sport & Tourism* 19 (2): 1–18.

Van Rheenen, D. 2017. "Promoting Responsible Sustainability in Sport Tourism: A Logic Model Approach." In *Routledge Handbook of International Sports Business*, edited by M. Dodds, K. Heisey, and A. Ahonen, 317–332. New York, NY: Routledge.

Van Rheenen, D., S. Cernaianu, C. Sobry, and F. Wille. 2017. "Sport Tourism Research in the 21st Century: Future Prospects for an Evolving Epistemology." In *Sport Tourism: New Challenges in a Globalized World*, edited by R. Melo and C. Sobry, 26–46. Newcastle upon Tyne: Cambridge Scholars Publishing.

Watson, N. 2007. "Nature and Transcendence: The Mystical and Sublime in Extreme Sports." In *Sport and Spirituality: An Introduction*, edited by J. Parry, S. Robinson, N. Watson, and M. Nesti, 95–105. London & New York: Routledge.

Watters, R. 1986. "Historical Perspectives of Outdoor and Wilderness Recreation." In *Outdoor Program Manual*, edited by R. Watters, 1–9. Pocatello: Idaho State University Press.

WCED. 1987. *Our Common Future: Report of the World Commission on Environment and Development.* Oxford: Oxford University press.

Weed, M., and C. Bull. 2004. *Sports Tourism: Participants, Policy and Providers.* Oxford: Elsevier.

Weiler, B., and D. Davis. 1993. "An Exploratory Investigation into the Roles of the Nature-based Tour Leader." *Tourism Management* 14 (2): 91–98.

Whannel, G. 2009. "Between Culture and Economy: Understanding the Politics of Media Sport." In *Marxism, Cultural Studies and Sport*, edited by B. Carrington and I. McDonald, 68–88. London: Routledge.

Wheaton, B. 2004. "Introduction: Mapping the Lifestyle Sport-scape." In *Understanding Lifestyle Sports: Consumption, Identity and Difference*, edited by B. Wheaton, 1–28. London: Routeledge.

Wheaton, B. 2013. *The Cultural Politics of Lifestyle Sports*. London: Routledge.

Wheaton, B. 2016. "Lifestyle Sport." In *Sport and Society: A Student Introduction*. 3rd ed., edited by B. Houlihan and D. Malcolm, 109–133. London: Sage.

Wittmann, M. 2011. "Moments in Time." *Frontiers in Integrative Neuroscience* 5: 66.

Nature sports: ontology, embodied being, politics

Douglas Booth

ABSTRACT

In nature sports athletes interact with the surfaces, textures and fluids of physical geographical features as well as the dynamic forces that create them. These interactions have largely been ignored by social constructionist thinking in the social sciences; social constructionism renders the natural environment inert, passive, and malleable for human meaning and use. In this article I argue that the elements of natural environments produce affects and sensations that inscribe themselves on, and transform and produce, bodies. Two questions arise from this argument. Firstly, what is the ontology of nature sports within Western philosophy that separates nature from culture as a primary divide in the organization of knowledge? Secondly, are theorists of nature sports correct in their view that participants are fostering a new ethic of care for the natural environment and facilitating a new environmental politics? Here I draw on surfing, an archetypal nature sport, to address both questions.

Today, the term nature sports sits alongside a collection of terms – alternative sports, *avant-garde* sports, conventional sports, established sports, extreme sports, lifestyle sports, traditional sports (Booth and Thorpe 2007; Honea 2007; Humberstone 2011; Krein 2008, 2014, 2015; Loy and Coakley 2007; Melo and Gomes 2017; Rinehart 2000, 2017; Thorpe and Rinehart 2010; Thorpe and Wheaton 2013; Wheaton 2004, 2010). Collectively, these terms remind us that sport is 'highly ambiguous' (Loy 1968, 1), socially constructed and contested (Andrews 2006), and continually emerging in new forms and configurations (Rinehart 2017). Nature sports, which include activities like hang-gliding and para-gliding, bouldering, kayaking, free diving and surfing, involve dynamic interaction between athletes and physical geographical features – mountains, forests, rivers, oceans, snow fields, ice sheets, caves, rock faces – as well as the dynamic forces that create them – gravity, waves, thermal currents, flowing water, wind, rain, sun (Rinehart 2017). Analyses of nature sports typically foreground participants' motor skills, emotional controls and willingness to take risks (Melo and Gomes 2017). Advocates of nature sports hold that these practices demonstrate a 'distinct pacing and feel' (Krein 2014, 193), convey a sense of adventure (Van Bottenburg and Salome 2010), are less constrained by formal rules (Humberstone 2011), contain a higher hedonistic content (Thorpe and Rinehart 2010), and promote less competitive relationships compared with established or traditional sports. Kevin Krein (2015) proposes that competition is not an essential component of nature sports,[1] although he adds that absence of competition does not mean that they are less intense or dramatic. Nature sports produce their own challenges and thrills as well as their own forms of unpredictability, tension, suspense and excitement.

Why investigate and analyze nature sports as a distinct category of sporting practice? Nature sports have a number of unique characteristics that differentiate them from other forms and make them interesting in their own right; some of these are apparent in the preceding paragraph. More saliently, nature sports are an ideal vehicle to delve into ontology and the grounding assumptions of sports analysis and in particular the embodied dimensions of sport (Section 1), to better understand the environments in which sports are practised (Section 2), and to explore some of the politics around those sporting environments. Nature sports are practised in the skies, across every imaginable terrain and even below the surface of the land and sea. Here, however, I focus on surfing (i.e. riding breaking waves, standing in an upright position, on surfboards), a (predominantly) oceanic pastime and sport that nicely illustrates the ontological, embodied, environmental and political issues associated with nature sports.[2]

The (embodied) ontology of sport

Ontology is concerned with the assumptions made about the nature, essence, and characteristics of things and, in particular, whether things exist objectively (i.e. independent of the mind and language), subjectively (i.e. dependent on the mind) or intersubjectively (i.e. dependent on language). Ontology focuses attention on our analytical concepts and categories, including their substantive properties and the relations between them. While questions of ontology have long been the preserve of philosophy, they are increasingly surfacing in the humanities and the social sciences. The receptiveness to ontology in these fields arises from two interrelated, albeit paradoxical, conditions: an emphasis on reflexive methods and approaches that call into question scientific claims to knowledge, and growing dissatisfaction with explanations of social phenomena that advance multiple representations and socially constructed worlds over fixed truths. In these contexts the turn to ontology constitutes a search for objective – pre-existing – situations that are not solely constructed (i.e. subjective and intersubjective) (Frost 2016; Law and Lien 2013; Van Heur, Leydesdorff, and Wyatt 2012; Woolgar and Lezaun 2013).

Since it became a field of scholarly interest in the 1960s, the study of sport has been moored to an analytical framework grounded in formalism, contextualization,[3] social theory, history and politics in which sport constitutes a set of socially constructed, regulated, formalized and contested physical practices.[4] Two streams are apparent in this framework. One emphasize the production of fit, healthy and productive citizens, the other examines sport as a site of social resistance. Although notions of objective, universal meaning carry little weight in either stream, they are not totally absent. For example, Loy and Coakley (2007) identify ludic and embodied content as veins of universal meaning across contemporary sporting forms. According to Loy and Coakley (2007, 4645) play 'precedes culture' and is a 'universal activity'. Following the Dutch theorist of play Johan Huizinga, they identify 'fun [as] "the essence of play"' (Loy and Coakley (2007, 4647). While Loy and Coakley (2007) acknowledge the difficulties associated with interpreting fun, and conclude that the institutionalization of ludic practices has largely removed play-like elements from contemporary elite and professional forms of sport, they nonetheless identify a number of sociological explanations of fun including 'sociability, euphoric interaction, quest for excitement and emotional dialectics' (4647).[5]

With regard to embodied content, Loy and Coakley (2007, 4643–4644) comment that 'the body constitutes both the symbol and the core of all sport participation' and that 'the essence of embodiment in sport' draws on 'many kinds and degrees of physicality' – aggression, combat, exercise, presence, prowess, sexuality, training, work. They elaborate on embodiment in their reflections on alternative sports that they observe are characterized by 'risk, speed and vertigo' and a 'desire by participants to maintain control of their bodies and physical activities without the intrusion of formalized administrative structures and hierarchical supervision' (Loy and Coakley 2007, 4652). Other scholars too have incorporated control of the body into their analyzes of sport. Roger Caillois (1961/2000) used the term *ilinx* to describe the euphoria generated by physical activities that involve gliding, precarious balance and rapid changes of direction. These movements are commonly associated with activities such as skateboarding, snowboarding and surfing. One of Caillois's four types of play, *ilinx* – from the 'Greek term for whirlpool' and 'from which is also derived the Greek word for vertigo, *ilingos*' – encompasses moments that 'destroy the stability of perception and inflict a kind of voluptuous panic upon an otherwise lucid mind' (Caillois 1961/2000, 23). In the same vein, Pierre Parlebas employs the term *ludomotricité* sports to refer to those physical activities in which pleasure derives from controlling one's body amid the vertiginous sensations of speed and movement (cited in Dant and Wheaton 2007). Biological research has further reinforced the embodied essence of sport by identifying a physiological dimension of *ilinx* and *ludomotricité* sports based on increased concentrations of neurotransmitters, notably epinephrine, norepinephrine and dopamine during activities that induce vertigo (Gill and Beaven 2007).

The analytical programme of social constructionism has paid scant attention to the sensuous experiences of embodiment. As Loy and Coakley (2007) remind us, sporting performances and practices are characterized by sensuous experiences (see also Thorpe and Rinehart 2010), and, even more fundamentally, in these experiences we express the agency that defines our capacities and enables us to reconstruct our material worlds (Turner 2008). In the following sections I grapple with the idea of nature sports as an interaction between performing bodies and objective features and forces in the physical environment. I argue that these interactions produce affects and sensations that inscribe themselves on, and transform and produce, bodies.[6] In *The Bodysurfers*, for example, Robert Drew (1983, 158) describes the 'astonishing … electric cleansing' power of the surf: 'the cold effervescing over the head and trunks and limbs' lifts the spirits, sharpens the brain, charges the body with agility, and sweeps away 'grubby lethargy'. But such interactions with geographical features and/or the dynamic forces that create them engage a radically different ontology to that propagated in Western thought. Since Descartes, Western philosophy has privileged anthropocentrism by separating human culture and meaning from nature, disabled nature's agency, and relegated nature to a passive recipient of human intervention (Anderson 2009).[7] While interactions between performing bodies and the physical environment open the door to thinking about embodiment, culture and nature, as well as the relationships between them, as an ontological enquiry it also raises issues of epistemology and representation. The abstract concepts and categories of ontology, that are typically presented as binary opposites, do not readily marry with lived experiences and practices (Thrift 2008) that are invariably complex, contextualized, nuanced and situational; nor are they necessarily 'proved' by empirical evidence, notwithstanding the common retreat into data to support ontological arguments.

Nature sports: co-constitutive relationships?

Early discussions tended to frame nature sports within an ontology of formal, institutionalized social relationships that foregrounded competition and conquest (e.g. the first to climb Mount Everest, the highest mountain, or the first to surf Waimea Bay, long renowned as the home of the biggest waves). Such frameworks, however, failed to capture the 'dynamic, rhythmical, harmonious, fluid and responsive interplay' between athletes and nature that characterized nature sports (Brymer and Gray 2009, 138). Thus new approaches emerged. Brymer and Gray (2009), for example, chose the metaphor of dance. The 'deep relationship with the natural world', in their words, is

> akin to an intimate 'dance' between actively engaged partners; aficionados do not simply view the natural world as a commodity, a stage for risk taking, or vehicle for self-gratification. On the contrary, … the natural world acts as a facilitator to a deeper, more positive understanding of self and its place in the environment. Nature [is] omnipresent and ubiquitous, and a source of innate power and personal meaning. (Brymer and Gray 2009, 135)

The dance metaphor suffuses surfing literature (e.g. Poirier 2003). Pierce Julius Flynn (1987, 400) provides an oft-cited account of surfing as a 'dance to and directly with a natural energy form' in which the surfer responds rhythmically – climbing and dropping along the wall, trimming, stalling, cutting-back – to the ever changing wave. The dance metaphor typically assigns control to one 'partner' or the other. Flynn recognises that the dance begins with the wave making the initial overture, but the surfer quickly takes the lead on what amounts to 'a blank canvas' that gives the rider absolute freedom to 'navigate … whatever lines … they choose' (Brennan 2017, 46).[8] Others place the wave firmly in command. Recounting his experience at 'exposed beach breaks', philosopher and surfer Daniel Brennan (2017, 46) says that he is 'yet to experience anything resembling the freedom of a blank canvas'.[9] Contest commentator and former world champion Martin Potter (2017a) believes that surfing is overwhelmingly reactive:

> There's no preconceived ideas, no premeditation; it's all about reacting. It's not like you [are] standing on the beach and you say 'ok, on this next wave I'm going to do a bottom turn, I'm going to do a cutback, I'm going to do a re-entry, I'm going to get tubed, I'm going to finish off with an aerial'. The wave doesn't allow that. The ocean is so unpredictable. Every wave is different.

Irrespective of which 'partner' the author privileges, and irrespective of the intensity of the relationship,[10] the (organic) dance metaphor ultimately separates the athlete from, and leaves the athlete outside, nature. These accounts continue to place human subjectivity and agency at the centre of analysis and effectively ignore the 'peculiar and distinctive' agency of matter that has 'its own impetus and trajectory' and which is 'neither a direct nor an incidental outgrowth of human intentionality' (Frost 2011, 70). Culture and nature, in other words, remain distinct ontological entities.

Could interactions between performing bodies and the physical environment in nature sports articulate an alternative ontology in which nature and culture embrace and form 'co-constitutive' relationships? Some scholars believe so. Rather than a world of 'discrete

pregiven forms that come together', they conceptualize the world as 'flows and connections within which things are continuously (re)constituted' (Anderson 2012, 582). In this
interactionist ontology moving and performing bodies converge with nonhuman material
entities in a process of 'mutual becoming' (Franklin 2014, 283; see also Schouwenburg
2015; Tuana 2008). An interactionist ontology transcends the dance metaphor; it shifts
thinking away from clear and stable entities toward a less-stable world 'composed of
flows and mutual interferences' and 'constellations' of nonhumans, humans and places
that 'continually merge and emerge' (Anderson 2012, 582).

   Although he does not employ the term interactionist ontology, geographer Jon Anderson (2012) offers a useful introduction to the notion, enhanced further by his references to
surfing.[11] Anderson (2012) begins by distinguishing between the concepts of assemblage
and convergence. An assemblage is 'formed by the coming together of many ... parts'
(578). An assemblage does not necessarily have an 'intention or design'; nor does it establish 'permanence'; rather, it is simply an 'aggregation' of parts that coalesce and 'form a
larger whole' (578). Ford and Brown (2006, 162), for example, identify surfing as an assemblage of 'genetics, neurophysiology, tools (surfboard, wetsuit, wax), life history, personal
dispositions, encultured narratives from the surfing subculture and media, and so on'.
These parts 'function ... together in brief instants of [a] non-cognitive slide along the
ephemeral wave'. The problem with this concept of assemblage, as Ford and Brown
(2006) note, and as Anderson (2012, 579) stresses, is the absence of surfing action and
the lack of clarity about the relationship between the 'physical constellation' of the surf
break – water, swell, weather system, bathymetry – and, the surfing body. The surfed
wave, in Anderson's (2012, 579–580) words, is not simply 'a "phenomenon but [also] a
relationship between phenomenon."'

   In order to address this problem, Anderson (2012) embraces the concept of convergence and associated notions of merging and emergence. In contradistinction to assemblage that denotes a 'connection' between the surfer, their board and the wave (for the
duration of the ride), the concept of convergence suggests that the 'constituent parts
... become blended and blurred into a converged entity/process' (571).[12] According to
Anderson (2012), rideable surf is 'never stabilised or normalised but conditional on the
intersection of a range of changing factors': 'sea, swell, wind, continental shelf, reef,
tide' (575) and so forth, and the surfed wave 'emerges through a *meeting* of surfer, sea,
and swell, which itself cannot be separated from the *movement* of its constituent parts'
(576, emphasis in original).

   In the context of nature sports, Anderson's (2012) concept of convergence and notions
of merging and emergence offer three important insights. First, while the surfed wave is
'*now*' and 'fixed only temporarily' before its 'constituent parts disengage and ... become
something else', convergence 'produces meanings, (re)presentations, and emotional
affects that outlive its existence' (Anderson 2012, 576, emphasis in original). For
example, Anderson (2012, 576) identifies the 'stoke' that surfers feel when riding a
wave,[13] as the source of a political economy of waves that become 'lived and photographed, yearned after, mythologised, and turned into component commodities for
other networks and systems (e.g. surf trips, surf clothing and equipment, and lifestyle
fashions, amongst other commodities' (see also Stranger 2011). Secondly, convergence
is a process far more substantial than the simple execution of riding skill or a heightened
level of absorption that overshadows all senses of space and time – what psychologists call

flow.[14] Rather, it signifies a sense of co-constitution in which the surfer feels at one with sea and the swell, 'merging' with them, and 'losing a coherent sense of self in being part of something larger' (Anderson 2012, 580). Thirdly, convergence, or co-constitution, conveys an ontological sense that the surfer and the wave are one: 'There is no longer a surfer and a wave ... only a surfed wave – for a short space of time this is now a singular entity/process, ontologically joined' (Anderson 2012, 581). However, Anderson (2012) adds a caveat: only the rider can experience an ontological sense of co-constitution. Those who watch a surfer riding a wave will see only 'an "ordinary" assemblage' (Anderson 2012, 581). Brymer, Downey, and Gray (2009) and Barbara Humberstone (2011) agree: one can only know nature, feel at one with nature, in the process of sensing its elements.

Is there evidential support for Anderson's concept of convergence as an ontological foundation of nature sports? While ontological assumptions are independent of, and invariably exceed, empirical evidence, Western intellectual practice nonetheless tends to favour and seek empirical support. Indeed, Anderson (2012) himself follows this approach, drawing empirical evidence for co-constitution from on an online questionnaire, in-depth interviews, and accounts in niche surfing magazines, books, autobiographies and biographies. Anderson's interviewees, for example, offered comments such as:

- 'I love the sea and so being able to spend time in it, and *be one with sea* is fantastic',
- 'It provides a unique way of enjoying myself that is *intimately connected to nature*', and
- Immersion in the fluid materiality of the sea facilitates a new 'sense of being a part of something that is timeless and much, much bigger than yourself, waves have been breaking since there has been water on the planet and that knowledge can ground me in a period of unease'. (Anderson 2012, 580; see also Brymer, Downey, and Gray 2009)

The personal reflections of surf studies scholar and surfer Clifton Evers (2010) and the historian of surfing and surfer Drew Kampion (2003) also offer empirical evidence of emerging and becoming bodies. Evers (2010, 75–76) describes the way surf locales, which include 'ever-changing weather patterns, coastline, rockwall, jetty, sea floor, reef and sand', inscribe themselves on surfers' bodies:

> each watery collision ... at my local surf break was another battering my body endured, tying it more tightly to the local environment. It became more than a place; it became my turf. The boundary between the place and me blurred; in fact the boundary was erased.[15]

We come from nature, says Kampion (2003, 125), which is the source of human spirit and which we experience with 'our eyes and ears and lungs and fingertips'. For the surfer, nature is 'the scrape of rock and shell on our cold bare feet', 'the chill sluice of brine down through [the] wetsuit', 'the early-morning offshore wind numbing [the] cheeks', 'the rising sun blind[ing] vision' (Kampion 2003, 125).

In contrast, Karin Amimoto Ingersoll (2016) challenges this ontology and epistemology. She doubts whether these connections with the ocean ever produce a fundamentally new understanding of the relationship between nature and culture. Ingersoll (2016, 46) admits that some surfers 'develop an intimate relationship with the ocean', but she relegates these relationships to surfing 'literacy'. Literate surfers can read the 'waves', 'shifting sand formations', 'circulating winds' and 'flowing kelp beds'. They intuitively understand the 'ocean's moods' and may even build their identities, careers, social structures, spirituality, and exercise regimes around surfing which may be profoundly significant in their lives (Ingersoll 2016, 46). Yet, surfing literacy does not transcend the ontological bifurcation of nature and culture; it does not emanate from the same deep ontological bond with the ocean that is experienced by, for example, the indigenous Hawaiian (Kanaka Maoli) surfer. The latter connects to the land and sea through an ontology that conjoins all matter, human and nonhuman, and proposes a perpetual state of balance between people and the environment (Ingersoll 2016).

Ingersoll (2016) concedes that the sea 'truly affects' surfing bodies and that surfing literacy engenders profound and intimate relationships with the ocean (76). As she explains, these relationships involve a 'rhythmical reconceptualization' of 'time and space' and harmonization with the 'pulses' of the ocean. Literate surfers 'listen [to], observe and sit inside waves' (76); they listen 'to the dominant ground swell' as they listen to a song – hearing and feeling sound – attuned to distortions or rearrangements that indicate changing patterns of waves as they arrive and break (132). Literate surfers read the sea and the surf – 'boils', 'water colour', 'reef outline' – and they adjust their positions in the line-up in anticipation of the next set (132). Literate riders experience waves with their muscles, ligaments, bones, joints, senses and memories. 'Ligaments in the surfer's feet and ankles' enable the surfer to slide across, and move around, the face of the wave.[16] 'The knees of the surfer crouch under the spitting tunnels of water' and 'redistribute' their body 'through space' and into spaces that 'constantly fluctuate' (133). Surfing, in Ingersoll's (2016, 77) words, is 'an enactment' that 'releases', 'digests' and 'rereleases' energy in an 'incessant cycle of rejuvenation and (re)connection'. Literate surfers are fully aware of the 'constantly evolving rhythms of the sea' and the 'constant regeneration of the seascape' as swells change direction, sand moves back and forth over the seabed, and waves adopt new shapes and appear and disappear at different locations (132).

Nonetheless, Ingersoll (2016) insists that indigenous ontology entangles the Kanaka Maoli surfer in a vastly different set of relationships. The Kanaka Maoli surfer connects to *ke kai* – the sea – in time and space through 'blood ties – kin': 'she is born from the seabed. *Ke Kai* is where she came from; it is part of her genealogy' (Ingersoll 2016, 47). Ingersoll (2016) questions whether the surfer whose relationship with the sea begins as a sporting practice will ever transcend the ontological gap between nature and culture.[17]

Here, then, we have two competing perspectives on the relationship between performing (surfing) bodies and the physical (natural – oceanic) environment: one that identifies the possibilities of an ontological convergence (e.g. Anderson 2012) and the other that recognises an enduring ontological separation between nature and culture in Western societies (e.g. Ingersoll 2016). Can we resolve or reconcile these two positions? In the next section I examine the environmental ethics and politics of nature sport athletes as an avenue to clarify the relationship between surfing bodies and the natural oceanic environment. Advocates of nature sports believe that through their relationships with nature participants readily subscribe to environmental ethics. While ontology and politics are rare bedfellows in the social sciences and humanities, they are inherently connected by virtue of the fact that no political action or analysis is ever ontologically neutral even if the ontological assumptions within the action/analysis remain implicit.

Nature sports: environmental ethics and politics

A key assumption in the nature sports literature is that the relational sensibilities of athletes to nature is 'politically significant' and provides 'new motivations' to protect the environment (Anderson 2009, 121: see, for example, Borne and Ponting 2015, 2017; Brymer, Downey, and Gray 2009; Hill and Abbott 2009; Humberstone 1998; Krein 2008; Melo and Gomes 2017; Olive 2017). Brymer, Downey, and Gray (2009) encapsulate the general sentiment when they write that feeling connected to nature fosters a desire to care for the natural world and contributes to more environmentally sustainable practices, while Greg Borne (2017) expresses the view from surfing studies that surfers have an acute sense of 'environmental awareness' by virtue of their 'direct contact with the ocean' and actively promote the environment (10–11). But evidence of political action among surfers is more ambiguous.

On the one hand, surfers have demonstrated their political commitments to 'keep[ing] the ocean environmentally, socially, politically and culturally healthy' through a raft of organizations (Ingersoll 2016, 75; see, for example, the case studies in Thorpe and Rinehart (2010) and Wheaton (2007)).[18] Some historical evidence supports the idea that bodies inscribed by nature have politically transformed social conditions and physical environments. In the late nineteenth century, bathers in Sydney began to spontaneously play among the waves. Arthur Lowe (1958), a self-proclaimed pioneer of surfbathing in Sydney, described how 'the big, white rollers' that he watched 'chasing each other into the beach' (19) lured him into the surf and enticed him to learn how to 'plunge' with the wave 'as it roll[ed] to the shore' (24). Lowe's (1958) accounts suggest that surfbathing began before cognition, in moments of experiential spontaneity and creative contingency, and in those moments that 'precede', and are 'separate' from and 'independent', of thought (Meillassoux 2012, 79). At the turn of the twentieth century, Sydney surfbathers successfully challenged the laws that then prevented them from bathing in daylight hours (Booth 2002) and within a few summer seasons, certainly by 1906 (Mills 1906), bathers who experienced the surf as Lowe had were describing themselves in a new realm of embodiment. The transformative power of these interactions should not be underestimated. Egbert Russell (1910, 262), an astute observer of the early surfbathing scene in Sydney, proclaimed that the surf 'represents a readjustment of all the classifications that history and politics and social conditions ever brought about'. Along the Sydney coastline, the surf inscribed itself on, and produced and reproduced bodies that in turn acted socially and politically to transform the urban beach into a new entity (Booth 2018).

On the other hand, a large body of evidence challenges the notion of surfers as active environmentalists who are willing to protect coastal environments because of their relational sensibilities with waves. Journalist Steve Barilotti (2001, 92) insists that the 'platonic love' for nature shown by surfers disguises a disturbing political reality:

> In their insatiable quest to find uncrowded quality surf, surfers have trekked to the most remote spits of the planet … But in the wake of the explorers inevitably follow the settlers. Outposts are set up, then villages, eventually, full-blown surfburbs. While the baseline activity of surfing is essentially non-exploitative, once surfers set up a collective around a marquee surf break, such as Jeffrey's Bay or Uluwatu, the impacts of human colonization—trash, roads, erosion, water pollution, development, environmental degradation, resource depletion—

inevitably follows. The list of soiled third-world surf paradises—Cloud Nine [Phillipines], Tamarindo [Costa Rica], Nias [Indonesia], Puerto Escondido [Mexico], Baja Malibu [Mexico], Cactus [South Australia]—is long and growing. (See also Laderman 2014)

The historian of surfing Matt Warshaw (2003, 162) relegates the 'vast majority of surfers' to 'dormant environmentalists at best' who are 'aroused to action only for a pressing local concern that might despoil their beach'. Heywood and Montgomery (2008) support Warshaw. Based on interviews with American boardriders, Heywood and Montgomery (2008, 169) argue that surfers are more likely to politically engage with environmental issues, such as water quality, when they occur at their local beach and touch their immediate world. Belinda Wheaton's (2007) oft-cited work on Surfers Against Sewage and my research on Bondi Beach (Australia) highlights the importance of context and local agents. For example, at Bondi local surfers were conspicuously absent from the community protests against ocean sewage outfalls in Sydney in the 1980s. Indeed, Kirk Willcox, an editor of the Australian surfing magazine *Tracks* and a member of STOP (Stop Ocean Pollution), chastized boardrider apathy in an article titled "Wake Up You Wankers" (cited in Booth 2016, 281).

The voices of surfers repeatedly subordinate the environment to personal pleasures that typically come 'at the expense of everyone and everything' (Davis 2015, 20).[19] Interestingly, Anderson (2017, 192) adds to this predilection in a recent piece where he writes that in the 'waterscape' of surfers' lives, the environment 'doesn't directly affect their internal goal – the experience of stoke, and their "own sense of self"' (see also Lazarow and Olive 2017). Evidence from current debates in surfing regarding the appropriateness of wave parks and artificial waves further supports the view that the quality of the wave is the primary focus of surfers and that they deem quality as independent of the natural environment. Greg Webber, of Webber Wave Pools, insists that 'the fulcrum for success in the industry can be distilled' to the quality of the wave: 'The critical thing that surfers look for is really just the wave itself. It's so narrow it's ridiculous. Place is irrelevant … It will come down to are the waves good or are they not good' (Ponting 2017, 227–228). Based on his research, Jess Ponting (2017, 228) concludes that surf parks are theoretically more consistent with the concept of '"flow" in which a person's focus of attention is entirely on the task at hand [to] the exclusion of other sensory inputs' than with a co-constitutive relationship with the wave. Observations by surf park developers Nick Hounsfield and Tom Lochtefeld add further weight to this notion. The greatest fear of the former is that artificial waves will remove surfers 'from important cultural experiences and [physical] reference points of the sport'; the latter believes that 'aspirational' surfers, as distinct from 'skilled' riders, will be the 'cash cows' of any successful wave park (Ponting 2017, 229). By this analysis, wave parks amplify bodily desires and economic calculations of hedonism, and do little to build co-constitutive relationships with nature. Rather than bridging the ontological divide between nature and culture, artificial waves replicate the confined, delineated and formally constituted spaces and the 'elements of control, predictability and calculability' (Van Bottenburg and Salome 2010) of established sports that are far removed from the free-flowing spatial, temporal and material conditions found in nature.

Conclusion

Scholars interested in the analysis of sport have tended to privilege the socially-constructed body over the performing body (Thorpe and Rinehart 2010). This is somewhat

surprising given that 'the body is both the *medium* and the *outcome* of their innate physical capital' and 'an entity' that, in the words of sociologist Bryan Turner (2008, 226), is
always 'in the process of becoming' (emphasis in original). Nature sports are an ideal
subject to investigate the performing body and the consequences of those performances
for being and becoming. The preceding discussion suggests that performing in nature
engenders very real relational sensibilities with the nonhuman material world.

What does this mean for ontological understanding? As far as Nigel Thrift (2008, 56) is
concerned, 'the ontology of nature and culture is merely a discourse that does not tell us
how nature is apprehended'. He believes that 'nature is apprehended' through particular
embodied experiences that in turn tell us 'what nature is'. Experiences – walking, swimming, cycling, climbing, surfing – form 'an embodied "unconscious"', or 'planes of affect
attuned to particular body parts (and senses) and corresponding elements of nature
(from trees and grass, to river and sky)', that construct nature not as a concept but as a
set of 'positions and orientations' addressed by posture. Critically, from a relational perspective, nature confirms its presence by 'pushing back' and 'speak[ing] in us as "infralan-
guage"' (Thrift 2008, 68): dropping down the face of a steep wave raises the heart rate,
tenses the leg muscles and releases dopamine. Thrift (2008, 68) sees bodily encounters
with nature 'fixing' affects, moods, emotions and feelings which, of course, are 'always
unique' and 'the phenomenological basis of individuality' (Turner 2008, 211–212).

Yet the choices we make as individual embodied agents, particularly those that conjure
transformative action, presuppose ontological notions of ideal meanings and relations
between universals and particulars and parts and wholes. Even in the iron cage of contemporary Western culture, surfers pursue 'feral' existences, travelling to remote surf locations
and living subsistence lives for extended periods (Booth 2011). Jeff 'Camel' Goulden embodies feralism: surviving on unemployment benefits, the West Australian surfer is proud that
he has 'never had a real job' which, he says, would mean 'losing touch with the ocean', 'the
one thing I'm definitely in tune with' (Kennedy 2009, 46; see also Hetzel 2003 and Jones
2015).[20] Less extreme are those who have the flexibility to organize their working lives
around the rhythms of tides and movement of storms. Teacher of writing and surfer
Thad Ziolkowski is a good example. He unashamedly cancelled his first writing class of
the new academic year in 2001 as waves generated by Hurricane Erin approached the
New York coastline. Ziolkowski (2017) admitted feeling pangs of guilt at sending 'eager'
learners away. Nonetheless, he insisted that he would have suffered more guilt had he
not cancelled the class: the latter 'could be made up' whereas 'a once-in-a-decade swell
was an evanescent natural miracle of sorts. I wanted to make a good first impression …
but I wanted to go surfing more'.[21] As ontological statements, the perspectives and
actions of Camel and Ziolkowski are something of a counterweight to the prevailing
social constructionist analyses. Additionally, the pair remind us of the value of nature
sports as a vehicle for embodied ontological and political enquiry.

Notes

1. Krein (2015, 278) refers to a continuum of competition in nature sports: 'the greater role formal
   competition plays in a nature sport, the less of a nature sport it is'.
2. Most contemporary analyses of surfing categorize it as a lifestyle sport (Wheaton 2004, 2010).
   Surfing also supports a substantial popular and burgeoning scholarly literature (e.g. Hough-

Snee and Eastman 2017; Moser 2008). The philosopher Aaron James (2017) recently described surfing as 'the zenith of all human endeavors: it's up there with the arts, friendship, love music, and even sex' (26), and 'the fullest expression of the free human's natural state of being' (49).

3. Formalist approaches 'maintain that the purpose, meaning and significance of sport practices can be read [from] their formal rules'; contextualist approaches 'maintain that sport is defined by both its rules and its ethos', that is, 'those social conventions that govern how the rules of a sport are to be interpreted in particular instances' (Morgan 2000, 207).

4. Bruce Kidd (1996) offers a prime example of contested meanings in *The Struggle for Canadian Sport* where he identifies four competing forms in the interwar period – amateur sport, professional sport, workers' sport and women's sport. These forms 'locked horns' and were 'rocked by internal conflict, often over basic principles' (Kidd 1996, 262). Of course, a form of ontological security can be found even within socially constructed forms of sport. Kidd (1996), for example, acknowledges common 'intentions and values' (262) across the competing forms of sport. Similarly, Loy and Coakley (2007, 4652) concede that formalization, institutionalization and regulation have generated 'dominant meanings'.

5. Huizinga took the view that 'the *fun* of playing, resists all analysis, all logical interpretation' (cited in Loy and Coakley 2007, 4647).

6. Such interactions rarely appear in social constructionist analyses of urban sporting spaces that sociologist Mike Silk (2013) calls 'sterile' and that geographer John Bale (2000, 180) refers to as 'placeless' 'machines' that produce 'rational' (i.e. scientific), largely disembodied, practices designed to measure and advance human performances (see also Bale 2004).

7. While this statement applies primarily to the analytic tradition in Western philosophy, readers should note that other schools of philosophy, including phenomenology and pragmatism, actively consider questions of ontology and the body. Gunnar Breivik (2017) offers a useful introduction to the subject in a recent analysis of three different perspectives on intentionality in sport. Although Breivik (2017, 206) also acknowledges that optimal reactions to the natural environment will be quite different to the context-specific rules, restrictions and obstacles of established/traditional sports.

8. In this regard, scholars of sport often cite the passage in Jean-Paul Satre's *Being and Nothingness* (1943) in which the philosopher likens human freedom to the skier who, in soft snow, chooses their own path. Aaron James (2017) argues that Satre would have drawn a different conclusion had he considered surfing in which 'no manoeuvre can be done at will, or on command, not without just the right, fleeting wave circumstances' (55).

9. Brennan (2017) further affirms the power of the surf in wipeout situations where the 'pull of the wave' takes total control of the rider's body (48). In an earlier piece, Brennan (2016) discusses big surf where the waves totally subsume the rider (919). This article is also important for introducing gender into the discussion.

10. Potter (2017b) beautifully captures a particularly intense relationship in another commentary: 'Julian Wilson timing that [wave] to perfection. You can see that as he stands up he doesn't let go of the right hand – the right hand holding that rail, the left hand feeling the face of the wave. You can see him touching it. Now he [adjusts his weight and] starts to slow down, [intuitively] understanding the dynamics of the wave – which way it is moving, and how fast he is going, how much speed he needs to wipe off. As he slides through this barrel, the thing starts to regurgitate, and in doing so fires him out [of the tube] like a cannonball out of a cannon'.

11. Anderson (2012) adopts a broader definition of surfing than that used here. He includes riding waves on any type of equipment – body boards, surf kayaks, surf skis – as well as long boards and short boards (576). The social history of surfing sharply distinguishes different wave riding craft (e.g. Booth 2002).

12. Anderson's (2012) convergence is synonymous with *agencement* (581, note 8), the term adopted by Deleuze and his peer Félix Guattari that has been widely translated into the English word assemblage (DeLanda 2016; Nail 2017). *Agencement*, Thomas Nail (2017) explains, conveys the idea of an arrangement or layout of heterogeneous elements that present as a multiplicity or as events as distinct from a unity or essence. 'A unity is an organic whole whose parts all work together like the organs of the human body. Each

organ performs a function in the service of reproducing its relations with the other parts and ultimately the harmony of the whole organism'. Instead of 'organic unities', Deleuze and Guattari advance the idea of 'multiplicity' which is 'neither a part nor a whole' but 'defined solely by their external relations of composition, mixture, and aggregation'. If a combination of heterogeneous elements 'are defined only by their external relations, then it is possible that they can be added, subtracted, and recombined with one another ad infinitum' (22–23).

13. Clifton Evers (2006, 230–231) defines stoke as 'a fully embodied feeling of satisfaction, joy and pride'. The Hawaiian word for stoke is *hopupu* (Poirier 2003).

14. The concept of flow often appears in the literature as a synonym of stoke to describe an athlete's 'peak' experience (e.g. Dant and Wheaton 2007, 11). However, Barbara Humberstone (2011) is critical of the concept that she argues masks our understanding of bodily experiences by hiding affective and embodied sensations and 'the sentience of the experience'. Critically, 'the notion of flow covers up a more insightful mobile and social understanding of body, nature, emotions nexus' and 'what is needed … is a sense of the senses in the body's engagement with nature in practice from the practitioner's experience' (501).

15. Game and Metcalfe (2011, 38) similarly cite a bather who found total relaxation while floating in the water at Bondi Beach. According to the bather, the boundaries between their body and the sea and air evaporated and they merged with the ocean and sky.

16. Elsewhere I refer to feet as 'the central organ' of surfing, the sharpest source of proprioception: 'standing on a thin layer of fibreglass-covered foam transported by an ocean wave transforms the feet from simple structures of locomotion into organs of affect. Through their feet, riders sense the power and energy of the ocean and, in the process of complex and intricate manoeuvres around, through and across the breaking wave, transform that energy into kinetic pleasures' (Booth 2008, 27).

17. Although Ingersoll (2016, 77) appears somewhat ambiguous on this point in her submission that the 'sensations felt by the surfer' have the power to 'radiate out' and 'reach those watching on the shore' and 'affect and pull them (even tourists) into the experience' (cf. Anderson 2012).

18. Among the organizations listed by Ingersoll (2016, 75) are 'the Groundswell Society, an ad hoc surfing think-tank that audits and analyses the culture and ethics of surfing and surf culture; the Surfrider Foundation, a non-profit environmental group (United States); Surfers Against Sewage, a non-profit environmental campaigning for clean, safe, and accessible recreational waters (Great Britain); SurfAid International, an international health care service working in surf-rich regions such as Indonesia (Australia); and Save Our Surf … a Hawai'i-based grassroots group, formed in the early 1960s … in response to increased environmental degradation and overdevelopment in the islands … by dredging'.

19. See also issue 339 of *Surfing Life* (2017). The lack of environmental perspective is stark in this edition devoted to 'surfers – who we are, who we want to be, and how we want to live' (cover).

20. Goulden has twice won the *Surfing Life* Oakley award for paddling-in to the biggest wave, in 2013 and 2014. The awards included cheques for AU$5000. In 2012 Goulden rescued a fellow surfer from a shark that had bitten him on the arm and stomach at a break in northern Western Australia.

21. Ziolkowski's college, too, cancelled classes that day – 11 September 2001 – which coincided with the attack on the Twin Towers; in the end Ziolkowski stayed home.

Acknowledgements

Sincere thanks to Mark Falcous and the anonymous reviewers for their constructive suggestions on this manuscript.

Disclosure statement

No potential conflict of interest was reported by the author.

References

Anderson, J. 2009. "Transient Convergence and Relational Sensibility: Beyond the Modern Constitution of Nature." *Emotion, Space and Society* 2 (2): 120–127.

Anderson, J. 2012. "Relational Places: The Surfed Wave as Assemblage and Convergence." *Environment and Planning D: Society and Space* 30 (4): 570–587.

Anderson, J. 2017. "Surfing: A Ritual with Consequences." In *Sustainable Surfing*, edited by G. Borne, and J. Ponting, 176–201. London: Routledge.

Andrews, D. 2006. *Sport, Commerce, Culture: Essays on Sport in Late Capitalist America*. New York: Peter Lang.

Bale, J. 2000. "Human Geography and the Study of Sport." In *Handbook of Sport Studies*, edited by J. Coakley, and E. Dunning, 171–186. London: Sage.

Bale, J. 2004. *Roger Bannister and the Four-Minute Mile: Sports Myth and Sports History*. London: Routledge.

Barilotti, S. 2001. "Lost Horizons: Surf Colonialism in the Twenty First Century." *The Surfer's Journal* 11 (3): 89–97.

Booth, D. 2002. *Australian Beach Cultures: The History of Sun, Sand and Surf*. London: Frank Cass.

Booth, D. 2008. "(Re)reading *the Surfers' Bible*: The Affects of *Tracks*." *Continuum* 22 (1): 17–35.

Booth, D. 2011. *Surfing: The Ultimate Guide*. Santa Barbara, CA: Greenwood Press.

Booth, D. 2016. "The Bondi Surfer: An Underdeveloped History." *Journal of Sport History* 43 (3): 272–289.

Booth, D. 2018. "Entangling Corporeal Matter and Geo Matter: Making and Remaking the Beach." In *Sport, Physical Culture, and the Moving Body: Materialism, Technologies, Ecologies*, edited by D. Andrews, H. Thorpe, and J. Newman, forthcoming. New Brunswick, NJ: Rutgers University Press.

Booth, D., and H. Thorpe. 2007. "The Meaning of Extreme." In *Encyclopedia of Extreme Sports*, edited by D. Booth, and H. Thorpe, 181–197. Great Barrington, MA: Berkshire.

Borne, G. 2017. "Sustainability and Surfing in a Risk Society." In *Sustainable Surfing*, edited by G. Borne, and J. Ponting, 3–20. London: Routledge.

Borne, G., and J. Ponting. 2015. *Sustainable Stoke: Transitions to Sustainability in the Surfing World*. Plymouth: University of Plymouth Press.

Borne, G., and J. Ponting. 2017. *Sustainable Surfing*. London: Routledge.

Breivik, G. 2017. "Searle, Merleau-Ponty, Rizzolatti – Three Perspectives on Intentionality and Action in Sport." *Journal of the Philosophy of Sport* 44 (2): 199–212.

Brennan, D. 2016. "Surfing Like a Girl: A Critique of Feminine Embodied Movement in Surfing." *Hypatia* 31 (4): 907–922.

Brennan, D. 2017. "Existentialism and Surfing." *Surfing Life* 339: 46–48.

Brymer, E., G. Downey, and T. Gray. 2009. "Extreme Sports as a Precursor to Environmental Sustainability." *Journal of Sport & Tourism* 14 (2): 193–204.

Brymer, E., and T. Gray. 2009. "Dancing With Nature: Rhythm and Harmony in Extreme Sport Participation." *Journal of Adventure Education and Outdoor Learning* 9 (2): 135–149.

Caillois, R. 1961/2000. *Man, Play, and Games*. Urbana: University of Illinois Press.

Dant, T., and B. Wheaton. 2007. "Windsurfing: An Extreme Form of Material and Embodied Interaction?" *Anthropology Today* 23 (6): 8–12.

Davis, W. 2015. "We'd Trip Our Own Mothers to Be Here Again." *Surfing Life* (April), 20.

DeLanda, M. 2016. *Assemblage Theory*. Edinburgh: Edinburgh University Press.

Drew, R. 1983. *The Bodysurfers*. London: Faber and Faber.

Evers, C. 2006. "How to Surf." *Journal of Sport and Social Issues* 30 (3): 229–43.

Evers, C. 2010. *Notes for a Young Surfer*. Melbourne: Melbourne University Press.

Flynn, P. J. 1987. "Waves of Semiosis: Surfing's Iconic Progression." *The American Journal of Semiotics* 5 (3/4): 397–418.

Ford, N., and D. Brown. 2006. *Surfing and Social Theory: Experience, Embodiment and Narrative of the Dream Glide*. London: Routledge.

Franklin, A. 2014. "On Why We Dig the Beach: Tracing the Subjects and Objects of the Bucket and Spade for a Relational Materialist Theory of the Beach." *Tourist Studies* 14 (3): 261–285.

Frost, S. 2011. "The Implications of the New Materialisms for Feminist Epistemology." In *Feminist Epistemology and Philosophy of Science Power in Knowledge*, edited by H. E. Grasswick, 69–83. Amsterdam: Springer.

Frost, S. 2016. *Biocultural Creatures: Toward a New Theory of the Human*. Durham: Duke University Press.

Game, A., and A. Metcalfe. 2011. "'My Corner of the World': Bachelard and Bondi Beach." *Emotion, Space and Society* 4 (1): 42–50.

Gill, N., and M. Beaven. 2007. "Physiology of Risk." In *Berkshire Encyclopedia of Extreme Sports*, edited by D. Booth, and H. Thorpe, 236–240. Great Barrington, MA: Berkshire.

Hetzel, Y. 2003. "The Camel Concept." *The Surfer's Journal* 12 (4): 43–51.

Heywood, L., and M. Montgomery. 2008. "'Ambassadors of the Last Wilderness'? Surfers, Environmental Ethics, and Activism in America." In *Tribal Play: Subcultural Journeys through Sport*, edited by M. Atkinson, and K. Young, 153–172. Bingley: Emerald JAI.

Hill, L., and A. Abbott. 2009. "Surfacing Tension: Toward a Political Ecological Critique of Surfing Representations." *Geography Compass* 3 (1): 275–296.

Honea, J. C. 2007. "Alternative Sport." In *Blackwell Encyclopedia of Sociology*, edited by G. Ritzer, 4653–4656. Hoboken, NJ: Wiley-Blackwell.

Hough-Snee, D. Z., and A. S. Eastman. 2017. *The Critical Surf Studies Reader*. Durham: Duke University Press.

Humberstone, B. 1998. "Re-creation and Connection in and with Nature: Synthesizing Ecological and Feminist Discourses and Praxis?" *International Review for the Sociology of Sport* 33 (4): 381–392.

Humberstone, B. 2011. "Embodiment and Social and Environmental Action in Nature-Based Sport: Spiritual Spaces." *Leisure Studies* 30 (4): 495–512.

Ingersoll, K. A. 2016. *Waves of Knowing: A Seascape Epistemology*. Durham: Duke University Press.

James, A. 2017. *Surfing with Satre: An Aquatic Inquiry into a Life of Meaning*. New York: Doubleday.

Jones, R. 2015. "Camel." *Surfing Life* 323 (August): 89–92.

Kampion, Drew. 2003. *The Way of the Surfer*. New York: Harry N. Abrahams.

Kennedy, L. 2009. "The Magnificent Seven." *Tracks*, November: 34–47.

Kidd, B. 1996. *The Struggle for Canadian Sport*. Toronto: University of Toronto Press.

Krein, K. 2008. "Sport, Nature and Worldmaking." *Sport, Ethics and Philosophy* 2 (3): 285–301.

Krein, K. 2014. "Nature Sports." *Journal of the Philosophy of Sport* 41 (2): 193–208.

Krein, K. 2015. "Reflections on Competition and Nature Sports." *Sport, Ethics and Philosophy* 9 (3): 271–286.

Laderman, S. 2014. *Empire in Waves: A Political History of Surfing*. Berkeley: University of California Press.

Law, J., and M. E. Lien. 2013. "Slippery: Field Notes in Empirical Ontology." *Social Studies of Science* 43 (3): 363–378.

Lazarow, N., and R. Olive. 2017. "Culture, Meaning and Sustainability in Surfing." In *Sustainable Surfing*, edited by G. Borne, and J. Ponting, 202–218. London: Routledge.

Lowe, A. M. 1958. *Surfing, Surf-Shooting and Surf-Lifesaving Pioneering*. Sydney: Lowe.

Loy, J. W. 1968. "The Nature of Sport: A Definitional Effort." *Quest* 10 (1): 1–15.

Loy, J. W., and J. Coakley. 2007. "Sport." In *Blackwell Encyclopedia of Sociology*, edited by G. Ritzer, 4643–4653. Hoboken, NJ: Wiley-Blackwell.

Meillassoux, Q. 2012. "Interview." In *New Materialisms: Interviews and Cartographies*, edited by R. Dolphijn, and I. Van der Tuin, 71–81. Ann Arbor: University of Michigan Library.

Melo, R., and R. Gomes. 2017. "A Socio-Cultural Approach to Understanding the Development of Nature Sports." In *Sport Tourism: New Challenges in a Globalized World*, edited by R. Melo, and R. Gomes, 47–76. Newcastle upon Tyne: Cambridge Scholars.

Mills, S. 1906. "Shooting the Breakers." *The Sydney Mail* (7 March): 606.

Morgan, W. 2000. "The Philosophy of Sport: A Historical and Conceptual Overview and a Conjecture Regarding Its Future." In *Handbook of Sport Studies*, edited by J. Coakley, and E. Dunning, 204–212. London: Sage.

Moser, P. 2008. *Pacific Passages: An Anthology of Surf Writing*. Honolulu: University of Hawai'i Press.

Nail, T. 2017. "What Is an Assemblage?" *SubStance* 46 (1): 21–37.

Olive, R. 2017. "Surfing, Localism, Place-Based Pedagogies and Ecological Sensibilities in Australia." In *Routledge International Handbook of Outdoor Studies*, edited by B. Humberstone, H. Prince, and K. Henderson, 501–510. London: Routledge.

Poirier, J.-E. 2003. *Dancing the Wave: Audacity, Equilibrium, and Other Mysteries of Surfing*. Translated by M. Kohn. Boston: Shambhala.

Ponting, J. 2017. "Simulating Nirvana: Surf Parks, Surfing Spaces, and Sustainability." In *Sustainable Surfing*, edited by G. Borne, and J. Ponting, 219–237. London: Routledge.

Potter, M. 2017a. Commentary at World Surfing League, Jeffreys Bay, South Africa, Round 3, Heat 5, Mick Fanning (wave score) 2.93. Retrieved from http://www.worldsurfleague.com/events/2017/mct/1900/corona-open-j-bay/heatanalyzer.

Potter, M. 2017b. Commentary at World Surfing League, Teahupo'o, Tahiti. Final, Julian Wilson (wave score) 9.73 slow. Retrieved from http://www.worldsurfleague.com/events/2017/mct/1920/billabong-pro-tahiti/heatanalyzer.

Rinehart, R. 2000. "Emerging Arriving Sport: Alternatives to Formal Sport." In *Handbook of Sport Studies*, edited by J. Coakley, and E. Dunning, 504–519. London: Sage.

Rinehart, R. 2017. "Alternative, Extreme (and Avant-Garde) Sport." In *The Routledge History of American Sport*, edited by L. Borish, D. Wiggins, and G. Gems, 414–428. Abingdon: Routledge.

Russell, E. 1910. "Australia's Amphibians." *Lone Hand* (January): 252–265.

Schouwenburg, H. 2015. "Back to the Future? History, Material Culture and New Materialism." *International Journal for History, Culture and Modernity* 3 (1): 59–72.

Silk, M. 2013. "Cities and the Cultural Politics of Sterile Sporting Space." In *A Companion to Sport*, edited by D. Andrews, and B. Carrington, 270–286. Chichester, UK: Wiley Blackwell.

Stranger, M. 2011. *Surfing Life: Surface, Substructure and the Commodification of the Sublime*. Farnham, UK: Ashgate.

Thorpe, H., and R. Rinehart. 2010. "Alternative Sport and Affect: Non-Representational Theory Examined." *Sport in Society* 13 (7-8): 1268–1291.

Thorpe, H., and B. Wheaton. 2013. "Dissecting Action Sports Studies: Past, Present and Beyond." In *A Companion to Sport*, edited by D. Andrews, and B. Carrington, 341–358. Chichester, UK: Wiley Blackwell.

Thrift, Nigel. 2008. *Non Representational Theory: Space, Politics, Affect*. London: *Routledge*.

Tuana, N. 2008. "Viscous Porosity: Witnessing Katrina." In *Material Feminisms*, edited by S. Hekman, and S. Alaimo, 188–213. Bloomington: Indiana University Press.

Turner, B. 2008. *The Body and Society*. 3rd ed. Los Angeles, CA: Sage.

Van Bottenburg, M., and L. Salome. 2010. "The Indoorisation of Outdoor Sports: An Exploration of the Rise of Lifestyle Sports in Artificial Settings." *Leisure Studies* 29 (2): 143–160.

Van Heur, B., L. Leydesdorff, and S. Wyatt. 2013. "Turning to Ontology in STS? Turning to STS through 'Ontology." *Social Studies of Science* 43 (3): 341–362.

Warshaw, M. 2003. *The Encyclopedia of Surfing*. Melbourne: Viking.

Wheaton, B. 2004. *Understanding Lifestyle Sports: Consumption, Identity and Difference*. London: Routledge.

Wheaton, B. 2007. "Identity, Politics, and the Beach: Environmental Activism in Surfers against Sewage." *Leisure Studies* 26 (3): 279–302.

Wheaton, B. 2010. "Introducing the Consumption and Representation of Lifestyle Sports." *Sport in Society* 13 (7-8): 1057–1081.

Woolgar, S., and J. Lezaun. 2013. "The Wrong Bin Bag: A Turn to Ontology in Science and Technology Studies?" *Social Studies of Science* 43 (3): 321–340.

Ziolkowski, T. 2017. "Not Surfing on 9/11." *New York Times* (*SundayReview*), September 9. https://www.nytimes.com/2017/09/09/opinion/sunday/surfing-9-11.html?emc=eta1.

Keeping it natural? challenging indoorization in Italian rock climbing

Raffaella Ferrero Camoletto and Davide Marcelli

ABSTRACT
This article explores the transformation of rock climbing in a North-Western Italian region, paying attention to the need for 'keeping it natural' in the process of authentication of the practice among a sample of climbers. Like other nature sports such as rafting, skydiving and surfing, rock climbing has been affected by processes of indoorization and sportivization, moving practice sites from mountain rocks to artificial walls. Mixing a post-subcultural perspective with the tourism and leisure studies debate on authentication, and drawing upon in-depth interviews with novices, experts and professional climbers and upon participant observation in climbing sites (both natural and artificial walls, contests, gatherings, etc.), this article focusses on how practitioners construct their authenticity as climbers and establish intra-group hierarchies by using, and giving meaning to, the naturalness of their practice.

Introduction

In many countries, nature sports have undergone development and expansion in terms of participants, services and commodities (Melo and Gomes 2016; Corneloup and Bourdeau 2004). Rock climbing is often grouped within this category, together with activities such as surfing, white-water kayaking and backcountry skiing, assuming that these practices share some common features.

Krein (2014) outlines two core dimensions of nature sports: first, nature must play a central role as opponent/competitor or partner/teammate of the human actors involved. Second, the kind of nature involved is what he names 'natural features', that is any part of the natural world that has not been shaped by, or is not under the control of, human action and that can be easily identified, for example in maps, guidebooks or sports handbooks. As a consequence, what distinguishes nature sports is that 'the features with which athletes interact are either changing as in the case of sports that take place in water, or are experienced as changing as the athlete moves through them, as in rock climbing' (2014, 198). This means that to apply the label of nature sport it is not sufficient that a sport practice take place in a non-urban and outdoor environment; nature must be the main subject of the interaction. Rock climbing has traditionally been strongly associated with mountains, wilderness and other natural elements, thereby representing an exemplary case of a nature sport. However, similar to other nature sports, rock climbing has undergone a double process of indoorization (Van Bottenburg and Salome 2010; Kulczycki and Hinch 2014) and sportivization (Challéat 2014).

The aim of this paper is to analyse how a sample of climbers (from different specialities as well as with different levels of expertise) active in Piedmont, North-Western Italy, authenticate their practices (Wheaton 2007) by making various appeals to their naturalness. We shall explore how nature is variously evoked and signified by practitioners: such as the environment in which the practice takes place; in terms of a distinctive lifestyle of hard-core climbers and how the body (Barratt 2011), both materially and emotionally, is involved. The analysis will show how naturalness is mobilized as a source of authentication for 'real climbers' (Kiewa 2002) to differentiate themselves from other users of indoor climbing facilities. In so doing, 'discourses of authenticity are used strategically by self-identified core members to identify and marginalize other participants' (Donnelly 2006, 220),[1] where core members may include not only practitioners but also rock-climbing service providers.[2]

Indoorization of climbing and the authentication of the practice: a review

Like other nature sports such as rafting, skydiving and surfing, rock climbing has been affected by processes of indoorization. That is 'the movement of adventurous, outdoor sports to artificial (most indoor) settings' (Van Bottenburg and Salome 2010, 70), such as artificial climbing walls and sportivization (Aubel et al. 2002, 2005; Suchet 2011; Challéat 2014), with a distinction being observed between 'adventure climbing' and 'sport climb-ing', together with new specialities (like bouldering), and the diffusion of formal sport com-petitions (mainly indoor) among climbers.[3]

The pluralization of climbing styles entails a mastery of various techniques and body skills and the valorization of different sensations and experiences (Kulczycki 2014). The emergence and co-existence of a variety of climbing activities and styles have triggered a debate, among both participants and researchers, about what a 'real climber' (Kiewa 2002; see also Senda-Cook 2012) is.

The issue of authenticity has been widely discussed in various streams of the literature (for a review on action sports, see Giannoulakis 2016[4]; within tourism studies, see Cohen 2010). Whereas Wang (1999) – overcoming the opposition between objective and con-structive authenticity – introduced the notion of existential authenticity as an activity-related definition focussed on the sense of reality of the intra-personal or inter-personal experience, Cohen and Cohen (2012) took another step forward by shifting attention from authenticity as a construct to authentication as a social process by which the auth-enticity is established. Their distinction between *cool* (explicit, formal and official, led by institutional actors, e.g. certifications) and *hot* authentication (informal and emotionally loaded, performed by lay participants, e.g. veneration of sites) is a useful heuristic tool.

Previous literature explored authentication processes among traditional or adventure rock climbers. Kiewa (2002) identified a set of features defining the symbolic boundaries of the 'real climber' as opposed to the 'pretender'. In her qualitative research on self-defined Australian traditional rock climbers, the core dimension is the 'go-for-it' attitude, the enjoyment of climbing for its own sake. One of the markers of this attitude is the adoption of exploratory behaviour, implying a personal search for climbing sites and criticism of the commercialization of climbing guidebooks and adventure tourism agencies.

Bogardus (2012) analysed the so-called 'bolt wars' engendered by the arrival in the USA of the 'French style' (namely, the adoption of bolts as a protection to be able to climb the most difficult routes more safely), where previously the traditional style was the improvization of an ascent from the ground up. The resulting debate showed the opposition of two different sources of authentication of the practices: voluntary and mastered risk for the American traditional climbers versus athletic and technical skills for French sport climbers. Traditional rock climbers interviewed by Bogardus tended to attribute more value to risk in the never-fully-under-control natural environment, thereby defining their practices as more authentic than those of sport climbers. Another example of the importance of nature in authentication processes is provided by Rickly-Boyd (2012). Focussing on a popular climbing site in the USA, Red River Gorge, Kentucky, she described a specific type of 'lifestyle climbers' (cf. also Rickly et al. 2018) whose distinctiveness is based upon their sober way of life, devoting all their resources to climbing, and upon their departure from a merely touristic approach to travelling. Recalling Wang (1999) notion of 'existential authenticity', Rickly-Boyd detected in lifestyle climbers a specific way of authenticating their practice, which can be summarized in the symbolic word 'dirtbagging'. 'Being a dirtbag is not only a discursive identity but also a performance of dedication, sacrifice, and lifeways' (2012, 97), in which a relationship with the outdoor environment and with the climber's embodied experience is central.

More recently, Rickly and Vidon (2017), analysing full-time travelling rock climbers and wilderness enthusiasts, showed how a sense of ethical commitment and responsible practices towards the natural environment are claimed as symbolic boundary makers of their authenticity, differentiating themselves, in terms of social distinction as well as of hierarchization, from fellow users of such natural environments.[5]

These studies suggest the relevance of the reference to naturalness in the authentication of the rock climbing experience, working as a central discourse in 'keeping it real' (Wheaton and Beal 2003). However, since those studies have focussed mainly on one aspect, the perspective of traditional and adventure climbers, the impact of indoorization and of sportivization in the authentication of different ways of climbing remains partially overlooked.

In this perspective, an important contribution is the work of Salome and Van Bottenburg (Salome 2010; Van Bottenburg and Salome 2010; Salome and Van Bottenburg 2012) on the indoorization of some lifestyle sports (skydiving, skiing, diving, white-water sports and also climbing) in the Netherlands. In her 2010 article, Salome pointed out that the relocalization of lifestyle sports from natural to artificial/indoors (in the case of climbing, from mountain rocks to indoor artificial walls) had promoted a double shift in the authentication process.

The first shift is 'from nature to scenery'. Whereas at the beginning there was an effort – in the structure and material of artificial settings – to simulate the natural environment as the main source of authenticity, gradually the reference to nature lost its importance, so that 'nature is now defined as a convertible and adjusted scenery' (Vanreusel et al. 2002, 185, cited in Salome 2010, 75). The authenticity of the practice seemed therefore to be decoupled from the naturalness of the context and to be associated with the experiential variety provided by indoor facilities. In other words, 'as these sports can be experienced in controlled and predictable environments, principles such as risk taking and sensation seeking are less relevant, as are the feelings of interacting with nature and escaping from reality' (Salome and Van Bottenburg 2012, 24).

A second shift moved the power to define authenticity from participants to the suppliers of indoor facilities and services, who would tend to acknowledge and welcome more inclusive and plural forms of participation in lifestyle sports, thereby downplaying the previous struggles for the construction of hierarchies among practitioners and portending a primacy of cool over hot authentication.

Another proof of the transformation under way is that striving for authenticity seemed to also decline among indoorized lifestyle sports practitioners. Salome and Van Bottenburg (2012), adopting a mixed-method approach (on-line questionnaires and in-depth interviews with indoorized lifestyle sports participants in the Netherlands), constructed a typology classifying their sample in 'exercisers' (29%), 'experiencers' (36%) and 'exceeders' (35%). 'Exercisers' (among whom rock climbers are overrepresented, 46%) are those who practise their sports mostly indoors, for a mixture of practical (the convenience of the site), health-oriented (keeping fit) and social (meeting other people) reasons. 'Experiencers' (more represented among kayaking, scuba diving and skydiving participants) tend to give more value to sensations such as freedom, kicks, flow and to the natural environment: 'For this group, the experience of being outdoors and the feeling of being at one with nature are essential elements of lifestyle sports' (Salome and Van Bottenburg 2012, 32). Despite their clear preference for natural environments, the majority of this category acknowledges the positive side of artificial facilities in providing easier, more convenient access to the practice. Finally, 'exceeders' (among whom climbers are widely represented) combine the convenience of training in artificial settings with the pleasure of experiencing outdoor settings. Salome and Van Bottenburg's research seems to lead to the conclusion that in new indoorized and commercialized lifestyle sports, including rock climbing, the source of authenticity has deviated from the reference to naturalness, and that the dichotomy between indoor and outdoor practices has declined, moving towards increasing legitimation, and often a widespread combination of both ways of practising.

In the following sections, we will further investigate the impact of indoorization on the way rock climbers make sense of, and authenticate, their practice. We will address some research questions: in the Italian context, is the reference to naturalness still relevant in the authentication of the experience carried out by practitioners attending indoor climbing halls? And does the reference to nature, however it is defined, continue to construct boundaries and hierarchies among different subgroups of practitioners in their authentication strategies?

Data collection

To plan our research design, we referred to Salome and Van Bottenburg's recent work on the impact of indoorization on the construction of the authenticity of indoorized lifestyle sport, trying to overcome two limitations of their research.

The first limitation is that little room had been given to how participants in indoorized sports construct the meaning of their experience and account for its authenticity. Salome (2010) focussed exclusively on suppliers of indoor sport facilities (18) and federations (7), while Salome and Van Bottenburg (2012), despite exploring the perspective of participants, relied on a quantitative (an on-line questionnaire answered by 372 subjects, of whom 76% practise rock climbing) more than on a qualitative (in-depth interviews with only 8 subjects, of whom 4 are rock climbers) data set. In this respect, in order to explore the transformations in the role given to nature in rock climbers' authenticity claims, we chose to focus on a larger, more comprehensive sample of both participants (divided according to gender, age and level of sport experience) and suppliers of sport and indoor climbing facilities (indoor climbing-hall managers, sport-climbing instructors, route-setters and referees).

The second limitation is the specificity of the context investigated. The Netherlands, because of its flat configuration, cannot provide easy access to natural sites for many of the lifestyle sports considered. This is particularly the case of rock climbing. Conversely, the context of our research, Turin, has a particular profile. It is a metropolitan city (in 2016, about 900,000 inhabitants in the municipal area, and about 2,300,000 in the greater metropolitan area, including 316 municipalities), but it is surrounded by mountains (mainly the Alps, about 1 h by car, with coach and train services). Notwithstanding its closeness to outdoor climbing sites, in the Turin metropolitan area there are six indoor climbing halls and some smaller indoor climbing facilities. Moreover, Turin has been one of most important centres in the history of Italian mountaineering and climbing. It is the city where the Club Alpino Italiano (CAI), the national association of mountaineering, was founded in 1863, and where some of the most famous Italian mountain climbers were born and grew up. The surrounding mountains hosted the first international sport-climbing competition in 1985, fostering the birth of the FASI (Federazione di Arrampicata Sportiva Italiana), the Italian Federation of Sport Climbing. Nowadays, Turin is also the headquarters of the Streetboulder Italia association.

We conducted a secondary analysis of qualitative empirical data collected during three different, albeit interconnected, research projects: two Masters dissertation research projects, carried out between September 2016 and February 2017 by two students who were methodologically trained and supervised by one of the authors,[6] and follow-up research in which we have tried to partially balance the two Masters research projects' sample composition by collecting new interviews between March and September 2017. In fact, in the first, female participants were overrepresented because of the focus on the construction of femininities in rock climbing, while in the second, there were more practitioners than instructors and climbing-facilities suppliers. Therefore, in the follow-up research we interviewed mainly male climbing instructors, referees and indoor climbing-facilities suppliers.

Participants

The whole qualitative data set is composed of 40 interviews, ranging from 40 min to 120 min of audio recording. In both the original Masters research projects and in the follow-up, the interviewees were selected through a combination of purposive, emergent, snowballing and convenience sampling (Patton 1990), intersecting gender, age, level of expertise and indoor and/or outdoor practice (see Table 1). Climbers of different levels of expertise were recruited in different climbing gyms in the Turin area. Moreover, interviewees provided connections for us to contact further potential informants.

All the interviewees, except one (a professional mountain guide living in the Aosta Valley), live in the Turin metropolitan area. Their ages range from 18 to 56, and their level of climbing expertise varies from suppliers of indoor and sport climbing facilities

Table 1. Interviewees' information.

Int	Pseudonym	Age	Gender	Profession	Level of expertise	Participant type
1	Ana	21	M	Undergraduate student	Expert amateur	Indoor & outdoor
2	Camilla	27	F	NGO trainer	Medium-experienced amateur	Indoor & outdoor
3	Ernesto	21	M	Instructor	Instructor and athlete	Indoor & outdoor
4	Enrica	37	F	Teacher	Expert amateur	Indoor & outdoor
5	Giada	24	F	Teacher	Novice amateur	Indoor & outdoor
6	Ilenia	18	F	Undergraduate student	Athlete	Indoor & outdoor
7	Mattia	24	M	Employee	Expert amateur	Indoor & outdoor
8	Gustave	27–29	M	Instructor	Instructor and route-setter	Mainly indoor
9	Leonzio	23	M	Athlete	Athlete	Indoor & outdoor
10	Maria	22	F	Instructor	Instructor	Mainly indoor
11	Michele	25	M	Masters student	Medium-experienced amateur	Mainly indoor
12	Mirco	27	M	Worker	Expert amateur	Indoor & outdoor
13	Riccardo	23	M	Masters student	Medium-experienced amateur	Mainly outdoor
14	Valentina	24	F	Masters student	Medium-experienced amateur	Mainly outdoor
15	Asia	26	F	Instructor	Instructor	Mainly outdoor
16	Antonia	45	F	Alpine guide	Expert amateur	Mainly outdoor
17	Barbara	28	F	Artisan	Expert amateur	Indoor & outdoor
18	Caterina	34	F	Employee	Expert amateur	Mainly indoor
19	Daniela	41	F	Oenologist	Medium-experienced amateur	Mainly indoor
20	Ester	49	F	Clerk	Referee and instructor	Mainly indoor
21	Enia	27	F	Physician	Expert amateur	Mainly outdoor
22	Francesca	46	F	Physiotherapist	Expert amateur	Indoor & outdoor
23	Fiorenza	21	F	Athlete and instructor	Athlete	Mainly outdoor
24	Lavinia	46	F	Teacher	Medium-experienced amateur	Indoor & outdoor
25	Lorenza	28	F	Instructor	Instructor	Indoor & outdoor
26	Liliana	41	F	Teacher	Medium-experienced amateur	Mainly outdoor
27	Loredana	27	F	Physician	Expert amateur	Mainly indoor
28	Miriam	26	F	Unemployed	Novice amateur	Mainly indoor
29	Monica	24	F	Instructor and athlete	Instructor and athlete	Indoor & outdoor
30	Melania	51	F	Journalist	Medium-experienced amateur	Mainly indoor
31	Martina	53	F	University professor	Medium-experienced amateur	Indoor & outdoor
32	Piera	56	F	Clerk	Medium-experienced amateur	Mainly indoor (now)
33	Stefania	32	F	Graphic designer	Expert amateur	Mainly outdoor
34	Sonia	50	F	Clerk	Novice amateur	Mainly indoor
35	Viviana	32	F	Unemployed	Medium-experienced amateur	Indoor & outdoor
36	Veronica	27	F	Lawyer	Medium-experienced amateur	Mainly outdoor
37	Dino	49	M	Software developer	Referee and instructor	Mainly outdoor
38	Cesco	30	M	Indoor climbing hall manager	Indoor climbing hall manager and route setter	Indoor & outdoor
39	Daniele	36	M	Indoor climbing hall manager	Indoor climbing hall manager and route setter	Indoor & outdoor
40	Pietro	40	M	University professor	Instructor	Mainly indoor

(10, of whom 2 are managers of indoor climbing halls, 2 referees and 6 sport-climbing instructors) to sport climbing athletes (3), expert amateurs (11), medium-experienced amateurs (13) and novice amateurs (3). The distinction between the different levels of expertise was constructed by taking into account how many years the subject had been climbing and what kind of climbing experiences he or she had undergone.

Data analysis

The available empirical material contains considerable internal variance due to the fact that the three research projects adopted different interview guide templates.[7] Interview transcriptions were therefore analysed using thematic analysis (Braun and Clarke 2006), being first coded then analysed (Sparkes and Smith 2014) in order to identify the main themes under discussion. Verbatim transcriptions of the audio-recorded interviews were uploaded in, and elaborated through computer-assisted qualitative data analysis software (CAQDAS), Atlas.ti version 7.5. The authors carried out the coding procedure together. The first step, open coding, allowed us to unearth the main themes. In the second step, we focussed on those themes referring to, and variously developing, the main topic of 'nature'. Since this topic was not always explicitly addressed in the different interview guide templates adopted, reference to nature emerged spontaneously.

In the following sections, we shall illustrate the main findings of the analysis. First we describe the themes in connection with which interviewees raise the issue of nature and naturalness as a relevant topic in accounting for their rock-climbing experience. Then we show how they use these references to naturalness in order to define what is a 'real climber', thereby engaging in an authentication process.

Results/findings

Away from nature? The indoorization of climbing

Artificial climbing walls represent the oldest (dating back to the 1960s) and best-known examples of artificial sport facilities, which moved the practice from natural outdoor to purpose-built indoor settings. The indoorization of climbing engendered an expansion of the number of its practitioners. Since its foundation in 1987, the Italian national federation of sport climbing (FASI) has gradually increased its membership (from 15,000 individual members and 200 sport associations in 2010 to, respectively, 33,460 and 262 in 2018).

The reasons for this success are summarized by Eden and Barratt (2010, 490): 'Indoor climbing was originally intended to be a rainy day alternative to the outdoors, so in terms of *comfort*, walls protect climbers from the weather and provide indoor heating as well as cafés, social areas and shops. Walls also offer a safer introduction to the sport of climbing for beginners, away from slippery or icy surfaces during bad weather. [...] Climbing walls are also more *convenient*. They allow climbers to visit and train at times when they cannot get out to the crags, whether because it is dark or because they live in cities far away from outdoor routes and cannot drive there easily between work or family commitments'.

In our interviewees' accounts, we find a convergence with the reconstruction of the recent history of climbing in international literature. Originally, artificial climbing walls were thought of as a safer more accessible site for teaching and training skills on rock walls. As an interviewee states:

> The evolution in my opinion, the first step was to shift from mountaineering to climbing, then climbing on artificial walls where you can climb in summer and winter, or attend courses any time during the day or at night. Think of the possibility of climbing as soon as you get out of the office. (Dino, referee and instructor)

Indoor climbing therefore began initially as a means to train for mountaineering. As a consequence, the initial artificial walls simulate natural rocks in their shape, in order to artificially reproduce how nature challenges the climber's movements.

> Artificial climbing walls were created to train people to go on the rocks. [...] Therefore the moves one reproduced indoors were the same as outdoors: fingers were trained a lot, because one should be able to grab onto small holds. (Gustave, instructor and route-setter)

As a result of their increasing popularity, artificial climbing facilities progressively became an essential part of rock climbing, promoting a shift to competitive sports events (Salome 2010). The indoorization and sportivization of rock climbing appear to be interconnected. As rock climbing becomes a sport with its own rules, competitions and scores, sport-climbing infrastructures gradually diverge from outdoor traditional climbing ones.

Artificial walls were then re-adapted to the new specific skills, moves, combinations of moves, and muscle groups to be trained in order to join climbing competitions. Climbing holds acquired new shapes and positioning, and climbing volumes ('those giant prism features that are attached to the wall like any other climbing hold'[8]) emerged as a revolutionary element of route-setting, turning what was once a static, flat feature into a dynamic, changing three-dimensional space.[9] Therefore, indoor walls not only became more 'consciously artificial' (Kulczycki and Hinch 2014), but also sport-climbing moves departed from natural climbing movements, becoming more sport-specific motor skills. The specialization of movement responded to the need for differentiating and ranking climbers' performances during competitions. As an interviewee explains:

> Competitions began with movements similar to those on the rocks. At some point, as many people in the know believe, it was impossible to establish a pecking order for those movements. [...] Therefore route-setters started to set out-of-balance movements [...] where the old-school climbers didn't feel comfortable and fell. [...] Reading the route, interpreting the boulder, and managing one's body have become more difficult. [...] I distinguish substantially between rock climbing and indoor climbing. Nowadays [...] moves adopted during competitions are very different from those on natural rocks. This is a little paradoxical; we started from moves which were an imitation ... taken from rock climbing, then we went beyond that [...] This was the big difference; on the rock you can't have these movements because there is no boulder-like shape. Now they set volumes that you would not consider climbing on the rocks, but during a competition you must do it. [...] Compared with natural movements on the rock, this makes it less natural. But in my opinion it makes it something apart - it's not more or less natural [...] it's simply something different, a sport. (Gustave, instructor and route-setter)

In accordance with Salome (2010), some of the interviewees (10 out of 40) acknowledge a decoupling of artificial settings from the natural environment as a taken-for-granted process. What makes indoor climbing sites attractive for participants is their technical features such as artificial walls, the variety of the holds and the quality of route settings. Therefore, a climbing site is evaluated in comparison with other artificial indoor facilities and not measured against the natural environment.

> I consider these wooden holds very kitsch, wood and stone [...] you are on an artificial wall, everything is fake, it is pointless to insert something recalling the natural [...]. (Pietro, instructor)

In our sample, route setters are particularly keen on discussing this issue, arguing that artificial walls tend to become increasingly spectacularized, with shocking colours and shapes in holds and volumes. Moreover, they tend to interpret any seeming return to nature (in materials, shapes, etc.) as a commercial initiative to attract new customers and to secure old ones' loyalty in a context of an expansion not only of demand, but also of competing suppliers. The use of natural material (like wood or stone) is therefore a commercial and aesthetic choice more than a technical or value-oriented option.

The guy who says "Well, in some rock climbing gyms the route-setting is far from the rock, while in others it seems you are climbing in the Susa Valley, on cliffs". The answer is simple; I tend to set routes to please the cliff-passionate climber who is only crimping[10] and the one who likes the boulder with little edges, where you put reverse fingers, a little old-school but no less entertaining or useful. […] Nowadays, to make things more and more spectacular, we work on the acrobatic side of the movement, and on the scenic impact of the set holds. (Cesco, artificial climbing hall manager and route-setter)

I think that brands have followed different attitudes. I saw very small holds […] which look fake, like fake rock to be fixed on the artificial wall. […] In that case it is an aesthetic choice, linked to pleasing, selling, providing something new. (Dino, referee and instructor)

But indoorization is not the whole story. In the next section, we will show how nature returns as a meaningful reference in climbers' accounts of both their indoor and outdoor practice.

Reclaiming the naturalness of climbing

Our interviewees revealed that climbing and nature remain closely connected. However, in their account practitioners evoke nature not only as a specific context for their practice (nature as an outdoor environment), but as a more general frame recalling the idea of naturalness, defining distinctive lifestyles and movements. In so doing, naturalness seems to be mobilized as a source of 'hot authentication'. Following Cohen and Cohen (2012), this mode of authentication is focussed on the high level of commitment and self-investment of practitioners, as well as on venerated climbing spots and on the emotions and sensations engendered by the outdoor practice.

The naturalness of the outdoor setting

The first way naturalness is portrayed by the practitioners is by addressing the importance of the outdoor environment. The majority of the interviewees (30 out of 40) explicitly define climbing as an activity that *should* take place in a natural, thereby outdoor, context qualified by its physical traits. The boundlessness of mountain and foothill areas, along with the different variety of rocks and the listing of the most famous climbing spots, are recalled in this respect. According to Kulczycki (2014), in this case the definition of the physical dimension of a certain site, as well as its attributes, occurs both at a macro stage – described by 'the broad site feature, layout and the atmosphere' (2014, 13) – and a micro stage where 'the geology (e.g. rock types), routes, and holds were features influencing place-meaning the most' (Kulczycki 2014).

For the above-mentioned reasons, some outdoor sites become ideal and mythical compounds in the climbing collective imaginary which our practitioners draw upon in their mapping of the ultimate, *par excellence*, must-do spots.

I like different sites where I come back often, maybe the Orco Valley or Finale Ligure, spots like these. But I also like to visit new places, discover new types of rock, follow strange routes. (Mattia, expert amateur)

Sometimes interviewees construct the naturalness of their climbing destinations beyond their physical features. The key point is not where to go 'within' the natural environment, but to escape from urban contexts.

[Climbing] to me is a way to get out the city, to be surrounded by green and emptiness, to hear from nobody. (Riccardo, medium-experienced amateur)

The city as a purpose-built space, thereby fully under human control, is framed as unnatural. Similarly, artificial climbing halls are criticized as 'highly managed spaces where the majority of risks are removed or designed out, thus providing comfort through safety and security' (Eden and Barratt 2010, 490).

On indoor walls the worst you can do is to break an ankle because you fall badly. On the rock it depends. It ranges from breaking an ankle to endangering your life. […] I am not just obsessed by making the grade in complete safety. […] Those who climb outdoors are more used to going on the mountains or coping with more difficult situations, containing higher risks … I feel those climbers are closer to my attitude because they do not pay so much attention to the level of difficulty but are more interested in the adventurous side of climbing rather than the technicalities of mere sport performance. (Mattia, expert amateur)

Traditional climbing and multi-pitching[11] are valued as practices where risk cannot be sanitized and within which different, more demanding, physical and mental involvement is required.

The naturalness of emotional and sensorial experience

Another way of attributing naturalness to outdoor environments is by mentioning the emotional and sensorial experience they trigger. We find repeated descriptions (in 26 out of 40 interviews) of what the climber's body feels palpably – including the senses of touch, smell and sight – during climbing experiences in a wild outdoor setting. The embodied sensations work as the markers of the naturalness of the outdoors.

I love climbing outdoors! When you feel the clean smell of the air and not the stink of the gym. (Ana, expert-amateur)

Climbing makes me feel peaceful … it makes me focus on one thing, on the rope especially. You feel the effect of the void while climbing on the rock face. I find that climbing really clears my mind. (Enia, expert amateur)

The involvement of multiple senses – evoked through the smell of the fresh air, the view of a beautiful landscape and the tactile pleasure of the real rock – is often enhanced by making reference to emotions. Respondents often outline different feelings which can be unleashed only within the natural environment. The rush triggered by the height reached or by falling; the mindfulness during outdoor climbing and the absolute flow while topping a boulder.

The naturalness of a climbing lifestyle

Naturalness, in addition to the physical–environmental frame, seems to be informed by an experiential and existential dimension conveyed by the idea of a particular natural lifestyle. Half of our interviewees (19 out of 40) stress the importance of an exploratory approach (Kulczycki 2014) to climbing. This requires trying different types of rocks, not confining oneself to must-do spots and better-known climbing sites, and constantly searching for new, not-easily-accessible places.

I like to go to different places so I bought a van with a friend and we go around as much as we can. He is a colleague of mine, therefore when we are free we take the van and go. This summer we went to Siena where we set several boulder and lead routes in a gym, with and without ropes. Then we moved on and reached Monte Amiata, climbed there and later took the ferry in Civitavecchia and went to Sardinia. [...] We came back to Turin, met other friends and hit the road again, heading for Switzerland and Austria. We travelled for over a month. (Daniele, indoor climbing hall manager and route-setter)

[...] You make choices that most people do not understand. They tell you: 'What the hell, you went to Thailand where there are the best beaches in the world and you looked for cliffs?' Yes, because everyone sees these beaches and nobody has ever seen the cliffs!' (Veronica, medium-experienced amateur)

Daniele and Veronica's quotes incorporate many interesting topics. While Daniele mentions some of the well-known, must-do destinations for climbers, namely Switzerland and Austria, both also adopt an exploratory approach by re-interpreting places such as Thailand, Sardinia and Monte Amiata, which are not included in climbing guidebooks, as enjoyable climbing sites. Veronica exemplifies the refusal and subversion of a touristic attitude. While normally people identify Thailand with its beaches she rather focusses her attention on cliffs as a feature usually ignored in the typical Thai postcard. Daniele, whilst moving from one place to another, notches up a lot of spots during a single climbing trip, thereby underlining a deliberate voracious nomadism, a distinctive trait of a real climber (Kiewa 2002). However, this nomadism conveyed by the number of destinations listed and the means of transportation quoted (the van, recalling the 'vanner' character in Rickly-Boyd 2012), also symbolizes a free gypsy spirit, a core element of a natural lifestyle.

Another component of this lifestyle is the rejection of any form of tourist facilities. Sleeping in a tent and eating low-price nutrient foods, as well as other simple-life choices, expresses the desire to abstain from any form of comfort or luxury.

The closer a cliff or a boulder area is to nature, the more beautiful it is. You can easily set yourself up there with a tent without the necessity of camping or accommodation facilities. (Camilla, medium-experienced amateur)

We can say that climbers are open-minded, they do not disdain sleeping in their knapsacks at the bottom of the cliff. They are a bit wild. We had a holiday in Spain and there were three of us in a small car. We spent fifteen days like this, two sleeping inside and one outside in rotation. Our kitchen table was the spare wheel. (Leonzio, athlete)

The naturalness of this gypsy lifestyle includes one more aspect; the inclination to seek ever-more direct contact with nature by normalizing and welcoming those adventurous and inconvenient elements that normal people would consider unpleasant and to-be-avoided (Rickly-Boyd 2012). For this aim, practitioners search for direct physical contact with the natural environment and often valorize the effects produced by the latter on their bodies – from wearing out their fingers to feeling pain in their backs because of sleeping on hard surfaces, from getting dirty because of the magnesite to wetting their shoes after having crossed a river in order to reach a boulder area.

Back to nature: climbing outdoors as a source of authentication

In traditional adventure sports, involvement in a natural setting and challenge was a core dimension of participation. It can be looking for big waves in surfing (Beal and Smith 2010), experiencing the countryside on mountain bikes (King & Church 2013) or backcountry skiing as a masculinized sportscape (Stoddart 2011), embodying nature as a spiritual space in windsurfing (Humberstone 2011) or as an intimate companion in extreme sports (Brymer and Gray 2010).

As we have already mentioned, some scholars identify a significant shift in those life-style sports which have seen recent growing indoorization (Van Bottenburg and Salome 2010). From the primacy of nature as a source of authenticity – leading to the effort to simulate the natural environment in designing artificial sport facilities – to the re-interpretation of nature as a backdrop to be staged and manufactured. In the specific case of sport climbing in an indoor setting, Salome (2010) gave some evidence of an increasing disassociation of indoor climbing walls from natural rocks, witnessed by the choice of materials, colours and shapes. Moreover, she pointed at a more varied participation profile in indoor settings compared with outdoor. Among indoor climbers, female and older participants tend to be more numerous. However, she also acknowledged that 'there are still tensions between core members of sport culture and the new consumers. These tensions are, especially in climbing centres, an issue' (Salome 2010, 81). For instance, 'real climbers' do not train indoors on average Saturdays when children's classes are scheduled.

In this final section, we will discuss how the above-described ways of talking about the naturalness of climbing work, for both indoor climbing facilities suppliers and users (a total of 25 out of 40), as a boundary marker in the authentication of their practice, defining 'real climbers' and making distinctions and hierarchies among different groups of climbing-facilities users.

Indoor and sport climbing-facilities suppliers tend to show a more positive, inclusive attitude towards not only the increasing participation in sport climbing, but also the pluralization of meanings attached to it. Some interviewees explicitly acknowledge the legitimacy of every kind of climbing, stressing the value of freedom in interpreting the practice.

> What's beautiful in this sport is that everybody can do it his/her own way, and it can be experienced in an incredible variety of ways: those who experience it as a lifestyle [...] because climbing is their passion and they connect all the aspects of their lives with it, travelling, leisure, holidays ... [...]; others who interpret it more as a competitive sport implying workout, competitive training, aiming at competitions, and therefore they don't climb outdoors [...]. (Cesco, artificial climbing hall manager and route-setter)

> In the majority of cases, [...] there is great reciprocal respect for, and considerable mixing between, those who came from sport climbing and moved to mountaineering, and those who came from mountaineering and discovered sport climbing. They are two sides of the same coin, not in contrast. (Dino, referee and instructor)

Such increasing participation is welcomed as a marker of commercial success and as a source of new profit, as well as evidence of growing social visibility and recognition. The recent inclusion of sport climbing in the forthcoming edition of the Olympic Games, in this perspective, is interpreted as a possible boost to further development of the practice, capable of attracting more funding and followers.

While expressing an inclusive attitude in acknowledging the variety of legitimate ways of climbing, when suppliers of indoor climbing facilities and services talk about their own practice as experts and committed climbers, the majority of them (7 out of 10) tend to stress the distinctiveness of climbing on the rocks. Going outdoors is perceived as a more pleasurable and comprehensive experience than when they methodically train or compete indoors, something that can be sometimes more relaxing, sometimes more challenging. Moreover, to attract people from indoor to outdoor climbing is, for some of these climbers, a sort of professional mission.

> I go on the rocks because I love climbing and sometimes I need to get rid of all that competitive atmosphere, to be fit on the day of the contest, to manage the course, to do it once without mistakes … When I go on the rocks I am more … not relaxed, but I have a different attitude, I go there to spend a full day out doing what I love most. (Gustave, artificial climbing hall manager and route-setter)

> I am still passionate about outdoor life, I am attending a course to become a mountain guide, to be certified to accompany people outdoors. My aim is, in the future, to be involved in indoor and sport climbing, […] but bringing people closer to this sport […] meanwhile working as a connection […] with the outdoor environment, the mountains surrounding our city […]. (Cesco, indoor climbing hall manager and rout-setter)

Among participants with different levels of expertise (expert, amateur, novice), we find a more conflictual mode of authenticating the different ways of climbing, adopting a more explicit indoor–outdoor polarization (20 out of 30). The interviewees insist on two of the above illustrated dimensions of authentication in defining what is natural; nature as an outdoor environment, and as a matter of a wild, gypsy-like lifestyle.

First of all, participants explicitly criticize those climbers who, having learned the practice on artificial walls, do not appreciate or try outdoor climbing (Eden and Barratt 2010). Restraining climbing experience to an indoor setting is described as a loss of its full (and legitimate) meaning, which is the exploration of the natural environment as well as one's own self.

> You should climb to discover, to explore … Outdoors and not only in an indoor centre. (Fiorenza, athlete)

> Surely those who climb only indoors miss the beauty of the mountains. (Antonia, expert amateur)

Therefore, indoor climbing, as a self-referential setting, risks being perceived as a closed context, with a symbolic shift from *indoor*, as a neutral connotation, to *artificial*, as a more derogatory label. In this critical perspective, even synthetic materials (plastic, resins) become the opposite of – and not something complementary with or preparatory to – *natural* rocks.

> Among them there are those who are just "plastic-pitchers", people who climb only indoors. They are not interested in going outdoors because outdoors is painful, tiring, difficult, dangerous […] Those who climb only indoors, on resin, with a comfortable crashpad below, they are the "comfy" ones. (Mirko, expert amateur)

Indoor climbing walls, losing their connection with the natural outdoors, can be (mis)understood as an average gym centre where participants are focussed only on toning up their bodies. A muscular body is acknowledged as a distinctive marker of a climber, but it is considered as a by-product of a practice whose aim is to probe one's embodied skills on a natural test-bench. An additional source of inauthenticity is the idea that climbing has become fashionable, and therefore can be approached by the typical poser, more focussed on appearance (the 'cool pose') than on attitude and commitment.

Climbing started on the rocks, and those who climb only indoors, saying "I don't like rocks" are practising a different sport, they are not climbing. They are "plastic-grabbers" … It's like doing pull-ups but using holds instead … Therefore those who climb only indoors and never go outdoors […] are not real climbers. (Fiorenza, athlete)

By a real climber I mean someone who climbs for love […] surely there are also inauthentic climbers who that do it as a fashion statement, because it's cool. (Francesca, expert amateur)

The reference to a *natural* way of performing (outdoor and within a committed lifestyle), as opposed to practising only within the artificial climbing walls setting, appears therefore to be still a core element in the process of authentication of real climbing.

Discussion and conclusion

The indoorization of climbing in Italy does not seem to have engendered the double shift in the sources of, and claim-makers for, authenticity described by Salome and Van Bottenburg (Salome 2010, Salome and Van Bottenburg 2012). In fact, our analysis has revealed that reference to nature is still a relevant dimension in the way Italian climbers define themselves and authenticate their practice. However, this reference appears to be more complex and nuanced than the mere outdoor/indoor binomial. We have chosen to adopt the notion of naturalness to try to account for this plurality of dimensions. Consequently, we have identified three main themes: nature as an outdoor environment; naturalness as a matter of the emotions and sensations involved; and naturalness as a wild lifestyle. These themes are mobilized as a battleground for a sort of 'hot authentication' (Cohen and Cohen 2012), allowing grassroots participants to debate who is, and what makes, a 'real climber', and therefore how to make distinctions and create hierarchies among authentic practitioners (Wheaton 2007; Wheaton 2000; Beal et al. 2003).

In line with Salome (2010), the suppliers of indoor facilities we interviewed, with respect to their professional positioning, seem to adopt a more inclusive attitude towards the increasing variety of climbing styles and types of participants, thereby blurring the hierarchical distinctions between hard-core participants and newbies, wannabees, posers and outsiders (Donnelly 2006). For this reason, these suppliers can be compared with the emerging type of participants Salome and Van Bottenburg (2012) named 'exceeders', combining the use of training in artificial settings with the search for a full experience in outdoor settings. The two scholars significantly described this type of participant as 'the most devoted and enthusiastic group with regard to their sports' (Salome and Van Bottenburg 2012, 37), with a high proportion of climbers.

On the other hand, when Italian suppliers account for their personal experience as expert and committed climbers, they acknowledge climbing on the rocks and outdoor life (Rickly-Boyd 2012) as a more meaningful aspect of their practice. However, they tend not to stress the reference to naturalness as an essential dimension for their authentication. We can provide a different interpretation of this outcome. On the one hand, we could follow Salome (2010) in saying that, for indoor suppliers, hierarchies among practitioners have become less relevant. On the other hand, since the suppliers we interviewed have a multi-layered professional profile (Dumont 2016) (i.e. indoor centre managers and/

or route-setters and/or instructors) they have such an established reputation within the local and national climbing community that they do not require any claim for their authenticity, which seems to be embodied and taken for granted.

Moving on to participants, we have found similarities with and differences from Salome and Van Bottenburg (2012). As in the Netherlands, in North-Western Italy climbing has become a more diversified practice including mainly-indoor, mainly-outdoor and both-indoor-and-outdoor practitioners. By exploring how different kinds of participants make sense of and authenticate their climbing experience some tensions, boundaries and hierarchies are re-emerging.

The naturalness of the outdoor context of practice and of a climbing-focussed wild lifestyle is evoked as a marker of the real – committed, passionate, engaged – climber (Kiewa 2002) when practitioners talk about their own experiences. Mirroring that, the lack of those two dimensions of naturalness is mobilized to label the (in)authenticity of those practitioners who, treating climbing as a sport like any other (Challéat 2014), risk de-naturalizing it.

To conclude, the investigation of Italian climbers (both indoor facilities suppliers and participants) has problematized the impact of indoorization on climbing as a practice, showing that, at least in the Italian context, the reference to naturalness is still a core dimension of the hot authentication of rock climbing (Cohen and Cohen 2012). Albeit with different emphases, for both climbing facilities suppliers and users, nature is not only perceived as the environment where climbing takes place, as an opponent (the pitch to be challenged and mastered) and as a partner (the rock to be in touch and to dance with). The naturalness of climbing also resides in the kind of emotions and sensations involved in the practice, and in the wild side of the existence a devoted lifestyle embodies.

Notes

1. Another example of an authenticity claim in climbing is provided by Clayton and Coates's (2015) analysis of narratives of parents who still climb 'seriously'.
2. Dupont (2014) provides an analysis of the different forms of participation in skateboarding. For an exploration of the new forms of multi-layered professionalism in rock climbing, see Dumont (2016, 2017).
3. Robinson (2008) distinguishes four types of rock climbing: traditional, sport, aid climbing and bouldering.
4. For an analysis of the authentication process, in Italy, of a recently emerged lifestyle sport, parkour, see Sterchele and Ferrero Camoletto (2017).
5. Similarly, Senda-Cook (2012) analyses the rhetorical practices through which "real" outdoor recreation is produced.
6. We want to thank Chiara Canova (interviews 15–36) and Matteo De Costanzi (interviews 1–14), the two Master's students who made their empirical material available to us and authorized our analysis for this article.
7. Despite the different lists of questions used as guideline in the three research projects, there were many shared topics under investigation.
8. http://blog.earthtreksclimbing.com/volumes-the-new-dimensions-of-indoor-climbing. See also http://blog.momentumclimbing.com/innovations-in-climbing-volumes/. (both accessed 15 September 2017).
9. http://blog.earthtreksclimbing.com/volumes-the-new-dimensions-of-indoor-climbing (accessed 15 September 2017).

10. A crimp is a hold which is only just big enough to be grasped with the tips of the fingers. Crimping is the process of holding onto a crimp. Source: https://en.wikipedia.org/wiki/Glossary_of_climbing_terms#C (accessed 12 December 2018).
11. Multi-pitching means climbing on routes that are too long for a single belay rope. Source: https://en.wikipedia.org/wiki/Glossary_of_climbing_terms#C (accessed 12 December 2018).

Disclosure statement

No potential conflict of interest was reported by the authors.

References

Aubel, O., O. Hoibian, and J. Defrance. 2002. "Les Enjeux de la Sportivisation de L'escalade Libre." In *Deux Siècles D'alpinismes Européens*, 273–291. Paris: L'Harmattan.
Aubel, O. 2005. *L'escalade Libre en France. Sociologie D'une Prophetie Sportive*. Paris: L'Harmattan.
Barratt, P. 2011. "Vertical Worlds: Technology, Hybridity and the Climbing Body." *Social & Cultural Geography* 12 (4): 397–412. doi:10.1080/14649365.2011.574797.
Beal, B., and M. M. Smith. 2010. "Maverick's: Big-Wave Surfing and the Dynamic of 'Nothing' and 'Something'." *Sport in Society* 13 (7–8): 1102–1116. doi:10.1080/17430431003780047.
Beal, B., L. Weidman, R. E. Rinehart, and S. Sydnor. 2003. "Skateboarding and Authenticity." In *To the Extreme: Alternative Sports, Inside and Out*, 337–352. New York: Suny Press.
Bogardus, L. M. 2012. "The Bolt Wars: A Social Worlds Perspective on Rock Climbing and Intragroup Conflict." *Journal of Contemporary Ethnography* 41 (3): 283–308. doi:10.1177/089121611426429.
Braun, V., and V. Clarke. 2006. "Using Thematic Analysis in Psychology." *Qualitative Research in Psychology* 3 (2): 77–101. doi:10.1191/1478088706qp063oa.
Brymer, E., and T. Gray. 2010. "Developing an Intimate 'Relationship' with Nature Through Extreme Sports Participation." *Leisure/Loisir* 34 (4): 361–374. doi:10.1080/14927713.2010.542888.
Challéat, S. 2014. "L'escalade, un Sport Comme les Autres Dans la Course aux Jeux?" *Grimper, Le Magazine de L'escalade* 159: 26–30. Hal Id: hal-01150150.
Clayton, B., and E. Coates. 2015. "Negotiating the Climb: A Fictional Representation of Climbing, Gendered Parenting and the Morality of Time." *Annals of Leisure Research* 18 (2): 235–251. doi:10.1080/11745398.2014.957221.
Cohen, E. 2010. "Tourism, Leisure and Authenticity." *Tourism Recreation Research* 35 (1): 67–73. doi:10.1080/02508281.2010.11081620.
Cohen, E., and S. A. Cohen. 2012. "Authentication: Hot and Cool." *Annals of Tourism Research* 39 (3): 1295–1314. doi:10.1016/j.annals.2012.03.004.
Corneloup, J., and P. Bourdeau. 2004. "Les Sports de Nature. Entre Pratiques Libres, Territoires et Logiques Institutionnelles." *Les Cahiers Espaces*, 117–125. Hal Id: halshs-00377043.
Donnelly, M. 2006. "Studying Extreme Sports: Beyond the Core Participants." *Journal of Sports and Social Issues* 30 (2): 219–224. doi:10.1177/0193723506287187.
Dumont, G. 2016. "Multi-layered Labor: Entrepreneurship and Professional Versatility in Rock Climbing." *Ethnography* 17 (4): 440–459. doi:10.1177/1466138116638677.

Dumont, G. 2017. "The Beautiful and the Damned: The Work of New Media Production in Professional Rock Climbing." *Journal of Sport and Social Issues* 41 (2): 99–117. doi:10.1177/0193723516686285.

Dupont, T. 2014. "From Core to Consumer: The Informal Hierarchy of the Skateboard Scene." *Journal of Contemporary Ethnography*, 43 (5): 556–581. doi:10.1177/0891241613513033.

Eden, S., and P. Barratt. 2010. "Outdoors Versus Indoors? Angling Ponds, Climbing Walls and Changing Expectations of Environmental Leisure." *Area* 42 (4): 487–493. doi:10.1111/j.1475-4762.2010.00943.

Giannoulakis, C. 2016. "The 'Authenticitude' Battle in Action Sports: A Case-Based Industry Perspective." *Sport Management Review* 19: 171–182. doi:10.1016/j.smr.2015.05.004.

Humberstone, B. 2011. "Embodiment and Social and Environmental Action in Nature-Based Sport: Spiritual Spaces." *Leisure Studies* 30 (4): 495–512. doi:10.1080/02614367.2011.602421.

Kiewa, J. 2002. "Traditional Climbing: Metaphor of Resistance or Metanarrative of Oppression?" *Leisure Studies* 21 (2): 145–161. doi:10.1080/02614360210158605.

King, K., and A. Church. 2013. "'We Don't Enjoy Nature Like That': Youth Identity and Lifestyle in the Countryside." *Journal of Rural Studies* 31: 67–76. doi:10.1016/j.jrurstud.2013.02.004.

Krein, K. J. 2014. "Nature Sports." *Journal of the Philosophy of Sport* 41 (2): 193–208. doi:10.1080/00948705.2013.785417.

Kulczycki, C. 2014. "Place Meanings and Rock Climbing in Outdoor Settings." *Journal of Outdoor Recreation and Tourism* 7-8: 8–15. doi:10.1016/j.jort.2014.09.005.

Kulczycki, C., and T. Hinch. 2014. ""It's a Place to Climb": Place Meanings of Indoor Rock Climbing Facilities." *Leisure/Loisir* 38 (3-4): 271–293. doi:10.1080/14927713.2015.1043710.

Melo, R., and R. Gomes. 2016. "Understanding Nature Sports Organizations in Portugal." *The Open Sports Sciences Journal* 9 (Suppl 1, M3): 13–25. doi:10.2174/1875399X01609010013.

Patton, M. 1990. *Qualitative Evaluation and Research Methods*. Beverly Hills: Sage.

Rickly, J. M., B. S. R. Grimwood, K. Caton, and L. Cooke. 2018. "Rock Climbing and the "Good Life": Cultivating an Ethics of Lifestyle Mobilities." In *New Moral Natures in Tourism*. London: Routledge.

Rickly, J. M., and E. S. Vidon. 2017. "Contesting Authentic Practice and Ethical Authority in Adventure Tourism." *Journal of Sustainable Tourism* 25 (10): 1418–1433. doi:10.1080/09669582.2017.1284856.

Rickly-Boyd, J. 2012. "Lifestyle Climbing: Toward Existential Authenticity." *Journal of Sport & Tourism* 17 (2): 85–104. doi:10.1080/14775085.2012.729898.

Robinson, V. 2008. *Everyday Masculinities and Extreme Sport*. Oxford: Berg.

Salome, L. 2010. "Constructing Authenticity in Contemporary Consumer Culture: The Case of Lifestyle Sports." *European Journal for Sport and Society* 7: 69–87. doi:10.1080/16138171.2010.11687846.

Salome, L., and M. Van Bottenburg. 2012. "Are They all Daredevils? Introducing a Participation Typology for the Consumption of Lifestyle Sports in Different Settings." *European Sport Management Quarterly* 12 (1): 19–42. doi:10.1080/16184742.2011.637171.

Senda-Cook, S. 2012. "Rugged Practices: Embodying Authenticity in Outdoor Recreation." *Quarterly Journal of Speech* 98 (2): 129–152. doi:10.1080/00335630.2012.663500.

Sterchele, D., and R. Ferrero Camoletto. 2017. "Governing Bodies or Managing Freedom? Subcultural Struggles, National Sport Systems and the Glocalised Institutionalisation of Parkour." *International Journal of Sport Policy and Politics* 9 (1): 89–105. doi:10.108019406940.2017.1289235.

Suchet, A. 2011. "La Sportivisation des Pratiques, Dites, Nouvelles." *Aspects Sociologiques* 18 (1): 1–17.

Sparkes, A. C., and B. Smith. 2014. *Qualitative Research Methods in Sport, Exercise and Health. From Process to Product*. London: Routledge.

Stoddart, M. C. 2011. "Constructing Masculinized Sportscapes: Skiing, Gender and Nature in British Columbia, Canada." *International Review for the Sociology of Sport* 46 (1): 108–124. doi:10.1177/1082690210373541.

Vanreusel, B., P. De Knop, B. Vanreusel, and J. Scheerder. 2002. "Naar een Socio-Economische Visie op Sportbeoefening in de Natuur: van Bambi tot Rambo." In *Sportsociologie. Het Spel en de Spelers*, 178–186. Maarssen: Elsevier Gezondheids-zorg.

Van Bottenburg, M., and L. Salome. 2010. "The Indoorisation of Outdoor Sports: an Exploration of the Rise of Lifestyle Sports in Artificial Settings." *Leisure Studies* 29 (9): 143–160. doi:10.1080/02614360903261479.

Wang, N. 1999. "Rethinking Authenticity in Tourism Experience." *Annals of Tourism Research* 26 (2): 349–370. doi:10.1016/S0160-7383(98)00103-0.

Wheaton, B. 2000. "'Just Do It': Consumption, Commitment, and Identity in the Windsurfing Subculture." *Sociology of Sport Journal* 17 (3): 254–274. doi:10.1123/ssj.17.3.254.

Wheaton, B. 2007. "After Sport Culture: Rethinking Sport and Post-Subcultural Theory." *Journal of Sport and Social Issues* 31 (3): 283–307. doi:10.1177/0193723507301049.

Wheaton, B., and B. Beal. 2003. "'Keeping It Real': Subcultural Media and the Discourses of Authenticity in Alternative Sport." *International Review for the Sociology of Sport* 38 (2): 155–176. doi:10.1177/1012690203038002002.

Nature sports: state of the art of research

Amador Durán-Sánchez, José Álvarez-García and María de la Cruz del Río-Rama

ABSTRACT

In the same way, as society has been experiencing significant changes in recent years, sport practice has evolved to acquire extraordinary importance, both socially and economically. At the moment, we are faced with a wide range of sports related to nature and outdoors as an alternative to sporting activities that were done traditionally. This diversity is precisely one of the reasons why there is still no unanimity between authors when it comes to establishing a single term that comprises such a large field of physical activities. Thus, these new sports can be denominated nature sports, adventure sports, alternative sports or lifestyle sports, among others. A descriptive and exploratory bibliometric study of the articles included in the multidisciplinary Scopus (Elsevier) database was carried out in order to analyse the current scientific production related to nature sports. Thus, it was found that of the 223 papers selected, a quarter of them use the term extreme sports to refer to sports practise in nature and only 5% use the term nature sports. The results obtained show the growing interest of the scientific community for the study of this subject in the last decade, mainly in the United States, United Kingdom and France and in the areas of social sciences, medicine and health care, business, administration and accounting.

Introduction

In recent years, the practice of physical activities in the natural environment has evolved from traditional and minority conceptions to more innovative and affordable forms for a broad social mass (Fuster and i Queixalós 2008). The increase in people's standard of living, the reduction of working hours, with the consequent increase in leisure time, improvement of communications, the increasing need of citizens to leave the stressful city routine in search of sensations and emotions, and the need to contact nature has contributed in some way to the gradual approach of the population to natural environments (Lacasa, Miranda, and Muro 1995).

If the combination of all of the above points is added to the importance of sporting phenomena in today's society, we are faced with the possible pillars on which the increase in the interest for physical and sporting activities in nature is supported, which has generated the production of a significant body of academic literature on the topic. More than ever, the systematic practice of physical activity is considered to be a solid alternative for promoting and improving the individual's quality of life (Morgan and Goldston 1987).

Physical activities in nature are motivated by a series of values and concepts that are part of the new cultural trends typical of the post-industrial and trans-modern society (Betrán and Betrán 1995; Corneloup 2005; Granero and Baena 2010). The potential sports participant looks for new sensations, variety and innovation, which are difficult to find in other sports (Lacasa, Miranda, and Muro 1995).

This universe of physical-sporting practices linked to the use and enjoyment of the natural environment receives several generic names depending on the most significant characteristics that define it and, in an attempt, to delimit this emerging sector in a genuine and precise way: adventure sports, nature sports, alternative sports, extreme sports, gravity sports, lifestyle sports, action sports, risk sports or outdoor sports are some of them.

Nature sports are the first term to emerge and groups a set of sport activities developed in direct contact with nature (Bessy and Mouton 2004). Subsequently, the terms adventure sports and risk sports appear, which offer a series of peculiar elements of motivation that make them particularly appealing to great parts of the population: facing the challenge of a difficult and risky task (challenge), doing an activity which is difficult for others success-fully (social recognition), overcoming self-limits (personal improvement) or feelings of competence (perceptions of self-efficacy) (Palmi & Martín, 2007).

Despite being recent, its rapid dissemination and economic and educational benefits have led to several investigations (Lacasa, Miranda, and Muro 1995). Therefore, it is necess-ary to stop to make an inventory of the work that has been done and at the same time to analyse and identify new directions and challenges for the future (Low and MacMillan 1988). Based on this fact, the objective of this article is to present an in-depth analysis of the current state of research related to nature sports through its bibliometric study. That is, by using mathematical and statistical methods to evaluate scientific production (Spinak 1996).

This article is divided into four main sections. Firstly, we proceed to review the academic literature in order to establish the theoretical framework of the research. Subsequently, in the third section, we describe both the sources and the methodological process used to obtain the references that form the empirical base of the study. In the fourth section, the main results obtained in the study of the basic bibliometric indicators are presented. In the fifth section, the main conclusions are discussed, while acknowledging the limit-ations of the research.

Theoretical framework

One of the main problems found when carrying out scientific work on sporting practices in nature is its theoretical delimitation, due in particular, to the fact that there is an infinite number of terms in the academic literature, with each one showing a set of theoretical assumptions to designate these practices (Melo 2009).

In response to this problem, some studies were carried out, whose aim was to clarify this definitional problem (Bessy and Mouton 2004; Betrán 1995; Turčová, Martin, and Neuman 2005; Wheaton 2004). However, no consensus was obtained and for the moment, there is no term that is unanimously accepted to designate the physical activities that take place in natural spaces, since each term has its semantic differences that represent distinctive ways of facing this phenomenon (Melo and Gomes 2017a).

According to Bessy and Mouton (2004), the term nature sports arose at the end of the twentieth century, with new sports areas in nature and an increase in the number of participants who need more organization, structuring and the ability to practice safety (Melo and Gomes 2017a). It comprises a set of sporting activities, both formal and informal, that are developed and experienced in different natural (air, land and water) or rural contexts and that can contribute to sustainable local development and its conservation (Melo 2009; Melo and Gomes 2017a). Furthermore, it incorporates sports that have as a central or essential component the natural environment (Howe 2012) and shares a fundamental structure in which human beings and features of the natural world are brought together (Krein 2014).

One of the first proposals to define the sport activity that takes place in natural spaces was elaborated by Palmi and Martín (2007). Its definition is built around four fundamental concepts: Adventure, in the sense that it is a type of physical activity with a significant amount of uncertainty (objective and subjective) and a clear connotation of challenge or defiance for the participant (self-improvement); Risk, as the danger of real or perceived loss (objective risk/subjective risk); Environment (natural environment), which provides a series of peculiar connotations that define them (open space, freedom sensation, evasion, fresh air); Competence, understanding this as the experience and/or ability that the subject has about a skill.

Later, Melo defined the concept of nature sports as

> all the physical and corporal activities that are done in direct contact with nature, presenting an organised format or not, whose objective is the expression or the improvement of the physical and psychological condition, the development of social relations, the goal of recreation and leisure, or obtaining results in competition at all levels, and contributing to the sustainability of local development in the environmental, economic and socio-cultural dimensions. (Melo 2009, 101)

These sports practices in natural spaces are also included under the concept of adventure sports or risk sports (Fuster and i Queixalós 2008). In this sense, Breivik (2010) considers the term adventure sports that contain a wide range of sports and is characterized as activities that (a) have elements of challenge, emotion and (in most sports) risk, (b) take place in natural environments, (c) are more freely organized than traditional sports, (d) represent a freedom or opposition to the dominant sports culture, (e) are individualistic but tend to form groups and subcultures around the activity. According to Fullonet (1995), this term is not the most adequate to refer to all activities that encompass the practice of sports in nature by introducing a typology of participants who seek risk and challenge when they should be considered as practices oriented to the bulk of the population.

More recently, Krein (2014, 193) defined the term nature sports as 'those sports in which a particular natural feature, or combination of natural features, plays at least one of the primary roles that human competitors or partners play in traditional or standard sports'. Melo and Gomes (2017b) highlight three fundamental elements that have contributed to the evolution of this concept: (a) a new sporting context that makes the sporting offer and diffusion in society possible, (b) the emergence of the concept of sustainable development, which attributes an important role to local economic development in sports activities and (c) the commercialization of nature activities through labels (products) related to adventure and ecology.

It is observed that sports practice constitutes an element of tourist motivation, linked to the rise of a new tourism modality from the synergy of sport and tourism called 'sport tourism'. The importance of this segment is shown by the increasing attention given by both the tourism and sports industry and by the development of numerous academic papers (Gibson 2005; Melo 2017). The connection between tourism and sport has been developing for several decades, generating a new field of scientific knowledge (Granero 2007). As in the case of nature sports, different terms are used indiscriminately to refer to the same typology: 'sports tourism in nature, active tourism, adventure tourism, active sports tourism or soft tourism' (Gil 2003, 137). In many studies, it is clear that both nature and sports done in nature are key elements of sports tourism (Hall and Page 2006).

Nature and sports done while travelling whose objective is the practice of sport in natural spaces are undoubtedly two of the main components of tourism (Hall and Page 2006). The relationship between nature sports and sports tourism (a term used in recent years to express sport-related leisure travel) is evident from the fact that the majority of these sports are done in places located at a great distance from the participant's home, promoting the need to travel and a number of tourist activities, resulting in a significant economic impact on tourist destinations (Melo and Gomes 2016a).

Another of the perspectives proposed by Melo and Gomes (2016b) that deserves special attention refers to the principle of sustainability that is imposed on the development of any type of activity, seeking not to degrade or exhaust the resources and that make this development possible, and its relationship with the development of rural areas (Gil 2003).

The research on nature sports, following the thematic classification made by Lacasa, Miranda, and Muro (1995), treats the discipline from different approaches: Sociology, psychology, management, performance, biomedical and others. The starting point, from a purely theoretical point of view, is the studies that aim to delimit the concept and contextualise it (Granero and Baena 2010; Howe 2012, 2017; Krein 2014, 2015). Taking into account the approach followed by the area of psychology, there are several studies that investigate the motivation to participate in different sporting practices in nature: horse riding activities (Daniels and Norman 2005), kite surfing, windsurfing (Hennigs and Hallmann 2014) and paragliding (Chang and Huang 2012; Woratschek, Hannich, and Ritchie 2007). Other studies analyse satisfaction with this sport practice (Mykletun and Rumba 2014).

Chazaud (2004) classified the different motivational factors to participate in sporting activities in nature into six groups: (a) nature/environment (enjoying the natural environment); (b) risk/adventure (new challenges and experiences); (c) social (personal relationships); (d) health; (e) competitiveness and (f) tourism. Buckley (2012), in his review of over 50 studies, identified 14 different categories of motivation that were grouped into three dimensions: (a) internal functioning of the activity (emotion, fear, control, skills, achievements, aptitude and risk); (b) interior/exterior, place in nature (nature, art, spirit) and (c) external, social position (friends, image, escape and competition).

Regarding the profile of participants in nature sports, Melo and Gomes (2017a) carried out a study to analyse their sociodemographic characteristics, demand profile, practice behaviours, motivations and restrictions. The results show that the participants in nature sports are mainly young men, with higher education, highly qualified work and high income, whose main motivation for the practice of these types of sports is nature and adventure, while the lack of time and money are the main limitations to their practice. Although these results are generic, the authors conclude that there are significant differences depending on the activity practised.

Following the management approach are several studies that seek to analyse nature sports and sport tourism connections (Bentley, Page, and Macky 2007; Bessy 2010; Bujdoso and David 2013; Dorville and Bouhaouala 2006; Melo and Gomes 2016a, 2017a). In this sense, Melo and Gomes (2016a) affirm that nature sports are a growing phenomenon in the sport tourism segment. Others deepen the relationship between nature sports and sustainability (Bourdeau, Corneloup, and Mao 2002; Extremera, López, and Gallegos 2008; Lauterwasser 2010; Rosa, Carvalhinho, and Soares 2017).

Methodology

This article presents the exploratory and descriptive bibliometric analysis of scientific production on nature sports. Bibliometric studies are an adequate means to organize and learn academic information, facilitating the description and assessment of the literature, guiding the reader and researcher to bibliographic sources with data of interest (Andrés 2009).

The Scopus database

As a source of primary information, the Scopus database of the publisher Elsevier was chosen. Its characteristics have been deeply analysed in papers such as those by Goodman and Deis (2005) and Bar-Ilan (2010). It is a base of abstracts and bibliographical references of peer-reviewed scientific literature, with over 64 million records, 21,500 peer-reviewed journals, of which more than 3656 are full gold open access,[1] 131,000 books (540 series of books) and more than 7.5 million conference papers. Scopus allows a multidisciplinary view of science and integrates all relevant sources for basic and applied research and innovation. In this way, it becomes a practical tool for bibliometric studies and evaluations of scientific production, not only due to its unique content but also because it has information regarding the profile of the author or institution while facilitating tracking of citations, knowing the *h* index and analysing scientific journals.

Tracking methodology

The terms used to designate and characterize the practice of physical activities in nature are vague, imprecise and hardly consensual, making it difficult to develop a single concept that can define and characterize these practices with some accuracy. Many terms have been used in a dispersed way and are not accepted by the entire scientific community, therefore, there are many concepts used to designate the same object of study (Dias and Alves Júnior 2007). According to Pimentel (2013), the concept of nature sports, for the moment, would be included under the more generic umbrella term adventure sports. This concept, in turn, comprises a wide range of activities that contain challenging elements, take place in natural or artificially conditioned places, and represent freedom in comparison with traditional sports culture. Thus, the concept of adventure sports covers a relatively broad field of physical activities termed as an alternative, extreme, X-sports, gravity, lifestyle and action sport (Breivik 2010).

Based on the above, in order to delimit the selection of documents to the field of nature sports, the following search equation was used (15 February 2017):

(TITLE ('Advent* sport*') OR TITLE ('natur* sport*') OR TITLE ('Alternat* sport*') OR TITLE ('extrem* sport*') OR TITLE ('gravity sport*') OR TITLE ('lifestyle sport*') OR TITLE ('action sport*') OR TITLE ('risk* sport*') OR TITLE ('outdoor sport*')) AND PUBYEAR < 2017 AND (LIMIT-TO (DOCTYPE, 'ar') OR LIMIT-TO (DOCTYPE , 'ip'))

This type of search has the advantage of allowing researchers to reach classified journals within all the thematic areas of knowledge (Corral and Cànoves 2013).

Following the outline of similar studies, only articles published in scientific journals are analysed for the development of bibliometric indicators, since these are the main means of transmission of the results of an investigation (Maltrás-Barba 2003) and constitute a representative sample of the academic activity at the international level (Benavides-Velasco, Guzmán-Parra, and Quintana-García 2011). Thus, comments, conference reports, press articles, editorials, notes, letters or errata contained in Scopus are excluded. Subsequently, after removing documents not related to the study area, the ad hoc database was made which was used for the calculation of each of the variables needed to obtain the bibliometric indicators.

Results and discussion

Volume indicators

The documents located by means of the search equation, and after the necessary removal of papers not related to the area of sport practice in the natural environment, are shown in Table 1.

As can be seen, only the search for gravity sports does not generate any articles for the set of papers selected to form the ad hoc database on which the different bibliometric indicators will be calculated. In this regard, extreme sports, with 54 studies (24.22% of the total), leads the ranking of concepts by a number of contributions.

Price (1956) found that scientific knowledge grew exponentially at such a rate that every 10–15 years the existing global information doubled (Price's law). However, as shown in Figure 1, each discipline goes through several stages following its own evolution: precursors (first publications); exponential growth (it becomes the focus of research); linear growth (growth slows down, review and knowledge archiving).

The graphical representation of the accumulated production of the selected articles on sport practice in nature is adjusted to an exponential equation with $R^2 = 0.9955$ (Figure 2) and indicates that the research in this particular area is in the exponential growth phase after a few initial years with little research activity.

Regarding the number of citations that the articles have received in Scopus (Table 2), 'Injuries in high-risk persons and high-risk Sports. A longitudinal study of 1818 school children' (Backx et al. 1991) is highlighted with 112 citations at the time of our study, but of which only 10 belong to the period 2014–2016. It is followed by 'Personality profile of

Table 1. Documents located in Scopus.

Concept	Articles	Conference papers	Books	Book chapters	Reviews	Letters	Notes	Art. in press	Editorial	Short survey	Σ
Adventure Sports	28	–	–	4	2	1	1	1	1	1	39
Nature Sport	12	–	–	1	1	–	–	–	1	–	15
Alternative Sports	15	1	–	1	–	–	1	–	–	1	19
Extreme Sports	54	3	3	26	13	4	2	–	2	1	108
Gravity Sports	–	1	–	–	–	–	–	–	–	–	1
Lifestyle Sport	12	–	1	2	1	1	–	–	–	–	17
Action Sports	24	1	–	2	1	1	–	–	1	–	30
Risk Sports	43	1	–	2	–	1	3	–	1	1	52
Outdoor Sports	35	21	–	3	2	1	1	1	–	–	64
Global Search	221	28	4	41	20	8	8	2	6	5	343

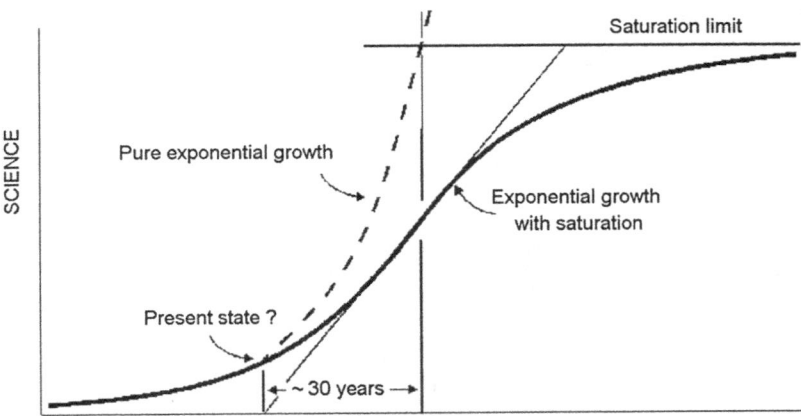

Figure 1. Graphical representation of the Price Growth Act. Source: Fernandez-Cano, Torralbo, and Vallejo (2004, 304).

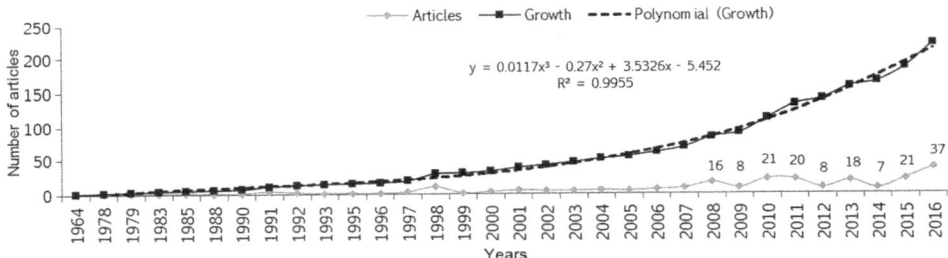

Figure 2. Evolution of the number of articles.

subjects engaged in high physical risk sports' (Freixanet 1991) with 101 citations and 'Sensation seeking among high- and low-risk sports participants' (Jack and Ronan 1998) with 98 citations. In the period 2014–2016, the article with the highest number of citations is 'Lead users and the option and diffusion of new products: Insights from two extreme sports communities' (Schreier, Oberhauser, and Prugl 2007) with a total of 35 citations.

Authors

Productivity of authors (both primary and secondary) is calculated based on the number of articles published by each of them. Following the criteria proposed by Lotka (1926), they are classified into three levels of production (Table 3).

There are no authors considered as large producers who have dealt with the subject of sports in nature in their work. Thus, the first author to appear in the ranking of the most productive authors (Table 4) is Thorpe, H. with 8 authorships, followed by Brymer, E., Collins, D. and Le Scanff, C. with 6. According to the classification made by Lotka, 89.79% (422) of the authors are occasional, as they only have a single published article and only 10.21% (48) are considered medium producers. This fact causes the average productivity per author to be 1.17.

Table 2. Most cited articles in Scopus about nature sports.

Author	Year	Title	<2014	2014	2015	2016	>2016	Σ
Backx, F.J.G., Beijer, H.J.M., Bol, E. and Erich, W.B.M.	1991	Injuries in high-risk persons and high-risk Sports. A longitudinal study of 1818 school children	100	6	4	-	2	112
Freixanet, M.G.	1991	Personality profile of subjects engaged in high physical risk sports	83	3	6	6	3	101
Jack, S.J. & Ronan, K.R:	1998	Sensation seeking among high- and low-risk sports participants	74	5	3	7	9	98
Schreier, M., Oberhauser, S. & Prügl, R.	2007	Lead users and the option and diffusion of new products: Insights from two extreme sports communities	48	10	15	10	6	89
Slanger, E. & Rudestam, K.E.	1997	Motivation and Disinhibition in High Risk Sports: Sensation seeking and Self-efficacy	63	5	3	6	5	82
Allegrucci, M., Whitney, S.L., Lephart, S.M., Irrgang, J.J. & Fu, F.H.	1995	Shoulder kinaesthesia in healthy unilateral athletes participating in upper extremity sports	69	1	5	4	3	82
Franques, P., Auriacombe, M., Piquemal, E., Verger, M., Brisseau-Gimenez, S., Grabot, D. & Tignol, J.	2003	Sensation seeking as a common factor in opioid dependent subjects and high-risk sport practicing subjects. A cross sectional study	52	3	3	4	3	65
Moehrle, M.	2008	Outdoor sport and skin cancer	38	7	5	8	3	61

Table 3. Lotka.

IP	Producers	No. of articles	Scopus	
			No. of authors	% of authors
IP ≥ 1	Large Producers	$n \geq 10$	0	0%
0 < IP < 1	Medium producers	$2 < n < 9$	48	10.21%
IP = 1	Occasional authors	$n = 1$	422	89.79%

Note: Productivity index.

Another bibliometric indicator to take into account, which is related to the authors, is the Collaboration Index. This is considered one of the professionalization signs of the field of research since papers with several authors have a greater impact than those with a single author due to increasing their citation scope (Granda-Orive et al. 2009). It is observed that although a percentage of the papers (35.43%, 79 articles) is single-authored, there is a clear tendency towards multiple authorship (64.57%, 144 articles).

Table 4. Ranking of the most prolific authors.

Author	Authorships	h-index	Lotka
Thorpe, H.	8	12	0.9031
Brymer, E.	6	8	0.7782
Collins, D.	6	28	0.7782
Le Scanff, C.	6	15	0.7782
Collins, L.	5	3	0.6990
Wheaton, B.	5	11	0.6990
Rinehart, R.	4	9	0.6021
Woodman, T.	4	16	0.6021

Table 5. Main countries of origin of the authors on nature sports.

Country	Authors	Authorships	Affiliation
United States	89	94	51
United Kingdom	47	61	23
France	46	57	33
Germany	28	28	24
Australia	27	33	16
Netherlands	25	29	11
Brazil	23	29	8
Poland	21	28	9

Table 6. Ranking of the most productive journals in nature sports.

Journal	Subject Area	Articles
Sport in Society	Social Sciences	7
Leisure Studies	Social Sciences	6
	Business, Management and Accounting	
International Review for the Sociology of Sport	Social Sciences	5
Journal of Sport and Social Issues	Social Sciences	4
Journal of Sports Sciences	Health Professions	4
	Medicine	
Perceptual and Motor Skills	Psychology	4
	Neuroscience	
Personality and Individual Differences	Psychology	4
6 Journals with 3 articles	–	18
20 Journals with 2 articles	–	60
131 Journals with 1 article	–	131

Together with authorship, affiliation is one of the determining factors for the correct identification and recovery of the intellectual production of a researcher in the different databases. In this respect, by country, and in the scientific production of work related to sport in nature, the United States stands out from the rest with 18.94% (89) of the authors affiliated to one of its centres, mainly academic (Table 5). It is followed by the United Kingdom and France with 10% each.

Journals

The set of 223 selected articles on sport in nature were disseminated through 164 different journals, 131 of them (79.88%) published a single paper (58.74% of the total), and only 33 (20.12%) included two or more papers (Table 6).

According to Bradford's Law (1934), a small number of journals group most of the published articles related to an area, a fact that helps us to identify the most used journals by researchers for the dissemination of their work (Figure 3). The Minimum Bradford Zone or Core (MBZ) is defined as the number of articles equal to half of the quantity that appears in the range of the list of journals sorted by production (those that produce a single article) (Spinak 1996).

$$MBZ = \frac{NR1a}{2}; \ MBZ = \frac{131}{2}; \ MBZ = 65.5$$

where MBZ is the Minimum Bradford Zone or Core, and NR1a is the total number of journals with a single published article.

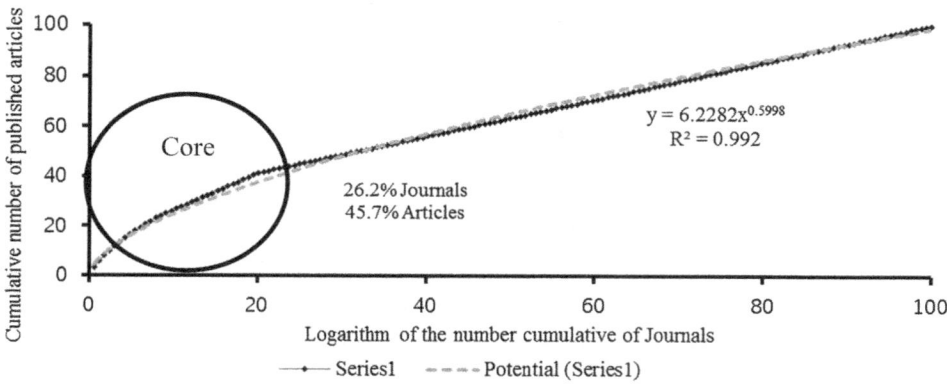

Figure 3. Core Bradford.

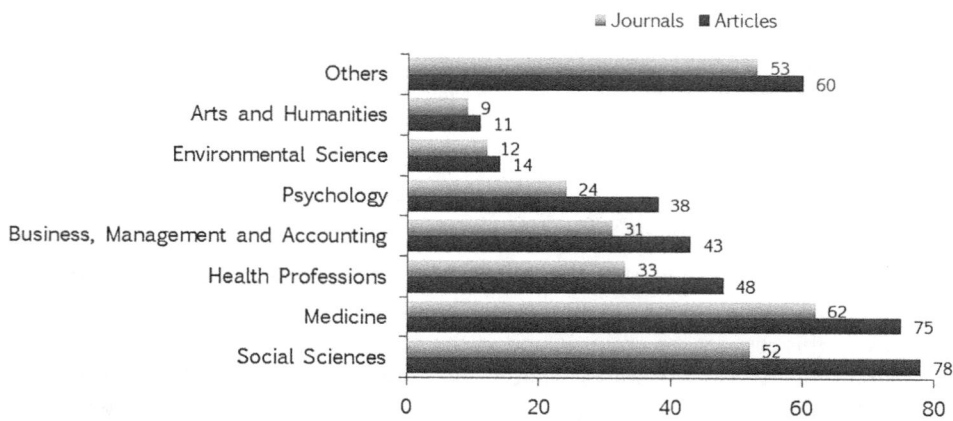

Figure 4. Main areas where articles about nature sports are collected.

After calculating the MBZ value, and from the ranking of journals sorted in descending order of productivity, the MBZ is made up of those journals whose sum of articles was equal to the MBZ value (66). In our bibliometric analysis, the MBZ consists of 20 journals, the most productive being Sport in Society (7), Leisure Studies (6) and International Review for the Sociology of Sport (5).

Thematic classification of the journal articles according to the areas the journals in which they are published belong (Figure 4) shows a wide range of areas (24). Two areas stand out from the rest: Social sciences with 78 articles and medicine with 75 articles, respectively. They are followed by health professions (48), business, management and accounting (43) and psychology (38).

Keywords

The correct selection of search terms is an essential issue when locating documents related to a specific field of research. The analysis of the keywords used by the

Figure 5. Cloud of keywords.

authors in their papers (Figure 5) shows *sports, risk, athletes* and *extreme* are the words that are most frequently repeated in the papers indexed in Scopus on nature sports.

Theme dealt with in the articles on nature sports in Scopus

Following the thematic classification made by Lacasa, Miranda, and Muro (1995) in his study of doctoral theses of physical activities in nature, as can be seen in Figure 6, four are the main areas in which themes dealt with in the selected articles can be included: Sociology (22.42%), psychology (21.97), management (20.63) and biomedical (20.18).

Table 7 shows the research areas most treated by the authors of nature sports articles are: various social groups, disability, education, diseases associated with the practice of these sports, and motivation and satisfaction of the athlete or the market associated with the product, for example, tourism (supply, demand, human resources, sustainability).

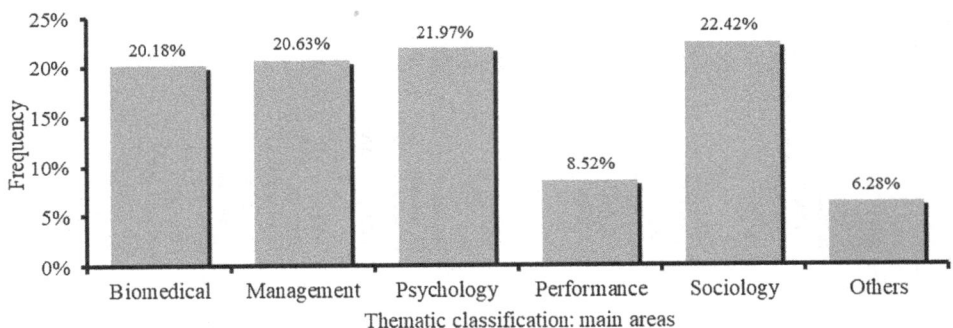

Figure 6. Main areas of research.

Table 7. Research areas.

Management	Marketing	Richez and Richez-Battesti (1991); Egner et al. (1998); Leese (1998); Shoham, Rose, and Kahle (1998); Bouhaouala and Chifflet (2001); Coontz (2001); Bourdeau, Corneloup, and Mao (2002); Egner (2002); Palmer (2002); Cianfrone and Zhang (2006); Dorville and Bouhaouala (2006); Mounet (2007); Schreier, Oberhauser, and Prugl (2007); Ferreira, Hall, and Bennett (2008); Mao and Bourdeau (2008); Soule (2008); Ujma-Wa,sowicz and Musioandl (2008) ; Kellett and Russell (2009); Bessy (2010); Edwards and Corte (2010); Lauterwasser (2010); Van Bottenburg and Salome (2010); Breivik (2011); Dubois and Terral (2011); Giannoulakis and Apostolopoulou (2011); Klaus and Maklan (2011); Suchet (2011); Burgin and Hardiman (2012); Falaix (2012); Salome and van Bottenburg (2012); Bujdoso and David (2013); Kruger et al. (2013); Parris (2013); Salome, van Bottenburg, and van den Heuvel (2013); Thorpe and Rinehart (2013); Yao (2013); Parris et al. (2014); Camoletto, Sterchele, and Genova (2015); Coulom (2015); Krein (2015); Giannoulakis (2016); Melo and Gomes (2016a); Plank (2016); Tian (2016); Melo and Gomes (2017a)
	Offer / Demand	
	HR	
	Ecological impact	
	Sustainability	
	tourism	
Psychology	Risk	Potgieter and Bisschoff (1990); Freixanet (1991); Slanger and Rudestam (1997); Jack and Ronan (1998); Zarevski et al. (1998); Breton (2000); Franques et al. (2003); Watson and Pulford (2004); Demirhan (2005); Opaschowski (2005); Lafollie and Le Scanff (2007); Self et al. (2007); Ko, Claussen, and Park (2008); Lafollie and Le Scanff (2008); Roger and Lee (2008); Willig (2008); Brymer (2009); Brymer and Oades (2009); Michel et al. (2009); Thorpe (2009); Brymer (2010); Cam et al. (2010); Castanier and Le Scanff (2010); Castanier, Le Scanff, and Woodman (2010); Guszkowska and Boldak (2010); Martha and Laurendeau (2010); Martha, Laurendeau, and Griffet (2010); Putsch and Job-Hoben (2010); Rhea and Martin (2010); Woodman et al. (2010); Langseth (2011); Tok (2011); Briki et al. (2012); Dean (2012); Brymer and Schweitzer (2013a); Brymer and Schweitzer (2013b); Woodman et al. (2013); Mykletun and Rumba (2014); Rinehart (2014); Strohle (2014); Tzetzis, Alexandris, and Kapsampeli (2014); Barlow et al. (2015); Mohamed et al. (2015); Siwek et al. (2015); Watson and Parker (2015); Dudek et al. (2016); Heirene et al. (2016); Hoffmannova et al. (2016); Leiter and Rheinberger (2016); Monasterio et al. (2016); Stops and Gropel (2016)
	Mental health	
	Cohesion Group	
	Self esteem	
	Satisfaction	
	Motivation	
Biomedical	Doping	Capener (1964); Israel (1978); Mitin and Tsar'kov (1979); Backx et al. (1991); Ljungqvist (1992); Igawa et al. (1993); Allegrucci et al. (1995); Jerosch (1996); Pope, Herbert, and Maher (1998); White (1998); Schafer, Gaulrapp, and Pforringer (1998); Sallis and Chassay (1999); Gugutzer (2001); Trubo (2001); Chumita (2002); Pain and Kerr (2004); Seppanen et al. (2004); Revuelta and Sandor (2006); Bentley, Page, and Macky (2006); Bentley, Page, and Macky (2007); Miller and Demoiny (2008); Fjell et al. (2007); Spanjersberg and Schipper (2007); Berrettini, Landolfi, and Patteri (2008); Moehrle (2008); Sytema et al. (2010); Mahe et al. (2011); Serrano, Canada, and Moreno (2011); Jankowski et al. (2012); Lawler et al. (2012); Ma and Dutch (2013); Serrano et al. (2014); Sharma et al. (2015); Thomson et al. (2015); Crawford et al. (2016); Faure and Fitzpatrick (2016); Gosteli et al. (2016); Greenberg et al. (2014); Janssen et al. (2016); Korobeynikov et al. (2016); Kramarz (2016); Li (2016); Ocampo and Klaus (2016)
	Nutrition	
	Injuries	
	Physiology	
	Medicine	
	Anthropometry	
Performance	Tests	Rudie (1997); Hritcu (2000); Dawson (2001); Vanstone (2003); DesMarteau (2004); Komilovich and Kiprina (2010); Houser, Wei, and Royer (2011); Duret and Anguao (2015); Fernando and Pinidiyaarachchi (2015); Bernardina et al. (2016); Ellmer and Rynne (2016); Gray and Collins (2016); Ha (2016); Harding, Lock, and Toohey (2016); Martinez-Nicolas, Muntaner-Mas, and Ortega (2017); Nath et al. (2016); Pluijms et al. (2016)
	training	
	Technology	
	Innovation	
	Biomechanic	
Sociology	Seniors	Glyptis (1985); Kerr (1991); Robinson (1992); Hachet (2003); Wheaton (2003); Penin (2004); Bette and Muller (2005); Skille and Waddington (2006); Burdsey (2008); Fletcher (2008); Laurendeau and Sharara (2008); Pimentel (2008); Schwier (2008); Baena Extremera and Rebollo Rico (2009); Breivik (2010); Brymer and Gray (2010); Lahire (2010); Thorpe and Rinehart (2010); Abdalad et al. (2011); Gilchrist and Wheaton (2011); Granero and Baena (2011); Olive and Thorpe (2011); Thorpe and Wheaton (2011); Rauter and Topič (2011); Kerr and Houge (2012); Baena-Extremera et al. (2013); Cardoso, Marinho, and De Assis Pimentel (2013); Collins and Collins (2013); Schwarz et al. (2013); Stanley (2013); Turner (2013); Zuev and Ivanov (2013); Collins, Collins, and Grecic (2015); Dos Santos et al. (2015); Green et al. (2015); King and Church (2015); Sisjord (2015); Thorpe (2015); Thorpe and Ahmad (2015); Wheaton (2015); Collins and Collins (2016a); Collins and Collins (2016b); Ferguson and Shapiro (2016); Hickman et al. (2018); Leather and Nicholls (2016); Lundberg et al. (2016) ; Rannikko et al. (2016); Schwartz et al. (2016); Thorpe (2016)
	Disability	
	Young boys	
	Ethnic groups	
	Education	
	Gender	
Others	Not classified	Ivanova and Terent'eva (1983); Kruger (1988); Franklin (1998); Shoham, Rose, and Kahle (2000); Donnelly (2006); Chandler (2007); Wheaton (2010); Navarro Gutierrez, Molina Jaime, and Lapresa Acosta (2011); Sokol (2011); Honea (2013); Rinehart (2014); Lebeau and Sides (2015); Lagos (2016); Simpson (2016)

Note: Subject disciplines.

Conclusions

At the beginning of this paper, it was proposed to carry out a review of the academic lit-erature contained within the Scopus database in order to better understand the state of research in the field of nature sports. Based on the analysis of the results, and the extensive literature consulted, below are the main conclusions:

(a) Within the different denominations that sport practice in nature can be situated under, extreme sports leads the ranking by number of articles recovered in the Scopus database.

(b) It is a new field of study in full growth and at the end of the first decade of the twenty-first century the theme aroused a real interest in the academic field. This suggests an upward tendency in the quantity of articles to be published in the following years.

(c) The productivity of authors, both primary and secondary, is close to one due to the fact that approximately 90% of authors are considered occasional (i.e. only one pub-lished article). Regarding the co-authorship analysis, although a large percentage of the work is done alone, there is a clear tendency towards multiple authorship.

(d) Within the scientific production of papers related to sport in nature, the United States stands out with almost a fifth of the authors affiliated to some of its centres, mainly academics. Other countries to highlight are United Kingdom, France and Germany.

(e) From the analysis of the journals in which the articles are published, it can be con-cluded that there is no defined core of journals considered as a reference in the area of sport practice in nature, only *Sport in Society* (7) and *Leisure Studies* (6) have published more than 5 articles each.

(f) The existence of a large number of different thematic areas such as social sciences, medicine, business, management and accounting, and psychology, together with the high number of articles included in several of them, demonstrate the multidisci-plinarity of the concept of sport in nature.

(g) Another indicator that expresses the relevance that this topic is taking is the number of citations that the articles receive. In this regard, there are 67 articles with 10 or more citations, highlighting injuries in high-risk persons and high-risk sports. A longitudinal study of 1818 school children (Backx et al. 1991) and the personality profile of subjects engaged in high physical risk sports (Freixanet 1991), being the only two studies that have received more than 100 citations.

(h) Although there are similarities between the research areas identified in this study and those found by Lacasa, Miranda, and Muro (1995) in his doctoral thesis on physical activities in nature, there are substantial differences between the two. The subject that most frequently dealt with the theses analysed was included in the area of man-agement, while the articles studied to deal with aspects related to psychology, soci-ology or medicine, dealing with issues such as education, youth, motivation, satisfaction or risk of injury.

In summary, nature sports has been referred to by several names since its origin as an academic field of study, being analysed from different areas of knowledge, which makes it a multi-disciplinary concept. At the moment, it is a subject that is clearly growing with respect to the number of published works, a tendency that is expected to be maintained in the next years. The United States, together with the United Kingdom and France, are at the forefront of research in this area.

As in any bibliometric study of this style, the limitations involved must be taken into account. When interpreting the results, it is necessary to opt for a given database and a particular search equation. In addition, the aim of this paper was not to evaluate the content quality of the selected articles, an objective that can be considered in later research but to undertake a descriptive-quantitative analysis of the papers related to the area of sports activities in the natural environment. In order to expand the present article, it would be interesting to examine indexed documents in other databases, together with the possibility of including comparative studies between them or to deepen the analysis of existing citations.

Notes

1. Gold Open Access is when publications are freely available online to all at no cost and with limited restrictions with regards reuse.

Disclosure statement

No potential conflict of interest was reported by the authors.

References

Abdalad, L. S., V. L. De Menezes Costa, L. Mourao, N. T. Ferreira, and R. F. Dos Santos. 2011. "Women and Risk Sports: Diving Into the Universe of Apneistas. [Mulheres e esporte de risco: um mergulho no universo das apneistas]." *Motriz. Revista De Educacao Fisica* 17 (2): 225–234.

Allegrucci, M., S. L. Whitney, S. M. Lephart, J. J. Irrgang, and F. H. Fu. 1995. "Shoulder Kinesthesia in Healthy Unilateral Athletes Participating in Upper Extremity Sports." *Journal of Orthopaedic and Sports Physical Therapy* 21 (4): 220–226.

Andrés, A. 2009. *Measuring Academic Research: How to Undertake a Bibliometric Study*. Oxford: Chandos.

Backx, F. J. G., H. J. M. Beijer, E. Bol, and W. B. M. Erich. 1991. "Injuries in High-Risk Persons and High-Risk Sports. A Longitudinal Study of 1818 School Children." *American Journal of Sports Medicine* 19 (2): 124–130.

Baena Extremera, A., and S. Rebollo Rico. 2009. "How People who Practise Adventure Sport Spend Their Free Time. [Uso del tiempo libre de los practicantes de deporte de aventura]." *Revista Internacional de Medicina y Ciencias de la Actividad Fisica y del Deporte* 9 (33): 1–13.

Baena-Extremera, A., J. M. Serrano Perez, R. Fernandez Banos, and J. Fuentesal Garcia. 2013. "Adapting new Adventure Sports to School Physical Education: Via Ferratas. [Adaptacion de nuevos deportes de aventura a la educacion fisica escolar: las vias ferratas]." *Apunts. Educacion Fisica y Deportes* (114): 36–44.

Bar-Ilan, J. 2010. "Citations to the 'Introduction to Infometrics' Indexed by WOS, Scopus and Google Scholar." *Scientometrics* 82 (3): 495–506.

Barlow, M., T. Woodman, C. Chapman, M. Milton, D. Stone, T. Dodds, and B. Allen. 2015. "Who Takes Risks in High-Risk Sport?: The Role of Alexithymia." *Journal of Sport and Exercise Psychology* 37 (1): 83–96.

Benavides-Velasco, C. A., V. Guzmán-Parra, and C. Quintana-García. 2011. "Evolución de la Literatura Sobre Empresa Familiar Como Disciplina Científica." *Cuadernos de Economía y Dirección de la Empresa* 14 (2): 78–90.

Bentley, T., K. Macky, and J. Edwards. 2006. "Injuries to new Zealanders Participating in Adventure Tourism and Adventure Sports: An Analysis of Accident Compensation Corporation (ACC) Claims." *New Zealand Medical Journal* 119 (1247): 1–9.

Bentley, T. A., S. J. Page, and K. A. Macky. 2007. "Adventure Tourism and Adventure Sports Injury: The New Zealand Experience." *Applied Ergonomics* 38 (6): 791–796.

Bernardina, G. R. D., P. Cerveri, R. M. L. Barros, J. C. B. Marins, and A. P. Silvatti. 2016. "Action Sport Cameras as an Instrument to Perform a 3D Underwater Motion Analysis." *PLoS ONE* 11 (8).

Berrettini, U., A. Landolfi, and G. Patteri. 2008. "The Heart in Extreme Sports: Hyperbaric Activity and Microgravity. [Il cuore nello sport estremo: Attivita iperbarica e microgravita]." *Giornale Italiano Di Cardiologia* 9 (10 SUPPL.1): 94S–98S.

Bessy, O. 2010. "*The Nature Sporting Activities, as Medium of the Renewal of Tourism Outlines.*" *Sud-Quest Europeen* 29: 105–114.

Bessy, M., and M. Mouton. 2004. "Du Plein air au Sports de Nature. Nouvelles Pratiques Nouveaux Enjeux." *Revue Education Physique et Sport* 309: 67–72.

Betrán, J. 1995. "Dossier. Las Actividades Físicas de Aventura en la Naturaleza: Análisis Sociocultural." *Apunts: Educación Física y Deportes* 41: 5–8.

Betrán, A. O., and J. O. Betrán. 1995. Propuesta de uma clasificación taxonômica de las actividades físicas de aventura em la naturaleza. Marco conceptual y análisis de los critérios elegidos In.: Dossier Las Actividades Físicas de Aventura en la Naturaleza: análisis sociocultural. *Apunts: Educación Física y Deportes, Barcelona*: Institut Nacional d'Educación Física de Catalunya, (41), 5–8.

Bette, K., and A. Muller. 2005. "X-treme: On the Sociology of Extreme and Risky Sports. [X-treme: Zur Soziologie des Abenteuer- und Risikosports]." *Sportwissenschaft* 35 (2): 212–216.

Bouhaouala, M., and P. Chifflet. 2001. "Functioning Logic of Instructors in Outdoor Sports: Hobby or Professional Occupation? [Logique d'action des moniteurs des sports de nature: entre passion et profession]." *Staps* 56 (3): 61–74.

Bourdeau, P., J. Corneloup, and P. Mao. 2002. "Adventure Sports and Tourism in the French Mountains: Dynamics of Change and Challenges for Sustainable Development." *Current Issues in Tourism* 5 (1): 22–32.

Bradford, S. C. 1934. "Sources of Information on Specific Subjects." *Engineering* 137: 85–86.

Breivik, G. 2010. "Trends in Adventure Sports in a Post-Modern Society." *Sport in Society* 13 (2): 260–273.

Breivik, G. 2011. "Dangerous Play with the Elements: Towards a Phenomenology of Risk Sports." *Sport, Ethics and Philosophy* 5 (3): 314–330.

Breton, D. L. 2000. "Playing Symbolically with Death in Extreme Sports." *Body & Society* 6 (1): 1–11.

Briki, W., R. J. R. Den Hartigh, F. C. Bakker, and C. Gernigon. 2012. "The Dynamics of Psychological Momentum: A Quantitative Study in Natural Sport Situations." *International Journal of Performance Analysis in Sport* 12 (3): 573–592.

Brymer, E. 2009. "Extreme Sports as a Facilitator of Ecocentricity and Positive Life Changes." *World Leisure Journal* 51 (1): 47–53.

Brymer, E. 2010. "Risk Taking in Extreme Sports: A Phenomenological Perspective." *Annals of Leisure Research* 13 (1-2): 218–238.

Brymer, E., and T. Gray. 2010. "Developing an Intimate "Relationship" with Nature Through Extreme Sports Participation." *Leisure/ Loisir* 34 (4): 361–374.

Brymer, E., and L. G. Oades. 2009. "Extreme Sports: A Positive Transformation in Courage and Humility." *Journal of Humanistic Psychology* 49 (1): 114–126.

Brymer, E., and R. Schweitzer. 2013a. "Extreme Sports are Good for Your Health: A Phenomenological Understanding of Fear and Anxiety in Extreme Sport." *Journal of Health Psychology* 18 (4): 477–487.

Brymer, E., and R. Schweitzer. 2013b. "The Search for Freedom in Extreme Sports: A Phenomenological Exploration." *Psychology of Sport and Exercise* 14 (6): 865–873.

Buckley, R. 2012. "Rush as a Key Motivation in Skilled Adventure Tourism: Resolving the Risk Recreation Paradox." *Tourism Management* 33: 961–970.

Bujdoso, Z., and L. David. 2013. "Extreme Sports and Other Activities in Tourism with Special Regard to the Matra Mountain." *Journal of Physical Education and Sport* 13 (1): 39–45.

Burdsey, D. 2008. "Contested Conceptions of Identity, Community and Multiculturalism in the Staging of Alternative Sport Events: A Case Study of the Amsterdam World cup Football Tournament." *Leisure Studies* 27 (3): 259–277.

Burgin, S., and N. Hardiman. 2012. "Extreme Sports in Natural Areas: Looming Disaster or a Catalyst for a Paradigm Shift in Land use Planning?" *Journal of Environmental Planning and Management* 55 (7): 921–940.

Cam, F. S., M. Colakoğlu, S. Tok, I. Tok, N. Kutlu, and A. Berdeli. 2010. "Personality Traits and DRD4, DAT1, 5-HT2A Gene Polymorphisms in Risky and non Risky Sports Participation. [Riskli ve risksiz sporlara kati{dotless}li{dotless}mda kişilik ozellikleri ile DRD4, DAT1, 5-HT2A gen polimorfizmleri]." *Turkiye Klinikleri Journal of Medical Sciences* 30 (5): 1459–1464.

Camoletto, R. F., D. Sterchele, and C. Genova. 2015. "Managing Alternative Sports: New Organisational Spaces for the Diffusion of Italian Parkour." *Modern Italy* 20 (3): 307–319.

Capener, N. 1964. "Adventure, Sport and Medicine." *The Medico-Legal Journal* 32: 73–84.

Cardoso, F. L., A. Marinho, and G. G. De Assis Pimentel. 2013. "Gender Issues in Universtity Practitioners of Adventure Sports. [Questoes de genero em universitarios praticantes de esportes de aventura]." *Revista Da Educacao Fisica* 24 (4): 597–608.

Castanier, C., and C. L. Le Scanff. 2010. "Who Takes Risks in High-Risk Sports? A Typological Personality Approach." *Research Quarterly for Exercise and Sport* 81 (4): 478–484.

Castanier, C., C. Le Scanff, and T. Woodman. 2010. "Beyond Sensation Seeking: Affect Regulation as a Framework for Predicting Risk-Taking Behaviors in High-Risk Sport." *Journal of Sport and Exercise Psychology* 32 (5): 731–738.

Chandler, D. L. 2007. "Space Diving: The Ultimate Extreme Sport." *New Scientist* 196 (2626): 46–49.

Chang, H., and Y. Huang. 2012. "Paragliding Adventure Recreation Consumers' Activity Motivation, Enduring Involvement and Their Involved Behaviour." *The Journal of Inter-National Management Studies* 7 (2): 61–74.

Chazaud, P. 2004. *Management du Tourisme et des Loisirs Sportifs de Pleine Nature*. Paris: Presses universitaires du sport.

Chumita, C. 2002. "Extreme Sports Injuries." *Emergency Medical Services* 31 (10): 129–131.

Cianfrone, B. A., and J. J. Zhang. 2006. "Differential Effects of Television Commercials, Athlete Endorsements, and Venue Signage During a Televised Action Sports Event." *Journal of Sport Management* 20 (3): 322–344.

Collins, L., and D. Collins. 2013. "Decision Making and Risk Management in Adventure Sports Coaching." *Quest* 65 (1): 72–82.

Collins, L., and D. Collins. 2015. "Integration of Professional Judgement and Decision-Making in High-Level Adventure Sports Coaching Practice." *Journal of Sports Sciences* 33 (6): 622–633.

Collins, L., and D. Collins. 2016a. "Professional Judgement and Decision-Making in Adventure Sports Coaching: The Role of Interaction." *Journal of Sports Sciences* 34 (13): 1231–1239.

Collins, L., and D. Collins. 2016b. "Professional Judgement and Decision-Making in the Planning Process of High-Level Adventure Sports Coaching Practice." *Journal of Adventure Education and Outdoor Learning* 16 (3): 256–268.

Collins, L., D. Collins, and D. Grecic. 2015. "The Epistemological Chain in High-Level Adventure Sports Coaches." *Journal of Adventure Education and Outdoor Learning* 15 (3): 224–238.

Coontz, P. 2001. "Managing the Action: Sports Bookmakers as Entrepreneurs." *Deviant Behavior* 22 (3): 239–266.

Corneloup, J. 2005. "La Place du Marché Dans le Fonctionnement des Loisirs Sportifs de Nature." *Téoros* 24 (1): 55–61. http://teoros.revues.org/1528.

Corral, J. A., and G. Cànoves. 2013. "La Investigación Turística Publicada en Revistas Turísticas y no Turísticas: Análisis Bibliométrico de la Producción de las Universidades Catalanas." *Cuadernos de Turismo* 31 (1): 55–81.

Coulom, J. 2015. "Nature Sports as Resource for Sustainable Development in a French Medium-Size Town Territory: The Case of pau. [Les sports de nature comme ressource de developpement territorial durable d'une ville-moyenne Francaise: Le cas de Pau]." *Bulletin d'Association De Geographes Francais* 92 (2): 258–276.

Crawford, J. J., J. K. Vallance, N. L. Holt, and K. S. Courneya. 2016. "Extreme Sport/Adventure Activity Correlates in Gynecologic Cancer Survivors." *American Journal of Health Behavior* 40 (2): 172–181.

Daniels, M. J., and W. C. Norman. 2005. "Motivations of Equestrian Tourists: an Analysis of the Colonial cup Races." *Journal of Sport Tourism* 10 (3): 201–210.

Dawson, D. 2001. "Composites Dive Into Protective Headgear for Adventure Sports." *Advanced Composites Bulletin* (DECEMBER): 6–7.

Dean, D. H. 2012. "Self-control and Perceived Physical Risk in an Extreme Sport." *Young Consumers* 13 (1): 62–73.

Demirhan, G. 2005. "Mountaineers' Risk Perception in Outdoor-Adventure Sports: A Study of sex and Sports Experience." *Perceptual and Motor Skills* 100 (3 II): 1155–1160.

DesMarteau, K. 2004. "Action Sports Success: Total Immersion Required." *Apparel* 45 (10): 12–13.

Dias, C. A. G., and E. D. Alves Júnior. 2007. "Notas Conceituais Sobre Esportes na Natureza." *Lecturas: Educación Física y Deportes* 12: 114–122.

Donn, A. 2011. "The Contribution of the Tauchseen-Portal Diving Lakes Portal to Environment-Friendly Sport Activities. [Der beitrag des tauchseen-portals zu einer naturvertraglichen sportausubung]." *Natur Und Landschaft* 86 (3): 120–125.

Donnelly, M. 2006. "Studying Extreme Sports: Beyond the Core Participants." *Journal of Sport and Social Issues* 30 (2): 219–224.

Dorville, C., and M. Bouhaouala. 2006. "The Part of Outdoor Sports in Tourism Development of Nord - pas-de-Calais Region. [Place des sports outdoor dans le developpement touristique de la region Nord-Pas-de-Calais]." *Territoire En Mouvement* (3): 3–13.

Dos Santos, P. M., M. N. Manfroi, J. De Paula Figueiredo, V. Z. Brasil, and A. Marinho. 2015. "Training and Perception of Skills Studentes of Physical Education: A Reflection from the Discipline of Adventure Sports. [Formacao profissional e percepcao de competencias de estudantes de educacao fisica: Uma reflexao a partir da disciplina de esportes de aventura e na natureza]." *Revista Da Educacao Fisica* 26 (4): 529–540.

Dubois, F., and P. Terral. 2011. "Companies of Outdoor Sports Tourism and Their Management. [De l'amateur sportif au dirigeant d'une petite entreprise. Le tourisme sportif de pleine nature]." *Travail Et Emploi* (126): 35–44.

Dudek, D., M. Siwek, R. Jaeschke, K. Drozdowicz, K. Styczeń, A. Arciszewska, A. A. Chrobak, and J. K. Rybakowski. 2016. "A Web-Based Study of Bipolarity and Impulsivity in Athletes Engaging in Extreme and High-Risk Sports." *Acta Neuropsychiatrica* 28 (3): 179–183.

Duret, P., and K. Anguao. 2015. "Two Norms for Innovation in Outdoor Sports: Technical and Social Innovation." *Loisir Et Societe* 38 (3): 372–382.

Edwards, B., and U. Corte. 2010. "Commercialization and Lifestyle Sport: Lessons from 20 Years of Freestyle BMX in 'pro-Town, USA'." *Sport in Society* 13 (7): 1135–1151.

Egner, H. 2002. "Moab, Utah - From the U.S. Capital of Uranium to an International top Spot for Outdoor Sports Tourism. [Moab/Utah - Vom Uranbergbau zum Natursport-Eldorado]." *Geographische Rundschau* 54 (12): 47–52.

Egner, H., A. Escher, M. Kleinhans, and P. Lindner. 1998. "'Extreme Nature Sports' - Spatial Component of an Active Style of Leisure Pursuits. [Extreme Natursportarten - die raumbezogene Komponente eines activen Freizeitstils]." *Erde* 129 (2): 121–138.

Ellmer, E., and S. Rynne. 2016. "Learning in Action and Adventure Sports." *Asia-Pacific Journal of Health, Sport and Physical Education* 7 (2): 107–119.

Extremera, A. B., M. G. López, and A. G. Gallegos. 2008. "La sostenibilidad del medio ambiente a través de las actividades físico-deportivas en el medio natural y su importancia en la educación ambiental." *Investigación Educativa* 12 (22): 173–193.

Falaix, L. 2012. "Outdoor Sports in the Landes Departement of France: From Controlled Development to the Promotion of a "Local Resource". [Les sports de nature dans le departement des Landes: Du developpement maitrise a la mobilisation d'une "ressource territoriale"]." *Annales De Geographie* 121 (686): 410–432.

Faure, C. E., and J. M. Fitzpatrick. 2016. "Professional Action Sport Athletes' Experiences with and Attitudes Toward Concussion: A Phenomenological Study." *Qualitative Report* 21 (10): 1836–1854.

Ferguson, B. R., and S. K. Shapiro. 2016. "Using a Naturalistic Sport Context to Train Social Skills in Children." *Child and Family Behavior Therapy* 38 (1): 47–68.

Fernandez-Cano, A., M. Torralbo, and M. Vallejo. 2004. "Reconsidering Price's Model of Scientific Growth: an Overview." *Scientometrics* 61 (3): 301–321.

Fernando, T., and U. A. J. Pinidiyaarachchi. 2015. "A Hybrid Algorithm for Player arm Biomechanics Evaluation in Outdoor Sporting Activities." *International Journal of Computer Science in Sport* 14 (1): 69–86.

Ferreira, M., T. K. Hall, and G. Bennett. 2008. "Exploring Brand Positioning in a Sponsorship Context: A Correspondence Analysis of the dew Action Sports Tour." *Journal of Sport Management* 22 (6): 734–761.

Fjell, A. M., M. Aker, K. H. Bang, J. Bardal, H. Frogner, O. S. Gangås, A. Otnes, N. M. Sønderland, A. K. Wisløff, and K. B. Walhovd. 2007. "Habituation of P3a and P3b Brain Potentials in men Engaged in Extreme Sports." *Biological Psychology* 75 (1): 87–94.

Fletcher, R. 2008. "Living on the Edge: The Appeal of Risk Sports for the Professional Middle Class." *Sociology of Sport Journal* 25 (3): 310–330.

Franklin, A. 1998. "Naturalizing Sports: Hunting and Angling in Modern Environments." *International Review for the Sociology of Sport* 33 (4): 355–366.

Franques, P., M. Auriacombe, E. Piquemal, M. Verger, S. Brisseau-Gimenez, D. Grabot, and J. Tignol. 2003. "Sensation Seeking as a Common Factor in Opioid Dependent Subjects and High Risk Sport Practicing Subjects. A Cross Sectional Study." *Drug and Alcohol Dependence* 69 (2): 121–126.

Freixanet, M. G. 1991. "Personality Profile of Subjects Engaged in High Physical Risk Sports." *Personality and Individual Differences* 12 (10): 1087–1093.

Fullonet, F. Q. 1995. "Propuesta de clasificación de las actividades deportivas en el medio natural." *Apunts: Educación física y deportes* (41): 124–129.

Fuster, J., and F. F. i Queixalós. 2008. "Características elementales de los nuevos deportes en el medio natural." *Ágora para la Educación Física y el Deporte* (7): 35–48.

Giannoulakis, C. 2016. "The "Authenticitude" Battle in Action Sports: A Case-Based Industry Perspective." *Sport Management Review* 19 (2): 171–182.

Giannoulakis, C., and A. Apostolopoulou. 2011. "Implementation of a Multi-Brand Strategy in Action Sports." *Journal of Product & Brand Management* 20 (3): 171–181.

Gibson, H. 2005. "Sport Tourism: Concepts and Theories. An Introduction." *Sport in Society* 8 (2): 133–141.

Gil, A. M. L. 2003. "La evaluación del medio para la práctica de actividades turístico-deportivas en la naturaleza." *Cuadernos de Turismo* (12): 131–150.

Gilchrist, P., and B. Wheaton. 2011. "Lifestyle Sport, Public Policy and Youth Engagement: Examining the Emergence of Parkour." *International Journal of Sport Policy* 3 (1): 109–131.

Glyptis, S. 1985. "Women as a Target Group: The Views of the Staff of Action Sport - West Midlands." *Leisure Studies* 4 (3): 347–362.

Goodman, D., and L. Deis. 2005. "Web of Science (2004 Version) and Scopus." *The Charleston Advisor* 6 (3): 5–21.

Gosteli, G., B. Yersin, C. Mabire, M. Pasquier, R. Albrecht, and P. Carron. 2016. "Retrospective Analysis of 616 air-Rescue Trauma Cases Related to the Practice of Extreme Sports." *Injury* 47 (7): 1414–1420.

Granda-Orive, J. I., S. Villanueva-Serrano, R. Aleixandre-Benavent, J. C. Valderrama-Zurían, A. Alonso-Arroyo, F. García-Río, C. A. Jiménez Ruiz, S. Solano Reinag, and G. González Alcaidec. 2009. "Redes de colaboración científica internacional en tabaquismo. Análisis de co-autorías a través del Science Citation Index durante el periodo 1999–2003." *Gaceta Sanitaria* 23 (3): 34–43.

Granero, A. 2007. "Las actividades físico-deportivas en la naturaleza y la industria turística." *Revista Internacional de Medicina y Ciencias de la Actividad Física y del Deporte/International Journal of Medicine and Science of Physical Activity and Sport* 7 (26): 111–127.

Granero, A., and A. Baena. 2010. "La búsqueda de la naturaleza como compensación del nuevo estilo de vida urbano." *Journal of Sport and Health Research* 2 (1): 17–25.

Granero, A., and A. Baena. 2011. "Games and Adventure Sports in Continuous Teachers Training Process. [Juegos y deportes de aventura en la formacion permanente del profesorado]." *Revista Internacional de Medicina y Ciencias de la Actividad Fisica y del Deporte* 11 (43): 531–547.

Gray, P., and D. Collins. 2016. "The Adventure Sports Coach: All Show and no Substance?" *Journal of Adventure Education and Outdoor Learning* 16 (2): 160–171.

Green, K., M. Thurston, O. Vaage, and K. Roberts. 2015. "'[We're on the Right Track, Baby], We Were Born This Way'! Exploring Sports Participation in Norway." *Sport, Education and Society* 20 (3): 285–303.

Greenberg, M. R., P. H. Kim, R. T. Duprey, D. A. Jayant, B. H. Steinweg, B. R. Preiss, and G. C. Barr Jr. 2014. "Unique Obstacle Race Injuries at an Extreme Sports Event: A Case Series." *Annals of Emergency Medicine* 63 (3): 361–366.

Griggs, G. 2011. "Ethnographic Study of Alternative Sports by Alternative Means: List Mining as a Method of Data Collection." *Journal of Empirical Research on Human Research Ethics* 6 (2): 85–91.

Gugutzer, R. 2001. "Die fiktion des naturlichen: Sportdoping in der reflexiven moderne." *Soziale Welt* 52 (2): 219–238.

Guszkowska, M., and A. Boldak. 2010. "Sensation Seeking in Males Involved in Recreational High Risk Sports." *Biology of Sport* 27 (3): 157–162.

Ha, A. S. 2016. "Student Learning Outcome and Teachers' Autonomy Support Toward Teaching Games for Understanding Through Adopting Accessible Technology and Alternative Sport Equipment: An Asian Experience." *Research Quarterly for Exercise and Sport* 87: S12–S13.

Hachet, P. 2003. "Facets of adolescent risks: Extreme sports, challenges and "crazy" behavior. [Visages du risqué a l'adolescence: sports de l'extreme, defis et actes "fous".]." *Soins.Pediatrie, Puericulture* (214): 18–21.

Hall, C., and S. Page. 2006. *The Geography of Tourism and Recreation Environment, Place and Space.* London: Routledge.

Harding, J., D. Lock, and K. Toohey. 2016. "A Social Identity Analysis of Technological Innovation in an Action Sport: Judging Elite Half-Pipe Snowboarding." *European Sport Management Quarterly* 16 (2): 214–232.

Heirene, R. M., D. Shearer, G. Roderique-Davies, and S. D. Mellalieu. 2016. "Addiction in Extreme Sports: An Exploration of Withdrawal States in Rock Climbers." *Journal of Behavioral Addictions* 5 (2): 332–341.

Hennigs, B., and K. Hallmann. 2014. "A Motivation-Based Segmentation Study of Kitesurfers and Windsurfers." *Managing Sport and Leisure* 20 (2): 117–134.

Hickman, M., P. Stokes, S. Gammon, C. Beard, and A. Inkster. 2018. "Moments Like Diamonds in Space: Savoring the Ageing Process Through Positive Engagement with Adventure Sports." *Annals of Leisure Research* 21: 612–630.

Hoffmannova, J., L. Šebek, P. Allison, M. Maina, and J. Toogood. 2016. "The Struggle for Individuality: Investigating a Long-Term Pursuit of a Lifestyle Sport Activity." *Acta Gymnica* 46 (2): 97–104.

Honea, J. C. 2013. "Beyond the Alternative vs. Mainstream Dichotomy: Olympic BMX and the Future of Action Sports." *Journal of Popular Culture* 46 (6): 1253–1275.

Hopkin, J., A. Mamourian, S. Lollis, and T. Duhaime. 2006. "The Next Extreme Sport? Subdural Haematoma in a Patient with Arachnoid Cyst After Head Shaking Competition." *British Journal of Neurosurgery* 20 (2): 111–113.

Houser, K. W., M. Wei, and M. P. Royer. 2011. "Illuminance Uniformity of Outdoor Sports Lighting." *Journal of Illuminating Engineering Society of North America* 7 (4): 221–235.

Howe, L. A. 2012. "Different Kinds of Perfect: The Pursuit of Excellence in Nature-Based Sports." *Sport, Ethics and Philosophy* 6 (3): 353–368.

Howe, L. A. 2017. "Intensity and the Sublime: Paying Attention to Self and Environment in Nature Sports." *Sport, Ethics and Philosophy*, 1–13.

Hritcu, I. 2000. "Textile Fabrics Which can 'Breath' for Outdoor Sporting Activities. [Materiale textile care respire destinate activitatilor sportive desfasurate in aer liber]." *Industria Textila* 51 (1): 20–24.

Igawa, S., H. Kibamoto, H. Takahashi, and S. Arai. 1993. "A Study on Exposure to Ultraviolet Rays During Outdoor Sports Activity." *Journal of Thermal Biology* 18 (5-6): 583–586.

Israel, S. 1978. "Quantification of Functional Differences of Extreme Sport Hearts and so-Called Normal Hearts." *Medizin Und Sport* 18 (6): 171–174.

Ivanova, O. G., and G. V. Terent'eva. 1983. " Year-Round Outdoor Sports in Sports Clothes as a Factor in Invigorating Preschool Children. [Kruglogodichnye zaniatiia fizkul'turoĭ na vozdukhe v sportivnoĭ odezhde kak factor zakalivaniia organizma deteĭ doshkol'nogo vozrasta.]." *Pediatriya - Zhurnal Im G.N. Speranskogo* (9): 49–53.

Jack, S. J., and K. R. Ronan. 1998. "Sensation Seeking among High- and low-Risk Sports Participants." *Personality and Individual Differences* 25 (6): 1063–1083.

Jankowski, K., E. Ozdzeńska-Milke, Ł. Jankowski, E. Rzewuska, P. Dul, E. Ilnicka, M. Kobylecka, and P. Pruszczyk. 2012. "Should the Patient with Myocardial Bridge be Advised not to Performe Extreme Sport Effort? Case of a Patient with Troponin I Elevation After Exercise. [Czy choremu z mostkiem mięśniowym nad tętnicą wieńcową należy zalecić zaniechanie uprawiania ekstremalnych wysiłków? Przypadek chorego z podwyższonym stężeniem troponiny I po wysiłku]." *Kardiologia Polska* 70 (11): 1161–1163.

Janssen, K. W., B. C. van der Zwaard, C. F. Finch, W. van Mechelen, and E. A. L. M. Verhagen. 2016. "Interventions Preventing Ankle Sprains; Previous Injury and High-Risk Sport Participation as Predictors of Compliance." *Journal of Science and Medicine in Sport* 19 (6): 465–469.

Jerosch, J. 1996. "Scene and Extreme Sports Varieties: The Injury Spectrum is Changing. [Szene- und Extremsportarten: Das Verletzungsspektrum Wandelt Sich.]." *Sportverletzung Sportschaden: Organ Der Gesellschaft Für Orthopädisch-Traumatologische Sportmedizin* 10 (3): VII–VIII.

Kellett, P., and R. Russell. 2009. "A Comparison Between Mainstream and Action Sport Industries in Australia: A Case Study of the Skateboarding Cluster." *Sport Management Review* 12 (2): 66–78.

Kerr, J. H. 1991. "Arousal-seeking in Risk Sport Participants." *Personality and Individual Differences* 12 (6): 613–616.

Kerr, J. H., and S. Houge. 2012. "Multiple Motives for Participating in Adventure Sports." *Psychology of Sport and Exercise* 13 (5): 649–657.

King, K., and A. Church. 2015. "Questioning Policy, Youth Participation and Lifestyle Sports." *Leisure Studies* 34 (3): 282–302.

Klaus, P., and S. Maklan. 2011. "Bridging the gap for Destination Extreme Sports: A Model of Sports Tourism Customer Experience." *Journal of Marketing Management* 27 (13-14): 1341–1365.

Ko, Y. J., C. L. Claussen, and H. Park. 2008. "Action Sports Participation: Consumer Motivation." *International Journal of Sports Marketing and Sponsorship* 9 (2): 111–124.

Kornilovich, A. V., and L. J. Kiprina. 2010. "Application of the Process Approach to the Design of Clothing for Extreme Sports." *Izvestiya Vysshikh Uchebnykh Zavedenii, Seriya Teknologiya Tekstil'Noi Promyshlennosti* (5): 75–77.

Korobeynikov, G., L. Korobeynikova, S. Iermakov, and M. Nosko. 2016. "Reaction of Heart Rate Regulation to Extreme Sport Activity in Elite Athletes." *Journal of Physical Education and Sport* 16 (3): 976–981.

Kramarz, S. 2016. "High-risk Sports During Pregnancy. [Risikosportarten in der Schwangerschaft]." *Gynakologe* 49 (9): 715–725.

Krein, K. J. 2014. "Nature Sports." *Journal of the Philosophy of Sport* 41 (2): 193–208.

Krein, K. 2015. "Reflections on Competition and Nature Sports." *Sport, Ethics and Philosophy* 9 (3): 271–286.

Kruger, M. 1988. "Was ist Alternativ am Alternativen Sport? - zur Analyse, Standortbestimmung und Kritik Einer Alternativen Spiel- und Bewegungskultur." *Sportwissenschaft* 18 (2): 137–159.

Kruger, O., U. Kalbe, E. Richter, P. Egeler, J. Rombke, and W. Berger. 2013. "New Approach to the Ecotoxicological Risk Assessment of Artificial Outdoor Sporting Grounds." *Environmental Pollution* 175: 69–74.

Lacasa, E., J. Miranda, and I. Muro. 1995. "Actividades físicas en la naturaleza: un objeto a investigar: dimensiones científicas." *Apunts: Educación Física y Deportes* (41): 53–69.

Lafollie, D., and C. Le Scanff. 2007. "Detection of High-Risk Personalities in Risky Sports. [Detection des personnalites a risque dans les sports a sensations fortes]." *Encephale* 33 (2): 135–141.

Lafollie, D., and C. Le Scanff. 2008. "Some Clues to Sensation Seeking, Disinhibition and the Practice of Risky Sports. [Recherche de sensations, desinhibition et pratique de sports a risque: quelques pistes de reflexion]." *Annales Medico-Psychologiques* 166 (10): 794–798.

Lagos, R. A. S. 2016. "Sedentary Lifestyle, Sports and Biopolitical Pressure for Healthy Living: Discourse Analysis on the "Choose to Live Healthy" System in Chile. [Sedentarismo, esporte e a pressao bio-politica por uma vida saudavel: Analise do discurso do programa "escolha uma vida saudavel"]." *do Chile] Movimento* 22 (2): 391–402.

Lahire, B. 2010. "Dispositions and Contexts of Action: Sport in Issues. [Dispositions et contextes d'action: Le sport en questions]." *Movimento* 16 (4): 11–29.

Langseth, T. 2011. "Risk Sports - Social Constraints and Cultural Imperatives." *Sport in Society* 14 (5): 629–644.

Laurendeau, J., and N. Sharara. 2008. ""Women Could be Every bit as Good as Guys": Reproductive and Resistant Agency in two "Action" Sports." *Journal of Sport and Social Issues* 32 (1): 24–47.

Lauterwasser, E. 2010. "Outdoor Sports: Towards Ecological Sustainability. [Natursport auf dem Weg zur okologischen Nachhaltigkeit]." *Natur Und Landschaft* 85 (9–10): 376–380.

Lawler, S., L. McDermott, D. O'Riordan, K. Spathonis, E. Eakin, E. Leslie, C. Gallois, N. Berndt, and N. Owen. 2012. "Relationships of sun-Protection Habit Strength with Sunscreen use During Outdoor Sport and Physical Activity." *International Journal of Environmental Research and Public Health* 9 (3): 916–923.

Leather, M., and F. Nicholls. 2016. "More than Activities: Using a 'Sense of Place' to Enrich Student Experience in Adventure Sport." *Sport, Education and Society* 21 (3): 443–464.

Lebeau, J., and R. Sides. 2015. "Beyond the Mainstream Versus Extreme Dichotomy: A Cyclical Perspective on Extreme Sports." *Sport in Society* 18 (6): 627–635.

Leese, P. 1998. "A More Varied and Exciting Outdoor Sports Scene." *Apparel International* 29 (1): 26–27.

Leiter, A. M., and C. M. Rheinberger. 2016. "Risky Sports and the Value of Safety Information." *Journal of Economic Behavior and Organization* 131: 328–345.

Li, M. 2016. "Investigation and Analysis on Outdoor Sports and Dietary Nutrition of College Students." *Carpathian Journal of Food Science and Technology* 8 (3): 160–167.

Ljungqvist, A. 1992. "Doping in Indoor and Outdoor Sports is an Increasing Abuse Problem. [Doping inom och utom idrotten ett stigande missbruksproblem.]." *Lakartidningen* 89 (30–31): 2491–2493.

Lotka, A. J. 1926. "The Frequency Distribution of Scientific Productivity." *Journal of the Washington Academy of Sciences* 16 (12): 317–323.

Low, M. B., and I. C. MacMillan. 1988. "Entrepreneurship: Past Research and Future Challenges." *Journal of Management* 14: 139–161.

Lundberg, N., S. Taniguchi, R. McGovern, and S. Smith. 2016. "Female Veterans' Involvement in Outdoor Sports and Recreation: A Theoretical Sample of Recreation Opportunity Structures." *Journal of Leisure Research* 48 (5): 413–430.

Ma, J. L. G., and M. J. Dutch. 2013. "Extreme Sports: Extreme Physiology. Exercise-Induced Pulmonary Oedema." *EMA - Emergency Medicine Australasia* 25 (4): 368–371.

Mahe, E., A. Beauchet, M. De Paula Correa, S. Godin-Beekmann, M. Haeffelin, S. Bruant, F. Fay-Chatelard, F. Jégou, P. Saiag, and P. Aegerter. 2011. "Outdoor Sports and Risk of Ultraviolet

Radiation-Related Skin Lesions in Children: Evaluation of Risks and Prevention." *British Journal of Dermatology* 165 (2): 360–367.

Maltrás-Barba, B. 2003. *Los Indicadores Bibliométricos: Fundamentos y Aplicación al Análisis de la Ciencia.* Asturias: Trea.

Mao, P., and P. Bourdeau. 2008. "A Contribution to Mapping Nature Sports, Recreational and Tourism Spaces. [Les lieux de pratique des sports de nature en France: Une geographie differenciee]." *Mappemonde* 89 (1): 1–13.

Martha, C., and J. Laurendeau. 2010. "Are Perceived Comparative Risks Realistic among High-Risk Sports Participants?" *International Journal of Sport and Exercise Psychology* 8 (2): 129–146.

Martha, C., J. Laurendeau, and J. Griffet. 2010. "Comparative Optimism and Risky Road Traffic Behaviors among High-Risk Sports Practitioners." *Journal of Risk Research* 13 (4): 429–444.

Martinez-Nicolas, A., A. Muntaner-Mas, and F. B. Ortega. 2017. "Runkeeper: A Complete app for Monitoring Outdoor Sports." *British Journal of Sports Medicine* 51: 1560–1561.

Melo, R. 2009. "Desportos de Natureza: Reflexões Sobre a sua Definição Conceptual." *Exedra* 2: 93–104.

Melo, R. 2017. "Understanding Nature Sports Participation: A Literature Review." In *Sport Tourism: New Challenges in a Globalized World*, edited by R. Melo and C. Sobry (Coords.), 241–275. Newcastle: Cambridge Scholars Publishing.

Melo, R., and R. Gomes. 2016a. "Understanding Nature Sports Organizations in Portugal." *Open Sports Sciences Journal* 9 (Suppl-1, M3): 13–25.

Melo, R., and R. Gomes. 2016b. "Nature Sports and Sustainable Local Development: Practitioners and Organizations Managers' Perspectives in Portugal." In *Sport Tourism and Local Sustainable Development*, edited by C. Sobry, 75–100. Lille: L'Harmattan.

Melo, R., and R. Gomes. 2017a. "Nature Sports Participation: Understanding Demand, Practice Profile, Motivations and Constraints." *European Journal of Tourism Research* 16: 108–135.

Melo, R., and R. Gomes. 2017b. "A Sociocultural Approach to Understanding the Development of Nature Sports." In *Sport Tourism: New Challenges in a Globalized World*, edited by R. Melo and C. Sobry (Coords.), 60–90. Newcastle: Cambridge Scholars Publishing.

Michel, G., N. Cazenave, C. Delpouve, D. Purper-Ouakil, and C. LeScanff. 2009. "Personality Profiles and Emotional Function in Extreme Sports: An Exploratory Study among BASE-Jumpers. [Profils de personnalite et fonctionnement emotionnel dans les sports extremes: a propos d'une etude exploratoire chez des BASE-jumpers]." *Annales Medico-Psychologiques* 167 (1): 72–77.

Miller, J. R., and S. G. Demoiny. 2008. "Parkour: A new Extreme Sport and a Case Study." *Journal of Foot and Ankle Surgery* 47 (1): 63–65.

Mitin, A. I., and V. M. Tsar'kov. 1979. "Optimization of a Four-Pole Lighting System for Outdoor Sports Installations." *Svetotekhnika* 2: 10–11.

Moehrle, M. 2008. "Outdoor Sports and Skin Cancer." *Clinics in Dermatology* 26 (1): 12–15.

Mohamed, S., V. Favrod, R. A. Philippe, and D. Hauw. 2015. "The Situated Management of Safety During Risky Sport: Learning From Skydivers' Courses of Experience." *Journal of Sports Science and Medicine* 14 (2): 340–346.

Monasterio, E., O. Mei-Dan, A. C. Hackney, A. R. Lane, I. Zwir, S. Rozsa, and C. R. Cloninger. 2016. "Stress Reactivity and Personality in Extreme Sport Athletes: The Psychobiology of BASE Jumpers." *Physiology and Behavior* 167: 289–297.

Morgan, W. P., and S. E. Goldston. 1987. *Exercise and Mental Health.* Washington, DC: Hemisphere.

Mounet, J. 2007. "Outdoor Sports, Sustainable Development and Environmental Controversies. [Sports de nature, developpement durable et controverse environnementale]." *Natures Sciences Societes* 15 (2): 162–166.

Mykletun, R. J., and M. Rumba. 2014. "Athletes' Experiences, Enjoyment, Satisfaction, and Memories From the Extreme Sport Week in Voss, Norway." *Sports, Business and Management* 4 (4): 317–335.

Nath, D., S. Mazumdar, J. K. Chandra, and A. K. Bag. 2016. "A Rough set-Based Method for Aiming Angle Tuning of Luminaires for Outdoor Sports Lighting." *Lighting Research and Technology* 48 (2): 126–154.

Navarro Gutierrez, S., J. A. Molina Jaime, and E. Lapresa Acosta. 2011. "Football Spectator: Risk Sport. [Espectador de futbol: Deporte de riesgo]." *Emergencias* 23 (3): 242.

Ocampo, R. P., and D. M. Klaus. 2016. "Comparing the Relative Risk of Spaceflight to Terrestrial Modes of Transportation and Adventure Sport Activities." *New Space* 4 (3): 190–197.

Olive, R., and H. Thorpe. 2011. "Negotiating the 'F-Word' in the Field: Doing Feminist Ethnography in Action Sport Cultures." *Sociology of Sport Journal* 28 (4): 421–440.

Opaschowski, H. W. 2005. "Crossing Borders. the Motivation of Extreme Sportsmen. [Grenzganger. Zur Motivation von Extremsportlern]." *Bundesgesundheitsblatt - Gesundheitsforschung - Gesundheitsschutz* 48 (8): 876–880.

Pain, M., and J. H. Kerr. 2004. "Extreme Risk Taker who Wants to Continue Taking Part in High Risk Sports After Serious Injury." *British Journal of Sports Medicine* 38 (3): 337–339.

Palmer, C. 2002. "'Shit Happens': The Selling of Risk in Extreme Sport." *Australian Journal of Anthropology* 13 (3): 323–336.

Palmi, J., and A. Martín. 2007. "Las Actividades Físico-Deportivas en el Medio Natural y sus Efectos Sobre la Salud y la Calidad de Vida: Factores Psicológicos Asociados." *Revista de Psicología del Deporte* 6 (2): 147–160.

Parris, D. L. 2013. "Conceptually Meeting Expectations of Generation y by Building Personalised-Customised Hybrid Bundles to Target Action Sports Consumers." *International Journal of Revenue Management* 7 (2): 138–154.

Parris, D. L., M. L. Troilo, A. Bouchet, and J. W. Peachey. 2014. "Action Sports Athletes as Entrepreneurs: Female Professional Wakeboarders, Sponsorship, and Branding." *Sport Management Review* 17 (4): 530–545.

Pedersen, D. M. 1997. "Perceptions of High Risk Sports." *Perceptual and Motor Skills*, 85 (3. PART I), 756–758.

Penin, N. 2004. "A Taste for Danger. A few Keys to Understanding Women's Involvement in Extreme Sports. ["l'amour du risqué". Modes d'engagements feminins dans les pratiques sportives a risques.]." *Staps* 66 (4): 195–207.

Pimentel, G. 2008. "Socio-cultural Aspects Regarding the Perception of Quality of Life Amongst People Engaging in Extreme (High-Risk) Sports. [Aspectos socioculturais na percepcao da qualidade de vida entre praticantes de esportes de aventura]." *Revista De Salud Publica* 10 (4): 561–570.

Pimentel, G. 2013. "Esportes na Natureza e Atividades de Aventura: uma Terminologia Aporética." *Revista Brasileira de Ciências do Esporte* 35 (3): 687–700.

Plank, A. 2016. "The Hidden Risk in User-Generated Content: An Investigation of ski Tourers' Revealed Risk-Taking Behavior on an Online Outdoor Sports Platform." *Tourism Management* 55: 289–296.

Pluijms, J. P., R. Canal-Bruland, M. J. M. Hoozemans, M. W. Van Beek, K. Bocker, and G. J. P. Savelsbergh. 2016. "Quantifying External Focus of Attention in Sailing by Means of Action Sport Cameras." *Journal of Sports Sciences* 34 (16): 1588–1595.

Pope, R., R. Herbert, and C. Maher. 1998. "Ankle Supports Prevent Ankle Ligament Injury During High-Risk Sporting Activities." *Australian Journal of Physiotherapy* 44 (2): 139–140.

Potgieter, J., and F. Bisschoff. 1990. "Sensation Seeking among Medium- and low-Risk Sports Participants." *Perceptual and Motor Skills* 71 (3 II): 1203–1206.

Price, D. J. S. 1956. "The Exponential Curve of Science." *Discovery* 17 (6): 240–243.

Putsch, M., and B. Job-Hoben. 2010. "Information Systems in the Field of Nature Conservation and Sports. [Fachinformationssysteme im Themenfeld Naturschutz - Sport]." *Natur Und Landschaft* 85 (9-10): 390–396.

Rannikko, A., P. Harinen, P. Torvinen, and V. Liikanen. 2016. "The Social Bordering of Lifestyle Sports: Inclusive Principles, Exclusive Reality." *Journal of Youth Studies* 19 (8): 1093–1109.

Rauter, S., and M. D. Topič. 2011. "Perspectives of the Sport-Oriented Public in Slovenia on Extreme Sports. [Ekstremni sportovi u percepciji Slovenske sportske javnosti]." *Kinesiology* 43 (1): 82–90.

Revuelta, R., and G. K. B. Sandor. 2005. "Degloving Injury of the Mandibular Mucosa Following an Extreme Sport Accident: A Case Report." *Journal of Dentistry for Children* 72 (3): 104–106.

Rhea, D. J., and S. Martin. 2010. "Personality Trait Differences of Traditional Sport Athletes, Bullriders, and Other Alternative Sport Athletes." *International Journal of Sports Science and Coaching* 5 (1): 75–85.

Richez, G., and J. Richez-Battesti. 1991. "Outdoor Sporting Activities in the Rural Areas of Corsica. [Les activites sportives de pleine nature dans l'espace rural corse]." *Mediterranee* 72: 21–31.

Rinehart, R. E. 2014. "Anhedonia and Alternative Sports." *Staps* 104 (2): 9–21.

Robinson, D. W. 1992. "The Risk-Sport Process: An Alternative Approach for Humanistic Physical Education." *Quest* 44 (1): 88–104.

Roger, S., and S. Lee. 2008. "Multiple Groups Confirmatory Factor Analysis of the Motivational Factors Affecting Individuals' Decisions About Participating in Action Sports and an Inquiry Into Participant Action Sports Participatory Fandom." *International Journal of Sport Management and Marketing* 3 (4): 348–357.

Rosa, P. F., L. A. D. Carvalhinho, and J. A. P. Soares. 2017. "Nature-based Sports and Sustainable Development: Perspectives of Development and Governance." *Movimento* 23 (1): 419–436.

Rudie, R. 1997. "Extreme Sports Spawn new Breed of 'Techno' Fabrics." *Bobbin* 38 (5): 10–14.

Sallis, R., and C. M. Chassay. 1999. "Recognizing and Treating Common Cold-Induced Injury in Outdoor Sports." *Medicine and Science in Sports and Exercise* 31 (10): 1367–1373.

Salome, L., and M. van Bottenburg. 2012. "Are They all Daredevils? Introducing a Participation Typology for the Consumption of Lifestyle Sports in Different Settings." *European Sport Management Quarterly* 12 (1): 19–42.

Salome, L. R., M. van Bottenburg, and M. van den Heuvel. 2013. "'We are as Green as Possible': Environmental Responsibility in Commercial Artificial Settings for Lifestyle Sports." *Leisure Studies* 32 (2): 173–190.

Schafer, J., H. Gaulrapp, and W. Pforringer. 1998. "Acute and Chronic Overuse Injuries in Extreme Sportclimbing. [Verletzungen und Uberlastungssyndrome beim extremen Sportklettern]." *Sportverletzung-Sportschaden* 12 (1): 21–25.

Schreier, M., S. Oberhauser, and R. Prugl. 2007. "Lead Users and the Adoption and Diffusion of new Products: Insights From two Extreme Sports Communities." *Marketing Letters* 18 (1–2): 15–30.

Schwartz, G. M., J. P. Figueiredo, L. M. Pereira, D. A. Christofoletti, and V. K. Dias. 2013. "Adventure Sports and Prejudice: The (no) Female Presence. [Preconceito e esportes de aventura: A (nao) presenca feminina]." *Motricidade* 9 (1): 56–67.

Schwartz, G. M., L. M. Pereira, J. D. P. Figueiredo, D. F. A. Christofoletti, and V. K. Dias. 2016. "Strategies for the Participation of Women in Adventure Sports. [Estrategias de participacao da mulher nos esportes de aventura]." *Revista Brasileira De Ciencias do Esporte* 38 (2): 156–162.

Schwier, J. 2008. "Commitment, Identity and Subcultural Media in Alternative Sport. [Inszenierungen widerspenstiger Korperlichkeit. Zur Selbstmediatisierung jugendlicher Sportszenen]." *Zeitschrift Fur Soziologie Der Erziehung Und Sozialisation* 28 (3): 271–282.

Self, D. R., E. De Vries Henry, C. S. Findley, and E. Reilly. 2007. "Thrill Seeking: The Type T Personality and Extreme Sports." *International Journal of Sport Management and Marketing* 2 (1-2): 175–190.

Seppanen, M., A. Virolainen-Julkunen, I. Kakko, P. Vilkamaa, and S. Meri. 2004. "Myiasis During Adventure Sports Race." *Emerging Infectious Diseases* 10 (1): 137–139.

Serrano, M., J. Canada, and J. C. Moreno. 2011. "Ultraviolet Exposure for Different Outdoor Sports in Valencia, Spain." *Photodermatology Photoimmunology and Photomedicine* 27 (6): 311–317.

Serrano, M., J. Canada, J. C. Moreno, and G. Gurrea. 2014. "Personal UV Exposure for Different Outdoor Sports." *Photochemical and Photobiological Sciences* 13 (4): 671–679.

Sharma, V. K., J. Rango, A. J. Connaughton, D. J. Lombardo, and V. J. Sabesan. 2015. "The Current State of Head and Neck Injuries in Extreme Sports." *Orthopaedic Journal of Sports Medicine* 3 (1): 1–6.

Shoham, A., G. M. Rose, and L. R. Kahle. 1998. "Marketing of Risky Sports: From Intention to Action." *Journal of the Academy of Marketing Science* 26 (4): 307–321.

Shoham, A., G. M. Rose, and L. R. Kahle. 2000. "Practitioners of Risky Sports: A Quantitative Examination." *Journal of Business Research* 47 (3): 237–251.

Simpson, W. 2016. "Easton Cowboys and Cowgirls: Anatomy of an Alternative Sports Club." *Soccer and Society* 17 (5): 721–731.

Sisjord, M. K. 2015. "Assessing the Sociology of Sport: On Lifestyle Sport and Gender." *International Review for the Sociology of Sport* 50 (4–5): 596–600.

Siwek, M., D. Dudek, K. Drozdowicz, R. Jaeschke, K. Styczen, A. Arciszewska, K. K. Akiskal, H. S. Akiskal, and J. K. Rybakowski. 2015. "Temperamental Dimensions of the TEMPS-A in Male and Female Subjects Engaging in Extreme or/and High Risk Sports." *Journal of Affective Disorders* 170: 66–70.

Skille, E. A., and I. Waddington. 2006. "Alternative Sport Programmes and Social Inclusion in Norway." *European Physical Education Review* 12 (3): 251–271.

Slanger, E., and K. E. Rudestam. 1997. "Motivation and Disinhibition in High Risk Sports: Sensation Seeking and Self-Efficacy." *Journal of Research in Personality* 31 (3): 355–374.

Sokol, D. K. 2011. "Boxing, Mixed Martial Arts, and Other Risky Sports: Is the BMA Confused?" *BMJ* (Clinical Research Ed.), 343. www.scopus.com.

Soule, B. 2008. ""Extreme Sports" as a Notion: Conceptual Analysis of a Successful Characterization. [Les "sports extremes": Analyse terminologique d'une caracterisation sportive a succes]." *Science Et Motricite* 63 (1): 83–90.

Spanjersberg, W. R., and I. B. Schipper. 2007. "Kitesurfing: When fun Turns to Trauma—The Dangers of a new Extreme Sport." *Journal of Trauma* 63 (3): E76–E80.

Spinak, E. 1996. *Diccionario Enciclopédico de Bibliometría, Cienciometría e Informetría*. Venezuela: UNESCO.

Stanley, F. 2013. "Teaching Artistry: Education's Extreme Sport." *Teaching Artist Journal* 11 (3): 161–167.

Stops, T., and P. Gropel. 2016. "Motivation for High-Risk Sports: A Qualitative Study with Professional Freeskiers. [Motivation zum risikosport eine qualitative untersuchung mit professionellen free-skiern]." *Zeitschrift Fur Sportpsychologie* 23 (1): 13–25.

Strohle, A. 2014. "Extreme Sport. [Extremsport]." *Psychiatrie* 11 (4): 271–274.

Suchet, A. 2011. "Adventure Sports and Tourism at the Beginning of the Construction of Europe in the Pyrenees: Cross-Border Cooperation Between France and Spain During the 1993 Pyrenees Adventure Games. [Sports d'aventure et tourisme au debut de la construction europeenne en pyr-enees: La cooperation transfrontaliere entre la France et l'Espagne durant les Jeux Pyreneens de l'Aventure 1993]." *Revue De Geographie Alpine* 99 (3): 1.

Sytema, R., R. Dekker, P. U. Dijkstra, H. J. Ten Duis, and C. K. Van Der Sluis. 2010. "Upper Extremity Sports Injury: Risk Factors in Comparison to Lower Extremity Injury in More Than 25 000 Cases." *Clinical Journal of Sport Medicine* 20 (4): 256–263.

Thomson, C. J., R. J. Power, S. R. Carlson, J. L. Rupert, and G. Michel. 2015. "A Comparison of Genetic Variants Between Proficient low- and High-Risk Sport Participants." *Journal of Sports Sciences* 33 (18): 1861–1870.

Thorpe, H. 2009. "Understanding 'Alternative' Sport Experiences: A Contextual Approach for Sport Psychology." *International Journal of Sport and Exercise Psychology* 7 (3): 359–379.

Thorpe, H. 2015. "Natural Disaster Arrhythmia and Action Sports: The Case of the Christchurch Earthquake." *International Review for the Sociology of Sport* 50 (3): 301–325.

Thorpe, H. 2016. "Action Sports for Youth Development: Critical Insights for the SDP Community." *International Journal of Sport Policy* 8 (1): 91–116.

Thorpe, H., and N. Ahmad. 2015. "Youth, Action Sports and Political Agency in the Middle East: Lessons From a Grassroots Parkour Group in Gaza." *International Review for the Sociology of Sport* 50 (6): 678–704.

Thorpe, H., and R. Rinehart. 2010. "Alternative Sport and Affect: Non-Representational Theory Examined." *Sport in Society* 13 (7): 1268–1291.

Thorpe, H., and R. Rinehart. 2013. "Action Sport NGOs in a neo-Liberal Context: The Cases of Skateistan and Surf aid International." *Journal of Sport and Social Issues* 37 (2): 115–141.

Thorpe, H., and B. Wheaton. 2011. "'Generation x Games', Action Sports and the Olympic Movement: Understanding the Cultural Politics of Incorporation." *Sociology* 45 (5): 830–847.

Tian, B. 2016. "Development Status of China's Outdoor Sports and Countermeasures Based on SWOT Analysis." *RISTI - Revista Iberica De Sistemas e Tecnologias De Informacao* 2016 (E11): 76–84.

Tok, S. 2011. "The big Five Personality Traits and Risky Sport Participation." *Social Behavior and Personality* 39 (8): 1105–1112.

Trubo, R. 2001. "Leptospira Brings Fresh Challenge to Adventure Sports." *The Lancet Infectious Diseases* 1 (2): 73.

Turčová, I., A. Martin, and J. Neuman. 2005. "Diversity in Language: Outdoor Terminology in the Czech Republic and Britain." *Journal of Adventure Education and Outdoor Learning* 5 (2): 101–118.

Turner, D. 2013. "The Civilized Skateboarder and the Sports Funding Hegemony: A Case Study of Alternative Sport." *Sport in Society* 16 (10): 1248–1262.

Tzetzis, G., K. Alexandris, and S. Kapsampeli. 2014. "Predicting Visitors' Satisfaction and Behavioral Intentions From Service Quality in the Context of a Small-Scale Outdoor Sport Event." *International Journal of Event and Festival Management* 5 (1): 4–21.

Ujma-Wa͵sowicz, K., and T. Musioandł. 2008. "Outdoor Sport in the City of the Future. Planning and Designing Issues." *WIT Transactions on Ecology and the Environment* 117: 13–22.

Van Bottenburg, M., and L. Salome. 2010. "The Indoorisation of Outdoor Sports: An Exploration of the Rise of Lifestyle Sports in Artificial Settings." *Leisure Studies* 29 (2): 143–160.

Vanstone, J. R. 2003. "Adrenalscapes: A Conceptual Design Model for Extreme Sport. [Des paysages adrenalesques: Un modele d'amenagement conceptuel pour sports extremes]." *Landscapes* 5 (2): 11–14.

Watson, N., and A. Parker. 2015. "The Mystical and Sublime in Extreme Sports: Experiences of Psychological Well-Being or Christian Revelation?" *Studies in World Christianity* 21 (3): 260–281.

Watson, A. E., and B. D. Pulford. 2004. "Personality Differences in High Risk Sports Amateurs and Instructors." *Perceptual and Motor Skills* 99 (1): 83–94.

Wheaton, B. 2003. "Lifestyle Sport Magazines and the Discourses of Sporting Masculinity." *Sociological Review* 51 (S1): 193–221.

Wheaton, B. 2004. *Understanding Lifestyle Sports: Consumption, Identity and Difference.* London: Routledge.

Wheaton, B. 2010. "Introducing the Consumption and Representation of Lifestyle Sports." *Sport in Society* 13 (7): 1057–1081.

Wheaton, B. 2015. "Assessing the Sociology of Sport: On Action Sport and the Politics of Identity." *International Review for the Sociology of Sport* 50 (4–5): 634–639.

White, J. 1998. "Alternative Sports Medicine." *Physician and Sportsmedicine* 26 (6): 92–105.

Willig, C. 2008. "A Phenomenological Investigation of the Experience of Taking Part in 'Extreme Sports'." *Journal of Health Psychology* 13 (5): 690–702.

Woodman, T., M. Barlow, C. Bandura, M. Hill, D. Kupciw, and A. MacGregor. 2013. "Not all Risks are Equal: The Risk-Taking Inventory for High-Risk Sports." *Journal of Sport and Exercise Psychology* 35 (5): 479–492.

Woodman, T., L. Hardy, M. Barlow, and C. Le Scanff. 2010. "Motives for Participation in Prolonged Engagement High-Risk Sports: An Agentic Emotion Regulation Perspective." *Psychology of Sport and Exercise* 11 (5): 345–352.

Woratschek, H., F. M. Hannich, and B. Ritchie. 2007. "Motivations of Sports Tourists: An Empirical Analysis in Several European Rock Climbing Regions." University of Bayreuth. http://www.fiwi.uni-bayreuth.de/de/download/WP_02-07.pdf.

Yao, X. K. 2013. "The Design and Brand Analysis of Outdoor Sports Casual Wear-Take Austrian Brand HEAD for Example." *Taiwan Textile Research Journal* 23 (1): 50–59.

Zarevski, P., I. Marušić, S. Zolotić, T. Bunjevac, and Z. Vukosav. 1998. "Contribution of Arnett's Inventory of Sensation Seeking and Zuckerman's Sensation Seeking Scale to the Differentiation of Athletes Engaged in High and low Risk Sports." *Personality and Individual Differences* 25 (4): 763–768.

Zuev, V. N., and V. A. Ivanov. 2013. "Youth Value Orientations When Choosing Extreme Sports Subcultures." *Teoriya i Praktika Fizicheskoy Kultury* 12: 14–16.

Conceptualizing adventurous nature sport: a positive psychology perspective

Susan Houge Mackenzie (iD) and Eric Brymer (iD)

ABSTRACT

Research and public policy has long supported links between traditional sports and well-being. However, adventurous nature sport literature has primarily focused on performance issues and deficit models of risk or sensation-seeking. This standpoint is limited by assumptions that participation is: (a) dependent on personality structures; (b) solely motivated by risk-taking and hedonism; (c) only attractive or accessible to a narrow demographic; and (d) widely perceived as dysfunctional or deviant. In contrast, recent research suggests that adventurous nature sports provide unique benefits due to their context. This paper critically assesses the validity of dominant perspectives against emerging literature to illustrate how nature sports can be conceptualized through a positive psychology lens as well-being activities that facilitate both hedonic and eudaimonic outcomes. The significance of this perspective is that nature sports may become an important consideration when designing health and well-being interventions for both people and the planet.

Introduction

> The secret for harvesting from existence the greatest fruitfulness and the greatest enjoyment is - to *live dangerously*! - Nietzsche (1974, 228)

Over the past two decades, interest in adventurous and 'extreme' nature sports, such as skiing, skydiving, rock climbing, and whitewater kayaking, has steadily increased (e.g. Brymer and Schweitzer 2017; Lyng 2005). While participation in many traditional organized sports has declined or stagnated, a wider range of nature-based sports have grown in popularity (e.g. Outdoor Foundation 2017). According to Puchan (2004, 177), involvement in these sports is 'not ... just a "flash in the pan" but a sign of the times in which people are looking for a new way to define their lives and to escape from an increasingly regulated and sanitized way of living.'

At the 'extreme' end of the nature sport spectrum (e.g. activities such as B.A.S.E. [Buildings, Antennae, Space, Earth] jumping, big wave surfing, waterfall kayaking, rope-free climbing), the most likely outcome of a mismanaged error or accident is death. Thus, many psychologists view this behaviour as irrational and deviant, resulting from ignorance or the inability to self-regulate (e.g. Lupton and Tulloch 2002). However, emerging research contests traditional definitions and models (Brymer and Oades 2009; Brymer and Schweitzer 2013; Kerr and Houge Mackenzie 2012). Traditional theoretical paradigms in adventurous nature sport literature are often narrowly focused on risk, danger, and/or physical or emotional discomfort, which limits their predictive power and depth. These accepted narratives preclude serious consideration of adventurous nature sport activities in mainstream health and well-being discourses and public health initiatives. Thus, the aim of this paper is to explain how adventurous nature sports can be conceptualized through a contemporary positive psychology lens. In particular, we propose that an improved frame of analysis can be developed from well-being models that integrate hedonic and eudaimonic dimensions. To demonstrate the potential of these positive psychology approaches, we critique dominant discourses in adventurous nature sport literature by illustrating how traditional models fail to encapsulate a range of research outcomes. We then suggest theoretical perspectives that may explain emerging findings.

Adventurous nature sports: traditional definitions & risk perspectives

Inherent in the concept of nature sports is an outdoor, natural context for these activities. Nature contexts can be quite varied and include water (e.g. surfing, whitewater kayaking), land (e.g. climbing, mountain biking), and wind-based activities (e.g. skydiving, paragliding). While examples of nature sports abound, clear definitions and models of these activities are difficult to ascertain. This may be due in part to the proliferation of terminology, such as 'extreme', 'high-risk', 'adventure', and 'alternative', across a range of disciplines including sport and exercise psychology, sociology, philosophy, tourism, leisure studies, business studies, experiential education and wilderness therapy (e.g. Bowen, Neill, and Crisp 2016; Castanier, Le Scanff, and Woodman 2011; Krein 2014; Melo and Gomes 2017). For the purpose of this discussion, the term *adventurous nature sports* (ANS) is used to encompass activities traditionally described as 'high-risk', 'adventurous', or 'extreme' nature-based sporting activities. These have typically been characterized by the following attributes: self-initiated, physical activities within a natural environment that provide opportunities to exercise personal skills in order to minimise real or apparent risk or danger, and thereby influence uncertain outcomes (e.g. Ewert and Hollenhorst 1989). In contrast to traditional sports, the primary challenge involved in ANS often lies not in defeating one's opponent, but in identifying and engaging with opportunities for challenges posed by the participant-environment relationship through use of personal and group competencies.

Adventurous nature sports have long been associated with risk and sensation-seeking. From an anthropological perspective, Clark (1986) differentiated between the inevitable risk-*taking* that occurs in life, and risk-*seeking* involved in adventure that is deliberate and easily avoidable. Clark (1986) and Foster (1993) identified risk-seeking through adventure as one way of attaining high levels of emotional arousal. 'Risk-seeking is a deliberate way of inducing the emotional arousal that risk-taking generates ... both pleasurable and unpleasurable excitement are involved in risk-seeking' (Foster 1993, 67). These perspectives remain prominent in research literature (e.g. Baretta, Greco, and Steca 2017; Kopp et al. 2016).

Traditional definitions and models of ANS have narrowly focused on risk, sensation-seeking, and 'pushing' participants out of their 'comfort zone'. For instance, risk-taking, danger and control were central to Ewert and Hollenhorst's (1989) initial model of adventure recreation; 'It is [the] positive valuation of risk and danger that makes adventure recreation fundamentally different from other recreation experiences' (127). Despite challenges to this view, many researchers and educators maintain that confronting risk, fear or danger produces optimal stress and discomfort, which in turn promotes outcomes such as improved self-esteem, character building, and psychological resilience (e.g. Ewert and Garvey 2007; Ewert and Yoshino 2011; Lupton and Tulloch 2002; Priest and Gass 2018). Although fear, risk and associated sensation-seeking have long been conceptualized as integral to ANS experiences (e.g. Kopp et al. 2016; Zuckerman 2007), the importance of these elements in ANS motivations and outcomes remains contested.

There are a number of problematic implicit assumptions embedded within traditional risk-taking approaches to ANS. Some researchers argue that paradigms focusing on risk have neglected the unpleasant experience of anxiety that accompanies risk perceptions (Brown 2009; Davis-Berman and Berman 2002). The risk paradigm also assumes that ANS will only appeal to a narrow demographic of individuals with particular personality structures. However, this is at odds with statistics demonstrating that participation rates are growing faster than many traditional sports and are increasingly attracting a broader range of participants (e.g. Outdoor Foundation 2017). The risk perspective has also tended to overlook more positive, developmental motivations and outcomes by characterizing participants as deviant, dysfunctional, or psychologically deficient. A possible explanation for these discrepancies is that investigations of ANS motivations and behaviour have generally applied models and theories developed to understand 'abnormal' behaviour in clinical contexts to disparate nature sport contexts. This approach also stems from a disproportionate focus on ill-being, rather than well-being, in psychology (Seligman and Csikszentmihalyi 2014). As a result, alternative, and potentially more appropriate, perspectives on the adventurous nature sport experience may have been overlooked.

Beyond risk: well-being and adventurous nature sports

Despite these traditional narratives, the risk-oriented paradigm has been increasingly questioned on multiple fronts. Ewert and Sibthorp's (2009) methodological critique identified a lack of quantitative, longitudinal, and randomized controlled studies and called for the development of context specific models that incorporate underlying processes. Brookes (2003) and Brown (2009, 2010) have repeatedly argued that research and theory should refocus to account for cultural, regional, historical, and social aspects of ANS experiences. Kerr and Houge Mackenzie (2012) identified several motivations beyond thrill-seeking across multiple adventure sports, a finding supported by studies reporting outcomes such as personal control, courage, attention restoration, personal growth, self-actualisation, achievement, and mastery (e.g. Fischer and Smith 2004; Lyng 2005; Pain and Pain 2005; Pearson and Craig 2014).

Barlow, Woodman, and Hardy (2013) further challenged the sensation-seeking perspective in a series of three studies. They concluded that different ANS involve distinct motivations (e.g. emotional regulation, agency) and highlighted how understanding these motivations can improve our understanding of human behaviour more generally.

Notwithstanding, Barlow et al.'s interpretations were still founded on a deficit model in which an adventurous nature sport (i.e. mountaineering) served as a compensatory activity through which to counteract difficulties with emotional regulation, personal agency and anxiety. Varley and Semple (2015, 77), although writing about adventure travellers specifically, eloquently summarized how current adventure conceptualisations ignore the 'holistic social nature of the [adventure] experience':

> Many theories of adventure (Ewert 1989; Keiwa 2002; Lewis 2000; Morgan 2014; Mortlock 1984; Priest and Bunting 1993) encapsulate the adventure motive as a desire for borderline experiences occupying the threshold between catastrophe and adventure. Such representations, with their almost fatalistic proximity to disaster seem essentialist and elitist, and intuitively are at odds with the motives of many contemporary adventure travelers.

Positive psychology approaches

In contrast to traditional risk and sensation-seeking perspectives, the emerging field of positive psychology provides an alternative way of understanding ANS that reflects current research findings. Positive psychology is concerned with understanding and fostering well-being by studying optimal experiences and functioning across individuals, communities, organizations and societies (Seligman and Csikszentmihalyi 2014). Researchers investigate concepts such as character strengths, positive relationships, meaning, autonomy, engagement and accomplishments. Prior to the establishment of positive psychology as an official branch of psychology, Ryff (1989) proposed a model of psychological well-being that included personal growth, self-acceptance, life purpose, mastery, autonomy and positive relationships. Well-being has since been conceptually developed to include multiple dimensions and domains (e.g. physical, psychological, emotional, social, financial) that are dynamic and function at various levels (e.g. individual, group) (Mental Health Commission of NSW 2017). This approach to well-being includes the effective management of unhelpful psychological phenomenon and nurturing of positive accomplishments, emotions, relationships, engagement and meaning.

In positive psychology literature, well-being has generally been approached from two distinct perspectives: hedonia and eudaimonia. Hedonic well-being consists of pleasure, positive emotions and avoidance of pain (e.g. Waterman, Schwartz, and Conti 2008). Conversely, eudaimonic well-being encompasses meaning, purpose, optimal functioning, self-realisation and flourishing (e.g. Huppert and So 2013; Ryan and Deci 2011). Although these perspectives seem to define well-being in distinct ways, research has increasingly supported less dialectical, more holistic approaches to well-being that incorporate both hedonic and eudaimonic elements (e.g. Hendeson and Knight 2012; Lomas and Ivtzan 2016). For example, Huta and Ryan (2010) argued that the pursuit of eudaimonic well-being results in a more complete and meaningful life and fosters more stable and enduring hedonic happiness. Eudaimonic benefits have been shown to stem directly from the immediate satisfaction of basic psychological needs for autonomy, competence, and relatedness (Ryan, Huta, and Deci 2013). Despite the volume of research supporting these models, critics argue that these predominantly western, anthropocentric approaches should be expanded to include connection to nature and community (Mental Health Commission of NSW 2017).

Hedonic and eudaimonic perspectives of well-being are both relevant to the expanded conceptualization of ANS presented in this paper. Indeed, given the seemingly paradoxical or divergent findings related to ANS participation (e.g. thrill or 'adrenaline'-seeking motives versus self-actualisation motives), incorporating both perspectives may help to explain these discrepancies in the literature and provide a fuller picture of ANS motives, experiences, and benefits. These perspectives may also help to explain how outcomes and motivations can change over time and through experience (e.g. Brymer, Downey, and Gray 2009). For instance, an individual might begin an ANS with hedonistic desires and develop more eudaimonic motivations and benefits through repeated experiences. In the following section, we explore research that supports this framework for understanding ANS from a well-being perspective.

Adventurous nature sports as well-being activities

A growing body of literature, typically using an inductive approach, supports the proposition that a well-being framework can expand current conceptualisations of ANS motivations and outcomes. Recent research suggests that adventurous nature activities enhance physical health and psychological well-being in a variety of ways, and that these experiences of well-being encourage further participation (Brymer and Schweitzer 2017). Participants report hedonic and eudaimonic outcomes that include: positive life transformations; optimal experiences; emotional regulation; development of emotional agency in interpersonal relationships; improved quality of life; goal achievement; social connections; escape from boredom; exploring personal boundaries; overcoming limitations imposed by fear; pleasurable kinesthetic bodily sensations; a sense of merging with nature; and transcendence (e.g. Brymer and Gray 2010; Willig 2008; Woodman, Cazenave, and Le Scanff 2008; Woodman et al. 2010). Studies of adventure education and wilderness therapy further underscore the eudaimonic benefits of these activities across a range of domains. Meta-analyses of hundreds of adventure education and adventure therapy studies demonstrate programme efficacy, particularly for longer programmes and younger participants, with outcomes that include improved self-concept, self-awareness and acceptance; chemical dependency recovery; and reduced behavioural and emotional symptoms (e.g. Gass, Gillis, and Russell 2012; Hattie et al. 1997).

A variety of mechanisms have been proposed to explain links between well-being and nature-based activities. The aesthetic, spiritual and novel qualities of natural environments have been found to promote personal development, self-awareness, and environmental consciousness (e.g. D'Amato and Krasny 2011; McKenzie 2000). ANS may restore person-environment relationships by, for example, restoring attentional resources and improving cognitive function (e.g. Berman, Jonides, and Kaplan 2008; Pearson and Craig 2014). Socioecological models suggest that nature-based adventure can promote healthy behavioural changes and eco-centric perspectives (Pryor, Carpenter, and Townsend 2012). Studies by Sibthrop and colleagues (e.g. Ramsing and Sibthorp 2008; Sibthorp and Arthur-Banning 2004) highlight the importance of autonomy and personal relevance in fostering positive outcomes. These findings challenge traditional risk-focused theories and suggest that natural settings and underlying psychological processes play an important role in promoting well-being through ANS.

Physical activity in nature

The additive effects of combining physical activity with natural settings may be an important mechanism through which ANS promote positive outcomes. Studies show the benefits of vigorous activity, particularly in outdoor contexts, for psychological function and well-being (e.g. Coon et al. 2011; Frumkin et al. 2017; Kamijo, Takeda, and Hillman 2011; Maller et al. 2002). For example, Herzog et al. (1997) found that an outdoor trip lasting only a few days decreased irritability, accidents, and mental fatigue, and improved problem-solving ability and concentration. Studies of 'green exercise' have suggested there are additive benefits of physical activity in outdoor settings over and above those accrued by physical activity alone (e.g. Pretty et al. 2007). Pretty et al. reported that even viewing pleasant natural settings during physical activity had superior physical and psychological benefits compared to viewing other settings (e.g. pleasant urban). In an experimental design across indoor, urban, and natural settings, Ryan et al. (2010) found increases in subjective vitality associated with natural settings despite equivalent levels of physical activity in each setting. Nevertheless, the majority of experimental studies have focused on one-off nature experiences in terms of immediate restorative benefits, rather than investigating relationships between repeated experiences and diverse well-being outcomes (Hartig et al. 2014). In recognition of this knowledge gap, recent reviews have called for further evidence evaluating (a) the diverse processes through which nature may promote health (Frumkin et al. 2017) and (b) the therapeutic effects of nature-based health interventions (Buckley and Brough 2017).

Fulfilling psychological needs

Another line of emerging research has focused on better understanding how ANS may actively support hedonic and eudaimonic well-being through the mechanism of basic psychological need fulfilment. ANS activities provide unique physical and psychological challenges resulting from the person-environment relationship, rather than other people or sporting situations that are 'contrived'. Successfully creating and mastering these challenges can stimulate feelings of competence and positive affect, increase self-efficacy, and facilitate 'optimal experiences' (e.g. Brymer and Oades 2009; Csikszentmihalyi and Csikszentmihalyi 1990; Delle Fave, Bassi, and Massimini 2003). In positive psychology models, these outcomes are recognized as essential components of well-being. The related concept of resilience, generally defined as a range of capacities that mitigate factors which threaten an individual's health (e.g. Kaplan 1999), has received increasing attention in positive psychology research. Adventure experiences in particular have been shown to foster resilience, which buffers the impact of stressful life events (e.g. D'Amato and Krasny 2011; Ewert and Yoshino 2011; Neill and Dias 2001).

In addition to building resilience and fulfilling the psychological need for competence, ANS provide opportunities to satisfy needs for autonomy and relatedness (as outlined in self-determination theory; e.g. Ryan and Deci 2011). There is evidence that adventure promotes autonomy, competence and relatedness both in the adventure context and in everyday life (Griffin, Meaney, and Podlog 2015; MacGregor, Woodman, and Hardy 2014; Sibthorp et al. 2008; Wurdinger and Paxton 2003). ANS participants arguably have greater opportunities for volitional choice about potential courses of action than they would in traditional sporting activities with more formalized 'rules'. These opportunities may support eudaimonic well-being by potentially increasing the salience of autonomous decision-making processes and personal meaning.

As ANS generally involve small groups working cooperatively in natural environments, it is also likely to support the need for relatedness in various ways. Nature itself has been shown to promote social connections (e.g. Maas et al. 2009), and ANS participants often work with others to reach common goals without the need to compete against others as traditional sports often require. For example, in a form of cooperative participation that Meier (1976) called the 'the kinship of the rope', rock climbers and mountaineers work together and trust climbing partners with their lives to complete difficult routes. Situations that necessitate cooperation are a common feature across ANS. Both the natural environment and the ANS activity pose unique challenges, ranging from physical discomfort or serious injury to psychological distress that participants must overcome together. Participants may also have prolonged contact with others in ANS contexts, as is common on multiday river, trekking, or mountaineering trips. Thus, adventurous nature sports have a number of characteristics conducive to forging strong, intimate connections to others that may not be as readily available in everyday social interactions. As meaningful connections to others has emerged as a fundamental dimension of health and well-being (Frumkin et al. 2017; Kawachi, Subramanian, and Kim 2008), and one of the most important predictors of successful aging (e.g. Waldinger and Schulz 2016), this aspect of ANS should be included in emerging frameworks and further investigated in relation to participant well-being.

Connections to the natural world

Although the need for relatedness is generally discussed and studied in terms of relationships with other people, this need may be met in other ways. Enhanced connections to nature, in addition to other human beings, may be another way that ANS fosters eudaimonic well-being. Even in the riskiest ANS activities, such as BASE jumping, participants report strong eudaimonic motivations to connect deeply with nature (Brymer and Gray 2010; Kerr and Houge Mackenzie in press). Albrecht (2012, 243) refers to this intimate connection as eutierria, 'a secular, positive feeling of oneness with the earth and its life forces where the boundaries between self and the rest of nature are obliterated and a deep sense of connectedness pervades consciousness.' Place attachment theorists maintain that these forms of intense emotional experiences and repeated visitation can facilitate strong bonds with the place(s) an activity occurs in, which in turn supports an individual's sense of purpose and well-being (Morgan, 2010). ANS are likely to promote place attachment and place identity, a related construct, as the distinct settings upon which these activities depend provide participants unique opportunities to validate their identity and values (Twigger-Ross and Uzzell 1996). Adventure participants report experiencing intense emotions during their activities and may repeatedly visit the same place to participate (e.g. Houge Mackenzie, Hodge, and Boyes 2011, 2013). These repeated experiences may facilitate identity formation and encourage connections to place and nature more generally. Put another way, positive hedonic experiences (e.g. positive emotions) can in turn foster positive eudaimonic experiences (e.g. place attachment, identity, eutierria) over time.

Studies of well-being and nature support these propositions and suggest that the outdoor context provides important affective, cognitive and experiential benefits (e.g.

Zelenski and Nisbet 2014). Relationships with nature have been linked to life satisfaction, high self-esteem, and subjective experiences of psychological well-being (Cervinka, Röderer, and Hefler 2012; Zhang, Howell, and Iyer 2014). Cleary et al. (2017) demonstrated how connecting with nature supports intrinsic value orientations (i.e. pursing goals congruent with personal growth, intimacy and community), which are essential to well-being. Feeling connected to nature has been shown to significantly correlate with lower levels of anxiety and higher levels of well-being (Martyn and Brymer 2016). Martyn and Brymer found that individuals who regularly engaged in outdoor physical activity had lower levels of somatic anxiety in comparison to participants engaged in indoor physical activity. Autonomy, a pillar of positive psychology research, significantly influenced this relationship. Thus, feeling connected to nature appears to support psychological well-being across multiple domains.

In summary, a growing number of studies show that ANS promote diverse hedonic and eudaimonic aspects of well-being. ANS appear to: (a) facilitate feelings of connection to nature; (b) foster physical and mental benefits associated with physical activity, (c) provide opportunities to overcome challenges and have optimal experiences; (d) increase positive psychological outcomes such as positive affect, self-efficacy, and resilience; (e) restore cognitive resources; (f) provide opportunities to experience self-determination (e.g. via psychological need fulfilment and intrinsic value orientations); and (g) promote social connectedness. This body of research suggests that positive psychology approaches can be applied to conceptualize ANS as activities that facilitate positive person-environment relationships and well-being.

Conclusion

Traditional risk-focused models have treated ANS as niche activities involving a small population of participants with specific personality characteristics. Contemporary research suggests that risk-focused approaches are narrow and do not account for the full range of motivations and outcomes associated with adventurous nature sports. In light of these findings, the current analysis suggested how positive psychology can be applied to conceptualize ANS as health and well-being activities. Specifically, we examined how ANS can support both hedonic and eudaimonic dimensions of well-being. This conceptual shift has a number of important implications, including ANS activities being considered in terms of their public health benefits and potentially used to foster mental and physical well-being across a broad population base. This shift also suggests that, given the unique characteristics and benefits of ANS discussed herein, further evaluation of their potential to foster short and long-term well-being relative to traditional sports is merited. Adopting the proposed health and well-being perspective would also mean expanding ANS frameworks to encompass and explain: (a) under-researched eudaimonic outcomes; (b) relationships between hedonic and eudaimonic motivations; and (c) more heterogeneous participants with diverse motivations and experiences.

Reframing our understanding of ANS has important implications for how these activities are viewed and facilitated by educators, schools, youth development workers, health promotion agencies, urban planners, and the general public. Researchers and policy makers may be better served by considering ANS as part of a broad well-being framework that promotes immediate hedonic benefits as well as long-term flourishing. From a practical perspective, ANS could be considered in preventative health approaches as vehicles for wellness promotion (Clough et al. 2016). This approach aligns with the movement toward 'green prescriptions' for health and may facilitate targeted well-being interventions for diverse populations (e.g. Buckley and Brough 2017; Buckley, Westaway, and Brough 2016). Better understanding the relationship between ANS and well-being can also inform the development of green environments and infrastructure in urban and rural areas. From a theoretical perspective, this shift is important in order to link nature sport research with existing bodies of work on motivation, well-being, health, and quality of life.

Given the wide range of ANS benefits identified in emerging literature, expanding our perspectives on these activities may have important implications for individual and social well-being. Although the current analysis focused on how positive psychology can be applied to conceptualize ANS from a health and well-being perspective, this represents one of many ways that ANS can be reconceptualised to better reflect participant experiences. For instance, a broader, more progressive framework of ANS might influence complementary avenues of theoretical development, such as skill development, leadership, and education perspectives. Future researchers should continue to critically examine traditional models of ANS and identify perspectives that can extend and strengthen these frameworks.

Acknowledgements

We wish to thank the two anonymous reviewers for their constructive feedback that helped to improve this manuscript.

Disclosure statement

No potential conflict of interest was reported by the authors.

ORCID

Susan Houge Mackenzie http://orcid.org/0000-0001-5660-6325
Eric Brymer http://orcid.org/0000-0003-0274-1016

References

Albrecht, G. A. 2012. "Psychoterratic Conditions in a Scientific and Technological World." In *Ecopsychology: Science, Totems, and the Technological Species*, edited by P. Kahn, and P. Hasbach, 241–264. Cambridge, MA: MIT Press.

Baretta, D., A. Greco, and P. Steca. 2017. "Understanding Performance in Risky Sport: The Role of Self-Efficacy Beliefs and Sensation Seeking in Competitive Freediving." *Personality and Individual Differences* 117: 161–165.

Barlow, M., T. Woodman, and L. Hardy. 2013. "Great Expectations: Different High-Risk Activities Satisfy Different Motives." *Journal of Personality and Social Psychology* 105 (3): 458–475.

Berman, M. G., J. Jonides, and S. Kaplan. 2008. "The Cognitive Benefits of Interacting with Nature." *Psychological Science* 19 (12): 1207–1212.

Bowen, D. J., J. T. Neill, and S. J. Crisp. 2016. "Wilderness Adventure Therapy Effects on the Mental Health of Youth Participants." *Evaluation and Program Planning* 58: 49–59.

Brookes, A. 2003. "A Critique of Neo-Hahnian Outdoor Education Theory. Part Two: 'The Fundamental Attribution Error' in Contemporary Outdoor Education Discourse." *Journal of Adventure Education and Outdoor Learning* 3: 119–132.

Brown, M. 2009. "Reconceptualising Outdoor Adventure Education: Activity in Search of an Appropriate Theory." *Australian Journal of Outdoor Education* 13 (2): 3–13.

Brown, M. 2010. "Transfer: Outdoor Adventure Education's Achilles Heel? Changing Participation as a Viable Option." *Australian Journal of Outdoor Education* 14 (1): 13–22.

Brymer, E., G. Downey, and T. Gray. 2009. "Extreme Sports as a Precursor to Environmental Sustainability." *Journal of Sport & Tourism* 14 (2–3): 193–204.

Brymer, E., and T. Gray. 2010. "Developing an Intimate 'Relationship' with Nature Through Extreme Sports Participation." *Leisure/Loisir* 34 (4): 361–374.

Brymer, E., and L. Oades. 2009. "Extreme Sports: A Positive Transformation in Courage and Humility." *Journal of Humanistic Psychology* 49 (1): 114–126.

Brymer, E., and R. Schweitzer. 2013. "Extreme Sports are Good for Your Health: A Phenomenological Understanding of Fear and Anxiety in Extreme Sport." *Journal of Health Psychology* 18 (4): 477–487. doi:10.1177/1359105312446770.

Brymer, E., and R. D. Schweitzer. 2017. "Evoking the Ineffable: The Phenomenology of Extreme Sports." *Psychology of Consciousness: Theory, Research, and Practice* 4 (1): 63–74. doi:10.1037/cns0000111.

Buckley, R. C., and P. Brough. 2017. "Nature, Eco, and Adventure Therapies for Mental Health and Chronic Disease." *Frontiers in Public Health* 5: 220.

Buckley, R. C., D. Westaway, and P. Brough. 2016. "Social Mechanisms to get People Outdoors: Bimodal Distribution of Interest in Nature?" *Frontiers in Public Health* 4: 257.

Castanier, C., C. Le Scanff, and T. Woodman. 2011. "Mountaineering as Affect Regulation: The Moderating Role of Self-Regulation Strategies." *Anxiety, Stress, & Coping* 24 (1): 75–89.

Cervinka, R., K. Röderer, and E. Hefler. 2012. "Are Nature Lovers Happy? On Various Indicators of Well-Being and Connectedness with Nature." *Journal of Health Psychology* 17 (3): 379–388.

Clark, M. 1986. "The Cultural Patterning of Risk-Seeking Behaviour: Implications for Armed Conflict." In *Peace and War: Cross-Cultural Perspectives*, edited by M. L. Foster, and R. A. Rubinstein, 79–90. New Brunswick, NJ: Transaction Books.

Cleary, A., K. S. Fielding, S. L. Bell, Z. Murray, and A. Roiko. 2017. "Exploring Potential Mechanisms Involved in the Relationship Between Eudaimonic Wellbeing and Nature Connection." *Landscape and Urban Planning* 158: 119–128.

Clough, P., S. Houge Mackenzie, L. Mallabon, and E. Brymer. 2016. "Adventurous Physical Activity Environments: A Mainstream Intervention for Mental Health." *Sports Medicine* 46 (7): 963–968. http://www.ncbi.nlm.nih.gov/pubmed/26895993.

Coon, J. T., K. Boddy, K. Stein, R. Whear, J. Barton, and M. H. Depledge. 2011. "Does Participating in Physical Activity in Outdoor Natural Environments Have a Greater Effect on Physical and Mental Well-Being than Physical Activity Indoors? A Systematic Review." *Environmental Science and Technology* 45 (5): 1761–1772.

Csikszentmihalyi, M., and I. S. Csikszentmihalyi. 1990. "Adventure and the Flow Experience." In *Adventure Education*, edited by J. C. Miles, and S. Priest, 149–155. State College, PA: Venture Publishing.

D'Amato, L. G., and M. E. Krasny. 2011. "Outdoor Adventure Education: Applying Transformative Learning Theory to Understanding Instrumental Learning and Personal Growth in Environmental Education." *The Journal of Environmental Education* 42 (4): 237–254.

Davis-Berman, J., and D. Berman. 2002. "Risk and Anxiety in Adventure Programming." *Journal of Experiential Education* 25 (2): 305–310.

Delle Fave, A., M. Bassi, and F. Massimini. 2003. "Quality of Experience and Risk Perception in High-Altitude Rock Climbing." *Journal of Applied Sport Psychology* 15: 82–98.

Ewert, A., and D. Garvey. 2007. "Philosophy and Theory of Adventure Education." In *Adventure Education: Theory and Applications*, edited by D. Prouty, J. Panicucci, and R. Collinson, 19–32. Leeds, UK: Human Kinetics.

Ewert, A., and S. Hollenhorst. 1989. "Testing the Adventure Model: Empirical Support for a Model of Risk Recreation Participation." *Journal of Leisure Research* 21 (2): 124–139.

Ewert, A., and J. Sibthorp. 2009. "Creating Outcomes Through Experiential Education: The Challenge of Confounding Variables." *Journal of Experiential Education* 31 (3): 376–389.

Ewert, A., and A. Yoshino. 2011. "The Influence of Short-Term Adventure-Based Experiences on Levels of Resilience." *Journal of Adventure Education and Outdoor Learning* 11 (1): 35–50.

Fischer, S., and G. T. Smith. 2004. "Deliberation Affects Risk Taking Beyond Sensation Seeking." *Personality and Individual Differences* 36: 527–537.

Foster, M. L. 1993. "Reversal Theory and the Institutionalization of war." In *Advances in Reversal Theory*, edited by J. H. Kerr, S. J. Murgatroyd, and M. J. Apter, 67–74. Amsterdam: Swets & Zeitlinger.

Frumkin, H., G. N. Bratman, S. J. Breslow, B. Cochran, P. H. Kahn Jr, J. J. Lawler, and S. A. Wood. 2017. "Nature Contact and Human Health: A Research Agenda." *Environmental Health Perspectives* 125 (7): 075001. doi:10.1289/EHP1663.

Gass, M. A., H. L. Gillis, and K. C. Russell. 2012. *Adventure Therapy: Theory, Research, and Practice.* New York: Routledge.

Griffin, K. L., K. S. Meaney, and L. Podlog. 2015. "Climb to Freedom: Autonomy, Competence and Relatedness in Rock Climbing." *SHAPE America National Convention and Exposition.* Seattle, WA, March 19, 2015. Reston, VA: SHAPE America.

Hartig, T., R. Mitchell, S. De Vries, and H. Frumkin. 2014. "Nature and Health." *Annual Review of Public Health* 35: 207–228.

Hattie, J., H. W. Marsh, J. T. Neill, and G. E. Richards. 1997. "Adventure Education and Outward Bound: Out-of-Class Experiences that Make a Lasting Difference." *Review of Educational Research* 67 (1): 43–87.

Hendeson, L. W., and T. Knight. 2012. "Integrating the Hedonic and Eudaimonic Perspectives to More Comprehensively Understand Wellbeing and Pathways to Wellbeing." *International Journal of Wellbeing* 2 (3): 196–221. doi:10.5502/ijw.v2i3.3.

Herzog, T. R., A. M. Black, K. A. Fountaine, and D. J. Knotts. 1997. "Reflection and Attentional Recovery as Distinctive Benefits of Restorative Environments." *Journal of Environmental Psychology* 17: 165–170.

Houge Mackenzie, S., K. Hodge, and M. Boyes. 2011. "Expanding the Flow Model in Adventure Activities: A Reversal Theory Perspective." *Journal of Leisure Research* 43: 519–544.

Houge Mackenzie, S., K. Hodge, and M. Boyes. 2013. "The Multiphasic and Dynamic Nature of Flow in Adventure Experiences." *Journal of Leisure Research* 45 (2): 214–232.

Huppert, F. A., and T. T. So. 2013. "Flourishing Across Europe: Application of a new Conceptual Framework for Defining Well-Being." *Social Indicators Research* 110 (3): 837–861.

Huta, V., and R. M. Ryan. 2010. "Pursuing Pleasure or Virtue: The Differential and Overlapping Well-Being Benefits of Hedonic and Eudaimonic Motives." *Journal of Happiness Studies* 11 (6): 735–762.

Kamijo, K., Y. Takeda, and C. H. Hillman. 2011. "The Relation of Physical Activity to Functional Connectivity Between Brain Regions." *Clinical Neurophysiology* 122: 81–89.

Kaplan, H. B. 1999. "Toward an Understanding of Resilience: A Critical Review of Definitions and Models." In *Resilience and Development*, edited by M. D. Glantz, and J. L. Johnson, 17–83. New York: Kluwer Academic.

Kawachi, I., S. V. Subramanian, and D. Kim, eds. 2008. *Social Capital and Health*. New York: Springer.

Kerr, J. H., and S. Houge Mackenzie. 2012. "Multiple Motives for Participating in Adventure Sports." *Psychology of Sport and Exercise* 13: 649–657.

Kerr, J. H., and S. Houge Mackenzie. in press. "I Don't Want to Die. That's Not Why I do it at All": Multifaceted Motivation, Psychological Health, and Personal Development in BASE Jumping." *Annals of Leisure Research*.

Kopp, M., M. Wolf, G. Ruedl, and M. Burtscher. 2016. "Differences in Sensation Seeking Between Alpine Skiers, Snowboarders and Ski Tourers." *Journal of Sports Science & Medicine* 15 (1): 11–16.

Krein, K. J. 2014. "Nature Sports." *Journal of the Philosophy of Sport* 41 (2): 193–208.

Lomas, T., and I. Ivtzan. 2016. "Second Wave Positive Psychology: Exploring the Positive Negative Dialectics of Wellbeing." *Journal of Happiness Studies* 17 (4): 1753–1768.

Lupton, D., and J. Tulloch. 2002. "Life Would be Pretty Dull Without Risk': Voluntary Risk-Taking and its Pleasures." *Health, Risk & Society* 4 (2): 113–124.

Lyng, S. 2005. "Sociology at the Edge: Social Theory and Voluntary Risk Taking." In *Edgework: The Sociology of Risk-Taking*, edited by S. Lyng, 17–50. New York: Routledge.

Maas, J., S. M. E. van Dillen, R. A. Verheij, and P. P. Groenewegen. 2009. "Social Contacts as a Possible Mechanism Behind the Relation Between Green Space and Health." *Health & Place* 15 (2): 586–595.

MacGregor, A., T. Woodman, and L. Hardy. 2014. "Risk is Good for you: An Investigation of the Processes and Outcomes Associated with High-Risk Sport." *Journal of Exercise, Movement, and Sport* 46 (1): 175.

Maller, C., Townsend, M., Brown, P., & St. Leger, L. (2002). "Healthy Parks, Healthy People: The Health Benefits of Contact with Nature in a Park Context." Report to Parks Victoria and the International Park Strategic Partners Group. Melbourne: Deakin University.

Martyn, P., and E. Brymer. 2016. "The Relationship Between Nature Relatedness and Anxiety." *Journal of Health Psychology* 21 (7): 1436–1445.

McKenzie, M. D. 2000. "How are Adventure Education Program Outcomes Achieved? A Review of the Literature." *Australian Journal of Outdoor Education* 5 (1): 19–28.

Meier, K. V. 1976. "The Kinship of the Rope and the Loving Struggle: A Philosophic Analysis of Communication in Mountain Climbing." *Journal of the Philosophy of Sport* 3 (1): 52–64.

Melo, R., and R. Gomes. 2017. "Nature Sports Participation: Understanding Demand, Practice Profile, Motivations and Constraints." *European Journal of Tourism Research* 16: 108–135.

Mental Health Commission of NSW. 2017. *Wellbeing language and definitions guide*. https://wbcnsw.files.wordpress.com/2017/09/language-and-definitions-guide-web.pdf.

Morgan, P. 2010. "Towards a Developmental Theory of Place Attachment." *Journal of Environmental Psychology* 30 (1): 11–22.

Neill, J. T., and K. L. Dias. 2001. "Adventure Education and Resilience: The Double-Edged Sword." *Journal of Adventure Education & Outdoor Learning* 1 (2): 35–42.

Nietzsche, F. 1974. *The Gay Science*. Translated by W. Kaufmann. New York, NY: Vintage.

Outdoor Foundation. 2017. *Outdoor recreation participation topline report*. https://outdoorindustry.org/wp-content/uploads/2017/04/2017-Topline-Report_FINAL.pdf.

Pain, M. T., and M. A. Pain. 2005. "Risk Taking in Sport." *The Lancet: Medicine and Sport* 366 (1): S33–S34.

Pearson, D. G., and T. Craig. 2014. "The Great Outdoors? Exploring the Mental Health Benefits of Natural Environments." *Frontiers in Psychology* 5: 1178. doi:10.3389/fpsyg.2014.01178.

Pretty, J., J. Peacock, R. Hine, M. Sellens, N. South, and M. Griffin. 2007. "Green Exercise in the UK Countryside: Effects on Health and Psychological Well-Being, and Implications for Policy." *Journal of Environmental Planning and Management* 50 (2): 211–231.

Priest, S., and C. Bunting. 1993. "Changes in Perceived Risk and Competence During Whitewater Canoeing." *Journal of Applied Recreation Research* 18 (4): 265–280.

Priest, S., and M. A. Gass. 2018. *Effective Leadership in Adventure Programming*. 3rd ed. Champaign, IL: Human Kinetics.

Pryor, A., C. Carpenter, and M. Townsend. 2012. "Outdoor Education and Bush Adventure Therapy: A Social-Ecological Approach to Health and Wellbeing." *Australian Journal of Outdoor Education* 9 (1): 3–13.

Puchan, H. 2004. "Living 'Extreme': Adventure Sports, Media and Commercialisation." *Journal of Communication Management* 9 (2): 171–178.

Ramsing, R., and J. Sibthorp. 2008. "The Role of Autonomy Support in Summer Camp Programs: Preparing Youth for Productive Behaviors." *Journal of Park and Recreation Administration* 26 (2): 61–77.

Ryan, R. M., and E. L. Deci. 2011. "A Self-Determination Theory Perspective on Social, Institutional, Cultural, and Economic Supports for Autonomy and Their Importance for Well-Being." In *Human Autonomy in Cross-Cultural Context: Perspectives on the Psychology of Agency, Freedom, and Well-Being*, edited by V. I. Chirkov, R. M. Ryan, and K. M. Sheldon, 45–64. Dordrecht, Netherlands: Springer.

Ryan, R. M., V. Huta, and E. L. Deci. 2013. "Living Well: A Self-Determination Theory Perspective on Eudaimonia." In *The Exploration of Happiness*, edited by A. Delle Fave, 117–139. Dordrech: Springer.

Ryan, R. M., N. Weinstein, J. Bernstein, K. W. Brown, L. Mastella, and M. Gagne. 2010. "Vitalizing Effects of Being Outdoors and in Nature." *Journal of Environmental Psychology* 30: 159–168.

Ryff, C. D. 1989. "Happiness is Everything, or is it? Explorations on the Meaning of Psychological Well-Being." *Journal of Personality and Social Psychology* 57: 1069–1081.

Seligman, M. E., and M. Csikszentmihalyi. 2014. "Positive Psychology: An Introduction." In *Flow and the Foundations of Positive Psychology*, 279–298. Dordrecht: Springer.

Sibthorp, J., and S. Arthur-Banning. 2004. "Developing Life Effectiveness Through Adventure Education: The Roles of Participant Expectations, Perceptions of Empowerment, and Learning Relevance." *Journal of Experiential Education* 27 (1): 32–50.

Sibthorp, J., K. Paisley, J. Gookin, and N. Furman. 2008. "The Pedagogic Value of Student Autonomy in Adventure Education." *Journal of Experiential Education* 31 (2): 136–151. doi:10.5193/JEE.31.2.136.

Twigger-Ross, C. L., and D. L. Uzzell. 1996. "Place and Identity Processes." *Journal of Environmental Psychology* 16 (3): 205–220.

Varley, P., and T. Semple. 2015. "Nordic Slow Adventure: Explorations in Time and Nature." *Scandinavian Journal of Hospitality and Tourism* 15 (1–2): 73–90.

Waldinger, R. J., and M. S. Schulz. 2016. "The Long Reach of Nurturing Family Environments: Links with Midlife Emotion-Regulatory Styles and Late-Life Security in Intimate Relationships." *Psychological Science* 27 (11): 1443–1450.

Waterman, A. S., S. J. Schwartz, and R. Conti. 2008. "The Implications of two Conceptions of Happiness (Hedonic Enjoyment and Eudaimonia) for the Understanding of Intrinsic Motivation." *Journal of Happiness Studies* 9 (1): 41–79.

Willig, C. 2008. "A Phenomenological Investigation of the Experience of Taking Part in Extreme Sport." *Journal of Health Psychology* 13: 690–702.

Woodman, T., N. Cazenave, and C. Le Scanff. 2008. "Skydiving as Emotion Regulation: The Rise and Fall of Anxiety is Moderated by Alexithymia." *Journal of Sport & Exercise Psychology* 30: 424–433.

Woodman, T., L. Hardy, M. Barlow, and C. Le Scanff. 2010. "Motives for Prolonged Engagement High-Risk Sports: An Agentic Emotion Regulation Perspective." *Psychology of Sport and Exercise* 11: 345–352.

Wurdinger, S., and T. Paxton. 2003. "Using Multiple Levels of Experience to Promote Autonomy in Adventure Education Students." *Journal of Adventure Education & Outdoor Learning* 3 (1): 41–48.

Zelenski, J. M., and E. K. Nisbet. 2014. "Happiness and Feeling Connected: The Distinct Role of Nature Relatedness." *Environment and Behavior* 46 (1): 3–23.

Zhang, J. W., R. T. Howell, and R. Iyer. 2014. "Engagement with Natural Beauty Moderates the Positive Relation Between Connectedness with Nature and Psychological Well-Being." *Journal of Environmental Psychology* 38: 55–63.

Zuckerman, M., ed. 2007. *Sensation Seeking and Risky Behavior*. Washington: American Psychological Association.

Nature sports, health and ageing: the value of euphoria

Ralf Buckley 🆔

ABSTRACT
Using autoethnographic approaches, I analyse ageing trajectories in 10 adventurous outdoor nature sports using boards, paddles, sails and wings in water, snow and air. Skill and risk are intermediate. Training, experience, and safety precautions are required, but risk of death is low. Chronic pain levels increase with age, and capabilities and challenges faced decline. These are offset, however, by greater attention and appreciation of natural surroundings. Of particular significance, enjoyment and opportunities for euphoria persist despite ageing, and euphoria can temporarily override chronic pain, stress and fatigue. In wealthy urbanised nations, chronic pain, and poor mental and emotional health, impose increasing social and economic costs as lifespans increase. By providing opportunities for euphoria as well as exercise, adventurous outdoor nature sports can make substantial contributions to the physical, mental and social health of older individuals, reducing the costs of aged care. Therefore, health policies should encourage lifelong nature sports.

Introduction

Social attitudes to adventurous outdoor nature sports, in wealthy urbanised nations, are divided and paradoxical. Research in this field is reviewed in the next section. In summary: for schoolchildren, and juveniles engaged in antisocial behaviours, these activities are considered beneficial, character building, and therapeutic. Adults who engage in formal competitive outdoor sports are also widely applauded. Adults who engage in non-competitive adventurous outdoor nature sports, however, are often criticised.

I argue here that participation in adventurous outdoor nature sports is at least as beneficial for adults as it is for children. These activities require high skill, extensive experience, and careful planning and safety precautions. Participants become physically, mentally and socially healthy and resilient; lead productive working lives; and contribute to their communities. These benefits extend to older individuals whose capabilities have decreased, but who can nonetheless continue to gain the same benefits, with adjustment of expectations. I argue that the key benefit of adventurous outdoor nature sports, not provided either by non-adventurous exercise or nature exposure, is that it can create euphoria, which can temporarily override chronic pain and psychological stress associated with other aspects of ageing.

In wealthy urbanised nations, average lifespan has increased substantially, but for many individuals the final years or decades are lived in poor health, and the costs of aged care and health care now represent a very substantial drain on national economies. I argue that by keeping older people healthy and happy, adventurous outdoor nature sports thus make large contributions to national economies, exceeding even their economic contributions through direct expenditure on equipment, travel and services.

Theoretical context

Social perceptions of participants in adventurous outdoor nature sports

Outdoor education, outdoor recreation, park visitation, nature tourism, ecotourism, adventure tourism, adventure recreation, adventure sports, extreme sports: each has slightly different connotations, but they all overlap. The choice of words depends on each author's background, the publication outlet, and the intended audience. Those same factors influence what previous literature any author is aware of, what professional experience they may have, and how they perceive the participants in any of these outdoor activities. In particular, these differences between authors, academic disciplines, and terminology adopted, influence how they think different individuals are motivated to take part in adventure activities, and whether they see those individuals as socially responsible or socially irresponsible.

Outdoor education, for example, has a very long practical history of school sports and camps, and adventure playgrounds and programmes. All of these approaches are seen both by teachers and parents as being good for the participants (i.e. the school children). They are seen as building self-esteem and self-reliance, physical and mental capability, and teamwork skills (Berman and Davis-Berman 2013; Bowen, Neill, and Crisp 2016; Epstein 2004; Ewert and Yoshino 2011; Hattie et al. 1997; Pryor, Carpenter, and Townsend 2012; Russell 2003; Sandseter and Kennair 2011; Scrutton and Beames 2015; Sibthorp et al. 2008; Sibthorp and Arthur-Banning 2004). Similarly, remedial outdoor programmes, for sub-adult individuals seen as socially delinquent, are treated as a positive influence (Gass, Gillis, and Russell 2012).

At the other end of the scale, however, many psychologists have written about adult adventure recreation and extreme sports as indicative of personality disorders. Why? Some of the terms used, such as sensation seeking personalities, are largely innocuous. Others, such as death wish, narcissism and regression (Elmes and Barry 1999), or egotism and recrimination, are less favourable (Puchan 2004). The actual activities, and the psychological experiences of the individuals taking part, are quite similar to those used for outdoor education, but the ways in which they are perceived and written about are very different.

In addition, both public and academic attitudes to adventure athletes depend on circumstances. Competitors in many Olympic and other international sports, for example, are praised, adored, and lionised, even though they face major risks, and many are injured severely and repeatedly during training and competition. Ski jumping and bobsled racing provide examples. The same applies for many highly physical competitive team sports, and for the various forms of organised competitive pugilism and other martial arts. As reviewed in the preceding paragraphs, however, individuals who measure their skills against the outdoors are admired by some, but criticised by others.

Attitudes and public perceptions can change, and I suggest that this is indeed happening at the moment, in regard to public perceptions of outdoor adventure. I suggest that there are three main reasons for this. The first reason is that participants have changed how they present themselves. Public perceptions of surfers and snowboarders, for example, have shifted over the past three to five decades, from social misfits to paid professional athletes. The second reason is that large and profitable industries have arisen to provide outdoor adventure opportunities, and these industries market their sponsored athletes and participants as people to be emulated. The commercial outdoor tourism industry has gradually taken over from individual outdoor recreation, to the point where it is now a trillion-dollar global sector (Buckley 2009), prepared to play a powerful role in major political controversies. This transition, from private nature and adventure recreation, to commercial nature and adventure sports and tourism, has been studied extensively elsewhere (Buckley et al. 2015) and is not my focus here.

The third reason for changing public attitudes and perceptions of outdoor nature and adventure sports and activities, relates to mental health. Research in mental health, and its relations with physical and social health and quality of life, has recently begun to credit outdoor activities, including associated emotional components, for their contributions to human health and well-being. As reviewed below, this applies particularly to office-bound urban individuals in the more wealthy and urbanised nations. This is my focus here: the importance of adventurous nature sports as outdoor therapies for mental health, and the economic value of the mental health outcomes achieved.

Motivations and experiences in adventure activities and nature sports

Many different motivations have been proposed and demonstrated for people to take part in adventurous outdoor nature sports: either individually; as members of recreational associations; or as clients of adventure tour operators. These motivations fall into two broad categories: external motivations associated with peer esteem and social capital, and internal motivations associated with self-esteem and emotional reward (Buckley 2012; Holm et al. 2017; Immonen et al. 2017; Melo and Gomes 2017; Pomfret and Bramwell 2016; Portugal et al. 2017). Skill and risk are important components of this mix, but by no means essential or even dominant.

Participant perceptions and emotions have now been analysed for a number of high-skill, high-risk adventure activities (Arijs et al. 2017; Baretta, Greco, and Steca 2017; Brannigan and McDougall 1983; Brymer 2013; Brymer and Mackenzie 2017; Brymer and Oades 2009; Brymer and Schweitzer 2013a, 2013b, 2017a, 2017b; Buckley 2012, 2015b, 2016a, 2016b; Holm et al. 2017; Holmbom, Brymer, and Schweitzer 2017; Immonen et al. 2017; Monasterio et al. 2016; Niedermeier et al. 2017; Niedermeier, Hartl, and Kopp 2017; Portugal et al. 2017; Seifert et al. 2017; Willig 2008). Overcoming fear is an important component (Buckley 2016a; Miesel and Potgieter 2003), but risk is generally seen as something to be minimised and managed, not as a motivation in itself. Parallel research in natural and other settings has also examined phenomena such as self-perceived near-death experiences (Moore and Greyson 2017; Thonnard et al. 2013); the functions of consciousness (Earl 2014); and the individual perception of slowed time when at high risk of immediate death (Arstila 2012; Buckley 2014; Stetson, Fiesta, and Eagleman 2007; Wittmann 2011).

The phenomenological concept of ineffability, experiences that are indescribable, has been examined extensively in the context of extreme sports (Brymer and Mackenzie 2017; Brymer and Oades 2009; Brymer and Schweitzer 2017a, 2017b; Holmbom, Brymer, and Schweitzer 2017). Buckley (2012) argued that at least some apparently ineffable adventure experiences could in fact be described, using the concept of rush, as a combination of thrill and flow. As an alternative to ineffability, emotions that are undescribable, Woodman et al. (2010) argued that individuals who take part in adventure activities suffer differentially from alexithymia, difficulty in describing one's emotions. Authors such as Hickman et al. (2016, 2017), Holmbom, Brymer, and Schweitzer (2017), and Wheaton (2017), however, report interviews with expert adventure practitioners who do indeed describe their emotions, albeit not in the terminology adopted in psychological research.

Effects of ageing on adventure participation and experiences

Ageing affects many human characteristics relevant to adventure activities, and it may also affect individuals' abilities to recall those activities. For most people, memory declines with age, though some individuals, known as super-agers, maintain the recall abilities of those 20–30 years younger (Sun et al. 2016). Cognitive abilities generally do not decline with age for those still in the workforce (Brough et al. 2011). They do, however, decline at later ages.

Laslett (1991) proposed four ageing stages in the human lifecycle: child, adult, third age, and fourth age. The third age is the age of 'bucket lists': individuals who have retired from full-time work, and have the means, time, and capabilities to pursue leisure goals. The fourth age begins when capabilities decrease so far that goals are no longer reachable, and individuals become 'dependent and decrepit' (Laslett 1991). This distinction led to the concept of 'successful ageing' (Boyes 2013), where individuals retain sufficient physical and psychological resilience to prolong their 'third age' as far as possible.

Extensive recent research has shown that continuing physical exercise is good for human health, even at advanced ages (DiPietro et al. 2017). Physical fitness also helps to maintain brain function in older individuals, as measured by gray matter volume (Erickson, Leckie, and Weinstein 2014). Older people take fewer risks (Boyes 2013) and this is associated with neuroanatomical changes (Grubb et al. 2016). Steptoe, Deaton, and Stone (2015) found that subjective self-assessed wellbeing, for individuals in wealthy Anglophone nations, is lowest at age 50, but highest at age 70. Their study did not survey respondents aged above 75. Individuals at age 70 reported more pain, but less worry or stress. Orth, Maes, and Schmitt (2015) found that self-esteem is highest at age 60, and begins to decline at greater ages. This applies irrespective of other demographic factors. Wooden and Li (2016) reported that life satisfaction in Australia remains approximately constant from age 25–65, but then falls abruptly.

There seem to be few recent qualitative studies that focus specifically on individual adventure athletes' perceptions of ageing. During the past 6 years, there have been interview-based studies of: 7 New Zealand hikers and bikers aged 63–80 (Boyes 2013); 8 Scottish rock-climbers and 7 sea-kayakers aged 65+ (Hickman et al. 2016); 10 climbers aged 65–75 (Hickman et al. 2017); and 11 British surfers aged 45–70 (Wheaton 2017).

Buckley (2017) argued that individual participants in adventurous outdoor nature sports go through a 'leisure lifepsychle' reflecting the psychological trajectory of ageing. Elaborating this, Buckley (2018) proposed that ageing adventure athletes pass through two major thresholds in self-esteem. The first occurs when individuals realise that younger friends and colleagues, previously less skilled than themselves, are now more skilled. That is, they themselves are no longer leaders. The second occurs when individuals realise that they are no longer even a neutral independent addition to a group. Instead, they have become a burden, someone whom the younger members respect for past achievements, but not current capabilities. Ageing adventure athletes must adjust their aspirations, and reassess their achievements, in order to avoid loss of self-esteem.

Nature, human health, & outdoor therapies

Nature contributes to human health at many scales, from planetary-scale ecosystem processes to individual people. Here I consider only the latter, focusing specifically on the health gains achieved by individuals who spend time in natural surroundings. These gains derive from both physical and psychological components. Exercise has demonstrated therapeutic benefits for at least 26 different physical and psychological conditions (Pedersen and Saltin 2015). This applies even for 'weekend warrior' exercise patterns (O'Donovan et al. 2017). Exercise can prevent depression (Harvey et al. 2017) and improve cognition (Gomez-Pinilla and Hillman 2013). In experiments with mice, Sah et al. (2017), and Vivar and van Praag (2017) found that the act of running causes detectable physical changes in the brain.

Young et al. (2017) identified a cascade effect, whereby exercise improves social and psychological as well as physical health. Lee, Brellenthin et al. (2017) showed that runners live 3 years longer, on average, than non-runners. Very detailed modelling by Lee, Adam et al. (2017) showed that current low levels of exercise amongst children in the USA will cost the US economy US$2.8 trillion (measured as net present value) over the course of their lifetimes. Exercise outdoors yields greater individual improvement than exercise indoors (Coon et al. 2011; Frühauf et al. 2016; Niedermeier et al. 2017; Niedermeier, Hartl, and Kopp 2017; Pasanen, Tyrväinen, and Korpela 2014). Adventurous activities in nature yield a range of health benefits (Biedenweg, Scott, and Scott 2017; Hendriks et al. 2016; Luttenberger et al. 2015; Mantler and Logan 2015; Niedermeier et al. 2017; Niedermeier, Hartl, and Kopp 2017; Oh et al. 2017; Seymour 2016).

These links between nature and health have been proposed as the basis for outdoor nature, eco and adventure therapies (Buckley and Brough 2017a; Buckley, Brough, and Westaway 2018; Clough et al. 2016; Frumkin et al. 2017). A range of research is still required to bring these therapies to fruition. For example, the effects of therapeutic outdoor interventions differ both between individuals (Blaschke et al. 2017; Wang et al. 2017) and environments (Immonen et al. 2017; Triguero-Mas et al. 2017; Wyles et al. 2017). Because of the high social and economic costs of poor mental health (Lee et al. 2017; Zeisel et al. 2016), the contribution of adventurous outdoor nature sports to mental health can create economic value for parks and other places particularly suitable for such activities (Buckley and Brough 2017b; Smith, Roux, and Hayes 2017). Such economic valuations are increasingly important in land allocation and policy (Jepson et al. 2017; Rabarison et al. 2015).

A number of recent reviews (Buckley and Brough 2017a; Frumkin et al. 2017; Seymour 2016) have assembled evidence from a very wide range of clinical, experimental, and correlational studies showing that nature exposure yields health benefits. These benefits accrue across a wide range of: exposure types and intensities; physical, mental and social health parameters; and human cultures, ages, socioeconomic statuses, and prior mental health conditions. Most of these studies have measured only a limited set of parameters, and considered only brief low-intensity exposures. With few exceptions (e.g. Niedermeier et al. 2017; Niedermeier, Hartl, and Kopp 2017), the effects of lifetime involvement in adventurous outdoor nature sports have received little attention in the healthcare literature.

The reviews mentioned above concluded that poor mental health imposes a range of social and economic costs on the economies of developed nations, in aggregate equivalent to around 10% of their GDP (Buckley and Brough 2017a, 2017b). These reviews also concluded that these costs could be alleviated through increased exposure to nature. Critical information to calculate the exact financial value is currently lacking (Buckley and Brough 2017b), though relevant research is under way. Estimates currently available indicate a greater value for nature through its contributions to human mental health, than that achieved through expenditure on tourism (Buckley and Brough 2017b).

To convert this value into realisable economic gains will require the routine incorporation of outdoor nature, eco and adventure therapies into clinical and public healthcare systems (Buckley and Brough 2017b; Buckley, Westaway, and Brough 2016; Clough et al. 2016). As for any other type of therapy, one of the steps needed to achieve this is to create menus of certified, insured, and prescribable outdoor therapies, customised to patient characteristics and mental health conditions. This needs an extensive programme of research that considers and tests a wide range of outdoor activities for different circumstances and patient groups (Frumkin et al. 2017). These activities will need to include adventure and nature sports, as well as passive nature contemplation.

To design and establish such a programme, we can first draw on existing research literature in outdoor education, recreation, tourism and leisure studies. Whilst little of that research set out to design or test therapeutic healthcare, it does consider much more intense experiences than the nature-health literature, and much longer timespans, often extended over entire lifetimes. What can we extract or deduce, in relation to the mental health of participants, from the literature on outdoor nature and adventure sports, education, recreation and tourism? Can we partition the results by age, cultural background, personality, or socioeconomic status; or by the type, intensity, risk, emotional components, frequency, duration, and setting of the activities? Here, as outlined above, I focus on the effect of ageing.

Methods

Intermediate skill & risk levels

In this contribution, I present an autoethnographic analysis of ageing trajectories in a set of adventurous nature sports, carried out at intermediate skill and risk levels (Table 1). Few of these, except for aerobatic hanggliding four decades ago, are extreme in the sense that miscalculation means death (Brymer 2013; Brymer and Mackenzie 2017; Brymer and Oades 2009; Brymer and Schweitzer 2013a, 2013b, 2017a, 2017b; Holmbom, Brymer, and Schweitzer 2017). At the levels described in this contribution, participants must

Table 1. Autoethnographic history of nature-based adventure activities.

Activity	Start age	Age of peak skill	End age	Current level of activity
Ski, telemark	5	40	45	Inactive, still have gear
Snowboard	45	50	55	Inactive, still have gear
Hangglide	20	25	25	Inactive, still have gear
Kayak, flatwater	10	18	n/a	Active, low key, local
Kayak, whitewater	35	45	n/a	Active, low skill, global
Seakayak & surfski	40	50	n/a	Active, mod skill, local
Sailboard, flatwater	20	25	25	Inactive, still have gear
Sailboard, waves	35	45	n/a	Very occasional, local
Surf	45	60	n/a	Frequent, skill declining
Kiteboard	58	63	n/a	Frequent, mod skill, local

routinely adopt measures to minimise risks of injury, but they are unlikely to die unless they are unlucky as well as unskilled (Buckley 2012, 2015a, 2016a, 2016b, 2017). The age range covered is from <10 years old, to >60 years old (Table 1).

Autoethnography of critical incidents

It took some time for autoethnographic methodologies to be accepted as part of the panoply of social science techniques (Anderson 2006; Pace 2016). Currently, however, they are used widely (Anderson and Austin 2012; Buckley 2012, 2016b; Chang 2016; Jones, Adams, and Ellis 2016; Scheidt 2016; Stahlke Wall 2016; Tolich 2010). In the study of adventurous nature sports, a key component of autoethnographic approaches is the ability to recall fine detail of events and emotions, even if these are difficult to describe (Brymer and Schweitzer 2017b; Buckley 2015b).

This fine recall is possible for two reasons. The first is that human brains can either perceive or remember potentially life-threatening events in enhanced detail and clarity: the subjective impression of 'slow time' (Arstila 2012; Buckley 2014; Stetson, Fiesta, and Eagleman 2007; Wittmann 2011). The second is that the human brain can recall memories of such 'critical incidents' in much greater detail than memories more generally, even after a considerable interval has elapsed (Brown and Kulik 1977; Buckley 2016a; Flanagan 1954). Whilst individuals typically express high confidence in these recollections, the recollections may not always prove to be objectively accurate (Bradburn, Rips, and Shevell 1987; Loftus 2017; Talarico and Rubin 2003; Winkler 2017). The level of detail recalled generally does not decline with age, and may increase (Gardner, Mainetti, and Ascoli 2015; Huber, Milne, and Hyde 2017; Knäuper et al. 2016).

Data, generalisation, abstraction

I adopted a retrospective analytical autoethnographic approach, as a person who has taken part in a range of outdoor adventure activities for over half a century. I aim firstly, to identify the health outcomes from these adventurous nature sports; and secondly, to track how these outcomes have changed with advancing age. There are thus four categories of primary data. The first category consists of recollections of critical incidents from different nature sports activities, which are sufficiently intense and detailed to include psychological components. The second category consists of recollections of confounding factors that may also have affected physical or mental health, such as injuries unrelated to adventurous nature sports. This information is needed in order to interpret changes in individual capabilities.

The third category consists of general long-term autoethnographic observations on changing motivations, capabilities, experiences and consequences associated with outdoor adventure activities. The fourth consists of reflective observations on: current levels of activity in each of the adventurous nature sports concerned; current levels of physical and mental health and capability; and self-perceptions of the links between nature sports and health at my current age. From these sets of data, I generalise across the different adventure activities, whilst recognising that I pursued different activities most intensely at different ages. I then extract a set of second-level abstractions, representing lifetime changes and trends in higher-tier parameters. These include physical health parameters such as fitness and flexibility, and mental health parameters such as emotional intensity and generalised self-esteem.

Ethics statement

Some of the data presented here were obtained during commercial adventure tours. Assistance and sponsorship of tour operators is gratefully acknowledged. All of the research reported here, including that drawn from previous publications by the same author as well as new research conducted specifically for the current analysis, was conducted in strict compliance with the research ethics requirements of the author's university. This includes adherence to the University Research Ethics Manual and the relevant National Statement on Ethical Conduct in Human Research, and approvals by the University Human Research Ethics Committee as required.

Results

The adventure activities involved, overall age spans over which they were practiced, and current levels of activity or inactivity, are summarised in Table 1. The relative level of intensity for each activity at different age brackets is shown in Table 2. This indicates successive replacement of activities, with some being carried out in parallel, others sequentially. These changes in relative priority of different adventure activities were due partly to

Table 2. Successive replacement of self-perceived priority adventure activities.

Activity	Age ranges and intensity of activity[+]					
	< 20	20–30	30–40	40–50	50–60	> 60
Ski, telemark	*	***	*	*		
Snowboard				***	***	
Hangglide		*****				
Kayak, flatwater	****	*	*	*	*	*
Kayak, whitewater			**	****	***	*
Seakayak & surfski				**	**	**
Sailboard, flatwater		**	*	*	*	
Sailboard, waves		*	****	****	**	*
Surf				**	****	****
Kiteboard						****

[+]Stars indicate relative intensity of activity cf. other age brackets within same activity. More stars indicates higher intensity.

changing interests, and partly to their different availability and accessibility in different geographic areas.

Tables 3 and 4 summarise the highest level of skill achieved in each activity, using two different sets of measures. Table 3 lists external recognition, such as competitions or sponsorships. Table 4 is a self-reflective evaluation, identifying specific events or incidents that in my own evaluation, required the highest degree of skill or generated the highest levels of fear or thrill. Comparison of Tables 3 and 4 shows that external measures of recognition are only weakly correlated with internal sense of achievement. Table 4 also shows that the internally assessed achievements are idiosyncratic. That is, even at summary level, such as in Table 4, these critical events or incidents can only be described with reference to very specific geographical sites and environmental characteristics, and prevailing conditions such as weather, river flow, or surf size. As noted by Buckley (2018), adventure practitioners want to know details, whereas theorists are interested in abstractions.

Table 5 provides these abstractions, summarising lifetime trends or trajectories of change across all activities, for a series of physical and psychological parameters. It includes four physical parameters: physical capability, including fitness; the effects of injuries from unrelated sources such as car crashes; chronic pain; and level of stamina and reserves of strength in adversity. It includes five psychological parameters: the ability to overcome fear, both prior to a risky activity and during the progress of the activity itself; the ability to assess one's limits accurately, both physical and mental; the experience of positive emotions such as thrill, joy, and awe; the degree of attention paid to the surrounding natural environment, unrelated to its role in performing the adventure activity; and the degree of self-awareness of how manoeuvres are performed and how new skills are gained. Also included in Table 5 are two contextual parameters. The first is the degree of difficulty of challenges faced or attempted. The second is the self-perceived importance of adventure activities, relative to other components of one's life such as work, social relationships, or other forms of leisure.

Comparing the ageing trajectories for the different parameters in Table 5 leads to the highest-level finding of this analysis. As age increases, one's abilities decrease; one's

Table 3. Intensity, skill levels, and measures of attainment in adventure activities.

Activity	Intensity	Skill	Achievement, external recognition
Ski, downhill & telemark	Intermittent	low	nil
Snowboard	Moderate	Moderate	Sponsored by manufacturer (Burton®) and heli companies (CMH, MWHS, etc)
Hangglide	Addicted*	Moderate	1 Australian, 1 international competition, 1 (brief) record, *circa* 1978
Kayak, flatwater	Moderate	Moderate	Cambridge University half-blue, for race against Oxford, *circa* 1973
Kayak whitewater	Moderate	Moderate	International travel, lead kayaker in first descents, sponsored by manufacturer
Seakayak, surfski	Moderate	Moderate	International travel to seakayak (e.g. Arctic × 2) supported & unsupported
Sailboard, flatwater	Moderate	Moderate	Invited to make a commercial for a major tobacco company, *circa* 1980
Sailboard, wavesailing	Addicted*	Moderate	Took part in world first international wave-sailing competition, *circa* 1980
Surf	Addicted*	Moderate	International travel, sponsored by surf tour companies, shaper (Byrning Spears)
Kiteboard	Addicted*	Moderate	Nil

*See Buckley (2012, 2015a). Intensities compare between activities, not within each.

Table 4. Highest self-perceived achievement in each adventure activity.

Activity	Highest self-perceived achievements, defined by personal pride
Ski, downhill & telemark	XC-ski snow camping, Yellowstone NP, −40°C; skied 'the Funnel', back side of Mt Carruthers, Kosciuszko NP, in lightweight tele gear.
Snowboard, freeride	High-speed tree runs as (rotating) lead of heliski groups, Canada; successful (small) jumps from cornices, outcrops, tree pillows, etc.
Hangglide	Cross-country thermal flights, cliff take-offs, wingovers (aerobatic manoeuvre), landing in strong wind with passenger riding on back.
Kayak, flatwater	Paddled racing ski on flatwater river in Anaconda multisport team event, passed >50% of competitors (but the slowest 50%).
Kayak whitewater	Infierno Canyon & Terminator, Futaleufu (guided); No Exit, Mekong (only kayak run); Maruia Falls, New Zealand; Las Leones, Chile.
Seakayak, surfski	10 days, Baffin Island, Arctic (commercial trip, but unsupported); surfing (small) ocean surf on racing surfski, Gold Coast, Australia.
Sailboard, flatwater	High-speed run (short, before crash) in 60 knot wind on Cobra carbon speedboard, Adelaide; overtaking jetski on same board, Gold Coast.
Sailboard, wavesailing	(Maybe 3–4 times in 25 years) rode ocean swells to twice mast height (8–10 m vertical face) during storms and cyclones on Gold Coast.
Surf, shortboard	Cyclone swells, Kirra, Snapper, Burleigh, Australia; surfed HT's, Icelands, Lighthouses etc, Mentawais, Indonesia (very cautiously!).
Kiteboard, twin-tip	(occasional) jumps to >10 m vertical altitude, in winds up to 40 knots, Gold Coast; riding cyclone swells.

attention to surroundings and skills increases; and one's enjoyment of adventure activities remains largely unchanged. Euphoria is achievable at any age, as long as one is physically able to take part in at least some type of adventurous outdoor nature sports at some level of capability. Nature sports can thus contribute to mental health at all ages.

For myself specifically, my abilities are now on the decline for every adventure activity, except perhaps kiteboarding. This applies even though my abilities were never more than intermediate, at best, for any of these activities. I have never learned skydiving (except tandem), let alone BASE jumping or proximity flying. I have never surfed the very large,

Table 5. Autoethnographic trajectory of physical and psychological parameters.

Parameter	Trajectory over time, as perceived autoethnographically
Physical capability including fitness	Peaked around age 20, declining ever since, currently (age 64) a very severe limitation, including cardiovascular, flexibility.
Effect of injuries (not from adventure)	Spinal injuries greatly restrict ability to travel to sites, and activities themselves; restrictions worsen greatly with age.
Stamina, reserves of strength in adversity	Persisted reasonably well until aged in forties, declined greatly in fifties, and now in sixties, shadow of former self.
Chronic pain (all sources)	Continuing expansion in intensity, extent, and debilitating effect, currently a significant restriction on all activities.
Overcoming fear (pre and in event)	Difficult to recall, except for the most severe moments of fear. Now, when avoiding challenges, is it realism or cowardice?
Recognising limits (physical, mental)	Two key thresholds: (a) no longer a leader; and (b) becoming a burden on others. Major adjustments to self-esteem needed.
Positive emotions (thrill, joy, awe)	Can recall instances of thrill and joy dating back to age in twenties, and still continue currently, so not sure of any trend.
Attention to nature, detail of setting	Detailed observation and attention to nature since early age, still continues currently, cannot detect any trend.
Awareness of skill (how it is gained)	Increases with age. At younger age, easier to gain new skills, but do not know how. When older, difficult, observe carefully.
Challenges faced (degree of difficulty)	Challenges faced at different ages for different activities (see Tables 1 and 2). For most, declined since age forties or fifties.
Importance in life (e.g. cf. work, other)	Always important implicitly, but with greater age and more restricted ability, importance recognised clearly & explicitly.

steep, hollow and powerful waves ridden by professional competitive surfers, and I never shall. I should add that I found it hard to type the final four words of the last sentence, to admit to myself 'out loud' that I shall never be capable of surfing Teahupo'o or Shipstern or Nazarre or Peahi or Mavericks or many other such famous waves. Analytically, I know perfectly well that my abilities are orders of magnitude too low to attempt even far smaller and easier waves. But I still do not like to let go of the imaginary possibility. Thirty years ago I was a confident Class IV and occasional Class V whitewater kayaker: currently, I am Class III at best. It is easy enough to admit this to others, and indeed, they know it already. It is hard to admit it to oneself.

The increasing attention paid to one's natural surroundings, as age increases and capabilities decrease, is unexpected. It seems to be a form of compensation, recognising that even though one may not be catching as many waves as the youngsters, one can better appreciate the crystal blue ocean, the dolphins surfing nearby, the sea eagles soaring over the headland, the gannets riding the rising airflow in front of each wave. This seems to be distinct from the very detailed high-speed perception of surroundings associated with high danger, described by Buckley (2016b) for hanggliding in dangerous conditions, and by Holmbom, Brymer, and Schweitzer (2017) for proximity flying, that is connected with the phenomenon of 'slow time' perception (Buckley 2014).

Discussion

Previous research in adventurous outdoor nature sports, and extreme sports in particular, has repeatedly revealed that participants value their experiences enormously. There seem to be three principal reasons. The first reason is that these experiences are: only available through these activities; far outside the realm of experience otherwise available; and so powerful as to transform lives. Brymer and Oades (2009) cited autobiographical reports from kayakers, sailboarders and mountaineers, where single events transformed the entire subsequent lives of those concerned.

Climbers interviewed by Willig (2008) reported that their entire attention was focussed on the present instant. A BASE jumper interviewed by Brymer and Oades (2009) described 'how frightening, how exciting, how peaceful and beautiful the sensation is.' Brymer and Schweitzer (2017b) quoted a BASE jumper: 'it's incredibly, incredibly intense ... you're at this level of alertness that you're not in a normal life.' Another BASE jumper said that: 'your awareness of one second expands enormously ... it feels like it's in slow motion ... you can see the tiny little creases in the rock and different colours in the sky and you're totally aware.' This is the slow-time perception examined by Arstila (2012) and Buckley (2014).

The second reason is that these experiences provide existential meaning. They lead participants to recognise and accept their mortality, and to appreciate and value their lives. Brymer and Oades (2009) quoted a BASE jumper, who said that it involves: 'accepting that you're mortal ... vulnerable ... like a piece of dust.' Holmbom, Brymer, and Schweitzer (2017) quoted proximity wingsuit flyers: 'We are all gonna die someday ... you admit that reality and choose to enjoy, live and love the rest of the tiny spark that is our short life in the infinite universe'. Or as another said: 'we are all going to die ... it is how we LIVE that matters'. My own autoethnographic experience suggests that this is the philosophy of most participants in all adventurous outdoor nature sports, not only those that pose immediate risks of death.

The third reason is that these experiences generate psychological strength, that can then be applied elsewhere (Hickman et al. 2017). Pain and Pain (2005, 33) argued that: 'despite the public's perception, extreme sports demand perpetual care, high degrees of training and preparation, and above all, discipline and control.' Brymer and Oades (2009) quoted a BASE jumper: 'fear is a constant companion that requires great psychological skill to overcome'. They also quoted a big-wave surfer, who said that 'nothing can upset you'. Similarly, Holmbom, Brymer, and Schweitzer (2017) quoted a proximity wingsuit flyer: 'no other challenge is too big.' Again, my own experience, albeit at far lower intensities, coincides with those findings.

Previous research on the effects of ageing on participants in adventurous outdoor nature sports has revealed two general effects. The first is that older individuals who are able to continue these activities despite their age are proud of doing so (Hickman et al. 2016; Wheaton 2017). They identify themselves with their preferred activities (Hickman et al. 2016, 2017), and remain addicted to them (Wheaton 2017). The second is that older participants pay more attention to nature and their surroundings, and savour each moment more intensely than their younger counterparts (Hickman et al. 2016). The results reported here are derived from far less extreme levels of skill and risk than those reported by Holmbom, Brymer, and Schweitzer (2017), though perhaps similar to those studied by Hickman et al. (2016, 2017) and Wheaton (2017). They are congruent with these previous findings.

The results reported here also add several new findings. The most important is that despite loss of capability in adventurous outdoor nature sports, older participants are still able to use those activities to experience euphoria. That euphoria allows them to overcome pain, temporarily. It gives them psychological strength to overcome the stresses of major life transitions, and provides them with continuing meaning to life. Those consequences have considerable value, not only for the health and happiness of individuals, but for the economies of wealthy urbanised nations with ageing populations. This conclusion, that adventurous outdoor nature sports can continue to provide euphoria even in ageing individuals, is the highest-level finding from the autoethnographic analysis presented here.

Conclusions

Continuing enjoyment, even at decreased capability, is the single most important finding from a health perspective. It means that even individuals in older age brackets, in the post-working 'Third Age' as defined by Laslett (1991), can maintain their mental health through the intermittent euphoric events associated with adventurous outdoor nature sports. From an economic perspective, it is these older individuals who currently pose the greatest new cost on the economies of wealthy urbanised nations (Buckley and Brough 2017a, 2017b).

Poor mental health of working-age individuals imposes costs on workplace productivity (Powell 2017); and poor mental health of children and young adults imposes costs through healthcare and antisocial behaviours that may persist throughout their lives (Lee, Adam et al. 2017). These can be counteracted through outdoor nature and adventure therapies, and in many cases they already are (Mojtabai, Olfson, and Han 2016). It is the older age brackets, however, where the therapeutic effect of adventurous outdoor nature sports has the greatest social and economic significance. People in wealthy urbanised nations are now living longer than in the past, but they are spending their extra years in an unhealthy state, imposing large social and economic costs through the need for physical and mental health care, aged care, paid or unpaid carers, and assisted living.

Larger proportions of these ageing individuals are now recognising for themselves, however, that they need not relapse into inactivity. They may not be as capable as once they were, but they can still get outdoors, take part in nature sports and adventure activities, and experience occasional euphoria as a consequence. The euphoric experiences achieved during those activities provide older individuals, myself included, with a continuing and convincing demonstration that life is still very well worth living, despite injuries, illnesses, chronic pain and stress, and advancing decrepitude. Adventure provides euphoria as well as physical health; euphoria provides positive mental health; and maintaining the mental health of older individuals has high economic value for modern societies.

Disclosure statement

No potential conflict of interest was reported by the author.

ORCID

Ralf Buckley ⓘ http://orcid.org/0000-0003-0442-5818

References

Anderson, L. 2006. "Analytic Autoethnography." *Journal of Contemporary Ethnography* 35: 373–395.

Anderson, L., and M. Austin. 2012. "Auto-Ethnography in Leisure Studies." *Leisure Studies* 31: 131–146.

Arijs, C., C. Stiliani, G. E. Brymer, and D. Carless. 2017. "Leave Your Ego at the Door: A Narrative Investigation Into Effective Wingsuit Flying." *Frontiers in Psychology* 8: 1985.

Arstila, V. 2012. "Time Slows Down During Accidents." *Frontiers in Psychology* 3: 196.

Baretta, D., A. Greco, and P. Steca. 2017. "Understanding Performance in Risky Sport: The Role of Self-Efficacy Beliefs and Sensation Seeking in Competitive Freediving." *Personality and Individual Differences* 117: 161–165.

Berman, D., and J. Davis-Berman. 2013. "The Role of Therapeutic Adventure in Meeting the Mental Health Needs of Children and Adolescents: Finding a Niche in the Health Care Systems of the United States and the United Kingdom." *Journal of Experiential Education* 36: 51–64.

Biedenweg, K., R. P. Scott, and T. A. Scott. 2017. "How Does Engaging with Nature Relate to Life Satisfaction? Demonstrating the Link Between Environment-Specific Social Experiences and Life Satisfaction." *Journal of Environmental Psychology* 50: 112–124.

Blaschke, S., C. C. O'Callaghan, P. Schofield, and P. Salander. 2017. "Cancer Patients' Experiences with Nature: Normalizing Dichotomous Realities." *Social Science & Medicine* 172: 107–114.

Bowen, D. J., J. T. Neill, and S. J. Crisp. 2016. "Wilderness Adventure Therapy Effects on the Mental Health of Youth Participants." *Evaluation and Program Planning* 58: 49–59.

Boyes, M. 2013. "Outdoor Adventure and Successful Ageing." *Ageing & Society* 33: 644–665.

Bradburn, N. M., L. J. Rips, and S. K. Shevell. 1987. "Answering Autobiographical Questions: The Impact of Memory and Inference on Surveys." *Science* 236: 157–161.

Brannigan, A., and A. A. McDougall. 1983. "Peril and Pleasure in the Maintenance of a High Risk Sport: A Study of Hang-Gliding." *Journal of Sport Behaviour* 6: 37–51.

Brough, P., G. Johnson, S. Drummond, S. Pennisi, and C. Timms. 2011. "Comparisons of Cognitive Ability and job Attitudes of Older and Younger Workers." *Equality, Diversity and Inclusion: An International Journal* 30: 105–126.

Brown, R., and J. Kulik. 1977. "Flashbulb Memories." *Cognition* 5: 73–99.

Brymer, E. 2013. "Risk and Extreme Sports: A Phenomenological Perspective." *Annals of Leisure Research* 13: 218–239.

Brymer, E., and S. H. Mackenzie. 2017. "Psychology and the Extreme Sport Experience." In *Extreme Sports Medicine*, edited by F. Felletti, 3–13. Berlin: Springer.

Brymer, E., and L. Oades. 2009. "Extreme Sports: A Positive Transformation in Courage and Humility." *Journal of Humanistic Psychology* 49: 114–126.

Brymer, E., and R. Schweitzer. 2013a. "Extreme Sports are Good for Your Health: A Phenomenological Understanding of Fear and Anxiety in Extreme Sport." *Journal of Health Psychology* 18: 477–487.

Brymer, E., and R. Schweitzer. 2013b. "The Search for Freedom in Extreme Sports: a Phenomenological Exploration." *Psychology of Sport and Exercise* 14: 865–873.

Brymer, E., and R. Schweitzer. 2017a. *Phenomenology and the Extreme Sport Experience.* Abingdon: Taylor & Francis.

Brymer, E., and R. D. Schweitzer. 2017b. "Evoking the Ineffable: The Phenomenology of Extreme Sports." *Psychology of Consciousness: Theory, Research, and Practice* 4: 63–74.

Buckley, R. C. 2009. *Ecotourism Principles & Practices.* Wallingford: CABI.

Buckley, R. C. 2012. "Rush as a Key Motivation in Skilled Adventure Tourism: Resolving the Risk Recreation Paradox." *Tourism Management* 33: 961–970.

Buckley, R. C. 2014. "Slow Time Perception can be Learned." *Frontiers in Psychology* 5: 209.

Buckley, R. C. 2015a. "Adventure Thrills are Addictive." *Frontiers in Psychology* 6: 1915.

Buckley, R. C. 2015b. "Autoethnography Helps Analyse Emotions." *Frontiers in Psychology* 6: 209.

Buckley, R. C. 2016a. "Qualitative Analysis of Emotions: Fear and Thrill." *Frontiers in Psychology* 7: 1187.

Buckley, R. C. 2016b. "Nature Fix: Addiction to Outdoor Activities." *Journal of Behavioural Addiction* 5: 557–558.

Buckley, R. C. 2017. "Analysing Adventure: a Leisure Lifepsychle?" *Annals of Leisure Research* 44: 1–6. doi:10.1080/11745398.2017.1361333.

Buckley, R. C. 2018. "Ageing Adventure Athletes Assess Achievements and Alter Aspirations to Maintain Self-Esteem." *Frontiers in Psychology* 9: 225.

Buckley, R. C., and P. Brough. 2017a. "Nature, Eco and Adventure Therapies for Mental Health and Chronic Disease." *Frontiers in Public Health* 5: 220.

Buckley, R. C., and P. Brough. 2017b. "Economic Value of Parks via Human Mental Health: An Analytical Framework." *Frontiers in Ecology and Evolution* 5: 1247.

Buckley, R. C., P. Brough, and D. Westaway. 2018. "Bringing Outdoor Therapies Into Mainstream Mental Health." *Frontiers in Public Health* 6: 119.

Buckley, R. C., U. Gretzel, D. Scott, D. Weaver, and S. Becken. 2015. "Tourism Megatrends." *Tourism Recreation Research* 40: 59–70.

Buckley, R. C., D. Westaway, and P. Brough. 2016. "Social Mechanisms to Get People Outdoors." *Frontiers in Public Health* 4: 257.

Chang, H. 2016. *Autoethnography as Method.* London: Routledge.

Clough, P., S. H. Mackenzie, L. Mallabon, and E. Brymer. 2016. "Adventurous Physical Activity Environments: A Mainstream Intervention for Mental Health." *Sports Medicine* 46: 963–968.

Coon, J. T., K. Boddy, K. Stein, R. Whear, J. Barton, and M. H. Depledge. 2011. "Does Participating in Physical Activity in Outdoor Natural Environments Have a Greater Effect on Physical and Mental

Well-Being Than Physical Activity Indoors? A Systematic Review." *Environmental Science and Technology* 45: 1761–1772.

DiPietro, L., Y. Jin, S. Talegawkar, and C. E. Matthews. 2017. "The Joint Associations of Sedentary Time and Physical Activity with Mobility Disability in Older People: NIH-AARP Diet and Health Study." *Journals of Gerontology Series A* 73: 532–538. doi:10.1093/gerona/glx122.

Earl, B. 2014. "The Biological Function of Consciousness." *Frontiers in Psychology* 5: 697.

Elmes, M., and D. Barry. 1999. "Deliverance, Denial, and the Death Zone: a Study of Narcissism and Regression in the May 1996 Everest Climbing Disaster." *Journal of Applied Behavioural Science* 35: 163–187.

Epstein, I. 2004. "Adventure Therapy: a Mental Health Promotion Strategy in Pediatric Oncology." *Journal of Pediatric Oncology and Nursing* 21: 103–110.

Erickson, K. I., R. L. Leckie, and A. M. Weinstein. 2014. "Physical Activity, Fitness, and Gray Matter Volume." *Neurobiology of Aging* 35: S20–S28.

Ewert, A., and A. Yoshino. 2011. "The Influence of Short-Term Adventure Based Experiences on Levels of Resilience." *Journal of Adventure Education and Outdoor Learning* 11: 35–50.

Flanagan, J. C. 1954. "The Critical Incident Technique." *Psychological Bulletin* 51: 327–358.

Frühauf, A., M. Niedermeier, L. R. Elliott, L. Ledochowski, J. Marksteiner, and M. Kopp. 2016. "Acute Effects of Outdoor Physical Activity on Affect and Psychological Well-Being in Depressed Patients–A Preliminary Study." *Mental Health and Physical Activity* 10: 4–9.

Frumkin, H., G. N. Bratman, S. J. Breslow, B. Cochran, P. H. Kahn Jr, J. J. Lawler, and S. A. Wood. 2017. "Nature Contact and Human Health: A Research Agenda." *Environmental Health Perspectives* 125: 075001-1.

Gardner, R. S., M. Mainetti, and G. A. Ascoli. 2015. "Older Adults Report Moderately More Detailed Autobiographical Memories." *Frontiers in Psychology* 6: 631.

Gass, M. A., H. L. Gillis, and K. C. Russell. 2012. *Adventure Therapy: Theory, Research, and Practice.* New York: Routledge.

Gomez-Pinilla, F., and C. Hillman. 2013. "The Influence of Exercise on Cognitive Abilities." *Comprehensive Physiology* 3: 403–428.

Grubb, M. A., A. Tymula, S. Gilaie-Dotan, P. W. Glimcher, and I. Levy. 2016. "Neuroanatomy Accounts for Age-Related Changes in Risk Preferences." *Nature Communications* 7: 13822.

Harvey, S. B., S. Øverland, S. L. Hatch, S. Wessely, A. Mykletun, and M. Hotopf. 2017. "Exercise and the Prevention of Depression: Results of the HUNT Cohort Study." *American Journal of Psychiatry* 175: 28–36. doi:10.1176/appi.ajp.2017.16111223.

Hattie, J., H. W. Marsh, J. T. Neill, and G. E. Richards. 1997. "Adventure Education and Outward Bound: Out-of-Class Experiences That Make a Lasting Difference." *Review of Educational Research* 67: 43–87.

Hendriks, I. H., D. van Vliet, D. L. Gerritsen, and R. M. Dröes. 2016. "Nature and Dementia: Development of a Person-Centered Approach." *International Psychogeriatrics* 28: 1455–1470.

Hickman, M., P. Stokes, C. Beard, and A. Inkster. 2017. "Doing the Plastic Fantastic: 'Artificial' Adventure and Older Adult Climbers." *Journal of Adventure Education and Outdoor Learning* 10: 1–11. doi:10.1080/14729679.2017.1308874.

Hickman, M., P. Stokes, S. Gammon, C. Beard, and A. Inkster. 2016. "Moments Like Diamonds in Space: Savoring the Ageing Process Through Positive Engagement with Adventure Sports." *Annals of Leisure Research* 38: 1–19. doi:10.1080/11745398.2016.1241151.

Holm, M. R., P. Lugosi, R. R. Croes, and E. N. Torres. 2017. "Risk-tourism, Risk-Taking and Subjective Well-Being: A Review and Synthesis." *Tourism Management* 63: 115–122.

Holmbom, M., E. Brymer, and R. D. Schweitzer. 2017. "Transformations Through Proximity Flying: A Phenomenological Investigation." *Frontiers in Psychology* 8: 229.

Huber, D., S. Milne, and K. F. Hyde. 2017. "Biographical Research Methods and Their use in the Study of Senior Tourism." *International Journal of Tourism Research* 19: 27–37.

Immonen, T., E. Brymer, D. Orth, K. Davids, F. Feletti, J. Liukkonen, and T. Jaakkola. 2017. "Understanding Action and Adventure Sports Participation: an Ecological Dynamics Perspective." *Sports Medicine - Open* 3: 18.

Jepson, P., B. Caldecott, S. F. Schmitt, S. H. C. de Carvalho, R. A. Correia, A. C. M. Malhado, and R. J. Ladle. 2017. "Protected Area Asset Stewardship." *Biological Conservation* 212: 183–190.

Jones, S. H., T. E. Adams, and C. Ellis, eds. 2016. *Handbook of Autoethnography*. London: Routledge.

Knäuper, B., K. Carriere, M. Chamandy, Z. Xu, N. Schwarz, and N. O. Rosen. 2016. "How Aging Affects Self-Reports." *European Journal of Ageing* 13: 185–193.

Laslett, P. 1991. *A Fresh Map of Life: The Emergence of the Third Age*. 2nd ed. Cambridge, MA: Harvard University Press.

Lee, B. Y., A. Adam, E. Zenkov, D. Hertenstein, M. C. Ferguson, P. I. Wang, and S. Falah-Fini. 2017. "Modeling the Economic and Health Impact of Increasing Children's Physical Activity in the United States." *Health Affairs* 36: 902–908.

Lee, D. C., A. G. Brellenthin, P. D. Thompson, X. Sui, I. M. Lee, and C. J. Lavie. 2017. "Running as a Key Lifestyle Medicine for Longevity." *Progress in Cardiovascular Diseases* 60: 45–55.

Loftus, E. F. 2017. "Eavesdropping on Memory." *Annual Review of Psychology* 68: 1–18.

Luttenberger, K., E. M. Stelzer, S. Först, M. Schopper, J. Kornhuber, and S. Book. 2015. "Indoor Rock Climbing (Bouldering) as a New Treatment for Depression: Study Design of a Waitlist-Controlled Randomized Group Pilot Study and the First Results." *BMC Psychiatry* 15: 201.

Mantler, A., and A. C. Logan. 2015. "Natural Environments and Mental Health." *Advances in Integrative Medicine* 2: 5–12.

Melo, R., and R. Gomes. 2017. "Nature Sports Participation: Understanding Demand, Practice Profile, Motivations and Constraints." *European Journal of Tourism Research* 16: 108–135.

Miesel, M. E., and J. R. Potgieter. 2003. "The Experience of Fear in High-Risk Sport." *South African Journal of Research in Sport, Physical Education and Recreation* 25: 49–56.

Mojtabai, R., M. Olfson, and B. Han. 2016. "National Trends in the Prevalence and Treatment of Depression in Adolescents and Young Adults." *Pediatrics* 138: e20161878.

Monasterio, E., O. Mei-Dan, A. C. Hackney, A. R. Lane, I. Zwir, S. Rozsa, and C. R. Cloninger. 2016. "Stress Reactivity and Personality in Extreme Sport Athletes: The Psychobiology of BASE Jumpers." *Physiology & Behavior* 167: 289–297.

Moore, L. E., and B. Greyson. 2017. "Characteristics of Memories for Near-Death Experiences." *Consciousness and Cognition* 51: 116–124.

Niedermeier, M., J. Einwanger, A. Hartl, and M. Kopp. 2017. "Affective Responses in Mountain Hiking: A Randomized Crossover Trial Focusing on Differences Between Indoor and Outdoor Activity." *PloS ONE* 12: e0177719.

Niedermeier, M., A. Hartl, and M. Kopp. 2017. "Prevalence of Mental Health Problems and Factors Associated with Psychological Distress in Mountain Exercisers: a Cross-Sectional Study in Austria." *Frontiers in Psychology* 8: 1237.

O'Donovan, G., I. M. Lee, M. Hamer, and E. Stamatakis. 2017. "Association of 'Weekend Warrior' and Other Leisure Time Physical Activity Patterns with Risks for all-Cause, Cardiovascular Disease, and Cancer Mortality." *JAMA Internal Medicine* 177: 335–342.

Oh, B., K. J. Lee, C. Zaslawski, A. Yeung, D. Rosenthal, L. Larkey, and M. Back. 2017. "Health and Well-Being Benefits of Spending Time in Forests: Systematic Review." *Environmental Health and Preventive Medicine* 22: 71.

Orth, U., J. Maes, and M. Schmitt. 2015. "Self-Esteem Development Across the Life Span: A Longitudinal Study with a Large Sample From Germany." *Developmental Psychology* 51: 248–259.

Pace, S. 2016. "Contested Concepts: Negotiating Debates About Qualitative Research Methods Such as Grounded Theory and Autoethnography." In *Constructing Methodology for Qualitative Research*, 187–200. Basingstoke: Palgrave Macmillan.

Pain, M. T., and M. A. Pain. 2005. "Essay: Risk Taking in Sport." *The Lancet* 366: 33–34.

Pasanen, T. P., L. Tyrväinen, and K. M. Korpela. 2014. "The Relationship Between Perceived Health and Physical Activity Indoors, Outdoors in Built Environments, and Outdoors in Nature." *Applied Psychology: Health and Well-Being* 6: 324–346.

Pedersen, B. K., and B. Saltin. 2015. "Exercise as Medicine–Evidence for Prescribing Exercise as Therapy in 26 Different Chronic Diseases." *Scandinavian Journal of Medicine & Science in Sports* 25 (S3): 1–72.

Pomfret, G., and B. Bramwell. 2016. "The Characteristics and Motivational Decisions of Outdoor Adventure Tourists: a Review and Analysis." *Current Issues in Tourism* 19: 1447–1478.

Portugal, A. C., F. Campos, F. Martins, and R. Melo. 2017. "Understanding the Relation Between Serious Surfing, Surfing Profile, Surf Travel Behaviour and Destination Attributes Preferences." *European Journal of Tourism Research* 16: 57–73.

Powell, K. 2017. "Work-Life Balance: Break or Burn Out." *Nature* 545: 375–377.

Pryor, A., C. Carpenter, and M. Townsend. 2012. "Outdoor Education and Bush Adventure Therapy: A Social-Ecological Approach to Health and Wellbeing." *Australian Journal of Outdoor Education* 9: 3–13.

Puchan, H. 2004. "Living 'Extreme': Adventure Sports, Media and Commercialisation." *Journal of Communication Management* 9: 171–178.

Rabarison, K. M., C. L. Bish, M. S. Massoudi, and W. H. Giles. 2015. "Economic Evaluation Enhances Public Health Decision Making." *Frontiers in Public Health* 3: 164.

Russell, K. C. 2003. "An Assessment of Outcomes in Outdoor Behavioural Healthcare Treatment." *Child & Youth Care Forum* 32: 355–381.

Sah, N., B. D. Peterson, S. T. Lubejko, C. Vivar, and H. van Praag. 2017. "Running Reorganizes the Circuitry of One-Week-Old Adult-Born Hippocampal Neurons." *Scientific Reports* 7: 10903.

Sandseter, E. B. H., and L. E. O. Kennair. 2011. "Children's Risky Play From an Evolutionary Perspective: The Anti-Phobic Effects of Thrilling Experiences." *Evolutionary Psychology* 9: 257–284.

Scheidt, R. J. 2016. "The Defense of My Aging Self: a Report From the Field." *The Gerontologist* 57: 110–115.

Scrutton, R., and S. Beames. 2015. "Measuring the Unmeasurable: Upholding Rigor in Quantitative Studies of Personal and Social Development in Outdoor Adventure Education." *Journal of Experiential Education* 38: 8–25.

Seifert, L., D. Orth, C. Button, E. Brymer, and K. Davids. 2017. "An Ecological Dynamics Framework for the Acquisition of Perceptual–Motor Skills in Climbing." In *Extreme Sports Medicine*, 365–382. Berlin: Springer.

Seymour, V. 2016. "The Human–Nature Relationship and its Impact on Health: a Critical Review." *Frontiers in Public Health* 4: 260.

Sibthorp, J., and S. Arthur-Banning. 2004. "Developing Life Effectiveness Through Adventure Education: The Roles of Participant Expectations, Perceptions of Empowerment, and Learning Relevance." *Journal of Experiential Education* 27: 32–50.

Sibthorp, J., K. Paisley, J. Gookin, and N. Furman. 2008. "The Pedagogic Value of Student Autonomy in Adventure Education." *Journal of Experiential Education* 31: 136–151.

Smith, M. K. S., D. J. Roux, and J. Hayes. 2017. "Adventure Racing Enables Access to Cultural Ecosystem Services at Multiple Scales." *Ecosystem Services* 28: 149–161.

Stahlke Wall, S. 2016. "Toward a Moderate Autoethnography." *International Journal of Qualitative Methods* 15. doi:10.1177/1609406916674966.

Steptoe, A., A. Deaton, and A. A. Stone. 2015. "Subjective Wellbeing, Health, and Ageing." *The Lancet* 385: 640–648.

Stetson, C., M. P. Fiesta, and D. M. Eagleman. 2007. "Does Time Really Slow Down During a Frightening Event?" *PloS ONE* 2: e1295.

Sun, F. W., M. R. Stepanovic, J. Andreano, L. F. Barrett, A. Touroutoglou, and B. C. Dickerson. 2016. "Youthful Brains in Older Adults: Preserved Neuroanatomy in the Default Mode and Salience Networks Contributes to Youthful Memory in Superaging." *Journal of Neuroscience* 36: 9659–9668.

Talarico, J. M., and D. C. Rubin. 2003. "Confidence, not Consistency, Characterizes Flashbulb Memories." *Psychological Science* 14: 455–461.

Thonnard, M., V. Charland-Verville, S. Brédart, H. Dehon, D. Ledoux, S. Laureys, and A. Vanhaudenhuyse. 2013. "Characteristics of Near-Death Experiences Memories as Compared to Real and Imagined Events Memories." *PLoS ONE* 8: e57620.

Tolich, M. 2010. "A Critique of Current Practice: Ten Foundational Guidelines for Autoethnographers." *Qualitative Health Research* 20: 1599–1610.

Triguero-Mas, M., D. Donaire-Gonzalez, E. Seto, A. Valentín, G. Smith, D. Martínez, and T. Martínez-Íñiguez. 2017. "Living Close to Natural Outdoor Environments in Four European Cities: Adults'

Contact with the Environments and Physical Activity." *International Journal of Environmental Research and Public Health* 14: 1162.

Vivar, C., and H. van Praag. 2017. "Running Changes the Brain: the Long and the Short of it." *Physiology* 32: 410–424.

Wang, R. A. H., S. K. Nelson-Coffey, K. Layous, K. J. Bao, O. S. Davis, and C. M. Haworth. 2017. "Moderators of Wellbeing Interventions: Why do Some People Respond More Positively Than Others?" *PloS ONE* 12: e0187601.

Wheaton, B. 2017. "Surfing Through the Life-Course: Silver Surfers' Negotiation of Ageing." *Annals of Leisure Research* 20: 96–116.

Willig, C. 2008. "A Phenomenological Investigation of the Experience of Taking Part in 'Extreme Sports." *Journal of Health Psychology* 13: 690–702.

Winkler, I. 2017. "Doing Autoethnography: Facing Challenges taking Choices, Accepting Responsibilities." *Qualitative Inquiry* 24: 236–247. doi:10.1177/1077800417728956.

Wittmann, M. 2011. "Moments in Time." *Frontiers in Integrative Neuroscience* 5: 66.

Wooden, M., and N. Li. 2016. "Ageing, Death and Life Satisfaction: Evidence From the Household, Income and Labour Dynamics in Australia Survey." *Australian Economic Review* 49: 474–482.

Woodman, T., L. Hardy, M. Barlow, and C. Le Scanff. 2010. "Motives for Prolonged Engagement High-Risk Sports: an Agentic Emotion Regulation Perspective." *Psychology of Sport and Exercise* 11: 345–352.

Wyles, K. J., M. P. White, C. Hattam, S. Pahl, H. King, and M. Austen. 2017. "Are Some Natural Environments More Psychologically Beneficial Than Others? The Importance of Type and Quality on Connectedness to Nature and Psychological Restoration." *Environment and Behavior*, doi:10.1177/0013916517738312.

Young, K. C., K. A. Machell, T. B. Kashdan, and M. L. Westwater. 2017. "The Cascade of Positive Events: Does Exercise on a Given Day Increase the Frequency of Additional Positive Events?" *Personality and Individual Differences* 120: 299–303. doi:10.1016/j.paid.2017.03.032.

Zeisel, J., B. Reisberg, P. Whitehouse, R. Woods, and A. Verheul. 2016. "Ecopsychosocial Interventions in Cognitive Decline and Dementia: A New Terminology and a New Paradigm." *American Journal of Alzheimer's Disease & Other Dementias* 31: 502–507.

Understanding nature sports: a participant centred perspective and its implications for the design and facilitating of learning and performance

Loel Collins 🆔 and Eric Brymer 🆔

ABSTRACT

Nature sports is a term used to describe a collection of physical activities that are frequently defined by characteristics of their environment or an inherent risk. These perspectives overlook new aspects of nature sports and motivations for participation, imposing an inaccurate perspective on the design and facilitation of learning experiences. Namely, that nature sports are undertaken by participants with an inherent need for risk. This paper presents an alternative perspective based on critiques of the traditional notions of the experience of participants which goes beyond notions of risk-taking and thrill-seeking. Adopting a participant focus provides insight into the constant evolution of techniques, participation, philosophies and the continuous striving for creativity and innovation. Effective learning design and facilitation in nature sports therefore demands adaptability, flexibility, cultural sensitivity, and the capacity to facilitate a participant's interaction with their environment.

Introduction

'Nature sport' has emerged as one of many terms (e.g. adventure sports, high-risk sports, action sports, outdoor sports, extreme sports to name the most popular) used to refer to a collection of physical activities that are surpassing many traditional sports in popularity (Pain and Pain 2005; Brymer and Schweitzer 2017a). Examples of such activities include kayaking, BASE (Building, Antennae, Space and Earth) jumping, skiing, climbing, walking and surfing. Additionally, the growth of adventure tourism and participation in nature sports has expanded possible participation beyond the well-researched and established realms of outdoor education (Peacock et al. 2017). Consequently, we take a position that reflects a leisure, tourism and participation perspective. The thread that binds the activities defined as 'nature' sports is that for the most part they are undertaken in relation to the natural environment and not bound by predetermined rules or artificially deter-mined physical boundaries. Understanding, more fully, the nature of nature sports seems paramount if we are to help leaders, coaches and instructors meet the demands of an increasingly diverse group of participants. We suggest three possible advantages

to this review (1) to challenge the theoretical perspectives that have surrounded participation in nature sports, (2) to distinguish between sub-groups within nature sports or
sports more widely, and (3) to focus academic research concerns.

In this paper, we argue that the traditional risk-based approach to nature sports is an
oversimplification and a more comprehensive understanding of nature sports that
focuses on the experience of the participant is needed to guide effective facilitation of
experiences and learning. Following an outline of the traditional perspective, we investigate and critique definitions of the variety of nature sports categories such as action
sports, adventure sports, extreme sports, lifestyle sports, and high-risk sports. We, then,
take an overview of current approaches to the facilitation of experiences and learning
to highlight how the traditional risk-focused approach has infiltrated the design and facilitation of learning experiences. Finally, we show how the notion of nature sports could be
understood from a participant perspective.

The typical theoretical perspective

The typical theoretical and popular perspective on nature sport activities emphasizes risk
and risk-taking. Activities are defined in terms of; (1) characteristics of the physical environment where the environment is assumed to be dangerous, dynamic or uncertain,(2) personality characteristics, where participants are described as risk-takers or adrenalin seekers
searching for novelty and uncertainty (Rossi and Cereatti 1993; Slanger and Rudestam
1997; Self et al. 2007; Brymer 2010a), (3) the socio-cultural environment where participants
are presumed to create a personal identity based on fitting in with risk-based counter-cul-
tural characteristics (e.g. lifestyle sports; Wheaton 2004).

A number of problems with the traditional approach that have a direct implication for
the design and facilitation of learning and experiences in nature sports have been identified (Brymer and Schweitzer 2017b). For example, a risk-focused perspective might
assume that participants are only interested in thrills and excitement and as consequence
providers of experiences are inclined to only focus on providing opportunities for thrills
and excitement. Notions of providing opportunities for enhancing health, connecting to
nature and developing expertise could be ignored. Equally, the provision of learning
opportunities might be primarily focused on risk management or providing the skills
required to undertake greater risk-focused challenges. From this perspective, learning
facilitators are less likely to be interested in designing experiences that address a
broader or more nuanced range of motivations for participation. From the risk perspective
nature becomes the competitor, a battleground or playground with the sole purpose of
providing a context for the participant to test capabilities (Brymer 2009; Brymer and
Gray 2009, 2010). An emphasis on the risk-focused approach in marketing is also more
likely to attract people who already wish to take risks and therefore create the potential
for unfortunate mishaps; a vicious circle.

The complex nature of nature sports: the traditional perspective

Nature sports, a relatively new term coined to describe those physical activities undertaken in the presence of nature or while being immersed in nature (Krien 2014; Melo
and Gomes 2017), are fast becoming the physical activity of choice across the world.

Nature sports are not bound by rules, regulations or set boundaries. Nor are they easily constrained by traditional notions of 'sport' as structured, competitive activities. Equally, nature sports do not easily comply with a modernist view of sport that originates in western Christian philosophies. Instead, nature sports are perhaps best allied with the original appreciation of sport as pastime and recreation (Immonen et al. 2017) and a postmodernist perspective on sport as multifaceted and including dimensions of self-development, recreation, social, historical, political and cultural discourses, and personal interpretation.

Perhaps because of these broad characterizations we know little about the complexities of nature sports. Developing an understanding of nature sports seems essential for business operators, learning designers and facilitators, and policymakers. Nature sport activities have become part of the tourism industry, the health industry, recreation and leisure industry, and remain an important aspect of the education sector. More recently, adapted versions of nature sports have infiltrated the traditional sporting sector (see 'sportification', Crum 1991). For the most part, attempts to define nature sports have been constrained by the context. However, mountain biking, climbing, snowboarding or surfing in an Olympic context where boundaries are constrained and regulations imposed might be different to mountain biking, climbing, snowboarding or surfing when undertaken as part of a health intervention or as a leisure pursuit or as a tourism activity. Indeed, the various terms used to describe seemingly similar activities seems to reinforce this perspective and make definitions challenging. While these different types of nature sports have some distinct, differentiating and unique elements, they also have common aspects that are pertinent and significant to the participant and the notion of nature sports.

In the following section, we review the key features of common types of sports captured by the main terms currently used to describe the varieties of 'nature' sports. The aim of this section is to investigate similarities and differences within the varieties of nature sports to highlight the complex nature of nature sports. In this process, we attempt to clarify the features of each category and highlight the crossover between the many types of nature sports. We have been careful to filter for nuances in the literature where activities might seem similar but do not refer to nature sports. For example, the literature on indoor alternatives to climbing, skiing, skydiving and sports that are mainly about competition is not considered.

Extreme and high-risk sports

The terms extreme sport and high-risk sport have often been used interchangeably to define activities where the likely outcome of a mismanaged mistake or accident is death (Frühauf et al. 2017; Brymer and Schweitzer 2017a). Examples of activities in this category that clearly involve interacting with nature include BASE jumping (including proximity flying), big wave surfing, mountaineering above the death zone (above 8000 m), waterfall kayaking and extreme skiing. Participation at this level has become highly specialized. Sports such as powerboat racing and stunt plane racing which have also been described as extreme have not been considered because of the low explicit nature component.

The traditional perspective presupposes that participation is about personality structures that mandate participation in risky activities. Participants are assumed to be young, male, and fearless with personality structures that mean they are motivated by thrill and the 'adrenaline buzz' The main personality theories that have been used to define these activities are sensation seeking, Type 'T' personality and psychoanalysis. Such theories have led to the adrenaline junkie misnomer that pervades social culture (Barlow, Woodman, and Hardy 2013). These theories suggest that learning and effective performance is about having, or developing, a personality structure that means a participant thrives because of the danger inherent in the activity.

Recent criticisms of this perspective argue it is overly simplistic and not reflective of the lived experience of participants (Brymer 2009; Brymer and Oades 2009; Brymer, Downey, and Gray 2009; Brymer and Schweitzer 2013). For example, this perspective does not reflect findings that indicate participant experiences of fear and freedom while participating are positive and transformational or that participants often report transcendent qualities intrinsic to the experience (Brymer and Schweitzer 2017b). Furthermore, personality research has produced inconsistent findings and has proven limited in its capacity to explain why participation rates are increasing so rapidly (Monasterio and Brymer 2015). Critics have also pointed out that an important aspect of extreme or high-risk sports, is often overlooked. Namely, that rules are not externally dictated and the environment is not generally artificially constrained. Both these factors might facilitate fast evolution of the sports and emergent possibilities that mean that participation can be taken, literally, to the extreme. The lack of these figurative boundaries also suggests a relationship between the performer and the environment that is experienced differently to other sports. The notion of conquering the environment, for instance the expression conquering Everest or battling the elements, used in everyday language, has been critiqued as simplistic and stemming from an inaccurate assessment that assumes sport must be about competition. However, mountains and waves are not aware of any competition against humans. Rather, research examining the relationship between extreme sport participants and nature suggests that participants are most often in harmony with nature, preferring to speak about the experience as immersive and relational (Brymer and Gray 2009; Brymer, Downey, and Gray 2009; Brymer and Gray 2010)

Adventure sports
Adventure sports, commonly referred to in a tourism context, have also been associated with risk (Peacock et al. 2017) and are increasingly the focus of sports coaching research (for example, Collins & Collins, 2013, 2015a, 2015b, 2016). In the tourism context, the range of adventure sports activities has been presented as a continuum (soft – hard) representing degrees of challenge, uncertainty, intensity, duration and perceptions of control (Varley 2006; Perdomo 2013). Activities include predictable, safe and reliable ones delivered by experienced facilitators with an element of perceived risk but little real risk (commodified adventure, Varley 2006; see also Loynes 1998 and Brown 2000) (example activities include, white water rafting, tandem parachuting, and bungy jumping). These commodified adventures contrast with those that require specialized activity and decision making skills, and greater participant commitment and responsibility (Cloke & Perkins 2002; Collins and Collins 2016). Example activities include white water kayaking, rock climbing, off-piste skiing and mountaineering. From a learning perspective adventure sport participation encompasses a broad range of demands; at the commodified end of the continuum the provider offers just enough information for the participant to undertake the activity and achieve what the provider assumes the participant wants from the

experience. While at the other, 'authentic' level (Valkonen, Huilaja, and Koikkalainen 2013), the learning experience focuses on the development of the technical and cognitive skills required to undertake the activity independently of the facilitator (see Collins, Collins, and Grecic 2015; Christian, Berry, and Kearney 2017). Nature in these types of activities is seen as a dynamic playground for testing physical and mental resources and possibly providing the thrills and excitement that are deemed to be part of the adventure sport activity.

Reflecting the potential breadth of participation, critics point to confusion over assumptions that certain sport or activity types are the same. An emphasis on risk and uncertainty ignores individual differences, the engagement with the culture of a particular adventure sport and role of the environment. In contrast, operators at the commodification end of the continuum most often minimize real risk to ensure safety, while exploiting perceived risk as an important aspect of adventure sport pedagogy. However, by emphasizing risk it is possible that organizations are less likely to build long-term relationships with participants and are more likely to feel impelled to provide the next thrill-seeking activity.

The emphasis on risk is hard to defend and leaves adventure synonymous with the narrow notion of extreme sports (highlighted earlier) and neglects participant lived experience, such as, for example, the quest for personal insight, knowledge, spirituality and enlightenment. Research points to a broader experience of nature in adventure sports described as feeling connected to nature (Kerr and Houge Mackenzie 2012 and often facilitating a deeper pro-environment identity (Sharma-Brymer, Gray, and Brymer 2017).

Action sports

The term action sport is used to describe a broad category of sports characterized by individuality and differentiated from competitive sports by the lack of rules and regulations (Collins and Collins 2016). For example, Rinehart (2005, 506) defines action sports as 'activities that either ideologically or practically provide alternatives to mainstream sports and mainstream sport values'. Action sports are often considered to be gender neutral and while they can occur on manufactured surfaces (e.g. indoor Climbing, skateboarding in the street) or constructed spaces (e.g. Skateparks) most are still undertaken in the natural world and retain close cultural and performance relationships with the natural world (Van Bottenburg and Salome 2010. Examples of nature-based action sports include BMX, kite-surfing, surfing, skydiving, parkour and snowboarding (Wheaton 2004; Booth and Thorpe 2007; Thorpe and Ahamed 2015). For the most part participants are assumed to be young, (most often generation Y), alternative, and searching for hedonistic outcomes associated, once again, with risk-taking. Participants are characterized by having a carefree perspective on life while living outside traditional society norms. Effective performance is measured by how successfully participants can develop the skills to chase increasing levels of performance, thrills, fun and risk. The relationship between action sports, the participant and nature has largely been ignored in the literature.

Critics of this perspective, point out that many participants are not generation Y and while initial motivations might include hedonism and risk-taking the importance of these aspects changes over time. For example, skill development and mastery, competition, aesthetics, and the desire to explore the limits of the body have also been associated with effective performance (Booth and Thorpe 2007). Further, research suggests that many action sports might be less dangerous than some traditional sports such as rugby, bicycling and swimming (Thorpe 2016). Equally, action sports have an enormous capacity to bring communities together and facilitate profound personal development (Thorpe 2016). Critics have also pointed out that many elements of action sports are part of traditional sports such as figure skating, gymnastics and diving. Similarly, to other terms above, the importance of the interaction between participants and their environment has barely been mentioned. For some participants, the interaction with the natural world is described as immersive and central to the development of identity and the value of their sport (Atkinson and Young 2008).

'Lifestyle' or alternative sports
Activities typically referred to when discussing lifestyle sports are similar to those discussed as action sports and include skateboarding, windsurfing (and related sports such as kiteboarding), surfing, sailing, alpine skiing, snowboarding, skydiving, and parkour. However, the focus of the lifestyle sports term is socio-cultural. For the most part research on the notion of lifestyle sports has assumed that participation stems from how sports are consumed and the how participants ascribe to particular sub-cultural norms. Often lifestyle sports are delineated by shared practice, dress codes, language and the notion of rebellion. While commercialization has enforced some regulation in recent years, lifestyle sports are often associated with a perceived lack of rules. Participants are often assumed to be childless, young, with high educational attainment, and reasonably affluent. Participation is a manifestation of identity and choice rather than the traditional organized structures associated with competition. From a lifestyle perspective learning is about the development of task-oriented skills for participation but also about how easily and effectively a participant embodies the sub-cultural norms. The natural world is rarely acknowledged even though participation in lifestyle sports is frequently undertaken in nature.

Critiques of this approach point to the myriad opportunities available to the participant and the realization that just because people undertake a sport does not mean that the sport has to be defined in terms of culture (Brymer 2005). Further, many activities have multiple versions, some of which are competitive and organized similarly to mainstream sport. For example, surfing has an international governing body and is now a competitive sport; climbing is now an Olympic sport and parkour has been recognized as a sport with its own governing body and regulation. The lack of an effective understanding of the importance of nature in lifestyle sports has been critiqued especially as the natural world is so important to many participants that they turn to active conservation (Wheaton 2007).

In summary, nature sports span a variety of activities. A traditional theoretical perspective links all these sports together by focusing on risk and risk-taking. Critical voices highlight a number of contradictory elements that reflect the assumptions and narrowness of definitions around the participants and their motivations. Nature sports herald from a variety of backgrounds. While in recent years some nature sports might be competitive for some participants, nature sports are different from traditional sports as they are not exclusively competitive and thus not constrained by predetermined rules, regulations and boundaries. For the most part nature sports involve a relationship with the natural environment with subcultural aspects. Despite these critical voices, the risk emphasis has had a profound influence on the design and provision of learning experiences in nature sports.

Learning in nature sports

Reflecting the traditional, yet criticized, focus on risk designers and facilitators of learning experiences in nature sports typically assume that participants focus on thrills and risk, possibly reflecting the facilitators' own motivation for participation. Consequently, risk management has been emphasized and other potential outcomes ignored (Muller and Cleaver 2000). This risk focus may reflect an increasingly litigious culture and adds to the perceived pressures from the participants. Initial research and social perception, supported by media and product marketing, has identified and perpetuated the association with risk and risk-taking. This infatuation with risk has logically led to, and implicitly justified, a focus on the technical management of risk. Consequently, and justifiably from the risk perspective, training for nature sports facilitators has both explicitly and tacitly prioritized technical risk management above the skills of facilitation. As an example, sixty percent of syllabus content for mountain leader training in the UK relates directly to technical risk management (Collins et al. 2017) with less than twenty percent addressing the facilitation (leadership) of the experience. Equally, one of the most often utilized textsafor developing leading and facilitating skills in an outdoor education context focuses on risk and risk management.

Reflecting the explicit risk management content of facilitator training a second, less obvious, aspect of learning design and facilitation has been an emphasis on the task aspects of nature sports. Implicitly, the performance of the activity is also an aspect of risk management. Notably, the teaching of facilitation skills, especially for novice facilitators, focuses on how to teach task and technical skills in a highly formulaic and rigid manner (e.g. www.britishcanoeing.org.uk/courses/level-1-certificate-in-coaching-paddlesport/#course-content).

A risk-focused emphasis has even led to calls to ban certain activities in some places (Monasterio and Mei-Dan 2008; Brymer and Schweitzer 2017b) and to restrict certain activities from formal learning experiences (Allman and Goldenberg 2012). In the US, National Parks have banned BASE jumping, and institutions such as Pennsylvania State University have banned some nature sport clubs arguing that they are too risky (see, www.bbc.co.uk/news/world-us–canada-43899183). One unfortunate consequence of these bans is that participants of certain sports are left with few places or ways to participate unless they undertake their activity illegally (Allman and Goldenberg 2012). The bans themselves might be contributing to the notions of sub-cultures, possibly causing accidents and even deaths, which in turn leads to the perspective that nature sports are dangerous and risk focused.

Contemporary research is now identifying a broad and more nuanced range of possible motivations and outcomes (Ryan et al. 2010; Woodman et al. 2010; Kerr and Houge Mackenzie 2012; Asfeldt and Hvenegaard 2013; Stott et al. 2015). In recent years scholars focusing on understanding learning design and facilitation in nature sports have pointed out that while the risk-based focus might be appropriate in a learning context for some people some of the time, the need to manage risk in order to optimize the experience for risk seekers and takers is no longer a primary factor. For example, even though the training of mountain leaders is predominantly based on technical risk management, qualified mountain leaders in the UK valued decision making as an aspect of leadership equally to the technical skills associated with risk management (Collins et al. 2017).

Instead, the design and facilitation of nature sports experiences have been described as a risk versus benefit balance (Collins and Collins 2013). From this perspective the poor comprehension of the benefit of a given course of action to the participant has been shown to skew crucial decisions in the learning context. Collins and Collins (2013) argued that perception and management of hazards and the associated risk is highly refined in nature sport facilitators. However, the imbalance between the comprehension of risk and the potential benefits of certain activities and actions in the learning context has contributed to a heuristic bias. In turn, this bias has negatively impacted on the decision making processes that drive the management of learning design and facilitation in nature sports. This does not mean that risk management should be overlooked, instead it should be one part of a broader requirement for those designing and facilitating learning experiences as an aspect of risk and benefit decisions. The broader requirement should not only reflect the critical perspectives of the different types of nature sports highlighted above but also, and perhaps most importantly, the lived experience of nature sport participants.

Participant experiences in nature sports: an overview

Nature sports are varied and diverse (Sibthorp, Paisley, and Gookin 2007; Brymer and Gray 2009; Kerr and Houge Mackenzie 2012; Stott, Zaitseva, and Cui 2012; Asfeldt and Hvenegaard 2013) but the image of the adrenaline junky lingers in the minds of researchers and the general public (Barlow, Woodman, and Hardy 2013; Frühauf et al. 2017). One reason that popular imagination and theoretical explanations have emphasized the risk and risk-taking perspective, at the expense of comprehending the benefits, is that conceptual definitions have stemmed from non-participant perspectives and from testing theories developed for unrelated contexts. For the most part participant experiences have been ignored (Brymer and Schweitzer 2017a). The lack of shared definitions, classifications or understanding among participants, activity facilitators and researchers has led to convoluted discourse. Consequently, discourse linking nature sports to the design and facilitation of learning experiences is both confusing and contradictory.

This oversimplification is challenged by many authors (Kerr and Houge Mackenzie 2012; Asfeldt and Hvenegaard 2013; Stott et al. 2015) who offer nuanced and contemporary perspectives on participation based on the lived experience of participants. For example, Kerr and Houge Mackenzie (2012) present a multidimensional perspective which includes 'pleasurable kinaesthetic bodily sensations from moving in water or air' (656). Additionally, Brymer and Gray's (2009) study of veteran extreme sport participants suggests that rather than trying to conquer the environment, participants describe profound engagement and connection with place, people and environment. A growing literature has also made links between nature sports participation and health and well-being, conservation, personal development and sustainability motivations. Nature sports have been linked with enhanced communitas amongst participants (e.g. Celsi 1992; Sharpe 2005), opportunities to develop courage and humility (Brymer and Oades 2009, freedom to explore fundamental human values (Brymer and Schweitzer 2013), transformational benefits (Brymer and Schweitzer 2013) and profound relationships with nature and other participants (Frühauf et al. 2017).

While individuals seem to seek a variety of seemingly, disparate experiences from their participation in nature sports, we can draw out key common ingredients across different iterations of nature sports. These commonalities can help to refine the conceptual under-standing of these activities and provide guidance for those designing and facilitating learning experiences. A participant centred perspective that takes into account a variety of sports undertaken in natural environments suggest that nature sports encompass a number of ingredients: (1) opportunities to connect with and feel part of nature (which often facilitates desires to protect or give back to nature), (2) opportunities to explore human potential, creativity and meaning, (3) opportunities to collaborate and develop communitas, (4) opportunities to explore mastery and development and (5) opportunities to experience enhanced health and well-being. We use the analogy of ingredients delib-erately as these can be varied to make a range of experiences.

From a learning perspective these ingredients suggest several key notions. Across all types of sports undertaken in natural environments the notion of sporting fields, risk, rules and competition are secondary. Instead, participants emphasize the experience, con-nection and well-being outcomes. From this perspective, learning facilitation and design needs to provide opportunities for participants to relate to the natural world, to explore human potential and relate effectively with others and the specific nature sport culture. The unconstrained environment is an important part of the learning experience. Rather than seeing this as an element to manage, learning designers could exploit this as the unmanaged environment obliges the participant to learn to adapt in order to interact with that environment in a manner that enables the participant to reach their objectives.

The lack of rules and regulations predetermined by a governing body or association also means that performance is most often determined by collaboration with peers and cultural perspectives that stem from within the grassroots of nature sports. This seems to also encourage evolution, creativity and adaptability while placing equal value on skilful performance and exploration of the potential for a given activity (Immonen et al. 2017). Nature sports from this perspective have been identified as ideal mediums for the development of subsidiary aspects such as health, community development and even peace. The nature of the individual's interaction with the physical and social environ-ment reflects the individual's motivation to participate in the activity. From this perspec-tive the learning designer must appreciate that a single size approach does not and cannot fit all participants.

In summary, traditionally there has been a lack of clarity about what defines a nature sport centred around five main issues. Firstly, activities requiring high levels of self-knowl-edge, personal skills, training, commitment, environmental knowledge and task knowl-edge are assumed to be in the same category as activities that require no previous experience or knowledge of the activity or environment. Secondly, the wide range of motives for participation, such as connection with nature, relieving boredom, pushing per-sonal boundaries, overcoming fear, social relationships, pleasurable kinaesthetic bodily sensations, control, mastery and skill, enhancing well-being and goal achievement has been ignored in favour of a risk perspective. Thirdly, sports differ in terms of activity dur-ation and intensity leading to different interaction effects on behaviour. Fourthly, there is an erroneous assumption that nature sports are synonymous with youth sports or sub-cul-tures; in fact, participants represent a broad demographic (Frühauf et al. 2017). Finally, a close look at the history and growth of each sport suggest that rather than being a hom-ogenous group, each has its own unique history, development pattern and focus (Frühauf et al. 2017). A more nuanced understanding of these activities based on the lived experience of participants provides a richer description of nature sports to guide the design and facilitation of learning experiences. By extension, this will enable facilitators to better meet participant needs and improve the quality of provision.

Facilitating learning in nature sports?

Ewert et al. (2013) suggested that it is incumbent upon adventure recreation providers to offer a range of adventure activities that allow for a complex and diverse set of motivational factors beyond just challenge and risk-taking. This advice seems to be relevant for nature sports more broadly. Clearly, this may be achieved by offering a full range of potential experiences to clients via carefully designed programmes or experiences. Effective facilitation in nature sports might also require a design that contains all ingredients in one activity or experience depending on individual requirements in the group. As such, learning designers and facilitators need to be capable of providing a variety of programmes and experiences within each programme that will help each learner develop in a manner that suits their needs. From this latter perspective, adaptable and flexible learning designers and facilitators are required. Delivery should be refined by facilitators skilled in meeting the diverse needs and motivations of participants.

A one-size-fits-all approach to facilitation and learning design that focuses on managing risk or assumes that participants take part for thrills and excitement is too simplistic (Brymer and Renshaw 2010). For example, an emphasis on task-relevant characteristics of nature sports, such as teaching new participants how to manage risks or how to undertake and implement particular technical skills, might be appropriate for some people some of the time but may fail to capitalize on opportunities for immersion or personal development for others. A one-size-fits all approach that assumes participants are a homogenous group of risk-takers from a single background can potentially result in the creation of barriers to learning for many potential participants (Brymer 2010b; Brymer and Renshaw 2010; Brymer and Davids 2013). Instead, the facilitator needs to develop adaptability and flexibility underpinned by nuanced judgement and decision making processes (Collins and Collins 2015a, 2016) that are dependent on an awareness of individual differences, situational demands (e.g. physical environment, the participants emotional state) (Collins and Collins 2015b, 2016; Aaland, Vikene, Varley & Moe, 2017), and the culture associated with participation in the activity.

The participant's relationship with the physical environment is central to the nature sport experience. Notions of immersion in nature, valuing nature, spirituality, and nature facilitating opportunities for identity development sit alongside desires to conserve and protect nature. Exploiting this relationship requires a recognition of it and the provision of opportunities for participants to realize multifaceted outcomes. Participants and facilitators need to understand salient aspects of the specific performance environment well enough to effectively achieve seemingly disparate goals such as recreation and health, for instance. The facilitator might need to design learning experiences that provide opportunities for interactions with environments that facilitate multi-goals within one group. The capacity to recognize individual characteristics, personal goals and opportunities within environments that facilitate those opportunities is important.

Research focusing on cultural intelligence (CI) highlights its significance as a factor in effective leadership and coaching. It appears logical that the facilitator of nature sports experiences would need a cultural sensitivity that reflects the individual participant, the group and the particular nature sport. Consideration of such influences appears pertinent given the culture within nature sports to place a value on seeking out latent potential (e.g. Zelenski and Nisbet 2012; Ewert et al. 2013; Wiersma 2014; Frühauf et al. 2017; Howlett 2017). Given such diversity and the limitations of a single approach (Collins, Wilmot, and Collins 2016), identification of the need for an equally diverse range of approaches to facilitation seems apt. The need for cultural sensitivity and alignment is demonstrated by Ojala and Thorpe (2015) who identified that some nature sports participants reject formal highly structured facilitation. While it would be an oversimplification to say all participants reject formal approaches to the design and facilitation of learning (Collins, Wilmot, and Collins 2016), this does support a need for breadth and range in facilitation skills.

Demonstrating cultural sensitivity that reflects the etiquette and norms of a particular nature sport culture appears imperative. For instance, participants of nature sports are increasingly being shown to integrate reflection into their practice as a way of learning (Frühauf et al. 2017; Howlett 2017). Other studies have identified informal collaborative developmental processes in action sports (Howlett 2017). Such informal collaborative interaction is also observable in adventure sports. Collaboration and reflection within a community of practice appear to exploit a social aspect to nature sports that many authors have identified (Zelenski and Nisbet 2012; Ewert et al. 2013; Wiersma 2014; Frühauf et al. 2017; Howlett 2017). Within these groups, social media and technology form part of informal facilitation and development (Stozkowski and Collins 2012; Howlett 2017). It seems logical that an effective facilitator of nature sports experiences will utilize teaching approaches that draw on the reflective and collaborative aspects that are inherent in the culture of these sports.

Arguably, the most important facilitators are those that introduce nature sports to relative novices. Often this is done by the least experienced facilitators who rely on certified training courses to gain qualifications that allow them to work with groups and individuals. If these courses provide a one-size-fits all approach based on a risk-taking perspective, then naïve soon-to-be facilitators will most likely follow the same route and perpetuate a risk-centric single approach. Courses that focus on teaching facilitators how to help others acquire technical skills or manage risk are in danger of assuming that nature sports participants are a homogenous group intent on risk and risk-taking. Instead, courses that aim to provide learning for facilitators need to focus on providing experiences and environments that develop a well-rounded, adaptable workforce capable of interpreting environmental information and individual requirements in a manner that encourages a relationship between the learner and the environment. Such highly individualized approaches place the participant at the centre of the process. Such approaches are, however, time consuming and dependant on facilitators that demonstrate a reflective and metacognitive capacity in addition to technical skills (Collins, Carson, and Collins 2016).

Such an approach may have several advantages for the designer, facilitator, and participant. Firstly, the facilitator would be capable of working to deliver a greater range of nature sports experiences. Secondly, a more diverse range of participants can therefore have nature sports experiences. Thirdly, aspects of such training can be designed across several activities, and as such, reduce training repetition across the industry. Fourthly, there would be an improvement in effectiveness and quality of provision.

From this perspective, those studying how best to develop new facilitators might be interested in exploring concepts such as what type of environmental information is relevant for what type of person with what type of goals. Equally, researchers might be interested in exploring how facilitators help learners identify environmental and cultural information.

Clearly, evaluation of the facilitator's capacity to fulfil this new diverse and complex role poses some challenges to the designer and facilitator of learning experiences. As highlighted earlier, assessment of a nature sports facilitator has prioritized and focused on technical skills to manage security. Such assessment can be competency based because the technical skills to assure safety are absolute (black and white), and we would not disagree. Our argument is that the facilitator's role must be beyond just risk management if the full range of participant motivations are to be met and that the assessment of potential leaders should reflect the expertise required (see, Collins et al. 2015). A mixed assessment, in which competencies and expertise are evaluated seems more appropriate. Sophisticated roles that require judgment skills would represent a greater proportion of an expertise evaluation.

Conclusion

Nature sports are a broad array of activities that have historically been associated with risk. Research increasingly recognizes that participants are not driven by risk alone but via a range of sophisticated and nuanced factors. In the past, the training of facilitators of nature sport clearly reflected the emphasis on risk and the demands and perceptions of the activity. In this paper, we argue that the comprehension of nature sports has developed and as a result there is a recognition that the nature sports facilitators' role requires a broad range of skills beyond the technical aspects of the activity. The requirements, training and assessment of the nature sports facilitators should reflect a broader set of practical skills and leadership needs. These processes and outcomes, in turn, require adaptable and flexible facilitators, as 'adaptive' experts (Hatano and Inagaki 1986; Tozer, Fazey, and Fazey 2007) with the skills and breadth of focus to respond to the highly diverse demands of participants.

Disclosure statement

No potential conflict of interest was reported by the authors.

ORCID

Loel Collins ⓘ http://orcid.org/0000-0002-7478-1140
Eric Brymer ⓘ http://orcid.org/0000-0003-0274-1016

References

Aaland, E., O. L. Vikene, P. Varley, and V. F. Moe. 2017. "Situation Awareness in Sea Kayaking: Towards a Practical Checklist." *Journal of Adventure Education and Outdoor Learning* 1 (3): 203–215. doi:10. 1080/14729679.2017.1313169.

Allman, T. L., and M. Goldenberg. 2012. "Should Extreme Sports, Such as BASE Jumping and Other High Risk Sports, be Included in Adventure Programming?" In *Controversial Issues in Adventure Programming*, edited by Bruce Martin and Mark Wagstaff, 165–183. Champaign, IL: Human Kinetics.

Asfeldt, M., and G. Hvenegaard. 2013. "Perceived Learning, Critical Elements and Lasting Impacts on University-based Wilderness Educational Expeditions." *Journal of Adventure Education and Outdoor Learning* 14 (2): 132–152. doi:10.1080/14729679.2013.789350.

Atkinson, M., and K. Young. 2008. *Tribal Play: Subcultural Journeys Through Sport*. London: Emerald.

Barlow, M., T. Woodman, and L. Hardy. 2013. "Great Expectations: Different High-risk Activities Satisfy Different Motives." *Journal of Personality and Social Psychology* 105 (3): 458–475.

Booth, D., and H. Thorpe. 2007. "The Meaning of Extreme." In *The Berkshire Encyclopaedia of Extreme Sports*, edited by D. Booth and H. Thorpe, 181–197. Great Barrington: Berkshire.

Brown, H. 2000. "Passengers, Participants, Partners and Practitioners. Working with Risk to Empower Groups." *Horizon* 12: 37–39.

Brymer, E. 2005. "Extreme Dude! A Phenomenological Perspective on the Extreme Sport Experience." PhD thesis, University of Wollongong. https://ro.uow.edu.au/cgi/viewcontent.cgi?referer; https:// www.google.co.uk/&httpsredir=1&article = 1379&context=theses.

Brymer, E. 2009. "Extreme Sports as a Facilitator of Ecocentricity and Positive Life Changes." *World Leisure Journal* 51 (1): 47–53.

Brymer, E. 2010a. "Risk and Extreme Sports: A Phenomenological Perspective." *Annals of Leisure Research* 13 (1–2): 218–239.

Brymer, E. 2010b. "Skill Development in Canoeing and Kayaking: An Individualised Approach." In *Motor Learning in Practice: A Constraints-led Approach*, edited by I. Renshaw, K. Davids, and G. Savelsbergh, 152–160. London: Routledge.

Brymer, E., and K. Davids. 2013. "Ecological Dynamics as a Theoretical Framework for Development of Sustainable Behaviours Towards the Environment." *Environmental Education Research* 19 (1): 45–63. doi:10.1080/13504622.2012.677416.

Brymer, E., G. Downey, and T. Gray. 2009. "Extreme Sports as a Precursor to Environmental Sustainability." *Journal of Sport & Tourism* 14 (2–3): 193–204.

Brymer, E., and T. Gray. 2009. "Dancing with Nature: Rhythm and Harmony in Extreme Sport Participation." *Journal of Adventure Education and Outdoor Learning* 9 (2): 135–149. doi:10.1080/ 14729670903116912.

Brymer, E., and T. Gray. 2010. "Developing an Intimate "Relationship" with Nature Through Extreme Sports Participation." *Leisure/Loisir* 34 (4): 361–374.

Brymer, E., and L. Oades. 2009. "Extreme Sports: A Positive Transformation in Courage and Humility." *Journal of Humanistic Psychology* 49 (1): 114–126. doi:10.1177/0022167808326199.

Brymer, E., and I. Renshaw. 2010. "An Introduction to the Constraints-led Approach to Learning in Outdoor Education." *Australian Journal of Outdoor Education* 14 (2): 33–41.

Brymer, E., and R. Schweitzer. 2013. "Extreme Sports are Good for Your Health: A Phenomenological Understanding of Fear and Anxiety in Extreme Sport." *Journal of Health Psychology* 18 (4): 477–487.

Brymer, E., and R. Schweitzer. 2017a. *Phenomenology and the Extreme Sports Experience*. London: Routledge.

Brymer, E., and R. D. Schweitzer. 2017b. "Evoking the Ineffable: The Phenomenology of Extreme Sports." *Psychology of Consciousness: Theory, Research, and Practice* 4 (1): 63–74.

Celsi, R. L. 1992. "Transcendent Benefits of High-risk Sports." In *NA – Advances in Consumer Research Volume 19*, edited by John F. Sherry, Jr. and Brian Sternthal, 636–641. Provo, UT: Association for Consumer Research.

Christian, E., M. Berry, and P. Kearney. 2017. "The Identity, Epistemology and Developmental Experiences of High-level Adventure Sports Coaches." doi:10.1080/14729679.2017.1341326.

Cloke, P., and H. C. Perkins. 2002. "Commodification and Adventure in New Zealand Tourism." *Current Issues in Tourism* 5: 521–549.

Collins, D., V. Burke, A. Martindale, and A. Cruickshank. 2015a. "The Illusion of Competency Versus the Desirability of Expertise: Seeking a Common Standard for Support Professions in Sport." *Sports Medicine* 45: 1–7. doi:10.1007/s40279-014-0251-1.

Collins, L., H. J. Carson, P. Amos, and D. Collins. 2017. "Examining the Perceived Value of Professional Judgment and Decision Making in Mountain Leaders in the UK: A Mixed-methods Investigation." *Journal of Adventure Education and Outdoor Learning*. doi:10.1080/14729679.2017.1378584.

Collins, L., H. J. Carson, and D. Collins. 2016. "Metacognition and Professional Judgment and Decision Making: Importance, Application and Evaluation." *International Sport Coaching Journal*. doi:10.1123/iscj.2016-0037.

Collins, L., and D. Collins. 2013. "Decision Making and Risk Management in Adventure Sports Coaching." *Quest* 65 (1): 72–82. doi:10.1080/00336297.2012.727373.

Collins, L., and D. Collins. 2015a. "Integration of Professional Judgement and Decision-making in High-level Adventure Sports Coaching Practice." *Journal of Sports Sciences* 33 (6): 622–633. doi:10.1080/02640414.2014.953980.

Collins, L., and D. Collins. 2015b. "Professional Judgement and Decision-making in Adventure Sports Coaching: The Role of Interaction." *Journal of Sports Sciences* (1–12). doi:10.1080/02640414.2014.953980.

Collins, L., and D. Collins. 2016. "Challenges in Adventures Sports Coaching." In *Routledge International Handbook of Outdoor Studies*. doi:10.4324/9781315768465.ch44.

Collins, L., D. Collins, and D. Grecic. 2015. "The Epistemological Chain in High Level Adventure Sports Coaches." *Journal of Adventure Education and Outdoor Learning*. doi:10.1080/14729679.2014.950592.

Collins, D., T. Wilmot, and L. Collins. 2016. "Over Egging the Pudding? Comments on Ojala and Thorpe." *International Sports Coaching Journal*. doi:10.1123/iscj.2015-0068.

Crum, B. J. 1991. "'Sportification' of Society and Internal Sports Differentiation." *Spelen Sport* 1: 2–7.

Ewert, A., K. Gilbertson, Y. Luo, and A. Voight. 2013. "Beyond "Because It's There": Motivations for Pursuing Adventure Recreational Activities." *Journal of Leisure Research* 44: 91–111.

Frühauf, A., W. Hardy, D. Pfoestl, F. G. Hoellen, and M. Kopp. 2017. "A Qualitative Approach on Motives and Aspects of Risks in Freeriding." *Frontiers in Psychology* 8: 1998. doi:10.3389/fpsyg.2017.01998netics.

Hatano, G., and K. Inagaki. 1986. "Two Courses of Expertise." In *Children Development and Education in Japan*, edited by H. Stevenson, H. Azuma, and K. Hakuta, 262–272. New York: Freeman.

Howlett, T. 2017. "Symbiotic Learning Partnerships in Youth Action Sports: Vibing, Rhythm, and Analytic Cycles Convergence." *The International Journal of Research into New Media Technologies*. doi:10.22318/cscl2017.88.

Immonen, T., E. Brymer, D. Orth, K. Davids, F. Felletti, J. Liukkonen, and T. Jaakkola. 2017. "Understanding Action and Adventure Sports Participation – An Ecological Dynamics Perspective." *Sports Medicine – Open*. doi:10.1186/s40798-017-0084-1.

Kerr, J. H., and S. Houge Mackenzie. 2012. "Multiple Motives for Participating in Adventure Sports." *Psychology of Sport and Exercise* 13 (5): 649–657. doi:10.1016/j.psychsport.2012.04.002.

Krien, K. J. 2014. "Nature Sports." *Journal of Philosophy in Sport* 41 (2): 193–208. doi:10.1080/00948705.2013.785417.

Loynes, C. 1998. "Adventure in a Bun." *Journal of Experiential Education* 21 (1): 35–39.

Melo, R., and R. Gomes. 2017. "A Sociocultural Approach to Understanding the Development of Nature Sports." In *Sport Tourism: New Challenges in a Globalized World*, edited by R. Melo and C. Sobry, 47–76. Newcastle: Cambridge Scholars Publishing.

Monasterio, E., and E. Brymer. 2015. "Mountaineering Personality and Risk." In *Mountaineering Tourism*, edited by G. Musa, J. Higham, and A. Thompson-Carr, 198–210. Abingdon: Routledge.

Monasterio, E., and O. Mei-Dan. 2008. "Risk and Severity of Injury in a Population of BASE Jumpers." *New Zealand Medical Journal* 121 (1277): 70–75.

Muller, T., and M. Cleaver. 2000. "Targeting the CANZUS Baby Boomer Explorer and Adventurer Segments." *Journal of Vacation Marketing* 6 (2): 154–169.

Ojala, A. L., and H. Thorpe. 2015. "The Role of the Coach in Action Sports: Using a Problem-based Learning Approach." *International Sport Coaching Journal* 2: 64–71. doi:10.1123/ iscj.2014-0096.

Pain, M. T. G., and M. A. Pain. 2005. "Essay: Risk Taking in Sport." *The Lancet* 366 (1): S33–S34.

Peacock, S., E. Brymer, K. Davids, and M. Dillon. 2017. "An Ecological Dynamics Perspective on Adventure Tourism." *Tourism Review International* 21 (3): 307–316.

Perdomo, Y. 2013. "Global Report on Adventure Tourism." doi:10.1017/CBO9781107415324.004.

Rinehart, R. 2005. "'BABES' & BOARDS: Opportunities in New Millennium Sport?" *Journal of Sport & Social Issues* 29: 232–255. doi:10.1177/0193723505277909.

Rossi, B., and L. Cereatti. 1993. "The Sensation Seeking in Mountain Athletes as Assessed by Zuckerman's Sensation Seeking Scale." *International Journal of Sport Psychology* 24: 417–431.

Ryan, R. M., N. Weinstein, J. Bernstein, K. W. Brown, L. Mistretta, and M. Gagné. 2010. "Vitalizing Effects of Being Outdoors and in Nature." *Journal of Environmental Psychology* 30: 159–168. doi:10.1016/j.jenvp.2009.10.009.

Self, D. R., E. D. V. Henry, C. S. Findley, and E. Reilly. 2007. "Thrill Seeking: The Type T Personality and Extreme Sports." *International Journal of Sport Management and Marketing* 2 (1–2): 175. doi:10.1504/IJSMM.2007.011397.

Sharma-Brymer, V., T. Gray, and E. Brymer. 2017. "Sport Participation to Create a Deeper Environmental Identity with Pro-environmental Behaviors." In *Routledge Handbook on Sport, Sustainability and the Environment*, edited by B. P. McCullough and T. B. Kellison, 330–339. New York: Routledge.

Sharpe, E. K. 2005. "Delivering Communities: Wilderness Adventure and the Making of Community." *Journal of Leisure Research* 37 (3): 255–280.

Sibthorp, J., K. Paisley, and J. Gookin. 2007. "Exploring Participant Development Through Adventure-based Programming: A Model From the National Outdoor Leadership School." *Leisure Sciences* 29 (1): 1–18. doi:10.1080/01490400600851346.

Slanger, E., and K. E. Rudestam. 1997. "Motivation and Disinhibition in High Risk Sports: Sensation Seeking and Self-efficacy." *Journal of Research in Personality* 31: 355–374.

Stott, T., P. Allison, J. Felter, and S. Beames. 2015. "Personal Development on Youth Expeditions: A Literature Review and Thematic Analysis." *Leisure Studies* 34 (2): 197–229. doi:10.1080/02614367.2013.841744.

Stott, T., E. Zaitseva, and V. Cui. 2012. "Stepping Back to Move Forward? Exploring Outdoor Education Students' Fresher and Graduate Identities and Their Impact on Employment Destinations." *Studies in Higher Education*: 1–23. doi:10.1080/03075079.2012.743116.

Stozkowski, J., and D. Collins. 2012. "Communities of Practice, Social Learning and Networks: Exploiting the Social Side of Coach Development." *Sport, Education and Society* 6: 773–788.

Thorpe, H. 2016. "Action Sports for Youth Development: Critical Insights for the SDP Community." *International Journal of Sports Policy and Politics* 8: 91–116.

Thorpe, H., and N. Ahamed. 2015. "Youth Action Sports and Political Agency in the Middle East: Lesson from a Grassroots Parkour Group Gaza." *International Review for the Sociology of Sport*. doi:19.1177/1012690213490521.

Tozer, M., I. Fazey, and J. Fazey. 2007. "Recognizing and Developing Adaptive Expertise Within Outdoor and Expedition Leaders." *Journal of Adventure Education and Outdoor Learning* 7 (1): 55–75. doi:10.1080/14729670701349780.

Valkonen, J., H. Huilaja, and S. Koikkalainen. 2013. "Looking for the Right Kind of Person: Recruitment in Nature Tourism Guiding Scandinavian." *Journal of Hospitality and Tourism* 3: 228–241.

Van Bottenburg, M., and L. Salome. 2010. "The Indoorisation of Outdoor Sports: An Exploration of the Rise of Lifestyle Sports in Artificial Settings." *Leisure Studies* 29 (2): 143–160. doi:10.1080/02614360903261479.

Varley, P. 2006. "Confecting Adventure and Playing with Meaning: The Adventure Commodification Continuum." *Journal of Sport and Tourism* 11 (2): 173–194. doi:10.1080/14775080601155217.

Wheaton, B. 2004. *Understanding Lifestyle Sports: Consumption, Identity and Difference*. London: Routledge.

Wheaton, B. 2007. "Identity, Politics, and the Beach: Environmental Activism in Surfers Against Sewage." *Leisure Studies* 26 (3): 279–302. doi:10.1080/02614360601053533.

Wiersma, L. D. 2014. "A Phenomenological Investigation of the Psychology of Big-wave Surfing at Maverick's Volume." *The Sport Psychologist* 28: 151–163.

Woodman, T., L. Hardy, M. Barlow, and C. Le Scanff. 2010. "Motives for Participation in Prolonged Engagement High-risk Sports. An Agentic Emotion Regulation Perspective." *Psychology of Sport and Exercise* 11: 345–352. doi:10.1016/j.psychsport.2010.04.002.

Zelenski, J. M., and E. K. Nisbet. 2012. "Happiness and Feeling Connected: The Distinct Role of Nature Relatedness." *Environment and Behavior* 46 (1): 3–23. doi:10.1177/0013916512451901.

Part II

Nature Sports: Development, Impact and Issues

Nature sports: current trends and the path ahead

Ricardo Melo, Derek Van Rheenen and Sean Gammon

Introduction

In the editorial (part one) of this special issue about nature sports (Melo, Van Rheenen, and Gammon 2019), we presented the main characteristics of nature sports and the connections between its related activities and other sectors, such as leisure, tourism, the environment, health and education. By providing an extensive review of the literature, we mapped out the numerous terms connected to nature sports in order to assemble them within a single unifying concept.

Moving on from the definitional and conceptual complexities of the term, the second part of the editorial will explore the developmental trends of nature sports – both in participation and scholarship. Furthermore, we will discuss the changing demographic taking place in nature sports involvement and participation, and reflect on how a more socially encompassing market may impact how these sports are managed and experienced.

The growth of nature sports

Evolving in a unique historical conjuncture, especially associated with global communication, corporate sponsorship and transnational entertainment industries, nature sports have experienced an exceptional growth, both in participation and their increased visibility across public and private space (Wheaton 2013). Since their emergence in the 1960s, these new forms of sport spread around the world much faster than most traditional sports (Wheaton 2016). The visibility of nature sports has been enhanced by media, through TV shows and broadcasts, specialist magazines, films and internet-based sites (Wheaton 2013). The most prominent examples are ESPN's X Games, which commanded a global audience of 50 million in 2003 (Wheaton 2013) and the movie 'Free Solo', winner of the 2019 Academy Awards for Best Documentary Feature. This is not to suggest that the origins of many nature sports, such as mountaineering and orienteering, did not evolve much earlier (Reinhart, part two of this special issue). Rather, it is only to highlight that current popularity figures have been fuelled by more recent cultural and technological developments.

The growth and development of some nature sports activities has led to a process of sportivisation (Aubel, Hoibian, and Defrance 2002; Suchet 2011), resulting in the incorporation of these activities into the Summer and Winter Olympic Games. Examples include sailing (since the first modern Olympic Games in Athens in 1896), skiing (since the first Winter Olympic Games in Chamonix in 1924), windsurfing (since the Los Angeles Olympic Games in 1984), mountain bike racing (since the Atlanta Olympic Games in 1996), snowboarding (since Nagano Winter Olympic Games in 1998), surfing (scheduled for the Tokyo Olympic Games in 2020), and rock-climbing (scheduled for the Tokyo Olympic Games in 2020).

The mediatization of some of these nature sports has helped to create global celebrities such as Shaun White (snowboarder), Kelly Slater (surfer), and, more recently, Alex Honnold (rock-climber) 'who, like other sport celebrities, transcend their subcultures and inhabit and apprise national and international space' (Wheaton 2013, 3).

Wheaton (2013) provides examples of the ever-expanding and diversifying ways in which consumers experience nature sports today, such as

> those who play video games, buy clothing and accessories, and devour the vast array of media products (from social media and internet based products to more traditional forms, such as DVDs, films and television shows) and experience activities through adventure tourism or as spectators. (3)

In short, like many other leisure pursuits, nature sports are now a multi-platform experience that helps support, sustain, and build worldwide markets.

A global phenomenon

The increased cultural visibility of nature sports has attracted a significant number of participants from all geographies (Rinehart and Sydnor 2003; Wheaton 2004, 2013). While the informal and itinerant structure of nature sports makes it hard to accurately measure participation levels (Melo 2013; Gomes et al. 2017), several examples demonstrate that the growth of nature sports participation has been consistent and widespread around the globe, outpacing the increase of most traditional sports in many Western nations (Wheaton 2013; Brymer and Schweitzer 2017).

In 1996, snowboarding was the fastest growing sport in the United States, with over 3.7 million participants (Howe 1998). By 2002, it was estimated that approximately 86 million individuals had taken up some sort of nature sports (Ostrowski 2002). In 2003, approximately 30 percent of all sporting goods sold in the USA, equating to a US$14 billion market, were nature sports-related (Liberman 2004). More recently, the *Outdoor Recreation Participation Report* (The Outdoor Foundation 2018) shows that 146.1 million (almost half of) Americans ages 6 and over participated in an outdoor activity at least once in 2017, a slight increase from 48.8% of the US population in 2016–49.0% in 2017. This continues three years of growth in outdoor participation.

In England, the *Getting Active Outdoors* study (Sports England and Outdoor Industries Association 2015) points to the increasing popularity of nature sports participation, highlighting that a total of 8.96 million citizens are active outdoors. 2.5 million (28%) of these are regularly active (once per week or more), and approximately 70% (1.7 million) of regular participants are engaged in nature 'adventure sports'. Moreover, the study by

Sports England (2015) stated that: (i) the British Mountaineering Council reported an overall 2% increase in membership (although club membership declined) in 2013, climbing competitions increased (18% increase from 2012 to 2013), as did social media and online traffic; (ii) Snowsport England had a 12% increase on domestic slopes for the period February to April 2013–2014 and an 11% increase for the period May to August 2013–2014; (iii) the Mountain Training Association has grown 15% in the last 12 months, demonstrating an example of the growth in independent niche providers; (iv) market research suggests that the outdoor activity industry continues to expand, demonstrated in recent years by the growth in outdoor activity tourism and the increase in the number of outdoor mass participation events (e.g. Great North Run, cycling challenges, and open water swimming challenges). There has likewise been an increase in the number of climbing walls (30% increase from 2010 to 2014) and total number of climbing wall visitors; (v) revenue sales across the outdoor commercial sector has grown in recent years. Indicators from commercial sales of equipment suggest outdoor sports enjoyed a 3% rise in 2014, while over 2013 and 2014 there has been a 39% increase in canoe and kayak sales.

In France, the Ministry of Health, Youth and Sports (MSJS 2015) reported in 2010 that 25 million of its citizens participated in some sort of nature sports. In 2014, more than 2.4 million licenses were issued by sports federations in the field of nature sports (unisport and multisport estimation), a growth trend over the past several years. Also in 2014, nearly thirty thousand (28,012) nature sports clubs were registered with national sports federations, corresponding to 23% of the total number of sports clubs. In addition, nearly 75,000 facilities, spaces and sites related to nature sports were identified (23% of the total number). Finally, one-third of all sporting events in France are estimated to involve nature sports activities.

In Portugal, similar indicators reflect an increasing number of participants and the sector's growth (Melo 2013). These indicators include: (i) higher participation rates of informal participants, which indicate a growing independence and autonomy in participation; (ii) greater participation of young people who begin to practice these activities at an earlier age, influenced by the integration of these activities in the curricula of primary and secondary education; (iii) women's increasing participation, particularly in younger age groups; (iv) diversified supply, offering different sport participation opportunities, ranging from more formal activities under the federative model (e.g. canoeing sports clubs, oriented for competition), to the more informal structures (e.g. mountain biking clubs oriented towards recreational practices), depending on the different motivations of the participants; (v) growth of a specialized market, targeted towards education and training of the participants, as in the case of most surf clubs; (vi) increases in the number of formal or organized sport events, such as orienteering federative competitions, but also informal events, such as mountain biking events organized by participants' clubs and associations; (vii) creation of new spaces for practice, such as networks of walking paths, nautical centres and centres of surfing high performance; (viii) creation of a positive image in the territories associated with mediatic sport events such as the case of Peniche from the surf world championship or Nazaré from the largest wave surfed (by Garrett McNamara); and (ix) growth tendency of the sector pointed to by the leaders of the nature sports organizations (Melo 2013).

This is not only a Western trend. There has been considerable growth in nature sport participation in other regions of the world (Brymer and Schweitzer 2017). Examples that reflect the penetration of nature sports in other geographies include, in 2016, approximately 130 million people engaged in nature sports activities in China. Also, Iran Surfing Federation became the 100th member of the International Surf Association (Brymer and Schweitzer 2017).

Nature sports participation: a shifting demographic

The rapid expansion of nature sports has been accompanied by a cultural fragmentation that supports a new profile of participation (Wheaton 2013). Initially, nature sports activities were predominantly practiced by young, educated males with highly qualified jobs and, consequently, high income levels (Dolnicar and Fluker 2003a; Barbieri and Sotomayor 2013; Portugal et al. 2017; Melo and Gomes 2017b) and high social capital (Pociello 1981). Today, the nature sports industry has witnessed a demographic shift as participation rates across the generations have grown (Brymer and Schweitzer 2017), thereby creating new and profitable niche markets that include not only teenage boys but also girls, women, men and an aging population, who have a broad range of interests and experiences (Wheaton 2016; Brymer and Schweitzer 2017). As Wheaton (2013) has stated:

> They range from occasional participants, perhaps taking part via the array of 'taster' activities being marketed through the adventure sport and travel industries, to the 'hard-core' committed practitioners who are fully familiarised to the lifestyle, argot, fashion and technical skill of their activity(ies), and spend considerable time, energy and often money doing it. (Wheaton 2013, 4)

Examples of this fragmentation in participation are given in the studies of Buckley (2018, part one of this special issue) about the transition of nature sports with trajectories of aging, and Hickman et al. (2018) about older adult participation in climbing and sea kayaking, giving expression to what Brymer and Schweitzer (2017) have stated about baby boomers who are enthusiastic participants of nature sports more generally.

The work of Kerr and Houge Mackenzie (part two of this special issue) demonstrates the significant opportunities for women to participate in nature sports on an equal footing with men, as previously suggested by Brymer and Schweitzer (2017). Statistical figures (Jarvie 2006; Comer 2010) support what Wheaton (2016) has claimed, that there has been a boom in women's and girls' interest in nature sports, including sports like surfing, previously seen as a bastion of hegemonic masculinity.

This growth and diversification of nature sports participation is linked to the technological evolution, which has allowed a greater fragmentation, development, differentiation and specialization within the many practices subsumed within nature sport activities. The materials and equipment are, in most cases, indispensable for the realization of participation, serving to mediate the relationship between the individual and the environment. This process of mediation allows for the transformation of nature's energy, such as wind speed (paragliding), the force of waves (surfboard), and the height or slope of the terrain (snowboard). The materials and equipment also help to promote safety (climbing ropes) and/or protection from meteorological agents (clothing for rain or snow). When analyzing these technological advances, there is a growing tendency towards the development of new materials and equipment to provide increasing individual adaptability, a greater ease of auto transport, and a greater personalization of nature sports activities (Melo 2013).

The diffusion of nature sports activities in society has been pointed out by Bessy and Naria (2005) as a series of historical phenomena: (i) manufacturers indicate that the revenue of sporting goods sales, positioned in the outdoor segment, has witnessed steady progression from 15% to 20% per year; (ii) there has likewise been an increase in the planning of numerous natural sites (routes, climbing routes, take-off and landing areas, etc.) and innovative sports equipment, such as surfing stations and artificial water multi-leisure parks; (iii) finally, there has been a multiplication of a new generation of sports events with a participative vocation (raids, challenges, adventure races, etc.). The growing number of commercial service providers associated with nature sports (e.g. the nature sport tourism sector), as evidenced in France (Corneloup and Bourdeau 2004) and Portugal (Gomes et al. 2017; Melo and Gomes 2017c).

In addition, the diversification of the nature sport market has in no small way been driven by global concerns over environmental and ecological sustainability (Mallen and Chard 2011). As detailed in part one of the editorial, a key motive for those participating in nature sports is a desire to get closer to the environment. However, sport-related interaction with the environment has the potential to damage it, an outcome that generates considerable disquiet among participants. Such anxieties have resulted in a call for more sensitive management approaches to particularly vulnerable sites, such as zoning and access-reduction initiatives (Bailey and Hungenberg 2018; Mach et al. 2018, part two of the special issue; Hutson and Howard 2015).

Increased diversification can also cause intra- and inter-generational conflict over how the environment should be used and managed. Whilst disagreement can often be resolved through cross-educational dialogue (King and Church 2019, part two of this special issue), we must be mindful that nature sport's sites will continue to raise disputes as participation numbers grow.

The following section highlights the contributions made for this second part of the special issue and, in this regard, we would like to thank the authors for their contributions that offer conceptual and empirical heft to the field of research on nature sports.

Volume two contributions

The second part of this special issue focuses on the benefits and outcomes of nature sport participation through selected case studies. For example, this collection of papers highlights the meaningful and challenging experiences of participants across numerous activities, ranging from surfing, mountain climbing, ultramarathon running and BASE jumping. These contributions address concerns of environmental impact and the need for an integrated approach to resource management and stakeholder engagement within the growing nature sport industry.

The first paper in the second part of this special issue follows the emergence, development and eventual politicization of rock climbing in the region of Saxon Switzerland. Kai Reinhart explains how in the nineteenth century Saxon Switzerland became one of the birth places of modern climbing. By 1911, the many clubs operating in the region founded the Saxon Mountaineering Federation, which adhered to the strong ethical traditions integral to free climbing. However, after the Second World War the region became part of the newly formed German Democratic Republic. The new socialist regime viewed climbing as a sport that prepared individuals as productive members of society. This led to much conflict with the climbers who saw climbing as an activity that transcended sport, viewing it as a pastime that represented freedom, friendship and adventure.

Andrew W. Bailey and Eric Hungenberg's paper draws attention to the complexities of economic impact assessment inherent in natural environments. Their study focuses on determining the economic stimulus that visiting climbers bring to the city of Chattanooga in Tennessee. As with many commodified natural environments across the world, the authors highlight the importance of maintaining a balance between the much needed income that active sport tourists bring to the area and the potential environmental damage that such activities can bring. The study finds that continued successful management of the natural adventure sites are largely dependent upon the involvement of a range of stakeholders from both inside and outside the region.

The paper by Leon Mach, Jess Ponting, James Brown and Jessica Savage discusses the impact of intra-seasonal demand upon natural environments, focussing primarily on surf tourism. The authors point out that whilst broad climatic factors undoubtedly influence travel to specific sites, it is the intra-seasonal demand, (predominantly influenced by domestic forecasts) which can accentuate the negative consequences surf-related crowding can cause. As a result, the paper recommends that destinations should consider utilizing the surfing forecasts in order to better prepare, and so benefit from, a sudden increase in visitor numbers.

The fourth paper of this special issue highlights the complex conflicts that arise between young mountain bikers and site managers. Katherine King and Andrew Church shed light on the importance of freedom and autonomy in young mountain biker's site choices and behaviours – and how such conduct is perceived and managed by those responsible for these leisure spaces. The authors recommend that a positive and inclusive dialogue be sought between both parties that encourages collective decision making, as well as opportunities for young people to learn trail building and design skills.

The paper by John H. Kerr and Susan Houge Mackenzie delves into the experiences of a veteran BASE jumper. Taking a case-study design of researching just one individual (a refreshing approach, that is underutilized) the study reveals that whilst such an activity is perceived as being high risk, the numerous psychological and emotion benefits help assuage any potential dangers. Furthermore, these positive experiences help the individual to cope palliatively with negative life events outside the sport. The key respondent in the research makes it clear that BASE jumping, for them, is not about having a death wish – but is more about life affirmation and celebration.

In the final paper of this special issue, Jim Cherrington, Jack Black and Nicholas Tiller adopt a collaborative auto-ethnographic approach to gain insights into the complex and dynamic experiences of an ultramarathon runner. The authors counter popular notions that emphasize the positive feelings of closeness and aesthetic appreciation that sport in a natural environment offers against alternative experiences that dwell in the darker, unforgiving features of nature, brought on by extreme exertion. By positioning these punishing experiences within dark ecology, the natural environment is perceived as a foe rather than a friend and can highlight the athlete's vulnerability and mortality. Whilst this paper focusses on experiences during an ultramarathon event, it would be fascinating to explore how such extreme practices impact on the athlete's life after the event is long over.

The path ahead

Just as there has been tremendous growth in nature sport participation globally, there has also been a growing body of literature on the subject area designed to better understand this social and historical phenomenon. To date, the body of work produced on nature sports has been dominated by Anglophone scholars, especially from the United States of America and the United Kingdom (Durán-Sánchez, Álvarez-García, and Del Río-Rama 2019, part one of this special issue).

The contributions developed by authors of other countries, especially those produced by French scholars, have tended to be overlooked by Anglophone scholars (Wheaton 2013), often because these publications have not been translated into English. As Wheaton (2013) has stated, a North American dominance is not surprising as the USA is considered the home of the nature sport phenomenon. Similarly, as Bourdieu (1979) pointed out, the spiritual base of many nature sports evolved in the United States, where commercialization and institutionalization processes developed rapidly and thoroughly, as demonstrated by the emergence and meteoric success of ESPN's X Games (Beal and Wilson 2004; Wheaton 2013).

Empirical work written in English (and other languages) is now emerging from all around the world. As we can see in this special issue (parts 1 and 2), the authors represent a diverse number of countries, including Europe (Germany, Italy, Portugal, Spain, United Kingdom), the Americas (Canada, Costa Rica, Panama, USA) and Oceania (Australia, New Zealand), illustrating both commonalities and differences in participants' experiences and outcomes (Durán-Sánchez, Álvarez-García, and Del Río-Rama 2019, part one of this special issue; Wheaton 2013).

Especially in the last decade, the academic interest in nature sport has broadened, encompassing a range of different academic (inter)disciplines, including leisure studies (Davidson and Stebbins 2011; Stebbins 2019, part one of this special issue), management and economy (Bayley & Hungenberg, part two of this special issue; Mach et al. 2018, part two of this special issue; King and Church 2019, part two of this special issue), philosophy (e.g. Booth 2018, part one of this special issue; McNamee 2006; Krein 2008, 2014, 2015, 2018), psychology (e.g. Kerr and Houge Mackenzie 2018, part one of this special issue; Houge Mackenzie and Brymer 2018, part one of this special issue; Lyng 1990; Thorpe 2009) and sociology (e.g. Pociello 1981, 1995, 1999; Wheaton 2004, 2013, 2014, 2016; Lyng 2005; Melo and Gomes 2017a, 2017b). This is stimulating the emergence of new theoretical developments and productive avenues of enquiry (Wheaton 2013; Melo, Van Rheenen, and Gammon 2019).

This two-part special issue on nature sports is an effort to encourage and stimulate, and document the most recent scholarship in this emerging field of enquiry. We expect that research into this unique area will continue to develop, challenging scholars to think globally and creatively to balance participation demand with environmental sustainability. Nature sports, a unifying set of physical practices experienced in relation to the natural environment, will continue to emerge in new forms and configurations. These configurations will certainly be in response to social, demographic and environmental changes and upheavals rapidly unfolding in the twenty-first century. While these practices will seek to preserve and/or foster a balance or harmony with our natural world, these activities will also embody the desire to stretch boundaries and defy the ever-dynamic contours of human limitation.

References

Aubel, O., O. Hoibian, and J. Defrance. 2002. "Les Enjeux de la Sportivisation de L'escalade Libre." In *Deux Siècles D'alpinismes Européens*, 273–291. Paris: L'Harmattan.

Bailey, A. W., and E. Hungenberg. 2018. "Managing the Rock-climbing Economy: A Case from Chattanooga." *Annals of Leisure Research*. doi:10.1080/11745398.2018.1488146.

Barbieri, C., and S. Sotomayor. 2013. "Surf Travel Behavior and Destination Preferences: An Application of the Serious Leisure Inventory and Measure." *Tourism Management* 35: 111–121.

Beal, B., and C. Wilson. 2004. "'Chicks Dig Scars': Commercialisation and the Transformations of Skate Boarders' Identities." In *Understanding Lifestyle Sports: Consumption, Identity and Difference*, edited by B. Wheaton, 31–54. London: Routledge.

Bessy, O., and O. Naria. 2005. "Les enjeux des loisirs et du tourisme sportif de nature dans le développement durable de la Réunion." In *Management et marketing du sport: du local au global*, edited by P. Boucher, and C. Sobry, 307–339. Paris: Éditions Septentrion.

Booth, D. 2018. "Nature Sports: Ontology, Embodied Being, Politics." *Annals of Leisure Research*. doi:10.1080/11745398.2018.1524306.

Bourdieu, P. 1979. *La Distinction: Critique sociale du jugement*. Paris: Editions de Minuit.

Brymer, E., and R. D. Schweitzer. 2017. "Evoking the Ineffable: The Phenomenology of Extreme Sports." *Psychology of Consciousness: Theory, Research, and Practice* 4 (1): 63–74.

Buckley, R. 2018. "Nature Sports, Health and Ageing: The Value of Euphoria." *Annals of Leisure Research*. doi:10.1080/11745398.2018.1483734.

Comer, K. 2010. *Surfer Girls in the New World Order*. Durham and London: Duke University Press.

Corneloup, J., and P. Bourdeau. 2004. "Les sports de nature. Entre pratiques libres, territoires, marchés et logiques institutionnelles." *Cahier Espaces* 8: 117–124.

Davidson, L., and R. Stebbins. 2011. *Serious Leisure and Nature: Sustainable Consumption in the Outdoors*. Houndmills, Basingstoke, UK: Palgrave Macmillan.

Dolnicar, S., and M. Fluker. 2003a. "Behavioural Market Segments among Surf Tourists – Investigating Past Destination Choice." *Journal of Sport Tourism* 8 (3): 186–196.

Durán-Sánchez, A., J. Álvarez-García, and M. Del Río-Rama. 2019. "Nature Sports: State of the Art of Research." *Annals of Leisure Research*. doi:10.1080/11745398.2019.1584535.

Gomes, R., N. Gustavo, R. Melo, and V. Pedragosa. 2017. *Private Sport Sector in Europe – A Cross-National Perspective*, edited by A. Laine, and H. Vehmas, 269–285. Cham: Springer.

Hickman, M., P. Stokes, S. Gammon, C. Beard, and A. Inkster. 2018. "Moments Like Diamonds in Space: Savoring the Ageing Process through Positive Engagement with Adventure Sports." *Annals of Leisure Research* 21 (5): 612–630.

Houge Mackenzie, S., and E. Brymer. 2018. "Conceptualizing Adventurous Nature Sport: A Positive Psychology Perspective." *Annals of Leisure Research*. doi:10.1080/11745398.2018.1483733.

Howe, S. 1998. *Sick: A Cultural History of Snowboarding*. New York: St. Martin's Press.

Hutson, G., and R. Howard. 2015. "Weaving Place Meanings into Outdoor Recreation Sustainability: The Case of the Niagra Glen." In *Landscapes of Leisure: Space, Place and Identities*, edited by S. Gammon, and S. Elkington, 176–191. Palgrave: Hampshire.

Jarvie, G. 2006. *Sport, Culture and Society: An Introduction*. London: Routledge.

Kerr, J. H., and S. Houge Mackenzie. 2018. "'I don't Want to Die. That's not why I do it at All': Multifaceted Motivation, Psychological Health, and Personal Development in BASE Jumping." *Annals of Leisure Research*. doi:10.1080/11745398.2018.1483732.

King, K., and A. Church. 2019. "Beyond Transgression: Mountain Biking, Young People and Managing Green Spaces." *Annals of Leisure Research*. doi:10.1080/11745398.2019.1571928.

Krein, K. 2008. "Sport, Nature and Worldmaking." *Sport, Ethics and Philosophy* 2 (3): 285–301.

Krein, K. 2014. "Nature Sports." *Journal of the Philosophy of Sport* 41 (2): 193–208.

Krein, K. 2015. "Reflections on Competition and Nature Sports." *Sport, Ethics and Philosophy* 9 (3): 271–286.

Krein, K. 2018. *Philosophy and Nature Sports*. London: Routledge.

Liberman, N. 2004. "New Heights or a Crash Landing?" *Street & Smith's Sports Business Journal* 12–18: 25. https://www.sportsbusinessdaily.com/Journal/Issues/2004/07/12/Special-Report/New-Heights-Or-A-Crash-Landing.aspx.

Lyng, S. 1990. "Edgework: A Social Psychological Analysis of Voluntary Risk Takking." *The American Journal of Sociology* 95 (4): 851–886.

Lyng, S. 2005. *Edgework: The Sociology of Risk-taking*. New York: Routledge.

Mach, L., J. Ponting, J. Brown, and J. Savage. 2018. "Riding Waves of Intra-Seasonal Demand in Surf Tourism: Analysing the Nexus of Seasonality and 21st Century Surf Forecasting Technology." *Annals of Leisure Research*. doi:10.1080/11745398.2018.1491801.

Mallen, C., and C. Chard. 2011. "A Framework for Debating the Future of Environmental Sustainability in the Sport Academy." *Sport Management Review* 14 (4): 424–433.

McNamee, M. 2006. *Philosophy, Risk and Adventure Sports*. London: Routledge.

Melo, R. 2013. "Desportos de Natureza e Desenvolvimento Local Sustentável: Análise dos praticantes e das Organizações Promotoras dos Desportos de Natureza" (Unpublished Doctoral Dissertation). University of Coimbra, Coimbra, Portugal.

Melo, R., and R. Gomes. 2017a. "A Sociocultural Approach to Understanding the Development of Nature Sports." In *Sport Tourism: New Challenges in a Globalized World*, edited by R. Melo, and C. Sobry, 60–90. Newcastle upon Tyne: Cambridge Scholars Publishing.

Melo, R., and R. Gomes. 2017b. "Nature Sports Participation: Understanding Demand, Practice Profile, Motivations and Constraints." *European Journal of Tourism Research* 16: 108–135.

Melo, R., and R. Gomes. 2017c. "Profiling the Typologies of Nature Sports Organizations in Portugal." In *Sport Management as an Emerging Economy Activity*, edited by M. Peris-Ortiz, J. Álvarez-García, and M. C. del Rio-Rama, 235–255. Cham: Springer.

Melo, R., D. Van Rheenen, and S. Gammon. 2019. "Editorial (Part I) - Nature Sports: A Unifying Concept." *Annals of Leisure Research* 22 (5): 587–604.

MSJS. 2015. *Sports de Nature: Repères & Actions*. Paris: MSJS.

Ostrowski, J. 2002. "Corporate America Makes Pitchmen of Pariahs." *Street & Smith's Sports Business Journal* 19: 26.

The Outdoor Foundation. 2018. *2018 Outdoor Recreation Participation*. Washington, DC: The Outdoor Foundation.

Pociello, C. 1981. "La force, l'énergie, la grâce et les réflexes. Le jeu complexe des dispositions culturelles et sportives." In *Sports et société*, edited by C. Pociello, 171–237. Paris: Editions Vigot.

Pociello, C. 1995. *Les Cultures Sportives*. Paris: Editions «PUF».

Pociello, C. 1999. *Sports et science sociales*. Paris: Editions Vigot.

Portugal, A., F. Campos, F. Martins, and R. Melo. 2017. "Understanding the Relation Between Serious Surfing, Surfing Profile, Surf Travel Behaviour and Destination Attributes Preferences." *European Journal of Tourism Research* 16: 57–73.

Rinehart, R., and S. Sydnor. 2003. *To the Extreme – Alternative Sports, Inside and Out*. Albany: State University of New York Press.

Sports England and Outdoor Industries Association. 2015. *Getting Active Outdoors: A Study of Demography, Motivation, Participation and Provision in Outdoor Sport and Recreation in England*. London: Sports England and Outdoor Industries Association.

Stebbins, R. 2019. "Sport and Nature: A Comment on Their Relationship." *Annals of Leisure Research*.

Suchet, A. 2011. "La Sportivisation des Pratiques, Dites, Nouvelles." *Aspects Sociologiques* 18 (1): 1–17.

Thorpe, H. 2009. "The Psycology of Extreme Sport." In *The Cultural Turn in Sport and Exercise Psycology*, edited by T. Ryba, R. Schinke, and G. Tenenbaum, 361–384. Morgantown: Fitnes Information Technology.

Wheaton, B. 2004. "Introduction: Mapping the Lifestyle Sport-Scape." In *Understanding Lifestyle Sports: Consumption, Identity and Difference*, edited by B. Wheaton, 1–28. USA and Canada: London: Routeledge.

Wheaton, B. 2013. *The Cultural Politics of Lifestyle Sports*. London: Routledge.

Wheaton, B. 2014. *The Consumption and Representation of Lifestyle Sports*. London and New York: Routledge.

Wheaton, B. 2016. "Lifestyle Sport." In *Sport and Society: A Student Introduction*, edited by B. Houlihan, and D. Malcolm, 3rd ed., 109–133. London: Sage.

Climbing in Saxon Switzerland (GDR): a path to freedom in a socialist dictatorship

Kai Reinhart

ABSTRACT

Saxon Switzerland (*Sächsische Schweiz*), a region close to the city of Dresden on the river Elbe, is in fact a small mountain range with steep rocks. Even in the nineteenth century, people started climbing the sandstone and developed a proud tradition of strict ethical rules. The use of ladders or any other devices was not allowed. Organized in small clubs, the climbers developed their own identity with a strong feeling of independence. After World War II however, the climbers were forced to join the new socialist sports organizations. The communist functionaries tried to re-define climbing as a conventional sport, but the climbers continued to dream of liberty, friendship, nature and adventure. There was thus considerable friction between the German Democratic Republic officials and the climbers. Climbing became a way of escaping from the socialist society. With the help of different sources, such as interviews with contemporary witnesses, magazine articles and summit registers, this conflict is described and analyzed in the present paper.

One of the oldest climbing areas of Europe – Saxon Switzerland (*Sächsische Schweiz*) – is situated about 30 kilometres southeast of Dresden. Romantic painters like Adrian Zingg and Caspar David Friedrich were among the first to depict the beauty of this landscape in the 18th and 19th centuries. Their paintings made it a popular destination and as early as 1801, when the first travel guide for Saxon Switzerland was published (Nikolai 1801). In 1912, Saxon Switzerland, also called *Elbsandsteingebirge* (sandstone mountain range on the river Elbe), became a nature reserve and has remained so until the present.

The historical background of Saxon Mountaineering in the GDR

Consisting of smooth sandstone and with over one thousand rocky peaks – some of them over 100 metres high – Saxon Switzerland became one of the birthplaces of modern rock climbing in the nineteenth century.[1] In 1864 five *Turners* (gymnasts) from the nearby city of Schandau were the first to climb a peak called Falkenstein (Schindler 1988). The first generations of Saxon climbers, including charismatic figures like the American adventurer Oliver Perry-Smith, the Alpinist Oscar Schuster and the visionary Rudolf Fehrmann, created strict ethics for free climbing. In contrast to the early Alpinism, the use of ladders, ropes, steps or any other artificial devices was strictly prohibited. The climbers founded small clubs (*Kletterklubs*), like the *Falkensteiner* (1895) and the club *Wanderlust* (1896), which were often not larger than a rope team (*Seilschaft*).[2] Nevertheless, they had their own charter, built their own huts in the mountain ranges and were a centre of social life. While there was a close fellowship in these clubs, there was also intense competition between the different clubs, which tried to outdo one other in terms of difficulty and first ascents.

Because their climbing style was very dangerous, the first rock climber fell to his death as early as 1900 (Hasse 2000). Nevertheless, Rudolf Fehrmann's mountain guide from 1913 only recorded routes that had been climbed without any artificial aids (Fehrmann 1913). This way the Saxon mountaineers developed excellent climbing skills and reached level VI according to today's UIAA scale (*Union Internationale des Associations d'Alpinisme*) at the beginning of the twentieth century (Ardito 2000; Messner 2002). In order to organize mountain climbing activities (Hasse 1979; Schindler 1988), the clubs founded the umbrella association of the Saxon Mountaineering Federation (*Sächsischer Bergsteigerbund, SBB*) in Dresden in 1911. The SBB grew quickly and consisted of 67 Clubs with 700 members only one year after its foundation (Schindler 2003). Even though there were workers and crafts-men among the SBB-members, it was dominated by the middle-class (Hasse 1979). The city of Dresden became the German capital of mountaineering (Hasse 1979; Schindler 1988). In 1914, there were more than 4.000 members of tourist organizations like the German and Austrian Alps Federation (*Deutscher und Österreichischer Alpenverein, DÖAV*). More climbing clubs from the working-class joined the SBB, and it committed itself to political neutrality, retaining its middle-class milieu. After the First World War, the numbers continued to grow and in the 1930s, about 30,000 people in Dresden were organized into about 300 tourist clubs and federations. Nine trade magazines sup-ported the enthusiastic following (Schindler 2001).

The Saxon mountaineers fascinated their contemporaries and formed a strong ethical climbing tradition of considerable international influence (Messner 2002). This was partly due to the famous mountain pioneer Fritz Wiessner (Gottfried 2000). In 1928/29, he emi-grated from Saxony to the USA, where the idea of climbing without technical equipment evolved (Wiessner 1979; see also Messner 2002). Until the mid-twentieth century, the climbing routes of the Elbsandsteingebirge remained the most difficult in the world (Wiessner 1979; see also Richter 1993; Hasse 2000; Messner 2002). Only then, did new centres of rock climbing, like the Yosemite Valley in California or the Grand Canyon du Verdon in France, take over.

During the Second World War, Saxon Mountaineering declined. In 1941/1942, all tourist-related magazines had to be closed down. More than half the members of the Saxon Mountaineering Federation (SBB) from 1943 lost their lives during the war (1943: 2050 members; after the war: about 1200 members) and after the allied firebombing of Dresden there were no more climbing activities (Hasse 1979).[3]

After the defeat of Germany, Saxony was occupied by the Soviet army and in 1949, it became a part of the newly formed German Democratic Republic (GDR). In the GDR, the nature reserve of Saxon Switzerland was expanded to more than 36,000 hectares, and it became one of the main tourist attractions for the population, which was not allowed to leave the country.[4] By the end of the 1980s, about 2.5 million tourists per year visited the Elbsandsteingebirge. Most of them came to walk and hike in the region and not to practice rock climbing. There are no exact numbers on mountaineering in East Germany, but Dresden remained the stronghold, with about 5200 organized climbers in 1974 (Hasse 1979). The numbers continued to grow and in 1989, the GDR Mountaineering Federation (*Stadtfachausschuss Dresden des DWBO*)[5] estimated that there were 8000 active participants in the city (Schwer 1989). Experts like Joachim Schindler and Rainer Schubert stated in an interview with the author of the present paper, that there must have been about 10,000–12,000 mountaineers in the whole of the GDR (see also Wobst-Wylezol 2005). Most of them not only went climbing in Saxon Switzerland, but also identified with the special traditions and the ethics of Saxon Mountaineering. This could cause conflicts with the socialist officials. Viewed from a socialist perspective, mountaineering was considered as an ordinary sport like athletics or football. This socialist perspective can be seen, for example in the rejection of a traditional, 'romantic' view of mountaineering and in the refusal of the traditional organizational structures of mountaineering in Saxon. Some of the main conflicts will be described and analyzed below.

The methodological approach

Several primary sources comprise the empirical data of this study. There were a number of magazines on mountaineering in the GDR, which served as the sponsored documents of the (governing) bodies, like *Der Tourist* (The Tourist) of the GDR Mountaineering Federation (DWBV/DWBO)[6] or the *Wandern und Bergsteigen* (Wandering and Mountaineering) of the Dresden Mountaineering Federation (KFA/SFA Dresden).[7] The mountaineers were not very enthusiastic about these magazines. In 1958, the GDR Mountaineering Federation (*Sektion Touristik der DDR*) complained that BSG[8] Empor Dresden-Löbtau had only ordered 80 issues for 594 members. Other BSGs did not order any at all. The Mountaineering Federation had to pressure its members into reading these organizational documents: 'Under the current circumstances, it is stipulated that the basis for the purchase order of the newsletter is to be for at least 50% of their members' (Illmer, Dachsel, and Schmidt 1958).

As the climbing scene of the GDR had a partly informal character, it is not possible to reconstruct its history only through written sources. Therefore, one of the most important information sources is interviews with contemporary witnesses. All interviews were conducted, transcribed and analyzed by the author. Even if the interviews were written down, they have to be considered as spoken language, including all kinds of linguistic mistakes. A systematic reflection on the opportunities and risks associated with oral history helped to provide a methodologically sound analysis of the interviews.[9] Some biographical information on the contemporary witnesses can be found at the end of the text. However, whenever written (documentary) historical sources were available, such as articles in magazines, letters, contemporary literature or summit registers, they were used.

The summit registers of Saxon Switzerland are a very special source in this field of research. Since the beginning of mountaineering in Saxon Switzerland in the nineteenth century, the climbers left messages on the rocky peaks (DWBV 1964). The first summit book was probably introduced by Oscar Schuster in 1893 (Schindler 2003). In 1914, the Saxon Mountaineering Federation (SBB) decided to archive full summit books and to replace full books with new ones. After 1945, the socialist Mountain Federation continued this tradition. In 1970, more than 800 rocks had their own summit register (Schindler 2003). They formed a unique public commentary that was accessible only to mountaineers. Unskilled persons simply were not able to reach the summits of the peaks. Therefore, many critical comments concerning the GDR state can be found in these books. The GDR Mountaineering Federation (Sektion Touristik der DDR) knew about these summit book scrawlings, but could do little about it, because it was not possible to control hundreds of rocky peaks. The socialist functionaries could therefore appeal only to the climbers, like Johann Frank (1955) in his article 'Something like this must never happen again!' Everyone should stand up against the summit book scrawlings. 'Keeping silent about the graffiti in our summit books means consent and tolerance of such subversive elements' (Frank 1955; see also Hänsel 1959, 12f.). In the name of all socialist mountaineers, Kurt B. Richter promised that, 'these enemies will be exposed and brought to justice' (Richter 1962, 248). But those threats did not change anything as the mountaineers refused to cooperate with the officials. Against this background, it is not surprising that many summit books suddenly got 'lost' and never found their way to the official archive (Heinicke 1976). After the German reunification in 1990, many hidden summit registers were included in the archive. Since then, it has been managed by the reestablished Saxon Mountaineering Federation (SBB), and is now open to the public.

In terms of theory, the study was inspired by the work of the French philosopher Michel Foucault and his concept of power and resistance as a bodily practice. In this perspective, conventional sports, such as gymnastics or athletics, can be seen as 'power technologies' that make people healthy and fit to support the economy and the politics of the state. It was not by chance, that the slogan of the GDR sports badge was 'ready for work and defense'[10] (Reinhart 2010a, 87–109). But sport or bodily practices could also be used in the opposite way – as a means of resistance.

Foucault considered the ways in which individuals in their projects and confrontations reject dictated practices and constitute themselves as subjects of their own practices, which he called 'technologies of the self'. He saw an example of such practices in the athletics and gymnastics of the ancient Greeks (Reinhart 2010a, 113–117). Can Saxon Mountaineering in the GDR also be described in terms of this concept? How did the regime deal with 'technologies of the self' among the mountaineers, as opposed to its own 'power technologies'? These were guiding questions of the study, which thus concentrated on the extremes on both sides. Indeed, rich empirical data on the conflict between the regime and the mountaineers could be found.

In the following discussion, some crucial conflicts will be analyzed that characterize both, the Saxon mountaineers and the socialist state of the GDR.

Clubs vs Cooperative Sports Collectives (BSG)

Even though many mountaineers had lost their lives or were prisoners of war, the Saxon tradition of the climbing clubs was still thriving and very much alive after the war. However, the new socialist regime saw them as a stronghold of the old bourgeoisie (H. Richter). Therefore, the council (Stadtrat) of Dresden banned the clubs on January 9, 1948. After extremely angry and numerous complaints, they had to drop the ban only one month later (Schindler 2001). However, the fight was not yet won. Franz Ruge, member of the Socialist Unity Party (Sozialistische Einheitspartei Deutschlands, SED) and head of the mountaineering organization in Dresden, warned: 'Those clubs and their members who do not join the new sport, but still get together will either be banned or reported to the police.' (quoted from Schindler 2001, 479). As a consequence, some social-ist mountaineers – those who believed in socialism – did leave their clubs and joined the sport association (*Sportgemeinschaft, SG*) Dynamo Dresden, which became a forerunner of the socialist sports movement and was therefore generally disliked among the mountai-neers (Eckert; Wobst-Wylezol 2005). In the summit books of the Saxon Switzerland, the names of the GDR Mountaineering Federation and well-known socialist Cooperative Sports Collectives (BSG) like Dynamo[11] Dresden or Lokomotive Dresden, were often crossed out and sometimes replaced with 'idiots' or other invectives and insults. With increasing political pressure, more and more climbers joined the Cooperative Sports Col-lectives (BSG).

In Dresden, many of the mountaineers went to the BSG Empor Dresden-Löbtau. Fritz Petzold, head of the mountaineers in this BSG, represented the middle-class tradition of climbing, which made it easier for many climbers to join the BSG. In December 1951, the organization had 352 mountaineers in 20 'rope teams', as the traditional climbing clubs were then officially called. Two years later, there were already 460 members (DWBO 1988). However, beneath the socialist surface the old structures remained alive: 'Officially they called themselves Empor Löbtau, but wrote TC [Tourist Club, K.R.] *Wander-lust* in their summit book entries' (H. Richter).

The functionaries of the new sport regime knew about this pretense and insincere show of integration. The question of how Marxism could be enforced in mountaineering was on the agenda of the first council meeting held by the GDR Mountaineering Federation (*Sektion Touristik der DDR*) on June 8, 1952. The Dresden delegate Harry Dürichen explained:

> One cannot stop the goings on of the clubs by banning them, they just continue illegally [...]. The ideological re-education of the Dresden climbers is a tough job, because they have been contaminated by the reactionary tradition of the former bourgeois climbing organizations (quoted from Schindler 2001, 502).

Two months later (August 25, 1952), the council members talked to representatives of the so-called 'rope teams' in the BSG Empor Dresden-Löbtau (DWBO 1988). As a result, the rope teams were tolerated but reinterpreted as 'one of the many small collectives in our democratic sport organization' (Richter 1962, 17). There would be a new kind of relationship between the climbers; not only fellowship, but also a mutual education according to the principles of socialism.

However, this was just wishful thinking. The functionaries' complaint in the mountai-neering magazine *Freundschaft* (Friendship) was as follows: 'Why do they hold their meet-ings on Mondays, when everyone knows that this is the day that the Workers' Party, the SED, uses for their training?' (Pankotsch 1953, 27). The president of the GDR Mountaineer-ing Federation (*Sektion Touristik der DDR*), Heinz Schlosser, explained with some frustration:

> There are clear signs of sectarianism here, whose roots are found in the adherence to old tra-ditions and club traits [...]. Everything which is new and corresponds to our advances toward a socialist physical education, which we are striving towards and implementing, is rejected by a majority of Dresden's 'mountaineer friends', due to false attitudes (Schlosser 1953, 70).

Being part of the official sport offered some advantages to the old clubs. Ropes and car-abiners, for example, were distributed by the BSGs: 'Using the name of the climbing club *Kreuztümer*, you couldn't expect any support, or demand any, but you could as BSG Chemie Meißen. This way, one lived a double life' (H. Richter). It was also possible to obtain insurance, receive free tickets for the GDR-railway or get a day off from work for a training course. Nevertheless, there was no loyalty to the GDR Mountaineering Federa-tion. Conversely, new climbing clubs were founded. At the beginning of the 1960s, there were at least 100 unofficial clubs in the tradition of Saxon Mountaineering (Richter 1993). Against this backdrop, it is easy to understand why the commemorative publication of the GDR Mountaineering Federation (DWBV) started with a quotation from General Secretary Walter Ulbricht: 'Whoever tries to preserve that which is old, historically obsolete, that which is destined to die, will fail, will go down with all else which does not survive' (DWBV 1964, 6). This was intended – among other things – to make a statement against the 'unprogressive' climbing clubs. Ulbricht's prediction was correct, but in a way that he probably did not expect. During the 'peaceful revolution' of 1989/1990, the socialist regime collapsed, and on December 21, 1989 the climbing clubs reestablished the traditional Saxon Mountaineering Federation (SBB).

Romanticism vs sport

In 1951, the Socialistic Unity Party (SED) introduced a programme for the development of body culture and sports in the GDR. To protect the people from US-imperialism, strong and determined citizens were needed. 'The purpose and content of the democratic sport movement is therefore the training and education of people who are prepared to work and defend peace' (printed in Teichler 2002, 200). One of the twelve points comprising the programme was – following the Soviet example – the standardized sports classifi-cation for outstanding performance. Three performance classes (*Leistungsklassen III-I*) and the title 'Master of Sport' were intended to motivate all athletes to increase their per-formance in training and competition. At the same time, the classification would help in gathering data relating to all top athletes (printed in Teichler 2002). Robert Otto Franz, head of the training commission, explained in the mountaineering magazine *Freundschaft* (Friendship): 'We thus gain the foundation for a planned strategic development of individ-ual sporting friends, whereby the performance level of all mountaineers will be raised' (Franz 1953, 7). Furthermore, the climbing functionaries may have hoped to break up the sworn community of mountaineers: 'It was certainly the political intention, to get the mountaineers under control [...]. We're going to control this now – that is sport – and now we're going to introduce classifications' (Klingner; see also H. Richter).

The performance classification had been developed and implemented without con-sideration of the mountaineers, who did not even consider themselves to be sportsmen. 'Bear in mind, that our mountains are more than a gymnasium' wrote Rudolf Fehrmann, one of the pioneers of Saxon Mountaineering in his mountain guide (quoted from Hoyer 1996, 36). In the magazine *Der Sächsische Bergsteiger* (The Saxon Mountaineer), it was written in 1938 that, 'we are particularly proud that we are not allowed to be counted as sportsmen' (Wächtler 1938, 4). This attitude continued in the post-war years: 'For us, the spirit of Saxon Mountaineering still applied, as characterized by the older gen-eration, with their romanticism and our own romanticism of the time' (Hasse 1969, 33).

The climbers dreamed of liberty, friendship, nature and adventure, as expressed in the following poem *Bergfreunde* (Mountain-Friends), written by Karl Heinz Gonda, a leading East German mountaineer of the post-war years:

> If two people strive together/in the open countryside of the mountains/accompanying each other all their lives/bonded through the traces of liberty//
>
> Then they are mountain-friends/two connected like one/and taking on the world./No one can ever separate them (quoted from Hel. Richter 2003, 21).[12]

As Erhard Klingner noted in an interview: 'Mountaineering is more than sport. You stand above everything.' The climbers loved the independence of mountaineering:

> Firstly, you had to make an effort to get all the gear together, in other words, ropes and car-abiners, etc. [...] You had say two, three friends, and took your pack, and then had to first drive somewhere and then walk to the peaks and mountains. Then you had to inform yourselves, [...] and that was great (Biock).

Thus, there was a substantial opposition between the socialist and the traditional understanding of mountaineering. The traditionalists regarded mountaineering as a way of life, characterized by freedom, friendship and adventure. The socialists saw mountaineering as a sport, observing the rules of efficient training and competition.

The conflict between socialist and traditional mountaineering can also be seen in the summit books. The Saxon mountaineers had turned the traditional salutation of the German Turners[13] *Gut Heil* (Good Health/Salvation) into *Berg Heil* (Mountain Health/Salvation). In opposition, the socialist mountaineers created the term *Berg Frei* (Mountain Liberty). In the GDR *Berg Frei* was the officially recommended form of salutation among mountaineers. Official Karl Däweritz (1979, 55) wrote, '"*Berg frei*" has survived the "*Berg heil*" salutation of the bourgeois period', but in fact it was the other way round. Many mountaineers insisted on the traditional *Berg Heil* (Schindler 2003; Eckert). Because, every new year, the summit books were opened with a mountaineer's salutation, there was a veritable race to be the first on a rocky peak in the New Year. Many of them were already climbed by New Year's Eve. Mostly the traditionalists won (Figure 1). A socialist *Berg Frei* could not be found very often in the books, as Dietrich Hasse (1969) recalled.

Of course, mountaineering changed over the course of the GDR. In the post-war years, mountaineers sang traditional songs on the peaks of the rocks. In the 1980s, the young climbers concentrated on the cliffs and often did not even finish climbing to the top. Witnesses of the younger generation constantly stated that there had been a strong 'sportization' of mountaineering, which can be seen in the specific training and in competitions. Nevertheless, the younger generation still felt that mountaineering was 'more'. For many of them, it was a self-determined, individual and holisitic experience. Bernd Arnold, one of the best climbers in the world in the 1970s and 1980s, explained in an interview: 'For me, although climbing is also sport, it is also a bit of an art, accordingly, I also want to express myself through climbing.'

One means of expression was to give new routes a special name. While the names in the 1960s, like *Nordwand* (Northwall) and *Ostwand* (Eastwall), were quite factual, they became more personal in the following decades. This was an international phenomenon (Messner 2002). For his routes, Bernd Arnold chose names like *Schallmauer* (Sound Barrier),

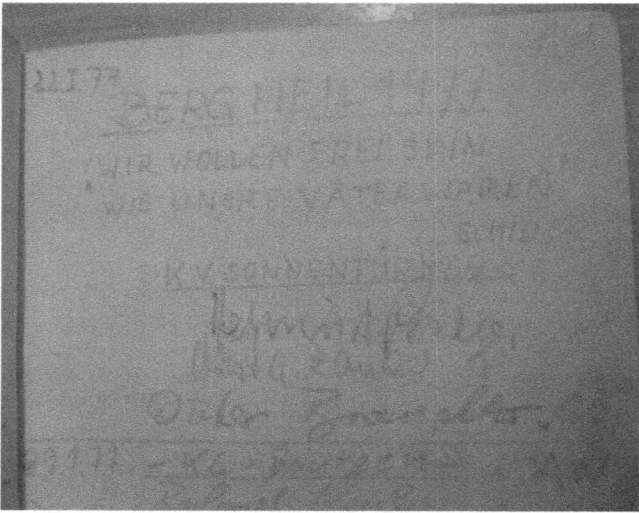

Figure 1. Summit book salutation and saying ('Mountain Health/Salvation: "We want to be free, just like our fathers were." Schiller'), (summit register Fensterturm, January 22, 1977)

Leben in den kleinen Felsen (Life among the small rocks), *Freudiges Ereignis* (Happy Event), *Garten Eden* (Garden of Eden) or *Weiße Taube* (White Dove).

According to Bernd Arnold, another important aspect of mountaineering is to spend time with your fellow mountaineers. The experiences of wandering, climbing and camping together deepens the emotional connection between the mountaineers. For him, mountaineering is an almost spiritual way of finding himself in the sense of the romantic German poet and philosopher Novalis (Arnold 1999). This was the exact opposite of the socialist understanding of mountaineering; Kurt B. Richter (1962) criticized the old-fashioned romantic picture of an adventurer who ignores the real world behind the mountains. 'Mountaineering *is* sport, no more and also no less!' he wrote (1962, 16). The GDR-officials knew that these opposing attitudes towards mountaineering would cause conflict. 'If the committee of the Mountaineering Federation [*Sektion Touristik der DDR*] has now decided to implement the sport classification for mountaineering, in other words, the performance assessment, we know that this will be, above all, a tough ideological struggle', wrote Franz (1953, 7), and he was right. At the start, almost no one wanted to take part in the classification system (Hasse 1979; Schindler 2001). The top climbers were consistently against it: 'It was like a silent wall that they couldn't break through' (Wünsche). The first attempt to implement a classification system in mountaineering failed (Wobst-Wylezol 2005).

Only in 1957, when many of the traditional mountaineers had already moved to Western Germany, and resignation spread among those who were still in the GDR, did the 'silent wall' begin to crumble (Hasse 1969). After the classification had been modified, Alfred 'Fred' Barth, Hans-Joachim Scholz and Heinz Urban from the socialist SG Dynamo Dresden accepted the honour of being the first Masters of Sport in rock climbing (September 29, 1957) (DWBO 1988). But most of the climbers remained true to their principles and even despised the 'classifiers'. For well-known traditional climbers, it would nonetheless have been difficult to become a 'Master of Sport'.

The GDR Mountaineering Federation (DWBV) stated in 1958 that the 'award [...] is an inalienable right of our socialist state. In particular, the political content of this measure is to be respected in all discussions' (DWBV 1958, 13). It became clear that the standardized sport classification was also a means of political education and disciplining. Therefore, it is no surprise that the state-loyal BSGs like Dynamo Dresden and Lokomotive Dresden received the most awards (Hempel 2002). Because the best climbers did not take part in the classification system, the standards were not very high. This frustrated the top mountaineers even more: 'Be better than the classifiers! That was something that we were proud of. We were the best' (H. Richter).

However, taking part in the classification was required more and more for those climbers who wanted to receive state support or to travel to mountain ranges and competitions outside the GDR. Functionary Hans Löwinger made it very clear: 'A list of participants for such enterprises must only comprise mountaineers who have achieved the corresponding standards in the sports classification, or are in the process of doing so' (Löwinger 1958, 9). This had consequences for the opponents of the classification:

> They said: "It's Commie rubbish, it's politics after all, I'm not going to do it. Climbing isn't just a sport. To me, climbing means getting into the outdoors, and it's more than that, I'm a mountaineer, I'm more than that too." And already there you had your problem that you weren't allowed to go with them [to mountain ranges outside the GDR, K.R.] (Klingner).

In 1960, being excluded from any state promotion, Fritz Eske, Herbert Richter and eleven other top climbers and opponents of the classification system (Richter 2006) decided to write an open letter to General Secretary Walter Ulbricht. At the same time, they sent it to 13 Sport Federations and magazines/newspapers of the GDR. At the beginning of the six pages, the authors expressed their pride in the GDR sport movement, but then harshly criticized the low standards of the classification that would paint a false picture of GDR rock climbing:

> It is appalling and ridiculous at the same time, what is presented to men of other sports (also on an international scale) as a Master of Sport. If all mountaineers acted according to the methods predominantly used by SG Dynamo Dresden, there would have to be more than a hundred Masters of Sport in rock climbing! (printed in Reinhart 2010a, 403–409, this quotation: 406)

The members of the state-loyal SG Dynamo Dresden benefited from state promotion without sufficient performance, which caused a stagnation of mountaineering. At the same time, there was a 'completely unsatisfactory magazine', 'outdated equipment' and an 'unsatisfactory composition of the governing bodies' (printed in Reinhart 2010a, 403–409, this quotations: 406). On the last few pages, the letter gets to the bottom of the conflict:

> They call our mountaineering "escapism" and believe that they have to, and can educate all mountaineers through the classification. But what have they then educated? Dogmatists, careerists! In the place of thinking, feeling and seeing people, they have put a catalogue. They promote dishonesty in our sport. They do not attempt to convince, but rather to coerce. They replace ethical principles with pure physical training (printed in Reinhart 2010a, 403–409, this quotation: 407).

The open letter was not published anywhere, but two months later, there was a meeting between top officials of the GDR Mountaineering Federation (DWBV) and the authors of the letter. The authors agreed to take part in the classification and hoped for improvements in mountaineering, but nothing really changed (Richter 2006).

In the 1960s and 1970s, the conflict lost its severity and the classification system became a widely accepted GDR-tradition, with the programme being opened up to children and less capable climbers. Young mountaineers thus grew up with the classification and took part to prove their performance level and to find recognition. In this way, it had a positive impact on mountaineering in the GDR, argued top climber Bernd Arnold. At the same time, pressure on the mountaineers to join the classification was maintained, especially through popular journeys to foreign countries. In the magazine *Wandern und Bergsteigen* (Wandering and Mountaineering), the following was written in 1970: 'The expert committee for foreign travel should make it their policy to award particularly sought-after Alpine trips only to those mountain friends who can either prove a classification, or at least commit to completing this in the present year' (KFA Dresden 1970, 2; see also FK Auslandsfahrten 1972). Accordingly, many climbers were willing to take part in the classification.

For the elite of the mountaineers, the classification standards remained too low. In the 1980s they made fun of it, as Alexander Adler remembered in an interview: 'Many of us almost found it amusing, well I also took part in this, to submit paths that were especially matched to these regulations, that reached such an astronomical number of points, that they no longer believed us.' Jörn Beilke said:

> On the evening you were given the award, there was a buffet, in that respect you thought to oneself: 'Oh well, at least I am able to enjoy the buffet' […]. I don't know who took it seriously […]. If anything, it brought you contempt, because you had colluded with the system (Beilke).

Individuality vs socialism

According to Heinz Schlosser, president of the GDR Mountaineering Federation (DWBV), the interests of the socialist state and the mountaineers were identical. They allegedly wanted to achieve the goal of 'knowing and learning to love their homeland […] and keeping oneself healthy, strong and prepared for defense as a means of social responsibility in the interests of progress' (Schlosser 1955, 483). In fact, the motives of the mountaineers were something entirely different. In the post-war years, the mountaineers were very suspicious of anything to do with politics, because of their experiences with political ideologies during the Third Reich. They simply wanted to enjoy freedom and individuality in a beautiful authentic landscape.

> This freedom, this deciding for oneself, there I will climb, I can choose the challenge, no one can stop me, it is my own decision, and I can enjoy the silence and view of the Elbe Valley, which was so incredibly breathtaking (Wünsche).

The chaotic circumstances in the defeated and largely destroyed country opened up a space of liberty. The group of young and active mountaineers was so small that almost everybody knew each other. Even though the material situation was extremely precarious, there was a unique atmosphere of freedom and friendship (see Hasse 1979; Wankerl 1979; Hasse 1993; Hel. Richter 2003).

Yet, when the new Socialist Unity Party (SED) was established and the chaos of the first few years was over, the free spaces began to shrink. The title page of the summit books, for example, was designed for propagandistic purposes. In the post-war years, it was written that 'Mountaineers have to be fighters for peace, and activists of work'. This provoked many of the rock climbers, so by crossing out and adding some words they changed the phrase into 'Mountaineers have to do nothing' (Hasse 1979, 180). Later, the propagandistic slogan conveyed a military attitude: 'The German Democratic Republic, our home country, and our mountains are what we love and what we are ready to defend anytime.' This was mostly changed to 'The German home country and our mountains are what we love' (Figure 2).

Over the years, it became more and more difficult to escape the influence of the SED. In 1958, the GDR Mountaineering Federation (DWBV) decided that political questions, the socialist perspective and the laws of the government must be discussed at the assemblies of the BSGs. In addition, the leading functionaries should study the basics of Marxism in courses given by the Socialist Unity Party (SED) or the Free German Youth (*Freie Deutsche Jugend, FDJ*), the youth organization of the GDR (DWBV 1958). The SED of Dresden

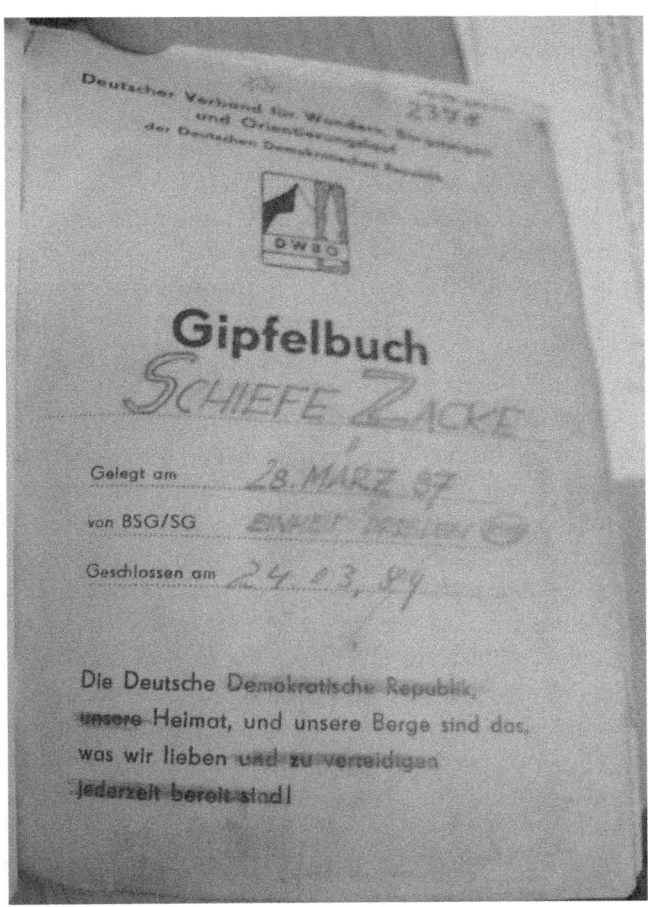

Figure 2. Title page of a summit book with graffiti (summit register Schiefe Zacke)

regarded the mountain rescue, the BSG Empor Dresden-Löbtau and the mountaineer choir *Bergfinken* as the main pillars of reactionary mountaineer culture.

GDR officials were very sensitive in understanding critical messages. 'When there is talk today of freedom only being found in the mountains, and those in the valleys being slaves, this is clearly an antisocialist statement' (Weinhold 1972, 3). This would be romantic escapism, and mountaineers ought to be aware of the political content:

> In this regard, there are some areas that have been neglected in our sections that need to be made up for. There is no apolitical mountain sport. It either serves the enemies of the state, as often was the case in the past, or otherwise, it satisfies the important needs of the working class and all working people in developed socialist society (Weinhold 1972, 4).

It could be dangerous to criticize the regime, and even convinced socialists like Hans-Joachim Scholz, could fall from grace. He allegedly disparaged the Soviet Union and in consequence was no longer allowed to work as a public prosecutor. He had to give up his leading function at the SG Dynamo Dresden and lost his title 'Master of Sport' (Wobst-Wylezol 2005).

However, such measures could not destroy the community of mountaineers, rather the contrary in fact: 'They didn't have any luck, because through their violent intolerance, a sworn "resistance group" of Saxon mountaineers was forged' (Hasse 1969, 33). Even if there were also mountaineers who believed in socialism and the new regime, 'on the whole, they were bourgeois or otherwise on the right [...]. That was still a group that the leaders of the GDR didn't trust' (Mempel). Erich Glaser, president of the GDR Mountaineering Federation (1966–1970) wrote in his unpublished memoirs that the re-education of the mountaineers had failed (Schindler 2003).

When the Berlin Wall was built (August 13, 1961), the freedom-loving mountaineers were trapped and they finally had to come to terms with the socialist state. Saxon Switzerland helped them to cope with the situation. Mountaineering became more and more a way to escape the structures of the state, at least for some time: 'In the mountains, you can forget the whole mess here, that was roughly the attitude' (H. Richter). Top climber Bernd Arnold lived in his parents' house in Hohnstein next to the Elbsandsteingebirge and worked as a self-employed book printer. He concentrated his climbing activities – the most important part of his life – on 'his paradise' (Arnold 1999, 11), where he felt safe and secure. He gave the name *Schneckenhaus* (snail shell) to one of his routes, as this expressed the feeling accurately and appropriately (see also Arnold 1999).

While the generation of the 1960s and 1970s often tried to come to terms with the socialist system, the young top mountaineers of the 1980s rejected any form of cooperation with the state. The GDR was in decline and the mountaineers were influenced by the US-climbing-scene of Yosemite Valley in California. Fritz Wiessner, a famous mountaineer from Dresden, who had migrated to the USA in 1929, visited Saxon regularly. In 1976, he even brought some friends with him, namely the American elite climbers Steve Wunsch, Henry Barber und Rick Hatch (Richter 1979; Wunsch 1979; Däweritz 1983). They had a substantial impact, especially on the young GDR climbers of the time. Many of them felt like outcasts from society: 'I think that a majority of them, at least those that were firmly established in the scene, were probably [...] dropout types. They just wanted out, for the main part, they couldn't identify with the system' (Adler). Climbing became a 'gathering place for people who wanted to get away from the mainstream, who used it as an outlet, to get outdoors, away from this permanent stress, this political, societal pressure' (Teubert). It was characteristic of this last decade of the GDR that people were taking great risks in climbing legendary and exposed routes without rope. 'I think that was also a reflection of the times, that you wanted to test yourself, and that was the only way. It was, in the 80s, so to say, also a certain way to live out increased individuality' (Adler; see also Lange 1993).

Many of the top climbers led a unique and dangerous life, with mountaineering as their only maxim (Lange 1993). During the warm season, they lived in huts and caves in Saxon Switzerland and only took simple jobs from time to time to earn some money and to avoid conflict with the state because of 'asocial behavior'.

> We were actually mainly those who then worked in church organizations, because you were also left alone there. I tended graves at the cemetery, as an alibi. There you were for just three days a week, did your job [...]. But you were left in peace and the rest of time was spent in Saxon Switzerland (Schelzel).

The relatively young scene was not clearly defined and people came and went, but there was nevertheless a shared identity: 'We did everything together: celebrating – philosophizing – climbing' (Lange 1993, 57). There was a climbers' football tournament, a sports festival with 'nonsense' disciplines, and so-called *Schrammelbands* (amateur music bands) gave concerts. The *Schlappseil-Fasching*, a carnival party, became so popular that a pub was no longer big enough and a large hall had to be hired. There was a special code of honour between the young mountaineers. You were respected when you

> had as little as possible to do with the system, and despised it, despite this went your own way and could climb well and remained relaxed at the same time [...]. The performance itself, to get to the top somewhere, that was unimportant (Beilke).

Opting out of GDR-society did not automatically lead the mountaineers to political resistance. They were not interested in direct political actions, said Gerald Krug. Uwe Schönfisch characterized climbing as an 'escape, where you could break rules, without landing in jail' (Schönfisch).

> It was maybe not active resistance, but it was simply ... , well not (really) resistance, like you might imagine with fliers or whatever, but it was simply a way of experiencing a kind of resistance. Everything was aimed to say: well, not like this! (Beilke).

Freedom vs. borders[14]

In the first post-war years, the border between Eastern and Western Germany was still open. By train, by hitchhiking or even by bike more and more Saxon mountaineers travelled to the Alps (Wankerl 1979). In the 1950s, however, the first well-known mountaineers, like Herbert Wünsche (1953) and Harry Schöne (1954), emigrated from the newly founded GDR. Their example encouraged others and from the mid-1950s, hundreds of mountaineers moved to the West, among them a lot of top climbers, like Lothar Brandler, Dietrich Hasse, Roland Wankerl and Harry Rost (Hasse 1979; Wankerl 1979). The reasons for leaving their Saxon home country entailed not only political frustration, but also a desire for adventure, 'the drive towards great Alpine rock and ice tours, the desire to be able to go wherever we wanted' (Wankerl 1979, 241). Most of the Saxons moved to Bavaria, close to the Alps, and caused an 'Invasion of Saxons' (Huber 1979, 257). The GDR Moutaineering Federation (DWBO) regarded the emigrants as 'traitors' (Däweritz 1979, 56) and a re-entry ban was imposed on the famous Dietrich Hasse. Socialist climber Hans Joachim Scholz wrote that the 'secret service agents of the West Germany' would headhunt mountaineers in an attempt to lure them to the West. 'It is really time to act decisively against all traitors, and to severely punish those, who are working against us on behalf of foreign powers' (Scholz 1958, 18). Letters from emigrants, such as one from Dietrich Hasse in 1958, were rejected by the mountaineering magazines: 'That is where mountain friendship ends' (Hammer et al. 1958, 11).

After Russian forces crushed the Prague Spring (August 21, 1968), the problems with the summit registers became so serious that the GDR Mountaineering Federation (DWBV) issued a statement: 'In various entries, our socialist German Democratic Republic has been defamed and the politics of the party and government dragged through the mud. We will address this graffiti strongly and distance ourselves firmly from such elements' (KFA Dresden 1969a, 1; see also KFA Dresden 1969b). These problems were even noticed in West Germany. The Munich magazine Alpinismus (1969, 58) wrote with a certain cynical glee, 'The responsible officials of the hiking and mountaineering organization had difficulties in quickly replacing the summit books that had been sullied in this way.'

At the beginning of the 1970s, the Ministry of State Security (MfS) started operation Bergsteiger (mountaineer). With the help of unofficial collaborators (Inoffizielle Mitarbeiter, IM), the summit books would be controlled regularly and replaced immediately in cases of graffiti. The handwriting was to be examined and compared with other writing from the summit book archive (Gliniorz 2003). 'All mountaineers should be careful about this', the official Martin Weinhold (1972) warned mountaineers. 'It may seem like only a few words crossed out of the summit book, but it means you are declaring yourself to be not for, but against, socialism'.

Against this background, it is not surprising that many summit books suddenly got 'lost' and never found their way to the archive (Heinicke 1976). However, the operation did not succeed and terminated after one year in 1976. 'If this had taken place in the guest book of any museum or something like that, they would have dug around until they had found the guilty party. But with 1,100 summit books, they were overstretched', argued Horst Mempel, a popular sports journalist, contemporary witness and unofficial collaborator (IM).

The summit registers became a popular place to make critical comments about the socialist state and its party, sometimes anonymous, often even with a signature:

> If mankind/ entwines itself in the clutches of tyranny,/ we will proclaim in the mountains/ the right to freedom. KCD 1959 (summit register Lößnitzturm, April 10 1966).[15]

> "To submit to this world, as if it were immutable,/ means to bow down in cowardice to the most shameful slavery,/ it means to suffocate the God in us with our own hands!" W. J. K. C. Lorenzsteiner, Sebnitz (summit register Goldstein, January 24 1970 [partially torn]).[16]

> "We want to be free, just like our fathers were." Schiller KV Sonnentürmer (summit register Fensterturm, January 22 1977).[17]

These entries show the perception of the mountains as refuges of liberty in a country in the hands of a dictatorship. They express a very idealistic view of man with divine attitudes. These attitudes compel him to fight for liberty. This liberty existed in the history of Saxon Mountaineering and the climbers sought to recover it once again. In the 1980s and especially during the 'peaceful revolution' (1989/1990), the slogans became more and more political and provocative:

Only a dead fish swims with the current! KC Bautzen (summit register Pilzturm, January 1 1982).[18]

All share the same sky, but not all the same horizon! Andreas Müller [and an illegible signature] (summit register Ganskopf, February 4 1986).[19]

The dinosaurs are extinct/ because they had too much "armor"/ and too little brain! Cato, Heijo (summit register Goldstein, March 29, 1987).[20]

From the coast to Saxony/ no mountain is a challenge for us./ From East to West/ that we cannot test! HSG WPU Rostock (summit register Falkenturm, February 16 1988).[21]

It is not enough to have no ideas, you also have to be incapable of realizing them! Jens Weinhold [and two illegible signatures] (summit register Kampfturmwächter, January 21 1989).[22]

Only a prisoner who moves [is not passive, K.R.], notices his chains. K.V. Sommerwand 1952 (summit register Schiefe Zacke, January 1 1989).[23]

"It is intolerable to live in a country where there is no sense of humor, but it is much more intolerable to live in a country, where you need your sense of humor (so much)." Brecht [two illegible signatures] (summit register Meurerturm, January 1 1989).[24]

The sun smiles on Spain, but the whole world laughs at the GDR!!! [four illegible signatures] (summit register Goldstein, January 2, 1989).[25]

Berg Heil [Mountain Health/Salvation] in the year of freedom 1990 AD. Heinz Renner [and an illegible signature] (summit register Wartburg, January 20, 1990).[26]

Many of the young mountaineers of the 1980s had already emigrated. For them, it was just a logical step towards a real escape (Adler; Schelzel). There are several names of climbing routes from those days, such as *Flüchtlingsgespräch* (The Refugee Talk) or *Visafrei* (Without a Visa), which express such thoughts and notions. Again, it was not only about political repression, but also the desire for new challenges in the mountain ranges of the world. Trying to flee the state was particularly dangerous. 'Over the border with its fences and mines – that was a risky business. You had to be really depressed or stand with your back to the wall so that you said, "I'll risk it now"' (Schelzel). However, there was a lot of frustration among the climbers, which were used to taking risks: 'We were prepared to take risks, we did it in our sport, and then also in real life' (Adler). Uwe Schönfisch planned his flight for a long time, organized a visa for Romania, went from there to Hungary and crossed the green border to Austria. But not all escapes worked out so well. Many attempts failed, which generally meant one or two years of prison (Schelzel; Adler; see also Wobst-Wylezol 2005).

It was less dangerous to apply for an emigration permit, but this led to severe discrimination against the relatives left behind. 'Well, my brother wouldn't have been admitted to the EOS [senior classes at school, K.R.], my father would have lost his job' (Beilke). The heads of mountaineering BSGs with many applicants could also get into trouble themselves. Arthur Treutler from BSG Empor Dresden-Löbtau was interrogated several times by the Ministry of State Security (MfS) (Wobst-Wylezol 2005). Nevertheless, in the 1980s a lot of young people applied for an emigration permit, as Uwe Schönfisch remembered: 'There was simply a large number of people, who had just had enough of this rotten system and wanted out' (Schönfisch). The effect was similar to the 1950s. 'You could just feel it. *He* had gone and *he* had gone, or a whole family of somebody's (just) disappeared one day' (Adler). Applicant Falk Schelzel saw a political dimension in this movement that grew like an epidemic and finally, at the end of the 1980s, destabilized the entire state.

Summary and interpretation

Saxon Mountaineering was a cradle of rock climbing. It started in the second half of the nineteenth century and developed a strong ethical climbing tradition. The use of ladders or any other devices was not allowed. Organized in small clubs, the climbers developed their own identity with a strong feeling of independence. After World War II, under the regime of the Socialist Unity Party (SED), the climbers were forced to join the new socialist Cooperative Sports Collectives (BSG). Because of the political pressure, the climbers agreed to do so, but this was just a pretense and an insincere integration. In fact, under the socialist surface, they still were organized in the form of the traditional clubs. Under the name of 'rope teams', they finally had to be tolerated by the GDR officials. The communist functionaries also tried to re-define climbing as a conventional sport. This can be seen, for example, in the standardized sports classification system, which was intended to motivate all athletes to increase their performance in training and competition. However, many of the mountaineers refused to take part and insisted that mountaineering was more than just a sport. For them, it was a romantic search for liberty, friendship, nature and adventure. Consequently, many of the climbers rejected any form of cooperation with the socialist state. In the 1950s, when the border was still open, the lucky few migrated to West Germany. In the 1980s, those who remained became social outcasts, leading a unique and dangerous life, with mountaineering as their only maxim and real outlet.

Similar conflicts between sportsmen and the GDR regime are evident in other maladjusted sport scenes like martial arts (Austermühle 1998), windsurfing (Wiese and Huster 2003) and skateboarding (Reinhart 2010b). They can also be found among the alpinists and adventurers who illegally crossed the borders of the Soviet Bloc in order to reach high mountain ranges, wild rivers or other spectacular landscapes (Reinhart 2014). Back in 1992, the sports sociologist Henning Eichberg proposed that these informal sport scenes were precursors of the revolution itself (Hietzge-Hof 1993). This can also be said of the Saxon mountaineers. They developed and established their own individualistic way of life: 'To be on a high peak, the sky so near, to determine everything yourself, to put oneself at risk or turn back, not to have any restrictions, that is a world with which I could identify', Herbert Wünsche explained. Forming their own identity, they rejected the way of life preached by socialist propaganda. The political effect of such a seemingly non-political attitude should not be underestimated. After the regime had built the Berlin Wall in 1961, the situation stabilized for a decade, but in the 1980s, there was a real exodus as contemporary witness Falk Schelzel remembered all too well:

Especially among the mountain climbers, there were a lot of people who wanted to leave the country […]. It was like an infection […]. You began to think about it for the first time, and then it started to grow. Mountaineering was really a calling, which made it a popular way to escape.

Tortured by wanderlust and a longing for freedom, the mountaineers of the GDR felt more and more like prisoners. In this manner and context, they can be regarded as precursors to the mass exodus of East Germans in 1989, which led to the 'peaceful revolution' of 1989/ 1990.

In the spirit of the French philosopher Michel Foucault, a further interpretation of Saxon Mountaineering is possible. He argued that reducing subversion to the fields of legislation and politics does not capture the true character of the power of the modern state. Far more so than the right, life itself became the subject of political struggles (i.e. the self-fulfillment and happiness of the people) (Foucault 1976). This describes very clearly the central conflict between the Saxon mountaineers and the GDR state. Resistance against modern 'power technologies' consists, according to Foucault, of replacing a way of living and identity prescribed by the state, with one's own forms of living and being (Foucault 1994). This is exactly what the Saxon mountaineers were seeking for and what they indeed practiced. Thus, Saxon Mountaineering in the GDR can be considered as a bodily 'technology of the self' and a practice of resistance.

Notes

1. The original term in Saxon is *Bergsteigen* (mountaineering). To distinguish between travel and climbing activities in high mountains, the term *Felsklettern* (rock climbing) can be used.
2. A rope team is a group of mountaineers who are linked together by a safety rope. In a more general sense, a group of mountaineers, travelling together, can also be called a rope team.
3. Some contemporary witnesses and experts like Joachim Schindler question the numbers of losses given by Hasse.
4. § (Paragraph) 8 of the passport law (*Pass-Gesetz*) and §213 of the penal code (*Strafgesetzbuch, StGB*) penalized any attempt to leave the country. The sentences extended from monetary penalties to eight years in prison. Between 1961 and 1989, several hundred people died while trying to cross the border illegally. The exact figures are not known (Hertle & Sälter 2006). Travelling to Western countries was only possible for people with special functions, like sportsmen, or retired persons. Travelling in states of the Eastern Bloc was possible, but for most of the countries, a special permission (Reiseanalge für den visafreien Reiseverkehr) was required to enter.
5. In the interest of simplification, only the English term (GDR) Mountaineering Federation will be used in this paper. The original German name is in brackets. There have been various different organizational structures and names, especially in the post-war years. For the purpose of this paper, they are not relevant.
6. DWBV: *Deutscher Wanderer- und Bergsteigerverband der DDR (1958–1970)*; DWBO: *Deutscher Verband für Wandern, Bergsteigen und Orientierungslauf der DDR (1970–1990)*.
7. KFA: *Kreisfachausschuss*; SFA: *Stadtfachausschuss*
8. Cooperative Sports Collectives (*Betriebssportgemeinschaft*). They represented the basic organization of mass sports, while the sport associations (*Sportgemeinschaft, SG*) and sport clubs (*Sportclub, SC*) were reserved for elite athletes.
9. A comprehensive reflexion on the potential and the problems of oral history can be found in Reinhart (2015).
10. *Bereit zur Arbeit und zur Verteidigung.*
11. Dynamo was the nationwide sports association of the Ministry for State Security (*Ministerium für Staatssicherheit, MfS*) and the police (*Volkspolizei*).

12. Wenn zwei zusammen streben / in der Berge freier Natur, / folgen durchs ganze Leben / verbunden der Freiheit Spur. // Bergfreunde sind sie dann, / zwei verbunden wie einer, / und stürmen gegen die Welten an. / Auseinander bringt sie keiner.

13. The German Turner [gymnastic] movement was started in the early 19th century when Germany was occupied by Napoleon. The Turners organized themselves in clubs and were as much athletic as they were politically active; fighting for democracy, liberalism and a national state.

14. The history of Alpinists and adventurers from Eastern Germany who crossed borders illegally and travelled to the high mountain ranges of the Soviet Bloc, such as the Pamir or the Caucasus, can be found in Reinhart (2014).

15. Mag sich die Menschheit/ auch in Tyrannenklauen winden,/ Wir werden von den Bergen/ der Freiheit Recht verkünden. KCD 1959 (summit register Lößnitzturm, April 10, 1966).

16. 'Sich in diese Welt, als in etwas Unabänderliches zu fügen,/ heißt feige unter die allerschimpflichste Knechtschaft sich beugen,/ heißt den Gott in uns mit eigenen Händen zu ersticken!'W. J. K. C. Lorenzsteiner, Sebnitz (summit register Goldstein, January 24, 1970 [partially torn])

17. 'Wir wollen frei sein/ wie unsere Väter waren.'Schiller KV Sonnentürmer.

18. Nur ein toter Fisch schwimmt mit dem Strom! KC Bautzen.

19. Alle haben den gleichen Himmel,/ aber nicht alle den gleichen Horizont! Andreas Müller [und eine unleserliche Unterschrift].

20. Die Saurier sind ausgestorben/ weil sie zuviel 'Panzer'/ und zu wenig Gehirn hatten! Cato, Heijo

21. Von der Küste bis nach Sachsen/ kein Berg ist uns gewachsen./ Von Osten nach Westen/ das könn' wir ja nicht testen! HSG WPU Rostock.

22. Es genügt nicht, keine Ideen zu haben, man muß auch unfähig sein, sie zu verwirklichen! Jens Weinhold [und zwei unleserliche Unterschriften].

23. Nur ein Gefangener der sich bewegt merkt seine Ketten. K.V. Sommerwand 1952.

24. 'Es ist unerträglich, in einem Land zu leben, in dem es keinen Humor gibt, aber noch viel unerträglicher ist es in einem Land, wo man Humor braucht.' Brecht [zwei unleserliche Unterschriften] (summit register Meurerturm, January 1, 1989).

25. Über Spanien lacht die Sonne über die DDR die ganze Welt!!! [vier unleserliche Unterschriften] (summit register Goldstein, January 2, 1989).

26. Bergheil im Jahre der Freiheit anno 1990. Heinz Renner [und eine unleserliche Unterschrift] (summit register Wartburg, January 20, 1990).

Disclosure statement

No potential conflict of interest was reported by the author.

References

Alpinismus. 1969. "Elbsandsteingebirge-Gipfelbücher mußten ausgetauscht werden." *Alpinismus* 7 (4): 58.

Ardito, Stefano. 2000. *Die Eroberung der Giganten: Von der Erstbesteigung des Montblanc bis zum Freeclimbing*. München: Bucher.

Arnold, Bernd. 1999. *Zwischen Schneckenhaus und Dom*. Köngen: Panico Alpinverlag.

Austermühle, Theo. 1998. "Konflikte und Konfliktlösungen im Sport." In *Alltagssport in der DDR*, edited by Jochen Hinsching, 135–159. Aachen: Meyer & Meyer.

Däweritz, Karl. 1979. Klettern im sächsischen Fels. Berlin (East): Sportverlag.

Däweritz, Karl. 1983. *Klettern im sächsischen Fels*. Seconf edition. Berlin, East: Sportverlag.

DWBO. 1988. Zeittafel zur Geschichte des DWBO der DDR, seines historischen Erbes und seiner Sportarten: Verbandsinternes Material. O. O. [Leipzig]: Deutscher Verband für Wandern, Bergsteigen und Orientierungslauf.

DWBV. 1958. "Arbeitsentschließung des 1. Verbandstages des DWBV im DTSB am 14. und 15. Juni 1958 in Dresden." *Skisport und Touristik* 2 (11): 12–13.

DWBV. 1964. *100 Jahre Bergsteigen im Elbsandsteingebirge. Festschrift*. Dresden: Druckerei Erich Zobler.

Fehrmann, Rudolf. 1913. *Der Bergsteiger in der Sächsischen Schweiz (2. Aufl.)*. Dresden: Siegel.

FK Auslandsfahrten. 1972. "Die FK Auslandsfahrten teilt mit." *Wandern und Bergsteigen* 18 (4): 8.

Foucault, Michel. 1976. *Histoire de la sexualité. Tome 1. La volonté de savoir*. Paris: Gallimard.

Foucault, Michel. 1994. "Interview de Michel Foucault." In *Dits et Écrits 1954–1988. Tome IV. 1980–1988*, edited by Daniel Defert, and Francois Ewald, 688–696. Paris: Gallimard.

Frank, Johann. 1955. "So etwas darf nicht wiederkehren!." *Sektion Touristik der Deutschen Demokratischen Sportbewegung – Kreis Dresden* 2 (12), without page number.

Franz, Robert Otto. 1953. "Über die Sportklassifizierung im Bergsteigen." *Freundschaft* 1 (1): 7–8.

Gliniorz, Heinz. 2003. "Sie nannten es "Gipfelbuchschmierereien"." In *Gipfelbücher und Bergsprüche*, edited by Joachim Schindler, and Gerd Uhlig, 69–71. Dresden: Selbstverlag.

Gottfried, Andreas. (Bearb.). 2000. *Fritz Wiessner 1900–1988*. Dresden: Sächsischer Bergsteigerbund.

Hammer, Rolf, Reiner Protze, Lothar Ulbricht, Günther Schultz, Erich Wauer, Martin Eisewig, Rainer Krahl, et al. 1958. "Da hört die Bergfreundschaft auf." *Skisport und Touristik* 2 (16): 11.

Hänsel, Hannes. 1959. "Schmierfinken auf den Gipfeln." *Skisport und Touristik* 3 (16): 12–13.

Hasse, Dietrich. 1969. "Bergheil – Bergfrei." *Alpinismus* 7 (5): 33.

Hasse, Dietrich. 1979. "Geschichte des Sächsischen Bergsteigens." In *Felsenheimat Elbsandsteingebirge. Sächsisch-Böhmische Schweiz: Erlebnis einer Landschaft und ihrer künstlerischen Darstellung; ein Jahrhundert sächsisches Bergsteigen*, edited by Dietrich Hasse, and Heinz Lothar Stutte, 133–210. Wolfratshausen/Obb: Stutte.

Hasse, Dietrich. 1993. "Erinnerungen an die Nachkriegszeit im Elbsandsteingebirge." In *Klettern im Elbsandsteingebirge*, edited by Frank Richter, 36–41. München: Berg.

Hasse, Dietrich. 2000. *Wiege des Freikletterns (2. Durchgesehene Aufl.)*. München: Bergverlag Rother.

Heinicke, Dietmar. 1976. "Alte Gipfelbücher noch im Privatbesitz?" *Wandern und Bergsteigen* 22 (7/8): 4.

Hempel, Lothar. 2002. "50 Jahre KC Lokomotive Dresden 1950." *Aus der Sächsischen Bergsteigergeschichte* 8 (8): 20–22.

Hertle, Hans-Hermann, and G. Sälter. 2006. "Die Todesopfer an Mauer und Grenze." *Deutschland Archiv* 39: 667–676.

Hietzge-Hof, Corinna. 1993. "Norbert Elias im Diskurs der Sportwissenschaften." *Sportwissenschaft* 23 (2): 219–221.

Hoyer, Siegfried. 1996. "Reaktion auf die 1. Publikation der IG." *Aus der Sächsischen Bergsteigergeschichte*. 2 (2): 34–36.

Huber, Hans. 1979. "Das sächsische Element im alpinen Nachkriegsbergsteigen." In *Felsenheimat Elbsandsteingebirge. Sächsisch-Böhmische Schweiz: Erlebnis einer Landschaft und ihrer künstlerischen Darstellung; ein Jahrhundert sächsisches Bergsteigen*, edited by Dietrich Hasse, and Heinz Lothar Stutte, 257–258. Wolfratshausen/Obb.: Stutte.

Illmer, Paul, Paul Dachsel, and Hans Schmidt. 1958. "An Alle!." *Sektion Touristik im Deutschen Turn- und Sportbund Stadtfachausschuss Dresden* 5 (6): 2.

KFA Dresden. 1969a. "Erklärung." *Wandern und Bergsteigen* 15 (1): 1.

KFA Dresden. 1969b. "Erklärung." *Der Tourist* 8 (2): 9.

KFA Dresden. 1970. "Entwurf zum Jahresprogramm." *Wandern und Bergsteigen* 16 (2): 2.

Lange, Uwe. 1993. "Selbstbefreiung durch Klettern: Unsere achtziger Jahre." In *Klettern im Elbsandsteingebirge*, edited by Frank Richter, 54–59. München: Berg.

Löwinger, Hans. 1958. "Kaukasusfahrt 1958." *Skisport und Touristik* 1 (15): 9.

Messner, Reinhold. 2002. *Vertical: 100 Jahre Kletterkunst*. München: BLV.

Nikolai, Karl Heinrich. 1801. *Wegweiser durch die Sächsische Schweiz. Nebst einer Reisekarte.* Pirna: Arnoldische Buch- und Kunsthandlung.

Pankotsch, Hans. 1953. "Antwort an BSG Empor Dresden-Löbtau." *Freundschaft* 1 (2): 27.

Reinhart, Kai. 2010a. *Wir wollten einfach unser Ding machen": DDR-Sportler zwischen Fremdbestimmung und Selbstverwirklichung.* Frankfurt/M.: Campus.

Reinhart, Kai. 2010b. ""I ollied the Berlin Wall" – An Empirical and Theoretical Study on Skateboarding in Socialist East Germany (GDR)." *Stadion* 36: 157–176.

Reinhart, Kai. 2014. "On Hidden Trails – Mountaineers and Adventurers in Communist Germany (GDR)." *The International Journal of the History of Sport* 31 (12): 1535–1554. doi: 10.1080/09523367.2014.922547.

Reinhart, Kai. 2015. "Oral History in der (Sport-)Geschichte." In *Sport - Geschichte - Pädagogik. Festschrift zum 60. Geburtstag von Michael Krüger,* edited by Emanuel Hübner, and Kai Reinhart, 267–285. Hildesheim: Arete.

Richter, Kurt Bruno. 1962. *Der Sächsische Bergsteiger.* Berlin, East: Sportverlag.

Richter, H. 1979. "Drei Amerikaner im Elbsandsteingebirge." In *Felsenheimat Elbsandsteingebirge. Sächsisch-Böhmische Schweiz: Erlebnis einer Landschaft und ihrer künstlerischen Darstellung; ein Jahrhundert sächsisches Bergsteigen,* edited by Dietrich Hasse, and Heinz Lothar Stutte, 269. Wolfratshausen/Obb: Stutte.

Richter, Frank. 1993. *Klettern im Elbsandsteingebirge.* München: Berg.

Richter, Helmut. 2003. "In memoriam Karlheinz Gonda." *Aus der Sächsischen Bergsteigergeschichte* 9 (9): 19–21.

Richter, Herbert. 2006. "Mein Weg zum Berg." *Aus der Sächsischen Bergsteigergeschichte* 12 (12): 14–17.

Schindler, Joachim. 1988. "Bildung, Entwicklung und Tätigkeit des Verbandes freier bergsportlicher Vereinigungen (VfbV): Zur Formierung einer proletarischen Dresdner Touristen- und Bergsteigervereinigung der zwanziger Jahre." In *Tourismus (2. durchges. Aufl.),* edited by Wolfgang Bagger, 147–167. Berlin, East: Wissenschaftsbereich Kultur der Sektion Ästhetik und Kunstwissenschaften der Humboldt-Universität zu Berlin.

Schindler, Joachim. 2001. "Entwicklung von Wandern und Bergsteigen in der Sächsischen Schweiz sowie zur Arbeit touristischer Organisationen Dresdens von 1945–1953." In *Aktionsfelder des DDR-Sports in der Frühzeit 1945–1965,* edited by Wolfgang Buss, and Christian Becker, 435–523. Köln: Sport & Buch Strauß.

Schindler, Joachim. 2003. "Gipfelbücher – geachtet oder missachtet?" In *Gipfelbücher und Bergsprüche,* edited by Joachim Schindler, and Gerd Uhlig, 5–102. Dresden: Selbstverlag.

Schlosser, Heinz. 1953. "Das Präsidium der Sektion antwortet." *Freundschaft* 1 (5): 69–73.

Schlosser, Heinz. 1955. "Die Touristik – ein Mittel zur patriotischen Erziehung unserer Jugend und der Werktätigen." *Theorie und Praxis der Körperkultur* 4: 481–488.

Scholz, Hans-Joachim. 1958. "Verräter." *Der Wintersport mit Touristik* 2 (1): 18.

Schwer, Siegfried. 1989. "Tradition und Verpflichtung" [Sonderheft]." *Wandern und Bergsteigen* 35: 1–2.

Summit register Falkenturm. February 16, 1988. Gipfelbucharchiv des Sächsischen Bergsteigerbundes (SBB) Archiv-Nr. 3555, 10.5.1987–8.10.2001.

Summit register Fensterturm. January 22, 1977. Gipfelbucharchiv des Sächsischen Bergsteigerbundes (SBB) Archiv-Nr. 2781, 9.12.1972–23.7.1993.

Summit register Ganskopf. February 4, 1986. Gipfelbucharchiv des Sächsischen Bergsteigerbundes (SBB) Archiv-Nr. 2631, 6.11.1971–29.9.1989.

Summit register Goldstein. January 24, 1970. Gipfelbucharchiv des Sächsischen Bergsteigerbundes (SBB) Archiv-Nr. 282, 7.10.1969–8.10.1972.

Summit register Goldstein. March 29, 1987 and January 2, 1989. Gipfelbucharchiv des Sächsischen Bergsteigerbundes (SBB) Archiv-Nr. 2483, 18.5.1984–15.5.1989.

Summit register Kampfturmwächter. January 21, 1989. Gipfelbucharchiv des Sächsischen Bergsteigerbundes (SBB) Archiv-Nr. 3173, 24.6.1978–23.7.1997.

Summit register Lößnitzturm. April 10, 1966. Gipfelbucharchiv des Sächsischen Bergsteigerbundes (SBB) Archiv-Nr. 2315, 11.11.1962–19.7.1987.

Summit register Meurerturm. January 1, 1989. Gipfelbucharchiv des Sächsischen Bergsteigerbundes (SBB) Archiv-Nr. 3323, 24.9.1988–3.4.1999.

Summit register Pilzturm. January 1, 1982. Gipfelbucharchiv des Sächsischen Bergsteigerbundes (SBB) Archiv-Nr. 2358, 10.10.1976–6.10.1989.

Summit register Schiefe Zacke. January 1, 1989. Gipfelbucharchiv des Sächsischen Bergsteigerbundes (SBB) Archiv-Nr. 2378, 28.3.1987–24.3.1989.

Teichler, Hans Joachim, ed. 2002. *Die Sportbeschlüsse des Politbüros: Eine Studie zum Verhältnis von SED und Sport mit einem Gesamtverzeichnis und einer Dokumentation ausgewählter Beschlüsse.* Köln: Sport & Buch Strauß.

Wächtler, Martin. 1938. "Freiwilligenmeldung zu den Gebirgsjägern für Herbst 1938." *Der Sächsische Bergsteiger* 19 (1): 4.

Wankerl, Roland. 1979. "Münchner Sachsen." In *Felsenheimat Elbsandsteingebirge. Sächsisch-Böhmische Schweiz: Erlebnis einer Landschaft und ihrer künstlerischen Darstellung; ein Jahrhundert Sächsisches Bergsteigen*, edited by Dietrich Hasse, and Heinz Lothar Stutte, 238–254. Wolfratshausen/Obb.: Stutte.

Weinhold, Martin. 1972. "Gedanken zu Gipfelsprüchen." *Der Tourist* 11 (5): 3–4.

Wiese, René, and Ronald Huster. 2003. "Brettsegeln in der DDR." In *Sport in der DDR. Eigensinn, Konflikte, Trends*, edited by Hans Joachim Teichler, 425–500. Köln: Sport & Buch Strauß.

Wiessner, Fritz. 1979. "Die Ausstrahlung des Sächsischen Bergsteigens auf das Bergsteigen in Nordamerika und in der Welt." In *Felsenheimat Elbsandsteingebirge. Sächsisch-Böhmische Schweiz: Erlebnis einer Landschaft und ihrer künstlerischen Darstellung; ein Jahrhundert Sächsisches Bergsteigen*, edited by Dietrich Hasse, and Heinz Lothar Stutte, 236–237. Wolfratshausen/Obb.: Stutte.

Wobst-Wylezol, Bettina. 2005. Bergsport in der DDR: Im Spannungsfeld zwischen sozialistischer Körperkultur und Tradition. Hagen: Fernuniversität. Unpublished Master thesis.

Wunsch, Steve. 1979. "Noch sind die Leistungen im freien Elbsandsteinklettern unübertroffen." In *Felsenheimat Elbsandsteingebirge. Sächsisch-Böhmische Schweiz: Erlebnis einer Landschaft und ihrer künstlerischen Darstellung; ein Jahrhundert sächsisches Bergsteigen*, edited by Dietrich Hasse, and Heinz Lothar Stutte, 263–268. Wolfratshausen/Obb.: Stutte.

Interviews with contemporary witnesses

Adler, Alexander, born 1968, grew up in Saxony, from the mid-1980s a top performer, first repeated the *action directe* route of W. Güllich (UIAA XI-), studied art, owner of a climbing and sport center, (interview on October 6, 2004)

Arnold, Bernd, born 1947, grew up in Saxon Switzerland, in the 1970s and 1980s outstanding developer of climbing in the GDR and world leader, single record holder with 872 first ascents in Saxon Switzerland, self-employed printer, owner of a climbing school and mountaineering shop (interview on August 4, 2004)

Beilke, Jörn, born 1968, grew up in Saxony, by the age of 16, already a top performer in Saxon Switzerland, doctorally qualified mechanical engineer, self-employed engineer (interview on October 25, 2004)

Biock, Martin, born 1942, grew up in Saxony, climbed to the limits of high-performance sport, several escape attempts, for this reason was imprisoned between 1965 and 1967, 1968 successful escape to West Germany, carpenter, self-employed filmmaker (interview on April 14, 2005)

Eckert, Walter „Backe", born 1937, grew up in Saxony, climbed to the limits of high-performance sport in the post-war years with SG Dynamo Dresden, active organizer of the club scene, locksmith (interview on October 5, 2004)

Klingner, Erhard, born 1943, grew up in Saxony, manufactured and sold private climbing gear on the black market, numerous expeditions, self-employed engineer (interview on August 4, 2004)

Mempel, Horst, born 1938, grew up in Saxony-Anhalt, GDR champion in decathlon, periodically active as an unofficial collaborator (IM) with the GDR system, sport and travel reporter in GDR television and for MDR radio (interview on October 4, 2004)

Richter, Herbert, born 1935, grew up in Saxony, member of the national alpine team from the early 1960s to his exclusion from the team in 1967, 'consummator' of classical Saxon Mountaineering, geophysicist (interview on October 6, 2004)

Schelzel, Falk, born 1963, grew up in Saxony, high-performance climber 1980–1983, 1984 left for Bavaria, self-employed master roofer (interview on November 22, 2004)

Schönfisch, Uwe „Schöni", born 1967, grew up in Berlin, high performance climber, development of
     boulder area Quackenwald near Ludwigsfelde/Berlin, 1989 escaped via Hungary, rooftop plumber,
     businessman, manager of a mountaineering shop (interview on July 30, 2004)
Teubert, Andersen, born 1962, grew up in Vogtland, owner of a mountaineering shop, manufacturer
     of climbing walls (interview on August 4, 2004)
Wünsche, Herbert, born 1929, grew up in Saxony, high performance climber of the post-war years,
     1953 relocation to Bavaria, numerous expeditions, model builder, top executive employee at BMW
     (interview on April 13, 2005)

Managing the rock-climbing economy: a case from Chattanooga

Andrew W. Bailey and Eric Hungenberg

ABSTRACT

Chattanooga is central to many rock-climbing locations that benefit the local economy. However, a lack of metrics quantifying the positive impacts render reliable access to and protection of land for the purpose of rock-climbing problematic. An influx of climbers also complicates land management policies and priorities. The purpose of this study was to determine the economic impacts of climbing in Chattanooga, and to clarify management preferences of activity participants.

Surveys were collected over nine months at five popular climbing areas. Information regarding demographics, climbing style and level, management preferences, and spending patterns were collected. Economic data were analyzed with IMPLAN software to determine indirect and induced impacts, as well as state and federal tax implications. An total impact of US$7 million was assessed, with another half-million in state and federal taxes. Management preferences differed by climbing site and number of visits, demonstrating the diversity of opinion within the climbing community.

Introduction

The growth of nature-based sports is an exciting and challenging phenomenon for participants and providers. The economic, social, and cultural impacts may be difficult to trace, due to relaxed permitting, remoteness of activity sites, and dispersed clientele. This study reports the methods and findings from an impact study on an emerging outdoor destination. Chattanooga is central to a variety of rock-climbing locations that have benefitted the local economy for decades. Having been described as 'America's dirtiest city' in 1969 (Neimark 2016), Chattanooga has successfully rebranded itself as an outdoor destination, recently winning a popular competition for the Best Outdoor Town Ever from Outside Magazine. This recognition has not come easily, and it brings with it many complications. Historically, climbers in this region have been tolerated but not courted (cf. Frank 2012). A lack of metrics quantifying the positive impacts have rendered it difficult to justify access to and protection of land for the purpose of rock-climbing. An influx of climbers also complicates land management policies and priorities. The purpose of this study was to determine the economic impacts of rock-climbers to the Chattanooga region, and to clarify management proposals and priorities of activity participants.

Literature review

Commodifying natural landscapes

Visionaries, Frederick Law Olmstead and John Muir, were among the first to reference the potential for natural landscapes, not just as a space to foster recreation, but as a means to ensure economic viability as well. In an 1865 report commissioned by the state of California, Olmstead asserted that natural scenes of impressive character represented a financial opportunity for governments based upon their ability to draw tourists seeking to escape the mundane in search of life experiences which were novel and unique.

> It is but sixteen years since the Yosemite was first seen by a white man. Several visitors have since made a journey of several thousand miles at large cost to see it, and notwithstanding the difficulties which now interpose, hundreds resort to it annually. Before many years, if proper facilities are offered, these hundreds will become thousands and in a century the whole number of visitors will be counted by millions (Carr 2014, 11).

However, if economic stimulus were to be realized, it would require that local governments provide access, conserve the landscape, and promote it so that physical spaces not become monopolized by the few and experienced only by the elite (Olmstead 1865).

Olmstead's recommendations for outdoor spaces were novel at the time, but have since had significant implications on the commodification of natural resources. Natural resources, according to Howe (1979), include settings and systems that are useful to humans *or could be* under plausible technological, economic, and social circumstances. When a place can be characterized according to desirable features, it establishes itself as a commodified space, as it possesses a competitive advantage over alternative locations (Cross 2001). This relationship is thought to be more cognitive and physical rather than emotional. In other words, the natural environment is the vital resource that enhances the experience of a desired activity (Williams and Roggenbuck 1989). Similarly, the meaning an individual associates with place becomes a product of the collective attributes and amenities that render the experience important to one's self (Williams et al. 1992). This commodified relationship of space triggered a change in how local communities, states, and regions utilized historical architecture or natural landscape aesthetics for economic stimulus through nature-based adventure sport tourism (defined as travelling for the purpose of participating in an activity that features a high level of danger).

There are innumerable ways in which outdoor settings, sport, and recreation enrich a community's status (Crompton 2007; Harnik and Crompton 2014), but the most widely acknowledged comes in the form of economic impact. A community or region will view forms of subsidized programming and facilities (e.g. climbing sites on state sponsored land) as inducing economic impact permitting that the spending originates from visitors travelling from outside their area, and come as a direct result of the leisure commodity (i.e. rock climbing, whitewater rafting, alpine skiing). Fundamental elements to this concept include: (1) the recreation commodity must be exported from the relevant area to bring in new money, which can then recycle through the area's economy, producing employment, income, etc.; and (2) the relevant area must be clearly delineated (Beardsley 1971). For instance, visitors travelling to Chattanooga from a neighboring state for a rock-climbing excursion may provide net gains to the Chattanooga area in the form of lodging, food, gas, and miscellaneous expenditures made throughout their stay. This money then has a residual effect on the local economy as initial spending recirculates as business recipients purchase supplies and pay employees. This rippling action is referred to as a multiplier effect (Crompton 2011).

Despite recent evidence of the efficacy for state and national parks to create economic stimulus through outdoor adventure sport tourism (c.f. Cullinane and Koontz 2017; Maples et al. 2017; Taylor et al. 2013), outdoor space continues to be a difficult sell to politicians. According to Jeong and Crompton (2015), outdoor spaces, particularly those which are not artificially constructed, have difficulty securing budgetary support for multiple reasons, with the more pertinent explanations relating to: (1) outdoor spaces rarely present a prominent issue in political campaigns, (2) they are heavily subsidized through local, state and/or federal taxes, and (3) costs are easily visible while their economic value is not. Further, unlike special events whereby net gains in economic activity can easily be observed, natural landscapes pose greater challenges. For instance, permits to rock climb cease to exist in many locations, rarely is parking monitored with fees or tracking procedures, and there is no database with contact information that can be used to survey rock climbers. As a consequence, parks and natural landscapes are perceived as being 'invisible assets,' commodities often times overlooked by legislators. When this occurs, Olmstead's recommendations fail to be realized because marketing dollars are not being allocated to promote visitation, landscape architectural work is not conducted to accelerate access, and conservation funds are not awarded to safeguard a destination's differentiating amenities. Thus, when the debate over opportunity costs occurs among public policy decision makers, outdoor spaces generally lose out in the context of utility unless credible and significant economic impact support is provided.

Application of destination tourism model

Tourism activities predominantly occur at destinations that offer a combination of tourism products for visitors, providing them an integrated and unique experience (Buhalis 2000). For instance, Kotler, Haider, and Rein (1993) summarize a destination as a place that incorporates a complementary set of attractions, events, services, and goods to enhance a value proposition to visitors. In this way, a sport tourism destination's product mix and subsequent benefits that a tourism location can offer are what distinguishes it from substitute choices. This may occur through a destination's unique qualities and/or benefits to visitors, or through the enhanced cache' that an event affords to a destination (Jago et al. 2003). In reference to the former, Pike (2002) insists that destination events have a significant advantage over manufactured tourism environments because of their inimitable natural resources (e.g. landscapes and terrain). Given the dynamic and competitive nature of destination tourism, the success of a destination, then, is often predicated on its ability to provide and maintain such resources in a way that enriches tourists' individual needs and desires (Teodorescu et al. 2012).

Nature-based adventure sport tourism provides an excellent example of natural resource commodification. For instance, mountain destinations may become an attractive choice among alpine ski enthusiasts seeking a particular ski resort which possesses distinctive topography and a history of smooth, dry, and abundant snow fall. Likewise, an avid kayaker may select a destination based on its close proximity to technical, big water rapids that offer unique challenges to paddlers. These examples reflect an opportunity for destination event marketers to promote environmental and geographical resources as successful sport attractions that offer 1) benefits, 2) perceived by a sizeable customer group, 3) which these customers value and are willing to pay for, and 4) cannot readily be obtained elsewhere (Day and Wensley 1988).

Chattanooga has experienced steady growth since its rebranding in the early 1980s with population growth outpacing the national average for the last 20 years (O'Neil 2012). Tourism growth demonstrated similar gains, often double the annual growth rates of other regional destinations such as Atlanta, GA and Asheville, NC (O'Neil 2012) and reaching the milestone of US$1 billion in economic impact in 2015 (Flessner 2016). Much of this has been driven by accolades from popular media sources, regarding the aesthetics and outdoor recreational opportunities in the region (cf. Davis 2016). In addition, high-profile special events have helped to highlight Chattanooga's natural and built environment. In 2017, for example, the city hosted three separate Ironman™ competitions, each drawing 2500 competitors and their families (Tanner 2017).

In regard to Butler's (1980) tourism life cycle model, Chattanooga has entered the 'development' stage, being an established tourism destination with a well-defined tourism market. Maturation of the local tourism industry is evidenced by the emergence of small businesses catering to visitors, including paddleboard rentals, bike tour vendors, and even boutique hotels, such as the climbing-centric 'Crash Pad' hostel. This growth has not come without complications. The city has experienced the issues of lagging infrastructure, localized inflation, and gentrification that are common to tourism destinations (Cook 2015b). In addition, many of the attractions and special events are natural-resource dependent. Hiking, climbing, whitewater kayaking, and adventure races all incur wear on green spaces and increase traffic to natural areas adjacent to the city. This has raised concerns from local residents and land managers, provoking fears of 'loving our natural treasures to death' (Cook 2017). Before entering Butler's (1980) stages of 'consolidation' and 'stagnation,' where visitor capacity is reached, resources are compromised and travel interests wane, an inclusive tourism/land management model should be explored.

Natural resource management

Land management policies vary by agency, region, and geographic disposition. State and national forests embrace a multiple-use mindset, where recreation coexists with conservation, timbering, and resource extraction (Newsome, Moore, and Dowling 2012). State and national parks adhere to preservationist principles, restricting activities that would grossly impact the natural environment. Private landowner principles range across the spectrum. Regional differences exist within the preservation-conservation continuum, often due to practical necessity. Many parks in the western United States, for example, require special-use permits that limit visitor traffic to popular destinations. The southeastern U.S., including Chattanooga, is less restrictive, possibly due to a combination of lower visitation and a cultural tendency to resist bureaucratic (i.e. governmental) oversight (Somin 2014). The local Access Fund director, for instance, was taken aback at the lack of concern expressed by locals when confronted with the fact that they were climbing in areas with no legal access (Z. Lesch-Huie, personal communication, 12 April 2015). This attitude can place climbers at odds with state and federal land agencies, who often prefer a top-down approach to land policy based on a one-size-fits-all perspective (Culhane 2013).

Many agencies have begun to experiment with a more participative approach to land management (Bello, Carr, and Lovelock 2016; Jansson and Lindgren 2012; Plummer and Fennell 2009). This method may be preferred in areas where heavy-handed policy enforcement meets resistance from user groups. Collaborating with users and non-profits when drafting and enforcing policies imparts a sense of ownership to those who frequent protected areas. Feedback from users informs managing agencies about appropriate messaging and pragmatic solutions, while a sense of ownership enhances awareness of ecological impacts and self-enforcement of policies (Kil, Holland, and Stein 2014; Smith, Siderelis, and Moore 2010). The process of developing best practices for recreational activities across boundaries can help create a clear, unified policy that benefits both users and managers.

Managing local climbing

The current lack of a cohesive land management policy across agencies complicates the execution of policy planning, and often confuses users who recreate across agency lines. Climbing regulations differ at each location in our study, though access is managed by the Southeastern Climbers Coalition (SCC) and a local chapter of the Access Fund, two non-profit advocacy groups responsible for maintaining climbing areas so that they remain open. Regulations and natural features also dictate the style of climbing at various locations. The most restrictive area (Sunset Park) is located within the Chattanooga Military Park, managed by the National Park Service. Access to this site is strictly monitored, and only *traditional* style climbing is permitted (i.e. no permanent bolts are affixed to the rock). Two areas are managed by the State, albeit through different agencies. Foster Falls, a popular *sport-climbing* area, lies within the Tennessee State Park system, while the Tennessee Wall, a well-known *traditional* and *sport-climbing* crag, exists in the bounds of a Tennessee State Forest. Unlike *traditional* climbing areas, *sport-climbing* locations have permanent bolts affixed to the rock, requiring less gear and expertise, and often attracting a different clientele. Rocktown, a *bouldering* area (i.e. climbing lower to the ground with no rope) south of Chattanooga, is managed by the Georgia Department of Natural Resources. Finally, the most-visited site in our study was the Stone Fort (aka Little Rock City) bouldering area, which is located on a private golf course north of the city.

The variety of climbing styles and management models demonstrates the complexity in generating a unified climbing policy in the region. Historically, climbing has been seen as a liability and access remains precarious (c.f. Frank 2012). Climbing-specific access trails, bridges, signage and bolted routes are typically established and maintained by the SCC and an army of volunteers. Funding for such projects comes from personal donations, grants, and, occasionally, matching funds from land management agencies. There is no recurring funding from city, county, or state agencies. Legal resources (i.e. liability consulting, private property rights, etc.) are managed in conjunction with the Access Fund. Both the SCC and the local chapter of the Access Fund are directed by a single paid employee, despite the tall order of managing climbing areas from Florida to Kentucky.

Given the unknown economic impact of climbing in a region renowned for its resources, the purpose of this study was to determine the scope of climbing tourism and its impact on the local economy (i.e. Hamilton County). A secondary purpose was to explore user preferences for management policies, in order to lay the foundation for a cohesive, inclusive, sustainable climbing plan that supports residents and tourists. The following section will detail the methods, measures, and analyses incorporated in this study.

Methods

Data collection

Procedures outlined in the subsequent sections were designed to estimate the economic impact of rock climbing to Hamilton County, Tennessee. To calculate net new spending to the local area, five climbing areas were surveyed which allowed visitor expenditure data to act as a foundation for formulating an overall estimate of climbers' stimulus to Chattanooga. A visitor was defined as any climber who had travelled 30 miles or more with the primary intention to rock climb in Hamilton County. Creating a 'non-local' delineation based upon miles travelled has been considered a more effective approach than county or zip code identifiers due to respondents' lack of awareness of state county boundaries (Jeong and Crompton 2015). A local vs. non-local delineation was assured with an initial question posed to prospective respondents upon greeting them and at the beginning of the survey. Following this initial screening, climbers completed a self-administered survey comprised of questions garnering information pertaining to demographics, climbing style and level, management preferences, travel habits, and spending patterns. Spending categories provided in the questionnaire included food, lodging, entertainment, shopping (including outdoor recreation-related expenditures such as gear, apparel, etc.), transportation (i.e. gas), and other miscellaneous retail items (un-related to outdoor recreational spending). Only those lodging in hotels, motels, hostels, and house rentals were calculated in the lodging estimate of the economic impact. Thus, no lodging impact was calculated for those who camped out during their stay.

Data were collected using procedures developed and refined by the Texas Park and Wildlife Department (TPWD). TPWD's model is considered to be an accurate regional, state, and national level approach to analyzing economic effects of natural environments (Kaczynski, Crompton, and Emerson 2003). This procedure relies on calculating personal spending, group size, as well as visiting days of those climbing within the geographical impact area. To give an example, an individual climber was first asked to report their personal spending with respect to the identified categories listed above. Then parties were asked to provide the total amount of individuals in their travelling party and to report how many days and nights they were intending to stay in Chattanooga. Thus, if a party of four climbers elected to spend three days in Chattanooga to climb, then the total amount of visiting days was 12. These data were used to inform average travel party size and number of visiting days for the study's sample.

Questionnaires were distributed on randomly selected weekdays and weekends over a period of nine months (September 2015–May 2016) at five climbing areas within a 30-minute drive radius of downtown Chattanooga. The nine-month period was established to ensure data was representative of times of year which could be characterized as peak and valley climbing seasons in the Southeast. Climbing sites were selected based upon advice given from a panel of individuals representing the SCC and the Access

Fund who were asked to identify areas which were most popular, accessible, and provided a variety of climbing options (i.e. degrees of difficulty, climbing type [sport, traditional, bouldering]). Further, previous experience in studying choice of climbing locations suggested that visitors to Chattanooga will climb at multiple sites surrounding the city rather than remaining at one site throughout their stay. This close proximity of sites is a benefit that Chattanooga provides climbers, with innumerable locales within a short drive time from the city. This also increased the likelihood of capturing climbers in the event one of the selected climbing destinations under study was not initially chosen by visitors.

Participants in the study were intercepted in parking lots located at trail heads used to enter and exit climbing locations. Additional surveys were collected at the base of climbing crags and at adjacent camp sites frequented by climbers staying overnight. Vocal checks were used to ensure duplicate surveys were not completed. Bias relating to estimation and population uncertainty was minimized by asking all climbers encountered by the research staff to complete the survey. Because probability sampling was not employed, visitors' homogeneity was further examined by conducting a statistical test (ANOVAs) that examined differences in spending behaviours across climbing sites. This examination rendered significant differences, $F(4,273) = 7.01$, $p = .000$ only in the lodging category of spending. Post hoc analyses using a Bonferroni adjustment indicated that Foster Falls and Rocktown location climbers reported spending significantly less than other locations. This is explainable as each resides greater distances outside of Chattanooga than other popular sites and historically attract day trip climbers from neighboring cities, Nashville and Atlanta. As a result, visitors to these sites tend to stay less frequently in Chattanooga than those climbing in nearby locations. Previous research (c.f. Jeong and Crompton 2015) indicates that day and overnight visitors will demonstrate disparate spending habits and should be examined separately. Thus, in the effort to provide a conservative estimate, the researchers include a 'potential impact' figure for locations likely to include day-trippers. This 'potential impact' estimate was based on parking lot data collected at these sites (e.g. car counts & license plates). A supplemental study would need to be conducted to estimate true impacts generated from regional sites and provided to regional counties.

Ultimately, a total of 530 surveys were completed (97% response rate), including 366 visitors and 164 local residents. Local residents were subsequently removed from the analysis, as economic impact estimates are only concerned with net new money entering into a community from outside the geographical impact area (in this case a 30 mile radius). Local spending is deemed displaced spending for it would have been spent in the community regardless of recreational choice, and is thus, not part of economic stimulus (Crompton 2006).

Climber demographics were in line with national data (OIA 2016). A slight majority (52%) were male with an average age of 28 years. The average group size was 3.7, with visitors typically staying two days and 1.5 nights. Climbers made an average of 4.7 visits to Chattanooga in the previous 12 months Nearly half (48%) camped out while visiting, with another 24% renting rooms at a hotel or hostel. Visitors and residents had a combined average of 5.7 years climbing experience, climbing traditional routes to 5.9+ (i.e. intermediate level), sport routes to 5.11 (i.e. intermediate to advanced), and bouldering at an average level of V5 (i.e.

intermediate to advanced). While some climbers to the area are undoubtedly beginners, the average skill level could be considered intermediate or higher.

Estimating overall spending

The reliability of expenditure estimates is largely dependent upon two factors: (1) the accuracy of the visitor count, and (2) methods of converting a sample's expenditures to a greater visitor population. Estimating visitation occurring in open spaces presents logistical challenges due to an inability to comprehensively track visitors vis-à-vis turnstile entry or attendance figures. Further, climbers' entrance into parks adjacent to Chattanooga is not tracked through visitation data. Such delimitations placed increased obligations on the researching team to establish measures by which to obtain visitation data and extrapolate the figures so that they may be representative of an overall spending estimation. To establish a pragmatic means of formulating estimations, researchers developed multipliers based on known visitor logs and sampled observations, similar to that utilized by the U.S. National Park Service (USNPS n.d.). Stone Fort climbing area was used as a constant by which other site visitation data could be formulated. Located on a private golf course, this location, unlike others, requires registration and a US$9 entry fee, allowing for an exact number of visitors to be provided by the site managers. From this data, a ratio of visitors was then created from counts at other climbing locations by comparing climbing frequencies to Stone Fort. This ratio was based on all site visits while distributing surveys (weekdays and weekends), to ensure reliability. Using this method, a formula depicting approximate annual counts of climbers at all regional sites could be established. For example, every 1 person at Stone Fort represented .47 at Tennessee Wall (TW) and .06 at Sunset Rock (SR). Using this ratio, the total number of people per year at each location and the percentage of overall climbers found to be non-residents (70%) was identified. The formula below illustrates how total visitors were estimated and final demographic comparisons with other research can be seen in Table 1.

$$SF + (.47)SF + (.06)SF + (.44)SF = 16,565.5(.70) = \text{Total Visiting Climbers}$$

Upon reaching an estimated calculation for total visiting climbers, further adjustments were needed to account for climbers who had reported making multiple trips to Hamilton

Table 1. Demographic comparison across studies.

Study	Maples and Bradley (2017)	Sims and Hodges (2004)	Chattanooga (current study)	Outdoor Participation Data (OIA 2016)
Gender	80% Male	70% Male	52% Male	54% Male
	20% Female	30% Female	48% Female	46% Female
Age	18–35: 56%	< 20: 15%	< 20: 18%	6–17: 22%
	36–50: 32%	20–30: 65%	20–30: 67%	18–24: 11%
	51–64: 11%	31–40: 8%	31–40: 9%	25–44: 33%
	> 65: 1%	41–50: 7%	41–50: 4%	> 45: 34%
		> 60: 5%	> 50: 2%	
Household Income	< $50k: 48%	< $50k: 86%	Not Available	< $50k: 35%
	$50k–100k: 33%	$50k–100k: 14%		$50k–100k: 34%
	> 100k: 18%	> 100k: 0%		> 100k: 31%
Education	< BA/BS: 15%	< BA/BS: 44%	< BA/BS: 58%	< BA/BS: 59%
	BA/BS: 48%	BA/BS: 36%	BA/BS: 29%	BA/BS: 26%
	> BA/BS: 37%	> BA/BS: 20%	> BA/BS: 14%	> BA/BS: 14%%

County throughout the year. To avoid inflating visitor estimates, unique visits to each location were determined by dividing total number of visits by average number of visits per year for each location (SF= 4.1, TW= 1.42, SR= 1.13). From this, unique climbing visits totalling 10,185 were found, with 7,130 of these visits being from persons who did not reside within the geographical impact area. Climbers also reported that for every climbing group ($M = 3.6$ people), there were, on average, 0.22 non-climbers accompanying them on their visit to Chattanooga. Given that non-climbers were not intercepted at the trailhead, they were added to the overall visitor numbers by multiplying the number of unique visitors by the average total expenditure, to arrive at the total direct expenditures for visitors on one visit.

Total Direct Expenditures = [Total Non-local visiting climbers

+((Total Non-local Visiting Climbers × % of Non-Climbers in Group/Group Size))]

× Average Expenditure per person

The Total Direct Expenditure value was then examined in relation to climbers' average trip per year. Average trip per year was determined by dividing annual climbing days in the region by average trip length. This formula is outlined below.

Total Expenditures = [Average Trip Per Year(9.5/2.0) × Total Direct Expenditures]

Analyzing climbers' economic impact

Total direct expenditures in each economic category were entered as inputs using IMPLAN software. IMPLAN software utilizes unique characteristics associated with individual counties (i.e. economic structures and multiplier valuations) to ascertain how initial tourism spending influences complementary economies. For instance, total Economic Impact is the result of a non-linear ripple effect generated from the direct spending of visitors in Hamilton County. In Table 2, the Direct Effect represents the marginal (non-leaked) money remaining in the region. Indirect Effects are the result of local businesses spending more on employment and materials, as a result of added business. Induced Effects include additional spending by local employees as a result of increased hours/income due to the activity. Further, these effects impact the region in various ways: 1) Employment: the number of full-year, full-time jobs supported by climbers, 2) Labour Income: added income for current employees, 3) Total Value: true profits after accounting for employment, taxes, and other everyday business expenses, and 4) Output: total overall sales and revenue from climbers. In the context of local interest, labour income is often deemed the most salient (and conservative) of induced effects for it reveals the economic benefits received by residents in relationship to costs invested (Crompton 2011). In contrast, sales-related outputs may have minimal interest for local governments due to it not directly affecting residents' standard of living.

Table 2. Illustration of direct, indirect, and induced impact for Hamilton county.

Impact Type	Employment	Labor Income (US$)	Total Value Added (US$)	Output (US$)
Direct Effect	65.6	1,648,918.8	2,666,340.9	4,624,607.1
Indirect Effect	8.5	436,858.4	726,019.7	1,202,435.0
Induced Effect	9.2	422,532.4	712,579.3	1,137,013.4
Total Effect	83.3	2,508,309.7	4,104,940.0	6,964,055.6

Management policies and preferences

Responses for land management preferences were analyzed mainly for descriptive purposes, to provide guidance to the SCC, local, state, and federal policymakers. Where
appropriate, correlations, X^2, and analyses of variance (ANOVA) were conducted to
determine significant relationships that may impact policy. For example, climbers who
visit sites more often may express more ownership of an area, which could be utilized
to aid in the drafting and enforcing of regulations in that area. Additionally, visitors and
residents may differ on management preferences, creating a conflict of stakeholders.
These items were developed with reference to similar surveys conducted at other climbing sites, and with the assistance of the SCC and Access Fund staff. The survey included
questions about demographics, frequency of visits to major climbing sites in the last
year, climbing destination preferences (five-point Likert scale; 10 items), responsibility
for maintenance of site (personal, non-profit, land manager; five-point Likert scale, 3
items), and preferences for sustainably managing regional climbing sites (three-point
scale; 7 items). Findings for all analyses are reported below, beginning with general
descriptive statistics, followed by economic impact and finishing with management
preferences.

Results

Economic impact

Chattanooga's surrounding landscape attracted over 16,565 non-resident visits during the
2015–16 climbing season, including 8,698 unique visitors. Sampling data estimates an
annual direct impact of US$6.4 million in local spending by participants, with indirect
and induced impacts adding another half-million in revenue (see Table 2). When climbing
areas, Foster Falls and Rocktown, were included in the analysis, a conservative impact of
US$10.3 million was deduced.

Table 3 provides an illustration of non-local climbers' average spending in each respective category. Among the downtown industries most affected by climbing tourism, restaurants and bars, hotels, and retail stores demonstrated the greatest total value added with
impacts of US$1.1 million, US$900 thousand, and US$550 thousand, respectively. Due to
the financial support to particular industries, climbing tourism is believed to support
roughly 83 full time equivalent jobs in Chattanooga.

In addition to local stimulus, climbing tourism provided a significant impact at the state
and national levels. Specifically, climbing in Chattanooga generates US$484,417 in state
taxes annually and over US$500 thousand in federal taxes. For comparison with other
economic impact research, industry statistics for Hamilton County, TN are presented in
the Tables 4 and 5.

Management preferences

According to collective responses from residents and tourists, factors most impactful in
determining their choice of climbing destination were aesthetics (i.e. classic lines and
nice views), variety of difficulty levels, novelty (i.e. new climbs, new experiences), and
ease of registration/permits. Access that is free of charge, and proximity to urban

Table 3. Average expenditures per discrete category.

IMPLAN Sector	Spending Categories	Average Spending (US$)	Total Spending (US$)
413	Food services & Drinking places	55.35	1,989,092.26
411	Hotels and Motels	42.56	1,529,296.68
410	Entertainment	18.64	669,740.41
328	Shopping (Outdoor Rec.- Related)	18.08	649.669.09
326	Transportation (Gas)	37.31	1,340,748.61
329	General Retail (Un-related to Outdoor Rec.)	6.73	241,843.50
	Total Direct Impact	178.67	6,420,494.41

Table 4. Hamilton county economic profile.

Model Information			
Model Year	2015	**Value Added**	
GRP	US$23,366,560,386	Employee Compensation	US$10,724,342,523
Total Personal Income	US$14,291,440,000	Proprietor Income	US$1,687,727,630
Total Employment	234,314	Other Property Type Income	US$9,685,591,575
		Tax on Production and Import	US$1,268,898,658
Number of Industries	277		
Land Area (Sq. Miles)	543	Total Value Added	US$23,366,560,386
Area Count	1		
		Final Demand	
Population	345,545	Households	12,139,279,201
Total Households	150,575	State/Local Government	US$1,938,646,299
Average Household Income	US$94,913	Federal Government	US$1,058,661,983
		Capital	US$5,084,902,517
Trade Flows Method	Trade Flows Model	Exports	US$21,226,922,421
Model Status	Multipliers	Imports	−US$17,358,855,836
		Institutional Sales	−US$722,995,954
Economic Indicators			
Shannon-Weaver Index	.71779	Total Final Demand:	US$23,366,560,631

Table 5. Top ten industries in Hamilton county.

Sector	Description	Employment	Labour Income (US$)	Output (US$)
413	Food services and drinking places	16,786	361,744,900	940,635,100
438	* Employment and payroll only (Educ only)	12,793	708,396,300	809,956,500
357	Insurance carriers	12,091	882,858,000	3,331,088,000
335	Transport by truck	10,093	488,825,500	1,367,557,000
394	Physicians, dentists, and other health	8,941	812,143,600	1,192,119,000
319	Wholesale trade businesses	7,672	576,134,900	1,564,165,000
382	Employment services	6,742	207,621,600	269,864,500
388	Services to buildings and dwellings	5,660	168,263,600	339,871,200
437	* Employment and payroll only (non-Educ)	5,035	321,957,800	366,903,500
397	Private hospitals	5,032	297,623,000	620,695,900

amenities were ranked lowest in the list of destination attractions (Figure 1). A one-way ANOVA between residents and visitors revealed no significant differences in destination preferences.

Some climbers make a single visit to Chattanooga with no intention to return. Additionally, climbers will visit some areas more often than others, typically driven by their preferred style of climbing. To determine site preferences of the most frequent visitors to each site, a correlation analysis was performed between site preferences and self-reported visits to each destination in the past 12 months (Table 6). This provides insight into management preferences of site stakeholders who may feel more ownership of particular

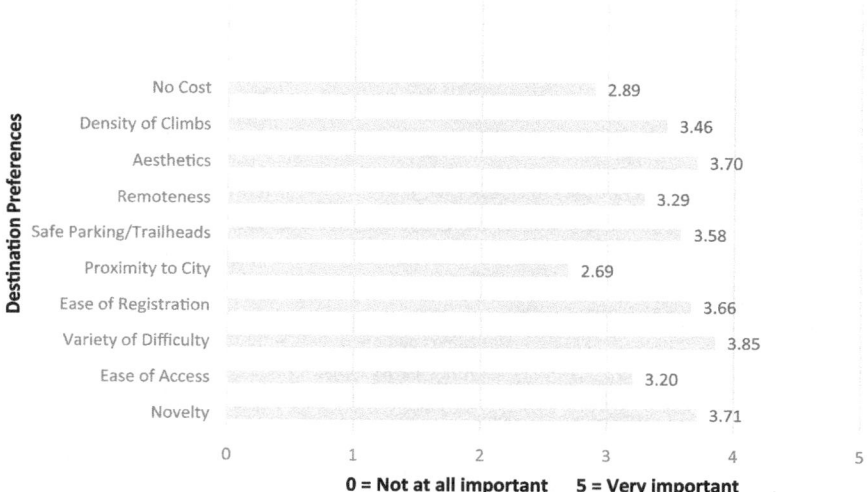

Figure 1. Destination preferences for all climbers.

crags. All significant relationships were negative, indicating that climbers who participate more frequently tend to care less about all factors. Put another way, newer climbers care more about these factors than seasoned climbers. Also of note is the lack of significance for any variables at both bouldering areas (Stone Fort and Rocktown).

Climbers in Chattanooga possess a sense of ownership for the crags in the area. Pairwise t-test comparisons support the belief that climbing area maintenance is more the responsibility of climbers ($M = 4.67$), than of the land manager ($M = 2.37$, $t = 36.755$, $p < .001$) or climbers' coalition ($M = 2.52$, $t = 35.591$, $p < .001$). A one-way ANOVA found no significant differences between residents and visitors on measures of responsibility. Commitment to the climbing sites is also evident in their actions, as the average climber donated 8.2 h of volunteering over the last year, for a total of 83,517 h, or the equivalent of US$605,502 of work at the rate of minimum wage in Tennessee.

Descriptive statistics for sustainability initiatives are presented in Figure 2. A X^2 analysis was conducted to aid with interpretation, revealed significant differences in opinion for all categories ($p < .01$), except for parking fees. Users strongly favoured donation boxes in the parking lot and reliance on non-profits to manage the site. They strongly opposed closing or selling off areas to private companies. The items 'reduce site maintenance' and 'increase restaurant taxes' may have been too vague to garner a clear response. Visitors demonstrated stronger support for donation boxes ($F = 7.423$, $p = .007$) and parking fees ($F = 13.677$, $p < .001$) than residents.

Discussion and implications

For several years, supporters of Chattanooga-based rock climbing have urged public policy decision-makers to create an outdoor recreation-specific budget that would ensure consistent funding for the promotion and conservation of outdoor space. Despite their pleading, no such line item exists in city, county, state or federal budgets, leaving broad initiatives (i.e. accessibility, marketing, maintenance, and land acquisition) insufficiently funded. It should

Table 6. Correlation analysis illustrating relationships between visits to each site (previous 12 months) and destination preferences.

	Well Cared For	Novelty	Access	Variety	Registration	Proximity	Safe	Wilderness	Aesthetics	Density	Cost
Foster Falls	−0.06	−0.11	−0.14**	−0.07	−0.16**	−0.14*	−0.05	0.01	−0.01	−0.11	−0.11
T Wall	−0.04	−0.21**	−0.23**	−0.17**	−0.18**	−0.20**	−0.09	−0.05	−0.07	−0.13*	−0.03
Sunset Rock	−0.05	−0.21**	−0.23**	−0.13*	−0.11	−0.20**	−0.17**	0.04	−0.06	−0.13*	−0.06
Stone Fort	−0.08	−0.02	−0.06	0.03	−0.04	0.03	−0.03	0.04	0.01	−0.07	−0.05
Rocktown	0.07	0.06	−0.04	0.03	−0.04	0.03	−0.07	−0.02	0.05	0.05	0.06

* = Significant at $p < .05$, ** = Significant at $p < .01$.

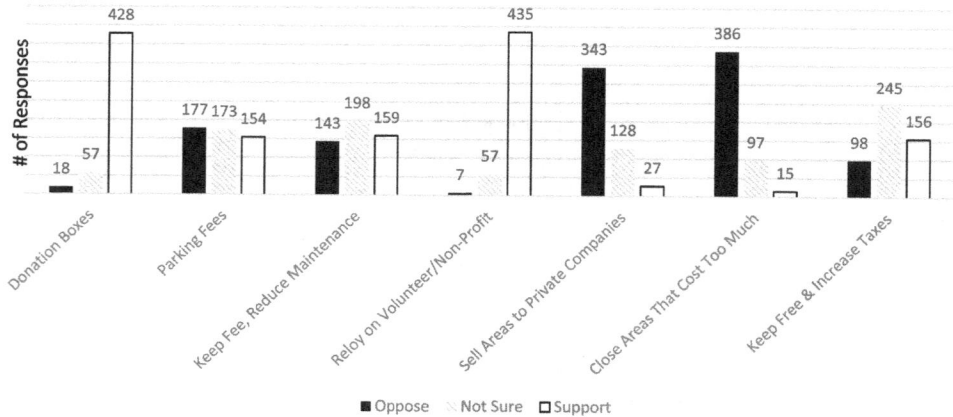

Figure 2. Preferences for sustainable management revenues.

be noted that park and recreational budgetary challenges are not isolated to Chattanooga, but rather appear to be quite ubiquitous. Crompton (2011) points out that such fiscal conservatism is largely attributable to parks' dependency on mere financial reporting to support their causes. As a consequence, recreational agencies are often mistaken for entities who merely take from the financial pot, while adding little in return. This is untrue, but without empirically revealing real value added, parks and recreation departments will continue to be overlooked. Thus, this study was conceptualized with the following goals which are all linked to the first one: (1) demonstrate economic stimulus, (2) derived from climbing pursuits, (3) in an attempt to provide leverage to those advocating for recreational land management and legislation. By demonstrating actual value added, outdoor adventure sports organizations can pursue financial support from government and/or grant-sponsoring agencies for preservation, access, and marketing, and other initiatives.

Cross promotional partnerships

The direct, indirect, and induced expenditure estimates illustrated from this research provide proof that climbing sites around Chattanooga create sizeable revenue to local, state, and federal budgets. This study's results, combined with recent work by Maples and Bradley (2017), who illustrated comparable impact figures for the Asheville, NC area, provide further evidence that economic impact can be used by parks and recreation to better position themselves at negotiating tables comprised of public, as well as private stakeholders. Each have much to gain from the US$7 million in estimated stimulus attributable to climbing tourism, and all should become vested in the promotion and sustainment of its popularity. As noted from the research findings, restaurants, bars, hotels, and retail shops are currently profiting from rock climbing, but only a few are currently engaged in regular promotions to this population. One restaurateur currently promotes the Southeastern Climbing Coalition through '10% nights,' whereby 10% of the night's profits are donated to climbing initiatives supported by the SCC. However, collaborative promotional strategies, such as this one, are rare in Chattanooga.

Given the growing outdoor culture in the region, it would seem feasible to expand this to a host of other local businesses. By doing so, a fund could be established to support a variety of initiatives. For instance, a one-day promotional event for climbing sustainment during Chattanooga's annual outdoor festival, RiverRocks, might be embraced by local restaurants and shops in the area, which in turn, may drive festival participants and local outdoor advocates to those locations. Support from the city and county, as well as the visitor's bureau, would increase visibility for such initiatives. However, indirect benefactors of rock climbing must be informed of economic data, or agencies responsible for managing climbing sites lose ammunition needed to successfully realize cross-marketing partnerships. Ultimately, as physical space becomes viewed as a commodity, preferentialism is bestowed, and land that was once perceived as 'invisible' emerges to the forefront.

Destination tourism

Aesthetics, novelty, and variety emerged as the most valuable assets sought out by climbers, while free access and proximity to city amenities ranked lowest. This establishes climbers as a discerning clientele who select destinations based on geographical assets and variety more so than cost and entertainment. Minimal fees associated with accessing climbing sites may not act as a constraint to climbers. Further, sites which are closer in proximity to cities may not be more desirable than sites in remote settings. This offers promise for rural regions that could seek to commodify their resources and become tourism destinations in their own right (Cross 2001; Teodorescu et al. 2012). In fact, the SCC director has made presentations to rural county mayors since the drafting of this economic impact report (C. Roney, personal communication, 7 March 2017), as they seek ways to attract climber travel to their lesser known sites.

Those who climb less in a particular area tend to care more about the destination assets than regular visitors. This could be an issue of expectations and site selection. Once climbers have been to an area, they tend to adjust their expectations to the site's given characteristics. Additionally, climbers will frequent sites that have their desired site characteristics. However, if the goal is to attract tourists to a certain destination, adequate signage, easy access and pain-free registration, as well as the development of crags closer to the city should be priorities. The impact of attraction density (i.e. close proximity to other tourist attractions) on the climbing economy of Chattanooga remains unclear. However, nearby restaurants and entertainment certainly influence spending patterns of users at climbing sites, and rural climbing destinations (e.g. Red River Gorge, KY) are making efforts to increase spending opportunities in their area (Maples et al. 2017). Chattanooga has not progressed to the 'development' phase of tourism (Butler 1980) solely because of its climbing assets, and the plausibility of climbing tourism to facilitate such growth remains dubious.

Management and sustainability

Climbers in Chattanooga clearly express a level of ownership over the climbing areas and agendas. Their commitment to site development and management is a grassroots success story. To this point, the lack of governmental support has largely been viewed cynically, leaving outdoor athletes feeling like little more than photo opportunities for the visitor's bureau (Cook 2015a). However, the level of grassroots ownership expressed by the climbers in this study represents an asset that may not have developed with governmental funding and oversight. Managers should seek to capitalize on the established culture, to maximize volunteer services on public lands. A more participative management approach could enhance the feeling of community ownership through inclusion in policy-making and enforcement (Bello, Carr, and Lovelock 2016). This currently happens on an ad-hoc basis, with the SCC and Access Fund drafting unique, one-off contracts for each new project (e.g. land acquisitions, trail building, parking lot development, etc.). A long-term participative relationship could benefit all parties.

Land managers should not expect to receive services and support entirely free of charge, either. Climbers expressed a willingness to expand parking lot donations, and were not vehemently opposed to parking fees or reduced maintenance. The vast majority of climbers (95%) would be willing to pay a fee for climbing access, with 62% expressing a willingness to pay $5 a day. Anecdotal feedback expressed while taking the surveys, though, indicated that they would only do so if the fees were largely 'earmarked' for climbing maintenance. This may be indicative of resentment stemming from the current situation at the Stone Fort Bouldering area; the only privately-owned location in our study. While the owner welcomes over 12,000 climbers onto his property annually at US$9 each, he still relies on the SCC to maintain the trails and signage during volunteer days. This may also explain the opposition to selling off climbing areas to private companies. Though few differences emerged from the data, visitors were more open to donations and parking fees than residents in this study. Policies established in this regard should recognize the added complexity in managing spaces for local recreation and tourism (Bailey, Kang, and Lewis 2017).

Mandatory fees at climbing sites are not uncommon, despite concerns about liability associated with fee-based services. However, 'pay-to-play' agreements typically come with improved amenities, such as restrooms, water access, well-developed trails and even emergency first aid stations. This generates consistent revenue for land managers and better access for users, and encourages buy-in from managing agencies. For instance, the Georgia Outdoor Recreation Pass is now required for entry to Rocktown (US$6/ weekend or US$19/year). When the road to Rocktown was recently washed out, state agencies were quick to act, as the closure directly influenced their bottom line, and they could justify the repair expenses based on revenues.

Conclusions

Nature-based sports and adventure tourism represent an increasingly popular market niche that can significantly influence the local economy. Historically, adventure athletes have been tolerated but not courted, likely due to misconstrued stereotypes based on anecdotal evidence. Additionally, outdoor recreationists have been slow to establish their case for inclusion at the economic 'table.' With the rise of national reports on the economics of the outdoor industry (OIA 2017) and recent signing into law of the Recreation's Economic Contribution (REC) Act in the USA (Beyer 2016), the impact of outdoor recreation is receiving due credit. Even so, national statistics do not always influence local politics. Objective, local impact reports must supplement the broader narrative to induce change. Accordingly, regional research is needed to guide the growth and development of nature-based sports tourism, while sustainably and responsibly managing outdoor recreation areas for local citizens (Bailey, Kang, and Lewis 2017). Utilizing nonprofits and grassroots initiatives to draft and enforce policies will ensure that all stakeholders have a voice and will encourage those who are most passionate about the activity and the place.

In summary, analyses attempting to engender positive change in the minds of policy makers cannot begin and end with mere economic impact reporting. Rather, future research which examines the implementation of plans and policies that originated from economic analysis is also necessary. For instance, this study not only highlighted the lucrative nature inherent with rock climbing tourism, but also attempted to delineate how and where private and public land operators should best respond to ensure its sustainability. Research that builds upon this premise is paramount to partnerships with land management organizations and accountability of economic data. As Olmstead (1865) professed, community members and government officials have pertinent roles to play in sustaining natural resource recreation through appropriate commodification, conservation, and management. Therefore, future research demonstrating the effectiveness of budgetary planning and resource allocation is warranted to evaluate their effectiveness and to inform other community inquisitions.

Disclosure statement

No potential conflict of interest was reported by the authors.

References

Bailey, A. W., H. K. Kang, and T. G. Lewis. 2017. "Outdoor Recreation and Adventure Tourism: Unique but Allied Industries." *Journal of Outdoor Recreation, Education, and Leadership* 9 (2): 244–247. doi:10.18666/JOREL-2017-V9-I2-8262.

Beardsley, W. G. 1971. "The Economic Impact of Recreation Development: A Synopsis." In *Recreation Symposium Proceedings*. N. E. For. Exp. Sta, 28–32. Upper Darby, PA: U.S. Forest Service.

Bello, F. G., N. Carr, and B. Lovelock. 2016. "Community Participation Framework for Protected Area-based Tourism Planning." *Tourism Planning & Development* 13 (4): 469–485. doi:10.1080/21568316. 2015.1136838.

Beyer, D. 2016. "H.R.4665 - 114th Congress (2015-2016): Outdoor Recreation Jobs and Economic Impact Act of 2016 [webpage]." December 8. Accessed October 16, 2017. https://www. congress.gov/bill/114th-congress/house-bill/4665.

Buhalis, D. 2000. "Marketing the Competitive Destination of the Future." *Tourism Management* 21: 97–116.

Butler, R. W. 1980. "The Concept of a Tourist Area Cycle of Evolution: Implications for Management Resources." *The Canadian Geographer/Le Géographe Canadien* 24 (1): 5–12.

Carr, E. 2014. "Frederick Law Olmstead: Designing America." http://www.pbs.org/wned/frederick-law-olmsted/learn-more/olmsted-and-scenic-preservation/.

Cook, D. 2015a. "The Best Outdoor City Deserves the Best Public Policy." *Timesfreepress.com*, June 2. http://www.timesfreepress.com/news/opinion/columns/story/2015/jun/02/best-outdoor-city-deserves-best-public-policy/307371/.

Cook, D. 2015b. "Missed opportunities in the Best Outdoor City." *Timesfreepress.com*, June 14. http://www.timesfreepress.com/news/opinion/columns/story/2015/jun/14/missed-opportunities-best-outdoor-city/309516/.

Cook, D. 2017. "Is More Publicity Good for Chattanooga's Beautiful Natural Areas? | Times Free Press." April 30 http://www.timesfreepress.com/news/opinion/columns/story/2017/apr/30/road-more-traveled/425550/.

Crompton, J. L. 2006. "Economic Impact Studies: Instruments for Political Shenanigans?" *Journal of Travel Research* 45: 67–82.

Crompton, J. L. 2007. *Community Benefits and Repositioning: The Keys to Park and Recreation's Future Viability*. Ashburn, VA: National Recreation and Park Association.

Crompton, J. L. 2011. *Measuring the Economic Impact of Park and Recreation Services*. Ashburn, VA: National Recreation and Park Association.

Cross, J. E. 2001. "What is 'Sense of Place'?." Paper presented at the archives of the twelfth headwaters conference. http://www.western.edu/headwaters/archivesheadwaters12_papers/cross_paper.html.

Culhane, P. J. 2013. *Public Lands Politics: Interest Group Influence on the Forest Service and the Bureau of Land Management*. New York, NY: Routledge.

Cullinane, T. C., and L. Koontz. 2017. *2016 National Park Visitor Spending Effects: Economic Contributions to Local Communities, States, and the Nation*. Natural Resource Report. Fort Collins, CO: National Park Service.

Davis, S. 2016. "Chattanooga: America's New Climbing Capitol." *Climbing Magazine*, June 28. https://www.climbing.com/places/chattanooga-americas-new-climbing-capitol/.

Day, G. S., and R. Wensley. 1988. "Assessing Advantage: A Framework for Diagnosing Competitive Superiority." *Journal of Marketing* 52: 31–44.

Flessner, D. 2016. "Tourism Pumped $1 Billion into Chattanooga Economy in 2015 | Times Free Press." *Chattanooga Times Free Press*, August 31. http://www.timesfreepress.com/news/local/story/2016/aug/31/tourism-tops-1-billihamiltcounty/384253/.

Frank, J. 2012. "Signal Mountain Considers Lifting Ban on Rock Climbing." *The Chattanoogan*, November 30. http://www.chattanoogan.com/2012/11/30/239632/Signal-Mountain-Considers-Lifting-Ban.aspx.

Harnik, P., and J. L. Crompton. 2014. "Measuring the Total Economic Value of a Park System to a Community." *Managing Leisure* 19 (3): 188–211.

Howe, C. W. 1979. *Natural Resource Economics*. New York, NY: John Wiley and Sons.

Jago, L., L. Chalip, G. Brown, T. Mules, and S. Ali. 2003. "Building Events into Destination Branding: Insights from Experts." *Event Management* 8 (1): 3–14.

Jansson, M., and T. Lindgren. 2012. "A Review of the Concept "Management" in Relation to Urban Landscapes and Green Spaces: Toward a Holistic Understanding." *Urban Forestry & Urban Greening* 11 (2): 139–145. doi:10.1016/j.ufug.2012.01.004.

Jeong, J. Y., and J. L. Crompton. 2015. "Measuring the Economic Impact of a State Park System." *Managing Sport and Leisure* 20 (4): 238–257.

Kaczynski, A. T., J. L. Crompton, and J. E. Emerson. 2003. "A Procedure for Improving the Accuracy of Visitor Counts at State Parks." *Journal of Park and Recreation Administration* 21 (3): 140–151.

Kil, N., S. M. Holland, and T. V. Stein. 2014. "Structural Relationships Between Environmental Attitudes, Recreation Motivations, and Environmentally Responsible Behaviors." *Journal of Outdoor Recreation and Tourism* 7–8 (Supplement C): 16–25. doi:10.1016/j.jort.2014.09.010.

Kotler, P., D. H. Haider, and I. Rein. 1993. *Marketing Place: Attracting Investment, Industry, and Tourism to Cities, States, and Nations*. New York; Toronto: Free Press; Maxwell Macmillan Canada; Maxwell Macmillan International.

Maples, J. N., and M. J. Bradley. 2017. "Economic Impact of Rock Climbing in the Nantahala and Pisgah National Forests." https://www.accessfund.org/uploads/OA_NPNF_ClimbingStudy_Oct-2017-FINAL.pdf.

Maples, J. N., B. G. Clark, R. Sharp, B. Gillespie, and K. Gerlaugh. 2017. "Climbing Out of Poverty: The Econoimic Impact of Rock Climbing in and Round Eastern Kentucky's Red River Gorge." *Journal of Appalachian Studies* 23 (1): 53–71.

Neimark, J. 2016. "The EPA Once Said this was the Dirtiest City in America. Now it's One of Our Greenest." *GOOD Magazine*, July 13. https://www.good.is/articles/chattanooga-dirty-to-green-city.

Newsome, D., S. A. Moore, and R. K. Dowling. 2012. *Natural Area Tourism: Ecology, Impacts and Management*. Tonawanda, NY: Channel View Publications.

OIA [Outdoor Industry Association]. 2016. *Outdoor Recreation Participation*. Topline Report. Boulder, CO: Outdoor Foundation. https://outdoorindustry.org/resource/outdoor-participation-report-2016/.

OIA [Outdoor Industry Association]. 2017. *The Outdoor Recreation Economy*. Boulder, CO: Outdoor Foundation. https://outdoorindustry.org/wp-content/uploads/2017/04/OIA_RecEconomy_FINAL_Single.pdf.

Olmstead, F. L. 1865. *Yosemite and Mariposa Grove: A Preliminary Report*. Yosemite National Park, CA: Yosemite Association.

O'Neil, C. 2012. "Chattanooga Tourism Officials Want Growth Trend to Continue." *Timesfreepress.com*, April 15. http://www.timesfreepress.com/news/business/aroundregion/story/2012/apr/15/destination-chattanooga/75552/.

Pike, S. D. 2002. "Destination Image Analysis – A Review of 142 Papers from 1973 to 2000." *Tourism Management* 23 (5): 541–549.

Plummer, R., and D. A. Fennell. 2009. "Managing Protected Areas for Sustainable Tourism: Prospects for Adaptive Co-Management." *Journal of Sustainable Tourism* 17 (2): 149–168. doi:10.1080/09669580802359301.

Sims, C. B., and D. G. Hodges. 2004. *Use, Demographics, and Economic Impacts of Rock Climbing in the Obed Wild and Scenic River Area*. Final Report submitted to National Park Service.

Smith, J. W., C. Siderelis, and R. L. Moore. 2010. "The Effects of Place Attachment, Hypothetical Site Modifications and Use Levels on Recreation Behavior." *Journal of Leisure Research* 42 (4): 621–640.

Somin, I. 2014. *Libertarianism and Federalism*. SSRN Scholarly Paper No. ID 2507519. Rochester, NY: Social Science Research Network. https://papers.ssrn.com/abstract=2507519.

Tanner, J. 2017. "How Chattanooga Became a Premier City for Ironman." *Timesfreepress.com*, September 3. http://www.timesfreepress.com/news/local/story/2017/sep/03/how-chattanoog became-premier-city-ironman/446966/.

Taylor, D. T., A. Nagler, C. T. Bastian, and T. Foulke. 2013. *The Economic Impact of Non-motorized Trail Usage on National Forests in Wyoming*. Laramie, WY: University of Wyoming.

Teodorescu, N., A. Stancioiu, A. Botos, O. Arsene, and C. Ditoiu. 2012. "Means of Assessing a Sport Tourism Destination's Competitive Advantage Sources." *Journal of Physical Education and Sport* 12 (4): 498–506.

USNPS. n.d. "Estimating Denali's Visitation (U.S. National Park Service)." Accessed February 13, 2018. https://www.nps.gov/articles/denali-visitor-estimation.htm.

Williams, D. R., M. E. Patterson, J. W. Roggenbuck, and A. E. Watson. 1992. "Beyond the Commodity Metaphor: Examining Emotional and Symbolic Attachment to Place." *Leisure Sciences* 14: 29–46.

Williams, D. R., and J. W. Roggenbuck. 1989. "Measuring Place Attachment: Some Preliminary Results." In *Abstracts: 1989 Leisure Research Symposium*, edited by L. H. McAvoy and D. Howard, 32–39. Arlington, VA: National Recreation and Park Association.

Riding waves of intra-seasonal demand in surf tourism: analysing the nexus of seasonality and 21st century surf forecasting technology

Leon Mach, Jess Ponting ⓘ, James Brown and Jessica Savage

ABSTRACT

This study examines the natural component of seasonality in surf tourism. Using survey responses collected globally, we first analyse how surfers report using forecasts to make travel decisions. Occupancy and head-count data were also collected in Pavones, Costa Rica and analyzed against surf forecast data to empirically assess intra-seasonal fluctuations. Despite a small and highly skilled subset of the surf population, most international travel is booked months in advance based on climatic factors. Case study results indicate, however, that intra-seasonal travel behaviour within a country is correlated to both mid-range (occupancy) and short range (head-counts in the water) forecasts. Combined, surf forecasts and observed natural conditions impact surf travel behaviours in nuanced ways that deserve further attention to better understand destination and hospitality management, as well as, host and guest satisfaction and how they relate to intra-seasonal and intra-regional travel patterns.

Introduction

The large differences in occupancy rates associated with seasonality have been found to exacerbate human resource challenges, reduce profitability, cause crowding and diminish service quality in tourism destinations (Butler and Mao 1997; Agnew and Palutikof 2006; Becken 2010). Climate and weather, natural (as opposed to institutional) dimensions of seasonality, act as both push and pull factors that impact when and where tourists travel (Gómez Martín 2005; Amelung, Nicholls, and Viner 2007; Ridderstaat et al. 2014). The relationship between tourism seasonality and weather and climate, and the managerial challenges they pose have become a growing focus in alpine/snow sports tourism (Pegg, Patterson, and Vila Gariddo 2012; Cocolas, Walters, and Ruhanen 2016) and nature based tourism (Yu, Schwartz, and Walsh 2010). However, no research to date has explored seasonality in surf tourism despite the highly specific and seasonal convergence of natural factors that surfers seek (Scarfe et al. 2009; Reineman, Thomas, and Caldwell

2017), increased quality of and access to surf forecast information (Mach 2017), and surfers' willingness to visit remote coastal regions (Dolnicar and Fluker 2003; Barbieri and Sotomayor 2013; Anderson 2014).

Surfers are one of the most hyper-mobile groups of nature sports enthusiasts (Reynolds and Hritz 2012; Barbieri and Sotomayor 2013; Melo and Gomes 2017b). Estimates suggest that there are roughly 35 million surfers who travel to coastal communities in more than 160 countries in pursuit of high quality and uncrowded surf-breaks (Martin and Assenov 2012; O'Brien and Eddie 2013). Barbieri and Sotomayor (2013) suggest that more than 90% of surfers have been on an international surf trip, and roughly 60% have been on more than ten in the last five years. This positions surf tourism as an important economic driver for coastal tourism development. A 2016 study found that high quality surf-breaks boost economic activity by $US 18–25 million per surf-break per year (McGregor and Wills 2016). This and other studies valuing surf-breaks (Murphy and Bernal 2008; Wagner, Nelson, and Walker 2011; Wright, Hodges, and Sadrpour 2013), however, do not consider the important issue of how fluctuating surf conditions within and between seasons can impact value. For example, an unusually long run of high quality swell in February 2016 on Australia's Gold Coast was estimated to have delivered an additional AUS$20 million boost to the local economy (McElroy 2016). This weather dependent windfall calls for a better understanding of how surfers respond to surf forecasts and surf conditions and the impacts and challenges presented by the associated visitation fluctuations.

Surf-break quality is dependent upon the convergence of relatively static factors (direction the surf area faces, headlands, coral reef size and positioning) and variable factors (swell height, period and direction; wind speed and direction; tide; breaking intensity and peel angle) (Butt, Russell, and Grigg 2004; Scarfe et al. 2009). A surf-break's consistency is measured by how often the confluence of these natural factors produce high quality surf. Many of the world's best and most iconic/highly sought-after waves, however, are often not very consistent, but instead rely on a very specific mix of infrequent conditions that occur within particular seasons. Surfers increasingly use powerful specialized surf forecasting sites, such as Magicseaweed.com, swell-info.com, and surfline.com to direct their travel. However, the impact of this phenomena in destinations has not yet been fully explored (Anderson 2014; Mach 2014, 2017).

Towns and villages adjacent to world-class surf breaks, particularly those that are remote and require a relatively rare confluence of variable factors, are forced to adjust to increasingly large peaks and troughs in demand as tourists arrive and depart with swells forecast well in advance. This study seeks to better understand this seasonal phenomena using Pavones, Costa Rica as a case study. Pavones was selected because it is often referred to as the best wave in one of the world's most popular surf destinations and the local economy is almost entirely reliant on surf tourism. And yet, surf travel forums are replete with comments like the following: 'Hey! if you like surfing with 100 people in the water, and being dropped in on, this spot is a dream wave …. I love Pavones, but the crowd kills me' (Anonymous 2006).

Literature review

Seasonality, weather, and nature sports tourism

Seasonality and tourism are inextricably linked (Commons and Page 2001; Becken 2013; Verbos and Brownlee 2017). Tourism seasonality has both natural and institutional dimensions (Butler and Mao 1997; Becken 2013). Institutional dimensions include public and religious holidays, cultural travel patterns and tastes, and events. Natural dimensions involve weather and climate. Climate is the prevailing condition of the atmosphere over long periods of observation, whereas weather is the manifestation of climate at a specific time and place (Gómez Martín 2005). While tourists' research and expect certain climate conditions when they travel to a place, they will experience the actual weather once there (Scott and Lemieux 2009; Becken 2010). The interplay of weather and climate act as critical factors in tourism generally (Gómez Martín 2005; Amelung, Nicholls, and Viner 2007; Ridderstaat et al. 2014). Tourist propensity to avoid certain conditions (i.e. cold temperatures and rain) and seek others, like sunshine, has been empirically demonstrated in different contexts (Agnew and Palutikof 2006; Falk 2014; Ridderstaat et al. 2014).

Methodologically, there has been limited consistency in evaluating the impact of climate and weather on tourism demand, and no approach has emerged superior to the others (Karamustafa and Ulama 2010). Most often studies use meteorological data in sending and receiving locations and analyse how well this information influences tourism demand (Agnew and Palutikof 2006; Becken 2013; Ridderstaat et al. 2014). These studies generally suggest that domestic travel is highly responsive to weather patterns within a given year or season. The frequency of international travel in a given year, however, is most highly correlated to the average weather documented in the previous. This means, for example, that a wet and cold summer season in the UK on average will encourage more international travel in the following year (Agnew and Palutikof 2006; Falk 2014).

Similar trends are found in analyses looking at seasonality as it relates to nature sports and outdoor recreation. This emergent field is concerned more with the natural conditions that facilitate the practice or viewing of sporting activities. Golf (Scott and Jones 2007; Nicholls, Holecek, and Noh 2008) and national park visitation (Yu, Schwartz, and Walsh 2010) have been examined and echo the importance of localized approaches to examining weather elements to provide accurate estimates in support of recreation and tourism planning, forecasting and decision making. The majority of studies, however, are dedicated to understanding how snow sports enthusiasts respond to weather conditions and climate change (Scott et al. 2006; Pegg, Patterson, and Vila Gariddo 2012; Cocolas, Walters, and Ruhanen 2016). Becken (2010) notes that the ski industry is a prime example of weather dependent tourism activity and in poor seasons, skiers change to more snow-reliable areas (typically higher altitude) (Elsasser and Buerki 2002). Seasons with less snow reliability have demonstrated significant losses of revenues (from both lift ticket sales and accommodation), which postpones investment and puts mountain destinations in recovery mode (Scott and Lemieux 2009). Cocolas, Walters, and Ruhanen (2016) found that while leisure based skiers, who are most concerned with the skiing conditions, are often displaced by poor weather conditions. Others, concerned more with the overall experience of the trip (i.e. bars, restaurants, shops, and concerts) than the skiing itself, are likely to visit particular mountian destinations regardless of the actual ski conditions.

When analyzed from an economic perspective, seasonality and the associated imbalances between low and peak visitation periods, impacts the efficient utilization of resources (Hudson and Cross 2005). When weather conditions are favourable during a high season, profits can soar. However, these favourable conditions also lead to overcrowding and congestion, which often overburdens infrastructure and places heavy demands on services. This in turn leads to reduced service quality and recreational satisfaction (Hudson and Cross 2005; Pegg, Patterson, and Vila Gariddo 2012). Nature sports literature suggests that as crowding increases, visitors with lower crowding thresholds and higher daily spending patterns are displaced by those with lower spending habits and higher crowding thresholds (Budruk et al. 2008; Vaske and Shelby 2008).

Resident involvement in the industry and resident goodwill towards tourists are critical to destination sustainability and success (Laws 1995; Bimonte and Punzo 2011; Bimonte 2013). Many studies have found that residents' attitudes towards tourism development began positive but declined as tourism increased (Doxey 1975; Teye, Sonmez, and Sirakaya 2002). Most studies found that in high seasons the use of community resources by large numbers of tourists, and the associated crowding, caused resentment towards tourists and lower resident satisfaction (Murphy 1985; Deery, Jago, and Fredline 2012; Vargas-Sanchez, Porras-Bueno, and Plaza-Mejia 2014). Most of these studies were cross-sectional and did not account for how seasonality may influence these perceptions (Uysal et al. 2015; Bimonte and Faralla 2016). Bimonte and Faralla (2016) found that residents reported lower personal hapiness and quality of life during the high season in comparison to the low season in the same year.

Conversely, off peak period problems are typified by underutilization of infrastructure, and work force reduction (Pegg, Patterson, and Vila Gariddo 2012). The seasonal nature of employment can place workers in positions with limited upward mobility and lead to voluntary unemployment (Commons and Page 2001). These down periods, however, can also facilitate recovery and investment in infrastructural improvements (Pegg, Patterson, and Vila Gariddo 2012). Some seasonal workers choose this type of employment so that they can have time-off to enjoy their nature sports pursuits (Marchant and Mottiar 2011).

Surf tourism as a nature sport and seasonality

Surf tourism is often defined as the act of travelling more than 40 kms from one's place of residence for at least one overnight stay (but less than 12 months) for the primary purpose of surfing (Buckley 2002; Dolnicar and Fluker 2003; Portugal et al. 2017). Surfing has been referred to as an art form, a lifestyle sport (Anderson 2014; Mach and Ponting 2017), an adventure sport (Buckley 2002; Reynolds and Hritz 2012), and a serious leisure sport (Barbieri and Sotomayor 2013; Portugal et al. 2017; Melo and Gomes 2017b). Melo and Gomes (2017a) define nature sports as those which are performed in different natural contexts (air, land, and water); range from formal to informal practices; and, may contribute to sustainable local development. As such, surfing can be contextualized as a nature sport.

Surfing is practiced formally through surf competitions, but most often informally by recreational surfers. The potential to contribute to local sustainable development is rooted in the idea that surf tourism brings relatively wealthy surf enthusiasts to remote coastal regions where there are few outlets for economic diversification (Dolnicar and Fluker 2003; Ponting, McDonald, and Wearing 2005). The desire to surf quality and uncrowded waves in warm exotic destinations drives this demand and remains an enduring theme in the specialized surf media and within the advertising campaigns of surf and adventure brands (Ormrod 2005; Ponting, McDonald, and Wearing 2005; Lawler 2011; Ponting and McDonald 2013; Canniford 2017). Surf travel has also become a critical component of the surfer habitus and a defining feature of the sub-culture, which also per-petuates the practice (Ford and Brown 2006; Krause 2012). Surfer numbers are reportedly growing at 30% per year (WSL 2016) and the inclusion of surfing in the 2020 Olympic Games in Tokyo is likely to further increase participation and government support for development of the sport. The global surf industry, inclusive of surf tourism (the fastest growing subset), has been estimated to be worth between AUS$70 and $130 billion annually (O'Brien and Eddie 2013).

Many studies, however, have found that surf tourism can also bring a host of social and environmental problems when local communities are excluded from the process of devel-opment and there is not proper planning. Such oversight calls for considering better tech-niques to control development, include local community members in the development process, and mitigate resource crowding (Tantamjarik 2004; Ponting, McDonald, and Wearing 2005; Krause 2012; Towner 2015, 2016; Anderson 2017). Studies of the social car-rying capacity of surf-breaks have found that higher quality surf often leads to more drastic coping mechanisms, such as violent forms of localism to control crowd numbers (Mixon 2014; Usher and Kerstetter 2014). Surfers also cope by avoiding crowded areas, which has impacts on tourism flows (Ponting and O'Brien 2015; Usher and Gomez 2016).

The literature on seasonality and nature sports tourism generally reveals that seasonal-ity is a complicated issue. Reineman, Thomas, and Caldwell (2017, 182) acknowlege that surf forecasts play a critical role in helping 'surfers choose where to surf given the day's current and expected conditions'. This study seeks to go beyond this fairly intuitive notion to explore how these forecasts impact surf travel domestically and internationally. The military parlance 'surgical strike' has been co-opted into the surfing vernacular to differentiate a particular surf trip, which can be domestic or international, where a surfer targets a specific surf-break based on detailed forecasting data and a deep under-standing of the variable factors that lead to the best possible conditions at that surf-break. Real Watersports (2014) describes them this way:

> 'Surgical strikes' are when you travel specifically for perfect weather conditions (swell/wind or both) rather than on a calendar like most humans do … . Recreational enthusiasts should partake in at least one surgical strike in their lifetime – and probably many more … If you only have two weeks off a year and you miss the epic score during your break, then you have to wait another year to roll those 2/52 odds again. Strike out too many years in a row and it starts to really eat at you.

Anecdotal evidence suggests surgical strikes are common practice and the exploits of pro-fessional surfers undertaking them are regularly and widely reported in the surf media. We seek to empirically understand who does this, how often, how far in advance they plan, how far they travel, and what impact these surf tourists have at the destination level. The temporal aspect of crowding and surf tourism demand is especially important in remote surf tourism destinations that are heavily reliant on this demand.

Methodology

Target population and survey data collection and analysis

This study began with a desire to better understand the intersection between nature sports, technology, and tourism and specifically the manner in which surf forecasts impact surfer travel behaviours generally. As an exploratory study, an online survey method was chosen because of the global dispersion of the surf population and because internet surveys can provide data of comparable quality with those generated from traditional mail or phone surveys (Gosling et al. 2004). The survey was disseminated using the online survey platform Qualtrics and the link was available between May 1 and July 22, 2015. The survey was initially applied to a convenience sample of self-ascribed surfers over 18 years old. The link was shared through email to authors' contacts and with surf clubs and associations. The authors' posted the link on social media (Facebook and Instagram) and surf-brands also posted the link on their social media platforms. A snowball sampling technique was also employed in that all respondents were asked to post or forward the link to others. In total, 3101 survey responses were gathered.

A portion of this large-scale questionnaire specifically asked surfers how often they use surf reports and then utilized a series of Likert-type scale questions to gain a better understanding on how technology influences surf travel behaviour domestically and internationally. Data were initially summarized using a series of key questions related to the research aims. Based on the results obtained from key questions, additional analysis was conducted on the critical factors driving the behaviour in choices regarding international and domestic travel habits and particularly surgical strikes. Subsequent Pearson's correlation analysis was conducted to ascertain relationships between income, age and surf ability and the number of surgical strikes.

Case study: Pavones, Costa Rica

Context and site rationale

Tourism is an important contributor to the Costa Rican economy. In 2015, tourism contributed US$1,043,500 to the GDP of Costa Rica (roughly 9%) (ICT 2015). In 2014, 2,527,000 tourists visited Costa Rica (ICT 2015), of whom 16.2% (409,000) identified surfing as the primary reason for travelling to the country (Krause 2012; Blanco 2013). Lazarow and Nelson (2007) estimated that surfing infused more money into the Costa Rican economy (US$816 million) than the coffee export industry in 2012. There are also an estimated five thousand national and foreign surfers living in Costa Rica (Blanco 2013). Foreign direct investment in Costa Rica in 2014 reached 2.2 billion USD (Sada 2015) and studies show that a large portion of this (roughly 34%) is in coastal real estate purchases (van Noorloos 2011). It has also been shown that the proximity to quality surf in other locations (Santa Cruz, California) leads to as much as a US$100,000 increase in real estate value compared to comparable homes not close to quality surf (Scorse, Reynolds, and Sackett 2015). We have observed similar trends in Costa Rica, though this has yet to be formally studied. Costa Rica's Caribbean and Pacific coasts are endowed with warm water and consistent surf breaks in close proximity to one another, appealing to surfers from beginners to experts. This, coupled with tourist-friendly national policies, incentives for foreign investment (van Noorloos 2011), the peaceful image associated with demilitarization, and improving infrastructure continue to shape the country's development (Honey 1999).

Pavones, shown in Figure 1, is a critical site for surf tourism in Costa Rica. It is known as the second longest left-hand point-break in the world, capable of delivering three-minute long rides on a solid south swell (Sanders n.d.). Evans (2015, vxii) says, 'the perfect swell

Original figure can be viewed in the journal article. Copyright permission could not be obtained for this figure.

doesn't happen often, but when it does, globetrotting surfers and the fortunate ones who happen to already be in Pavones spring into action.' The several communities that comprise Pavones are located in the municipality of Golfito, in the Puntarenas province. Rio Claro de Pavones (the town encompassing the main point-break referred to as Pavones) has a population of roughly 400 local Costa Rican and expatriates who have been drawn to surf or begin surf related enterprises (Usher and Gomez 2016). The initial phase of Costa Rican settlement in the area occurred between 1955 and 1985 when the United Fruit Company (UFC) was headquartered in Golfito and settlement branched south towards Pavones. Since the UFC closure, some residents who did not migrate have adopted fisheries-based livelihoods, but the majority now work in surf tourism, working in or running cabinas, restaurants, hostels or other tourist services (Usher and Gomez 2016).

Visiting surfers must travel a long way to get to Pavones. The town is two hours away from Golfito on a gravel road with sections flooded by rivers. Golfito is infrequently serviced by air and is a 7-hour bus ride from San Jose. Usher and Gomez (2016, 17) suggest that between 80 and 160 surfers can be counted in the water at the main point-break in Pavones when 'crowds generated by increasingly accurate swell prediction threaten the sustainability of the destination.' While Usher and Gomez (2016) found that crowding in Pavones leads locals (Costa Ricans) and resident locals (expatriates) to adopt different coping strategies – the former subtler and the latter more overt – an empirical connection between surf reports and crowding has yet to be made. Understanding the linkages between surf forecasts and surf tourism demand can have practical planning implications for surfers, business operators, government and community organizations considering regulating surf tourism in Pavones.

Onsite data collection and analysis

Individual case studies help to develop, expand, and generalize theories (Yin 2009). The Pavones case is illustrative of surf tourism and other nature sports destinations reliant upon precise (and rare) natural conditions. Previous tourism seasonality studies have compared occupancy data provided by governments and tourism agencies to publicly available weather information to empirically demonstrate tourism seasonality (Becken 2010; Karamustafa and Ulama 2010). Because no method for analysing tourism seasonality has emerged as empirically superior, trying different methods for different cases is critical (Karamustafa and Ulama 2010). Due to the lack of publicly available data, we relied on physically counting surfers in the water, the occupancy information provided from one lodging establishment (other businesses approached viewed this information as proprietary), and daily surf report data and forecasts for Pavones from Magicseaweed.com.

One author engaged in data gathering in Pavones for one summer surf season from June 2015 through September 2015 (87 days). This timeframe was chosen because the surf in Pavones requires a large, long period swell from the south/southwest, which occurs most frequently during these summer months. Because we were examining intra-seasonal travel behaviour, we decided to analyse a particular surf season to monitor how occupancy and the number of surfers in the water correlated to surf reports during the season. In order to approximate the number of surfers in the water each day, the author administered a headcount of all the people surfing at three separate times per day and the mean count was taken. The first observation was made at 8:00am, the second observation at 12:00pm, and the third observation at 5:00pm. The mean was chosen for analysis because it encapsulates fluctuations within a given day, which is a critical component of resource crowding.

One hospitality establishment agreed to anonymously share their occupancy data for this study. The daily occupancy percentage was obtained by documenting how many rooms were occupied on a given day, and dividing it by the total number of rooms. This establishment has roughly 14 dorm beds and 4 private rooms with a maximum capacity of around 26 guests. As a 'surf hostel,' we argue that it can act as a proxy for overall town occupancy rates because it is reflective of the movement of surfers in and out of town. There are 15 small hotels in Pavones with approximately 200 beds in total. In addition, there are camping options and approximately 28 private houses available to rent.

In order to test the relationship between the swell forecast and the influx of tourists, the daily and extended forecasts on the website magicseaweed.com were photographed and documented daily. Magicseaweed.com was chosen for analysis because most surfers in Pavones reported using this site and also because the competing site (surfline.com) only provides three-day forecasts for free and our survey revealed that only 18% of surfers pay for premium forecast services. Magicseaweed.com creates a surf quality index by converting the way certain weather conditions match the ideal conditions for Pavones and ascribe a certain number of stars, as a proxy for surf quality (0 being the worst and 5 the best). The site suggests the ideal surf conditions for Pavones are experienced when there is a long period (>10 s) swell, between 2 and 12 feet in height, from the South-Southwest and with light winds from the North-Northeast. A day predicted to have these conditions will be considered a 5-star day. The site publishes the observed conditions of each day, as well as, a surf-forecast prediction for each of the subsequent 10 days and we recorded these values for each day during the observational period.

To analyse this data, for each observed day, we selected the surf reports for that day and the day prior, as well as, three, five, seven and ten days prior. These were selected rather than each forecast observation to reduce multicollinearity issues. A multiple linear regression analysis using backwards selection testing was then undertaken to analyse the predictive influence of these reports on mean daily surfer headcount and hotel occupancy.

Limitations: The opt-in internet-based survey portion of this study is not generalizable and cannot be argued to be representative of the entire surf population (Couper 2004). These unsupervised responses must also assume respondents understood each question in their entirety. In addition, it must be noted that many respondents did not complete all questions in the survey (only a part of which is looked at in this paper). We decided to count every credible answer (after discarding duplicate IP addresses) to every question examined in this study rather than throwing out responses based on non-completion of the entire survey. Despite these limitations, the results offer important insights into surf forecast use and the influence these reports have on travel behaviour of a very large sample of the travelling surf population. They also justify analysing surfer behaviour with respect to natural conditions at a location reliant on specific weather conditions.

As for the onsite data collection, this study covers one surf season in Pavones, uses one forecast site and relies on occupancy data from one hotel. The use of one season is justified because it demonstrates surfers' response to weather within a season rather than climate. However, multiple uniform summers worth of data would lead to more robust findings. For occupancy percentage, ideally information from more lodging establishments of varying price and quality would have been collected, but this was not offered voluntarily after multiple solicitations. Counting surfers from the beach also did not allow us to distinguish between local and tourist surfers in the water, which was another limitation. As an exploratory study, the findings that can be derived from this information are a starting point to inspire future analysis.

Results

Survey respondents were mostly intermediate and advanced male surfers from North America, Australasia, and Europe. Results from the large-scale online surfer survey

Table 1. Demographic information on participants in large-scale online surf survey calculated from a total of 3101 respondents.

Variable	n	Categories	Percentage
Gender	2762	Male	80%
		Female	20%
Age	2765	18–25	17%
		26–34	27%
		35–54	48%
		55 or over	8%
Geographic Region	2714	North America	58%
		Europe	17%
		Australasia	21%
		Other	4%
Self-described surf ability	3093	Beginner	13%
		Intermediate	30%
		Experienced	48%
		Advanced	9%
Household Income	2664	$0–25,000	15%
		$25–50,000	19%
		$50–100,000	32%
		$100–175,000	22%
		More than $175,000	12%

(summarized in Tables 1 and 2) indicate that respondents typically plan international surf trips a few months to a year ahead of travel and do not, with high regularity, perceive that surf cameras and forecasts have much of an impact when making international travel plans. A subset of the population does make international surgical strikes based on surf forecasts and the data outlined in Table 3 suggests a significant positive relationship between self-described surf ability, and number of surgical strikes undertaken over the last five years. Contrastingly, there was not a significant correlation between either household income or age, and number of international surgical strikes.

Table 2. Summary of responses to selected questions extracted from large-scale online surf survey.

Survey Questions	n	Participant Reponses		
Use of Surf forecasts				
		Agree	*Neutral*	*Disagree*
Surf cams and forecasts influence if I go surfing each day	2960	68%	18%	12%
Surf cams and forecasts influence where I go surfing each day	2947	68%	20%	12%
I plan my international trips based on surf forecasts	2876	27%	40%	33%
Surf cams and forecasts contribute to my enjoyment of surfing	2980	54%	30%	16%
Surf cams and forecasts can cause crowding at my local surf break	2948	59%	31%	10%
		Once a day or more	*A few times a week*	*Once a week or less*
Frequency of surf cameras and forecast use	2980	60%	22%	18%
Travel Habits				
		Less than 1 month	*A few months to 1 year*	*More than 1 year*
How far in advance do you plan international trips?	2898	21%	70%	9%
		None	*Less than 4*	*More than 5*
In 5 years how many international surgical strikes have you made?	1400	56%	37%	7%
In the last five years, how many domestic surgical strikes have you made (>40 km)?	1334	6%	36%	58%

Table 3. Results of Pearson correlation analysis. NS = Nonsignificant.

Comparison	Pearson's Correlation Coefficient (r)	Statistical Significance (P)
Number of international surgical strikes in the last 5 years and Age	0.018	NS
Number of international surgical strikes in the last five years and Income	0.02	NS
Number of international surgical strikes in the last five years and Self-prescribed surf ability	0.131	<0.001

Participants do use surf cameras and forecasts very often (often multiple times a day) and perceive that surf forecasts and cameras impact their behaviour in terms of, if and where they surf. In response to surf forecasts and cameras, surfers also show a high propensity to participate in domestic surgical strikes (travelling more than 40 kms within one's home country in response to a favourable surf report) and perceive that surf cameras and reports contribute to crowding at their local surf-breaks.

In order to validate the results found within the large-scale surf questionnaire and examine intra-regional travel behaviour to an actual surf-break, data from the case study in Pavones, Costa Rica were analyzed to determine the interactions between surf forecasts and both in-water surfer headcounts and hotel occupancy. Results indicated that surf forecasts are a significant predictor of the maximum daily surfer headcount, with 45.3% of the variation explained by a combination of on-the-day forecasts, and forecasts one day in advance (Table 4), though only the on-the-day forecast has statistical significance. Importantly, analysis suggests that surf forecasts are also a relatively weak, but statistically significant predictor of hotel occupancy rates, with 11.7% of hotel occupancy determined by surf forecasts 5 and 7 days in advance (Table 5).

Discussion

International travel planning, surf forecasts, and climate

Results of the macro-study analysis reveal that international surf travel decisions are not typically made on short notice based on surf forecasts. While the surf media glorifies the notion of surfers dropping everything to chase swells forecasted around the globe, in reality, only a relatively small proportion of international surf trips are surgical strikes and most (nearly 80%) are planned sometime between three months and one year in advance of travel. This finding suggests that the climactic factors, or the general likelihood

Table 4. Results of multiple linear regression analysis using backwards selection. Predictive surf report versus in-water headcount.

Predictor Variable	Model				
	1	2	3	4	5
On the Day	0.406*	0.403*	0.400*	0.401*	0.434*
1 day prior	0.335	0.336	0.363*	0.351*	0.264
3 days prior	0.48	.46	–	–	–
5 days prior	−0.098	−0.155	−0.098	−0.119	–
7 day prior	−0.31	–	–	–	–
10 days prior	−0.38	−0.48	−0.44	–	–
Adjusted R^2	0.425	0.432	0.439	0.444	0.453

*$P = <0.05$.

Table 5. Results of multiple linear regression analysis using backwards selection. Predictive surf report versus hotel occupancy.

Predictor Variable	Model				
	1	2	3	4	5
On the Day	0.156	0.101	–	–	–
1 day prior	−0.087	–	–	–	–
3 days prior	0.20	0.171	0.321	0.197	–
5 days prior	−0.385*	−0.389*	−0.410*	−0.405*	−0.315
7 day prior	0.624*	0.627*	0.643*	0.526*	0.580**
10 days prior	−0.185	−0.091	−0.186	–	–
Adjusted R^2	0.119	0.129	0.132	0.127	0.117

*$P = <0.05$.
**$P = <0.01$.

of surf consistency is most significant when it comes to surfers' international travel decisions. This is consistent with previous studies that have found international travel decisions can be best explained by climactic variables (in both sending and receiving areas), while domestic tourism is more responsive to weather (Agnew and Palutikof 2006; Falk 2014; Ridderstaat et al. 2014). Previous studies have further demonstrated that potential tourists experiencing bad weather at home do not often book international travel within the season they are experiencing these conditions, but that experiencing bad weather encourages them to plan international trips the following year (Agnew and Palutikof 2006; Falk 2014). Further investigation might examine the way poor domestic surf seasons influence international surf travel in the following year. Costa Rica, for example, which is most often visited by surfers from the northeast of the U.S (Reynolds and Hritz 2012), may be able to prepare for an influx of surf travellers in the summer of 2019 after a poor fall season in 2018. This knowledge could be valuable in terms of target marketing and national destination management.

These findings also suggest that international tourism flows may be highly sensitive to shifts in swell consistency related to climate change. Much like alpine tourists (and particularly serious leisure enthusiasts) who have been found to shift toward higher altitude locations in response to general climatic shifts in snow reliability (Elsasser and Buerki 2002; Cocolas, Walters, and Ruhanen 2016), surf tourists are likely to be responsive to consistency changes in their travel planning. In short, areas of surf tourism interest may change depending upon the way in which climate influences surf consistency. It is beyond the scope of this paper to discuss this with any geographic specificity, but our findings suggest that these changes could have a significant impact on global surf travel flows and warrant further research. It is also worth noting that international surgical strikes do happen and that they are unique to surfing and similar nature sports. While more than half of our respondents have never participated in an international surgical strike, others have with varying degrees of regularity. Of those who have participated in one or more international surgical strike in the last five years, only surf ability was found to be positively correlated (with statistical significance) with this behaviour. This is suggestive of a small (7% of respondents participating in one or more international surgical strikes each year), but significant niche of highly skilled surfers who make fairly regular international surgical strikes based on forecasts, suggesting that very specific weather conditions provide a high likelihood of optimum conditions at high quality surf-breaks. Given that highly skilled surfers, and particularly professional surfers are anecdotally apt to take more than their fair share of waves on any given session, this small niche may have a disproportionate impact on perceptions of crowding amongst surfers of more modest ability. Future research could seek out and examine these skilled surfers to learn more about their motivations and desires, spending habits, mobility, behaviour and relative impact on perceptions of crowding. The macro-survey findings help to contextualize the relative importance of surgical strikes in relation to international surf forecast responsiveness and thereby validate further research into the intra-regional and intra-seasonal mobility of surf travellers.

Intra-seasonality and intra-regional tourism flows

Our analysis shows a high frequency of surf forecast use, surf forecasts determining whether and where people go surfing, and surfers willing to engage in surf tourism in response to forecast surf conditions. Previous studies finding a correlation between positive weather attributes and domestic overnight stays analyzed average occupancy against average observed conditions to examine how weather influenced visitation fluctuations between seasons (Agnew and Palutikof 2006; Falk 2014; Ridderstaat et al. 2014). This article exposes how forecasts influence intra-seasonal behaviours, which is useful for influencing real-time decision making within destinations. This case study reveals the different, but also interconnected ways in which mid-range (occupancy) and short-range (daily surf decisions) forecasts influence behaviour and highlights the impacts these forecast related behaviours may have on surf crowding, peak town visitation, resident well-being, and tourist satisfaction.

Firstly, we find that occupancy rates can be best explained by 5 and 7-day surf forecasts, with the 7-day forecast being the strongest predictor. This suggests surfers (Costa Ricans, other resident foreigners, and surf tourists) engaging in domestic travel from other areas of Costa Rica to Pavones to stay overnight, are most responsive to favourable forecasts within this time horizon. Tourism literature demonstrates how peaks in visitation within a high season can lead to overcrowding and congestion, reduced service quality (Murphy 1985; Hudson and Cross 2005; Pegg, Patterson, and Vila Gariddo 2012), and lower quality of life for residents (Ap and Crompton 1993; Bimonte and Punzo 2011; Bimonte and Faralla 2016). Predicting general occupancy variability is critical for mitigating these negative impacts. Lodging providers can look to 5 and 7-day forecasts to accurately plan for an influx of surfers chasing a predicted swell event. They can have staff prepared for increased numbers and also provision things like water (often scarce in the region) and food. Conversely, hospitality businesses can be prepared for gaps in visitation when surf reports in this time horizon do not show the likelihood of quality surf. We found this occupancy correlation while analysing a low-end establishment. Future studies, however, could examine how occupancy in mid-range and high-end establishments correlate to surf forecasts in order to make stronger assertions about overall destination level impacts.

When examining head counts at the main point-break in Pavones on any particular day, 45.3% of the variability was explained by the combined effects of the on-the-day forecast and the forecast from the day prior. This is important because it shows that while mid-range forecast data may influence travel to Pavones and occupancy, and create the general conditions for severe crowding, natural conditions are still most important in determining actual daily surf behaviour in situ, as well as, localized and regional resource crowding issues.

Lazarow and Olive (2017) found that the majority of surfers avoid crowded surf-breaks, especially if there is any potential threat of violence. Nature sports studies have also shown that crowding displaces high paying tourists in favour of a higher number of lower paying tourists (Budruk et al. 2008; Vaske and Shelby 2008). Usher and Gomez (2016) found that crowding in Pavones has led to violent episodes and puts pressure on other nearby surf-breaks as surfers seek to avoid crowds by travelling a few kilometers outside of Pavones to surf other places. Local anamosity towards visiting surfers was exacerbated at these once 'secret' spots (Usher and Gomez 2016), a result that echos studies finding residents' have negative perceptions of peak tourism and well-being when local resources are stressed (Bimonte and Punzo 2011; Bimonte and Faralla 2016).

Our study adds another layer of understanding that is useful for considering the potential of preserving a statisfying surf experience for both residents and visitors, which is critical for destination success and sustainabiltiy. Nearby surf-breaks may receive hightened use pressure when mid-range weather reports encourage travel to Pavones, but this may be exacerbated when surf conditions do not match forecast predictions. When there is a good surf report for Pavones roughly a week in advance, surfers will travel from afar to get there and if the conditions match up on a particular day, many surfers will paddle out and compete for rides causing local resource crowding at the main-break. In this instance, many surfers cope with crowding by exploring other local surf-breaks. When quality surf is predicted a week out and does not happen, surfers in situ will potentially abandon Pavones, or travel locally to surf other breaks putting pressure on 'local secrets' and also greatly impacting residents well-being and goodwill towards tourists. Only when examining the combined influence of mid and short-range reports can a robust understanding of the interrelationship between resource crowding and destination visitation fluctuations be formulated. Combined, surf forecasts and observed natural conditions impact surf travel behaviours in interesting and nuanced ways that deserve further attention. Such studies will help us better understand destination and hospitality management, as well as, host and guest satisfaction and how they relate to intra-seasonal and intra-regional travel patterns.

Conclusion

Combining the macro survey with the case study in Pavones provides valuable insights for researchers, entrepreneurs, destination management, and surfers. When exploring the natural component of seasonality in surf tourism, we found that climactic factors associated with surf consistency influence when surfers travel to certain places and where surfers choose to live (often seasonally) and visit on holidays. Most of these decisions are made three months to a year ahead of travel. However, a highly skilled subset of the population was found to make frequent international surgical strikes, which may have a disproportionate impact on tourist and resident perceptions of crowding in places like Pavones. We also demonstrated intra-seasonal travel behaviours involving the flow of surfers between surf-breaks or surf destinations within a region based on surf forecasts, which is critical, especially for locations requiring specific natural conditions. We found surfers make intra-regional travel decisions with regards to booking lodging based on mid-range surf reports, but are also immediately responsive in their behaviours to daily reports and conditions while in-situ at a particular destination. Combined, the interplay of mid-range and short-range weather reports greatly influence surf behaviour and resource crowding, which has been found to have detrimental impacts in Pavones and other similar locations. Incorporating and expanding on these findings can lead to more intricate hospitality management practices and surf management plans, that help build an understanding of how surf tourists are likely to respond to swell event forecasts within a region.

The articulation of intra-regional and intra-seasonal travel behaviour, we argue, makes a compelling case for destinations to consider regional surf tourism governance. Currently, surf tourists and residents seek optimality by following reports to iconic sites requiring specific conditions, but clustering in towns and on waves is threatening the quality of the experience. To date, regional governance, where surf zones are delineated and quotas of surfers allowed per zone are determined and monitored, has only been successfully implemented in Papua New Guinea, though several attempts have been made in Indonesia's Mentawai Islands (O'Brien and Ponting 2013). Marquee surf-breaks like Pavones add to overall destination appeal, but if unmanaged, resident animosity towards tourism will grow and word-of-mouth perceptions of crowding may limit tourist willingness-to-pay to visit the area. This is particularly critical as two large condominium projects are currently being erected in Pavones when water shortages and inadequate waste disposal during peak visitation periods are widespread and crowding has been reported to cause social issues and contentious responses from both local Costa Ricans and resident foreigners (Usher and Gomez 2016). Surfers are willing to travel to remote locations, which can provide considerable economic benefits to areas with few other outlets for diversification. Understanding that the surf population is hyper-responsive to surf forecasts (while in a country) reveals the importance of understanding the ways in which technology and temporal natural factors influence surf tourism flows and provide opportunities to manage surf tourism more effectively.

Disclosure statement

No potential conflict of interest was reported by the authors.

ORCID

Jess Ponting http://orcid.org/0000-0002-8528-7498

References

Agnew, M. D., and J. Palutikof. 2006. "Impacts of Short-term Climate Variability in the UK on Demand for Domestic and International Tourism." *Climate Research* 31: 109–120.

Amelung, B., S. Nicholls, and D. Viner. 2007. "Implications of Global Climate Change for Tourism Flows and Seasonality." *Journal of Travel Research* 45: 285–296.

Anderson, J. 2014. "Surfing between the Local and the Global: Identifying Spatial Divisions in Surfing Practice." *Transactions of the Institute of British Geographers* 39 (2): 237–249.

Anderson, J. 2017. "A Ritual with Consequence." In *Sustainable Surfing*, edited by G. Borne, and J. Ponting, 176–201. New York: Routledge.

Anonymous. 2006. *wannasurf.com*. Accessed September 28, 2017. https://www.wannasurf.com/spot/Central_America/Costa_Rica/Pacific_South/pavones/comment/index.html?wdaction=lib.WDPageComment.show&page=4.

Ap, J., and J. Crompton. 1993. "Residents' Strategies for Responding to Tourism Impacts." *Journal of Travel Research* 32 (1): 47–50.

Barbieri, C., and S. Sotomayor. 2013. "Surf Travel Behavior and Destination Preferences: An Application of the Serious Leisure Inventory and Measure." *Tourism Management* 35: 111–121.

Becken, S. 2010. *The Importance of Climate and Weather for Tourism*. Literature Review, Lincoln University, Canterbury, NZ: Land Environment and People.

Becken, S. 2013. "Measuring the Effect of Weather on Tourism: A Destination and Activity-based Analysis." *Journal of Travel Research* 52 (2): 156–167.

Bimonte, S. 2013. "Sustainable Tourism: an Interpretive and Management Paradigm." In *Tourism as a Tool for Development*, edited by P. Diaz, 83–99. Southampton: WIT Press.

Bimonte, S., and V. Faralla. 2016. "Does Residents' Perceived Life Satisfaction Vary with Tourist Season? A Two-step Survey in a Mediterranean Destination." *Tourism Managment* 55: 199–208.

Bimonte, S., and L. F. Punzo. 2011. "Tourism, Residents' Attitudes and Perceived Carrying Capacity with an 'Experimental' Study in Five Tuscan Destinations." *International Journal of Sustainable Development* 14 (3/4): 242–261.

Blanco, C. 2013. "Surf deja a Costa Rica más de 400 mil millones al año." *La Prensa Libre*, 5 January.

Buckley, R. 2002. "Surf Tourism and Sustainable Development in Indo-Pacific Islands: The Industry the Islands." *Journal of Sustainable Tourism* 10 (5): 405–424.

Budruk, M., S. A. Wilhem-Stanis, I. E. Schneider, and J. J. Heise. 2008. "Crowding and Experience Use History: A Study of the Moderating Effect of Place Attachment among Water-based Recreationists." *Environmental Management* 41: 528–537.

Butler, R. W., and B. Mao. 1997. "Seasonality in Tourism: Problems and Measurement." In *Quality Management in Urban Tourism*, edited by P. Murphy, 9–23. Chichester: Wiley & Sons.

Butt, T., P. Russell, and R. Grigg. 2004. *Surf Science: An Introduction to Waves for Surfing*. Honolulu: University of Hawaii Press.

Canniford, R. 2017. "Branded Primitives." In *The Critical Surf Studies Reader*, edited by D. Z. Hough-Snee, and A. S. Eastman, 365–385. Durham: Duke University Press.

Cocolas, N., G. Walters, and L. Ruhanen. 2016. "Behavioural Adaptation to Climate Change among Winter Alpine Tourists: An Analysis of Tourist Motivations and Leisure Substitutability." *Journal of Sustainable Tourism* 24 (6): 846–865.

Commons, J., and S. Page. 2001. "Mana Seasonality in Peripheral Tourism Regions: The Case of Northland, New Zealand." In *Seasonality in Tourism*, edited by T. Baum, and S. Lundtorp, 153–172. New York: Pergamon.

Couper, M. 2004. "Web Surveys: A Review of Issues and Approaches." *Public Opinion Quarterly* 64: 464–494.

Deery, M., L. Jago, and L. Fredline. 2012. "Rethinking Social Impacts of Tourism Research: A new Research Agenda." *Tourism Managment* 33 (1): 64–73.

Dolnicar, S., and M. Fluker. 2003. "Behavioural Market Segments among Surf Tourists: Investigating Past Destination Choice." *Journal of Sport & Tourism* 8 (3): 186–119.

Doxey, G. V. 1975. "A Causation Theory of Visitor-Resident Irritants, Methodology and Research Inferences." Sixth annual conference proceedings of the travel research association. San Diego: Travel and Tourism Research Association, 195–198.

Elsasser, H., and R. Buerki. 2002. "Climate Change as a Threat to Tourism in the Alps." *Climate Research* 20: 253–257.

Evans, J. 2015. *The Battle for Paradise: Surfing, Tuna, and one Town's Quest to Save a Wave*. Lincoln and London: University of Nebraska Press.

Falk, M. 2014. "Impact of Weather Conditions on Tourism Demand in the Peak Summer." *Tourism Management Perspectives* 9: 24–35.

Finger, R., and N. Lehmann. 2012. "Modeling the Sensitivity of Outdoor Recreation Activities to Climate Change." *Climate Research* 51: 229–236.

Ford, N., and D. Brown. 2006. *Surfing and Social Theory: Experience, Embodiment and Narrative of the Dream Glide*. Abingdon: Routledge.

Gómez Martín, M. B. 2005. "Weather, Climate and Tourism, a Geographical Perspective." *perspective. Annals of Tourism Research* 32 (3): 571–591.

Gosling, S., S. Vazire, S. Srivastava, and O. John. 2004. "Should we Trust Web-based Studies? A Comparative Analysis of Six Preconceptions About Internet Questionnaires." *American Psychologist* 59: 93–104.

Honey, M. 1999. *Ecotourism and Sustainable Development: Who Owns Paradise?* Washington, D.C: Island Press.

Hudson, S., and P. Cross. 2005. "Winter Sports Destinations: Dealing with Seasonality." In *Sport Tourism Destinations, Issues, Opportunities and Analysis*, edited by J. Higham, 188–204. England: Elsevier/Butterworth-Heinemann.

ICT. 2015. *Tourism Figures, Gasto Medio por Persona (GMP) En US$ de los Turistas no Residentes 2009-2015*. http://www.ict.go.cr/en/documents/estad%C3%ADsticas/cifras-tur%C3%ADsticas/gasto-y-estadia-media/846-todas-las-vias/file.html.

Karamustafa, K., and S. Ulama. 2010. "Measuring the Seasonality in Tourism with the Comparison of Different Methods." *EuroMed Journal of Business* 5 (2): 191–214.

Krause. 2012. "Pilgrimage to the Playas: Surf Tourism in Costa Rica." *Anthropology in Action* 19 (3): 37–49.

Lawler, K. 2011. *The American Surfer: Radical Culture and Capitalism*. New York: Routledge.

Laws, E. 1995. *Tourist Destination Management: Issues, Analysis and Policies*. New York: Routledge Topics for Tourism.

Lazarow, N., and C. Nelson. 2007. "The Value of Coastal Recreation Resources: A Case Study Approach to Examine the Value of Recreational Surfing to Specific Locales." Paper presented at the Coastal Zone, Portland.

Lazarow, N., and R. Olive. 2017. "Culture, Meaning, and Sustainabiltiy in Surfing." In *Sustainable Surfing*, edited by G. Borne, and J. Ponting, 202–218. New York: Routledge.

Mach, L. 2014. "From the Endless Summer to the Surf Spring: Technology and Governance in Developing World Surf Tourism." *Dissertation*, University of Delaware, Newark, DE.

Mach, L. 2017. "Surfing in the Technological era." In *Surfing and Sustainability*, edited by D. Borne, and J. Ponting, 41–71. New York: Routledge .

Mach, L., and J. Ponting. 2017. "A Nested Socio-ecological Systems Approach to Understanding the Implications of Changing Surf-reef Governance Regimes." In *Lifestyle Sports and Public Policy*, edited by D. Turner, and S. Carnicelli, 137–156. New York: Routledge.

Marchant, B., and Z. Mottiar. 2011. "Understanding Lifestyle Entreprenuers and Digging Beneath the Issue of Profits: Profiling Surf Tourism Lifestyle Entrepreneurs in Ireland." *Tourism Planning and Development* 8 (2): 171–183.

Martin, A. S., and I. Assenov. 2012. "The Genesis of a New Body of Sport Tourism Literature: A Systematic Review of Surf Tourism Research (1997–2011)." *Journal of Sport and Tourism* 17 (4): 257–287.

McElroy, N. 2016. *Pumping surf adds $20 million to the Gold Coast economy in two months.* 1 March. Accessed January 14, 2017. http://www.goldcoastbulletin.com.au/lifestyle/beaches-and-fishing/pumping-surf-adds-20-million-to-the-gold-coast-economy-in-two-months/news-story/53d2ab7d bae9b5177fb07352d2cdc56f.

McGregor, T., and S. Wills. 2016. *Natural Assets: Surfing a Wave of Economic Growth.* OxCarre Working Papers 170, Oxford Centre for the Analysis of Resource Rich Economies, University of Oxford. https://EconPapers.repec.org/RePEc:oxf:oxcrwp:170.

Melo, R., and R. Gomes. 2017a. "A Sociocultural Approach to Understanding the Development of Nature Sports." In *Sport Tourism: New Challenges in a Globalized World*, edited by R. Melo, and C. Sobry, 47–76. Cambridge: Cambridge Scholars Publishing.

Melo, R., and R. Gomes. 2017b. "Nature Sports Participation: Understanding Demand, Practice Profile, Motivations and Constraints." *European Journal of Tourism Research*, 16:108–135.

Mixon, F. 2014. "Bad Vibrations new Evidence on Commons Quality and Localism at California's Surf Breaks." *International Review of Economics* 61 (4): 379–397.

Murphy, P. E. 1985. *Tourism: A Community Approach.* New York: Methuen.

Murphy, M., and M. Bernal. 2008. *The Impact of Surfing on the Local Economy of Mundaka, Spain.* San Francisco: Save the Waves Coalition.

Nicholls, S., D. F. Holecek, and J. Noh. 2008. "Impact of Weather Variability on Golfing Activity and Implications of Climate Change." *Tourism Analysis* 13: 117–130.

O'Brien, D., and I. Eddie. 2013. "Benchmarking Global Best Practice: Innovation and Leadership in Surf City Tourism and Industry Development." The global surf cities conference. Kirra Community Center Austrialia.

O'Brien, D., and J. Ponting. 2013. "Sustainable Surf Tourism: A Community Centered Approach in Papua New Guinea." *Journal of Sport Management* 27: 158–172.

Ormrod, J. 2005. "Endless Summer (1964): Consuming Waves and Surfing the Frontier." *Film and History* 35 (1): 39–51.

Pegg, S., I. Patterson, and P. Vila Gariddo. 2012. "The Impact of Seasonality on Tourism and Hospitality Operations in the Alpine Region of New South Wales, Australia." *International Journal of Hospitality Management* 31: 659–666.

Ponting, J., and M. G. McDonald. 2013. "Performance, Agency, and Change in Surfing Tourist Space." *Annals of Tourism Research* 43: 415–434.

Ponting, J., M. McDonald, and S. L. Wearing. 2005. "De-constructing Wonderland: Surfing Tourism in the Metawia Islands, Indonesia." *Society and Leisure* 28 (1): 141–162.

Ponting, J., and D. O'Brien. 2015. "Regulating 'Nirvana': Sustainable Surf Tourism in a Climate of Increasing Regulation." *Sport Management Review* 18 (1): 99–110.

Portugal, A., F. Campos, F. Martins, and R. Melo. 2017. "Understanding the Relation between Serious Surfing, Surfing Profile, Surf Travel Behavior and Destination Attributes Preferences." *European Journal of Tourism Research*, 16: 57–73.

Real Watersports INC. 2014. *Surgical Strike: Diaries of a Professional Recreational Surfer.* 1 May. Accessed January 20, 2018. http://www.realwatersports.com/news/surgical-strike-puerto-rico/.

Reineman, D., L. Thomas, and M. Caldwell. 2017. "Using Local Knowledge to Project Sea Level Rise Impacts on Wave Resources in California." *Ocean & Coastal Management* 138: 181–191.

Reynolds, Z., and N. Hritz. 2012. "Surfing as Adventure Travel: Motivations and Lifestyles." *Journal of Tourism Insights* 3 (1), 1–15.

Ridderstaat, J., M. Oduber, R. Croes, P. Nijkamp, and P. Martens. 2014. "Impacts of Seasonal Patterns of Climate on Recurrent Fluctuations in Tourism Demand: Evidence from Aruba." *Tourism Management* 41: 245–256.

Sada, J. M. 2015. *The Curious Case of Costa Rica: Can an Outlier Sustain its Success?* September 7. http://hir.harvard.edu/the-curious-case-of-costa-rica-can-an-outlier-sustain-its-success/.

Sanders, M. n.d. *Pavones - Travel Guide.* Accessed September 14, 2017. http://www.surfline.com/surfdata/report_breakdata.cfm?id=5796&sef=true.

Scarfe, B. E., T. R. Healy, H. G. Rennie, and S. T. Mead. 2009. "Sustainable Management of Surfing Breaks – an Overview." *Reef Journal*, 1: 44–73.

Scorse, J., F. Reynolds, and A. Sackett. 2015. "Impact of Surf Breaks on Home Prices in Santa Cruz, CA." *Tourism Economics* (Sage Journals) 21 (2): 409–418.

Scott, D., and B. Jones. 2007. "A Regional Comparison of the Implications of Climate Change of the Golf Industry in Canada." *The Canadian Geographer* 51 (2): 219–232.

Scott, D., and C. Lemieux. 2009. "Weather and Climate Information for Tourism." White paper, World Meteorological Organisation.

Scott, D., G. McBoyle, B. Mills, and A. Minogue. 2006. "Climate Change and the Sustainability of Ski-based Tourism in Eastern North America." *Journal of Sustainable Tourism* 14 (4): 376–398.

Tantamjarik, P. A. 2004. "Sustainability Issues Facing the Costa Rica Surf Tourism." *Manoa: Unpublished Master's thesis*, University of Hawaii, Manoa, HI.

Teye, V., S. F. Sonmez, and E. Sirakaya. 2002. "Residents' Attitudes Towards Tourism Development." *Annals of Tourism Research* 29: 668–688.

Towner, N. 2015. "Surf Tourism and Sustainable Community Development in the Mentawai Islands, Indonesia: A Multiple Stakeholder Perspective." *European Journal of Tourism Research* 11: 166–170.

Towner, N. 2016. "Community Participation and Emerging Surfin Tourism Destinations: A Case Study of the Mentawai Islands." *Journal of Sport & Tourism* 20 (1): 1–19.

Usher, L., and E. Gomez. 2016. "Surf Localism in Costa Rica: Exploring: Exploring Territoriality among Costa Rica and Foreign Resident Surfers." *Journal of Sport Tourism*, 20 (3–4): 195–216.

Usher, L., and D. Kerstetter. 2014. "Residents' Perceptions of Quality of Life in a Surf Tourism Destination: A Case Study of Las Salinas, Nicaragua." *Progress in Development Studies* 14 (4): 321–333.

Uysal, M., M. Sirgy, E. Woo, and H. Kim. 2015. "Quality of Life (QOL) and Well-being Research in Tourism." *Tourism Managment* 53: 244–261.

van Noorloos, F. 2011. "Residential Tourism Causing Land Privatization and Alienation: New Pressures on Costa Rica's Coasts." *Development* 54 (1): 85–90.

Vargas-Sanchez, A., N. Porras-Bueno, and M. Plaza-Mejia. 2014. "Residents' Attitude to Tourism and Seasonality." *Journal of Travel Research* 53 (5): 581–593.

Vaske, J. J., and L. B. Shelby. 2008. "Crowding as a Descriptive Indicator and an Evaluative Standard: Results from 30 Years of Research." *Leisure Sciences: An Interdisciplinary Journal* 30 (2): 111–126.

Verbos, R., and M. Brownlee. 2017. "The Weather Dependency Framework (WDF): A Tool for Assessing the Weather Dependency of Outdoor Recreation Activities." *Journal of Outdoor Recreation and Tourism* 18: 88–99.

Wagner, S., C. Nelson, and M. Walker. 2011. *A Socioeconomic and Recreational Profile of Surfers in the United States.* San Diego: Surf-First & The Surfrider Foundation.

Wright, J. P., T. E. Hodges, and N. Sadrpour. 2013. *Economic Impact of Surfing on the Local Economy of Pichelemu, Chile.* Santa Cruz: Save the Waves Coaliltion. https://www.savethewaves.org/wp-content/uploads/SURFONOMIC_PICHILEMU_07_29_15_SPREADS.pdf.

WSL. 2016. *Sponsorship: The World Surf League: A partnership like no other. Why?* Accessed January 13, 2017. http://www.worldsurfleague.com/pages/sponsorship.

Yin, R. 2009. *Case Study Research, Design and Methods.* 4th ed. Thousand Oaks, CA: Sage Publications Inc.

Yu, G., Z. Schwartz, and J. Walsh. 2010. "Climate Change and Tourism Seasonality." *Journal of Tourism* VI (2): 51–65.

Beyond transgression: mountain biking, young people and managing green spaces

Katherine King ⓘ and Andrew Church ⓘ

ABSTRACT
The importance of regular participation in physical activity in youth has seen attention turn to the role of lifestyle sports. Existing research on lifestyle sports lacks consideration of young people's use of green spaces and the approaches of managers to conflicts in these spaces. Young people's experiences of leisure are closely tied to those who oversee their use of leisure spaces and this paper is a rare example of research that draws upon qualitative methods from 40 mountain biking participants and 9 managers to explore both perspectives. Findings reveal young people seek opportunities for autonomy in green spaces through mountain biking but contest normative management practices. Managers recognized the benefits of engaging young people in mountain biking and discussed experimenting with various strategies to accommodate their practices. The paper therefore discusses the importance of moving beyond constructions of young people's participation in lifestyle sports as transgressive and troublesome.

The choices young people make during their leisure time are becoming widely recognized as crucial to their physical, psychological and social development. Participation in physically active leisure is recognized as a key to improving quality of life (Sato, Jordan, and Funk 2014). For example, the importance of regular participation in physical activity in youth for preventing non-communicable diseases and supporting psychological well being has been recognized on a global scale (cf. WHO 2004). Participation in sport is considered important for the future development of healthy lifestyles (Thompson, Rehman, and Humbert 2005) and can play a role in addressing youth anti-social behaviour and reducing youth crime (Nichols 2007; DH 2010).

In England, as in many other countries (e.g. WHO 2007, 2010; HHS 2008), the benefits of being physically active through sport has resulted in many national policies focusing on increasing sport participation by young people between the ages of 16 and 25 years (DH 2010; DCMS 2012). In order to engage hard to reach young people and those currently disengaged from conventional team or school-based sports, delivery of activities now includes a more wide ranging profile of sports and organizations, including more informal forms of participation such as those offered by lifestyle sports (cf. Tomlinson et al. 2005; Rowe 2012). Lifestyle sports are defined as activities that enable participants to express themselves as individuals through recognizable styles, attitudes and other cultural prefer-ences such as music, art and fashion alongside the sport itself (Wheaton 2010). Club-based sport has been recognized as exclusive and out of touch with modern forms of consump-tion (Goretzki, Esser, and Claydon 2008) and attention has turned to creating a socially, psychologically and physically beneficial sporting habit that can be embedded alongside other choices young people make about the ways in which they live their lives (DCMS 2012; Sport England 2014).

In addition to the type of sports young people choose to undertake to be physically active, the spaces in which they spend their leisure time have been identified as a further means to improve young people's wellbeing. Green spaces are considered to be beneficial to the physical and mental health and social development of young people (Cooper 2005; Milligan and Bingley 2007; Gardsjord, Tveit, and Nordh 2014; Gill 2014). Of particular interest is the potential role of performing sporting activities in rural and green spaces, referred to as 'nature sports' (Melo and Gomes 2017).

The recognition of the potential benefits of lifestyle sport participation and use of green space by young people amongst policymakers and leisure space managers has been accompanied, however, by an emerging academic literature that has simultaneously high-lighted some of the key social problems that have arisen when public spaces are used by young people for lifestyle sports. This body of research reveals how young people can often experience the public spaces they wish to access for lifestyle sports as a battle-ground between themselves, managers, landowners and other users as they pursue activi-ties which are perceived as risky or problematic, even when the managers of these spaces are encouraging their use (cf. Borden 2001; Beal and Weidman 2003; Németh 2006; Gilchr-ist and Wheaton 2011; King and Church 2017).

An extensive body of research has developed seeking to understand user conflicts in outdoor recreation and how these conflicts can be managed (see Watson et al. 2016 for summary). Previous research has tended to understand conflict as a form of competition between user groups often based on goal interference. Ewert, Dieser, and Voight (1999, 337) defined conflict linked to recreation as being 'when one person, or group of people, experience or perceive an interference of goals or the likelihood of incompatible goals'. A related conceptual model of recreational conflict is the social values approach, which views conflict as stemming from differences in norms, beliefs and values (Vaske et al. 1995). Education is often considered an appropriate policy response when conflict is values based whereas zoning can be used to deal with goal interference (Watson et al. 2016). The social values and goal interference theorizations both understand the conflict from a social or psychological perspective based on the nature of intergroup or interpersonal relationships. Church, Gilchrist, and Ravenscroft (2007) have argued, however, that these conceptual approaches tend to pay little attention to the context in which conflicts take place and the related role of resource settings, power relations or property rights in influencing the types of conflict that occur.

The research questions framing this study are what are the key issues in the use of space and the management of tensions and conflicts associated with young people's involvement in lifestyle sport and how are these experienced by both young people and green space managers? The paper provides a distinct contribution to existing debates as it not only focuses on the sport of mountain biking, which is recognized as under-researched within the field of youth lifestyle sports compared to activities such as surfing and skateboarding (Wheaton 2010), but also is a rare example of where the findings presented are based on primary data derived from both youth participants and the managers of green spaces.

Youth lifestyle sports and spaces

Research in a variety of disciplines has revealed some important and distinct relations between youth lifestyle sports and the spaces in which they are situated. Youth is considered an ambiguous state: between, but in tension with the realms of adulthood and childhood. Such an ideological state creates uncertainty for young people, who are challenged to become active members of society but instead occupy a liminal state (Valentine 2004; Wood 2012). This is exemplified most notably through the interaction between young people and the everyday spaces in which they live out their leisure lifestyles in which they are now encouraged to participate but often on terms defined by adults.

The shaping of youth leisure activities is a spatially situated process for young people and the freedom to assert ownership is central to the youth leisure experience (Shildrick, Blackman, and Macdonald 2009). Young people draw a sense of ownership from their collective occupation of leisure spaces (Robinson 2009) yet a lack of access to backstage spaces such as local streets and neighbourhoods where they are free to enact their lifestyles has seen youth groups accused of transgressing what is acceptable in public leisure spaces and creating youth territories (Matthews, Limb, and Taylor 2000; Owens 2002; Brown 2013). Gidlow and Ellis (2011) highlight how urban green spaces are valued by young people as a point of congregation but this is often congruent with adult concerns about anti-social behaviour. As a result young people report feeling ownership over green spaces they visit but often this is accompanied by other feelings of persecution for what they perceive as unjust blame for tensions and conflicts linked to vandalism and misuse (Gidlow and Ellis 2011).

Young people participating in lifestyle sports encounter similar tensions and conflicts. The youth-based cultures associated with lifestyle sports have been found to be characterized by a departure from the values of mainstream sport such as competition, rules or team participation. Instead, they privilege individuality, informality, non-conformity and freedom from rules, including often the rules imposed by the managers of public space (cf. Rinehart and Grenfall 2002; Beal and Weidman 2003; Wheaton 2010; Gilchrist and Wheaton 2011). Sports such as skateboarding, parkour and BMX are popular with young people, yet, the alternative and unstructured nature of participation activities and their associated spaces can mark them as transgressive, deviant, and antagonistic to the urban environment (Borden 2001; Owens 2001; Beal and Weidman 2003; Németh 2006; Gilchrist and Wheaton 2011). It is argued therefore that youth participation in these sports is often the subject of passive marginalization by urban planners who lessen conflict and tensions by restricting these activities in certain civic locations, or diverting them to state funded, indoor, or corporate sites where behaviour and activities can be packaged, observed and controlled (Owens 2001; Van Bottenburg and Salome 2010; Taylor and Kahn 2011; Woolley, Hazelwood, and Simkins 2011).

Despite these tensions between youth lifestyle sports and urban space management previous research has revealed positive interconnections between lifestyle sport participants and the spaces utilized. For example, management in relation to parkour spaces that seek to address the lifestyle dimension of these sports has been found to create a sense of ownership of the spaces amongst young people involved (Gilchrist and Wheaton 2011). This reflects the general argument in outdoor recreation that it is important to examine the experiential variables of outdoor activities in order to inform and improve management strategies (Hallo, Manning, and Stokowski 2009). Thus, it is important to explore, as the empirical research in this paper does, how the management of spaces for youth lifestyle sports can increase participation and provide opportunities for the aspects of lifestyle sports that young people seek and find physically, mentally and socially beneficial whilst managing tensions, transgression or anti-social behaviours.

To date, youth lifestyle sport writings which explore the interconnection between participants and their leisure spaces have been almost entirely urban centred. There is little written about young people's use of green spaces for lifestyle sports, including spaces in urban parks away from formally designated areas, woodlands and the wider natural environment. There has been extensive research on the opportunities for young people to experience risk through formally managed adventure in green spaces (e.g. Cater 2006; Hinds 2011; Lekies, Yost, and Rode 2015) and a small body of work also identifies a preference by young people for using certain green spaces for informal leisure activities (cf. Bell, Ward Thompson, and Travlou 2003; Milligan and Bingley 2007; Lloyd, Burden, and Kiewa 2008). Nevertheless, research that considers the management issues of young people's use of green spaces tends to be from a youth perspective and there continues to be insufficient understanding of the consequent response by managers and landowners to the activities of young people who choose to visit urban, peri-urban and rural green spaces to take part in lifestyle sports (King and Church 2017). These knowledge gaps may limit the effectiveness of policies to increase lifestyle sport participation.

Mountain biking and the spaces of lifestyle sports

Mountain biking is one example of a lifestyle sport which presents an opportunity to increase young people's engagement with physical activity and green spaces. It is also a sport which is increasing in popularity internationally (Hardiman and Burgin 2013), and within the U.K. has seen an increase in participation post-Olympics (Sport England 2016). It is estimated to account for 9% of all outdoor recreational activities in England (Sport England & Outdoor Industries Association 2015). Mountain biking, however, is not a homogenous activity with disciplines continually evolving and new styles emerging.

Mountain biking can provide valuable insights into the relationships between youth lifestyle sport and space because it is a highly mobile activity yet these spaces are also typically environments which are subject to competing demands from different recreational groups. Unlike other lifestyle sports which may be dependent upon specific landscapes or fixed facilities, provision for mountain biking in the U.K. is formed largely of formal pay to ride or club owned mountain bike parks for dirtjump, downhill and freeride disciplines, or trail centres or open access state managed land for cross country riding. In addition, mountain biking is practised informally in rural green spaces, peri-urban or urban environments such as in freely accessible parks and woodlands, street spaces or on privately owned land accessed with or without landowner permission. It is in these informal environments that participants are able to create their own jumps, trails and apparatus.

The majority of research into mountain biking has been conducted within a North American context (Leberman and Mason 2000; Zajc and Berzelak 2016) although notably, research also originates from Australia and New Zealand. Within this literature, mountain biking has often been described in terms of 'controversy and discord' (Hollen-horst et al. 1995, 41) and has received substantial scrutiny over its negative impacts. Mountain bikers are often held responsible for ecological degradation of sensitive rural environments (c.f. White et al. 2006; Quinn and Chernoff 2010) and for causing conflict with other recreational user groups (c.f. Carothers, Vaske, and Donnelly 2001; Cessford 2003). An important challenge for mountain biking management, therefore, involves the conflicts between mountain bikers and other users in green spaces (Zajc and Berzelak 2016) and balancing the preferences of users against management concerns to reduce environmental impacts, particularly through the creation and use of unofficial trails (D'Antonio et al. 2016).

Mountain bikers of all ages have been positioned as non-traditional recreationists whose activities require complex management strategies (Brown 2016). The negative characterization of mountain biking can, however, be problematic if it results in a limited understanding of the social benefits young people gain from the activity and also the undervaluing of the successes of managers in influencing mountain biking behaviours to ensure positive experiences for youth participants whilst addressing the demands of other users and owners of the leisure space. Zajc and Berzelak (2016) stress that mountain bikers are not a homogeneous group of outdoor recreationists. Rather, they differ in skill levels, motivation, equipment, riding styles, as well as other characteristics which will affect the mountain biking experience and consequently the management approach required. More generally it is argued that understanding the values mountain bikers hold and the social benefits they gain from their sport are important issues for managers of green spaces to take account of in devising initiatives (Pickering and Rossi 2016).

This paper, therefore, presents insights based on primary research into both participant and management experiences of mountain biking that addresses the general lack of research on mountain biking management, especially in European locations. Specifically, it focuses on youth mountain biking in a range of peri-urban and rural green spaces in the South of England, a particularly densely populated region, to consider some of the critical debates surrounding youth lifestyle sports, the tension and conflicts that arise around these sports and the resulting implications for management of green spaces for encouraging physical activity.

Methodology

This article draws upon two sets of data collected as part of a sequential qualitative study set in the South of England to explore youth lifestyle sports activities and the resulting implications for managers of green spaces addressing what Hallo, Manning, and Stokowski (2009) identify as underrepresentation of qualitative methodologies in assessing outdoor recreational experiences.

In the sequential research design, the results of the first phase of the study inform the subsequent phase with the analysis building upon the findings of the first phase (Mason 2002). A two phased approach embeds reflective practice within research, positioning the research process as cyclical and reflexive through which the researcher can learn, reflect and respond. Unlike a purely management focused approach, the rationale for this approach was to share the feedback from young people who are traditionally marginalized from mainstream management of green spaces with the managers of those environments. The approach sought to obtain new perspectives from leisure managers on key themes which were derived from analysis of the first research phase with users themselves. Whilst a sequential approach is most commonly adopted for mixed methods research (cf. Creswell 2003; Mason, Augustyn, and Seakhoa-King 2010), in this study qualitative methods were administered in both phases under an interpretative framework which offered credibility, dependability and transferability of the data through the interaction between the two phases (Lincoln and Guba 1985). In the first phase, qualitative research was adopted to provide an in-depth account of the embodied and performative characteristics of participation by young people not readily captured by structured approaches (Monrad 2013). Similarly, the second phase of the study invited managers to reflect on their own subjectivities in their approaches to management of youth mountain biking activities in green spaces.

The first data set was drawn from ethnographic research with 40 participants aged between 13 and 25 years who participated in mountain biking across a range of urban, peri-urban and rural locations during 2008 and 2009. The study was sensitive to the ethics of working with young people, adopting a youth centred approach to the research that empowered young people to voice their own experiences. The research design adhered to a U.K. university research ethics code of practice and sought written consent and parental permission from those participants under 16 years of age. The purpose of this part of the study was to investigate the role of green spaces for youth lifestyle sport participation. The methodology sought to be inclusive of a range of youth experiences and following Roberts (2006), acknowledges the prolonging of youth to include those up to 25 years of age. Age, however, is accepted as a fluid category and it was important to recognize the variation in experiences that occurs within a wide age range. Respondents were recruited through their participation at a large publically managed destination which offered facilities for freeride, dirtjump and cross-country mountain biking and was well used by young people. It must be noted, however, that mountain biking participants rarely limit their participation to one location. Instead they concurrently access multiple sites according to skill level, accessibility, social factors, cost, etc. and results therefore reflect this multi-site perspective. Purposive theoretical sampling was employed to select individuals according to their expected contribution of insights for the development of theory (Flick 2005). In this case all participants were required to have participated in mountain biking at the designated study site in the previous six months. Recruitment of the participants was achieved primarily through the ethnographic presence of the researcher at the designated study site (see Table 1) and performed secondarily through snowballing as there was no accessible sampling frame for the population (Bryman 2015). The sample included members of formally recognized mountain biking clubs ($n = 13$) and those that participated without any club affiliation ($n = 27$). Respondents differentiated themselves according to their cycle discipline and included cross-country, dirtjump, downhill and freeride mountain bikers, BMX riders and some young people who participated across these disciplines (see Table 1). This typifies the heterogeneity of mountain bikers in terms of skills and activities (Zajc and Berzelak

Table 1. Phase 1 research methods.

Method of participant recruitment		No of participants
	Online advertisements	6
	On site advertisements	3
	Cycle club meets	12
	Leisure cycling encounters	10
	Snowballing (Existing contacts)	9
	Total	40
Participant observation		
	Accompanied mobile methods	10
	Unaccompanied mobile methods	5
	Accompanied participant observation in cycle space	25
	Total	40
Semi structured interviews		
	Group	19
	Individual	21
	Total	40
Participant disciplines		
	BMX dirt jump	2
	MTB dirt jump	5
	Dirt jump/downhill/freeride (DDF)	12
	Cross country	14
	Cross country/downhill/freeride/DDF	7
	Total	40

2016). Approximately 90% of respondents were male, replicating similar gender profiles of participation in mountain biking in the U.K. (Ruff and Mellors 1993).

In line with youth centred approaches to research (Holland et al. 2010) all participants took part in semi-structured interviews individually or in groups according to their own preference, and participants also chose the setting for interviews which was usually within the leisure space itself. Interviews sought to explore the lifestyle and identity formation of young people who visit countryside spaces for leisure. In addition, each participant took part in participant observation activities such as a mobile interview or observation where respondents participated in the sport whilst documenting their own reflections on their practices either with or without the researcher present. All data recordings were transcribed alongside fieldnotes taken by the researcher as part of the participant observations and were subjected to a process of thematic analysis whereby themes and sub-themes were developed, reviewed and defined. The analysis process revealed four themes surrounding young people's use of green spaces for mountain biking which related to the management of green spaces and reflect debates in the literature discussed earlier in the paper. The first theme identified was the importance of developing a sense of ownership and belonging for green spaces. The second was liminal and transgressive activities that occur as part of young peoples' mountain biking in green spaces. The third theme relates to the conflict which occurred between young people and other user groups in green spaces and the final theme explored young peoples' experiences of formal management processes. These four themes were then explored from a leisure management perspective in the second phase of the sequential study.

The second phase of research was subsequently conducted with actors involved in managing green spaces for mountain biking in the South of England during 2012. Following the themes identified in the first phase, interviews focused on interactions between managers and local user communities, specifically addressing the development of ownership and belonging amongst users, the management of user conflict and transgressive activities, and engaging young people in the management of green spaces. Semi-structured interviews were conducted face to face or via telephone with nine participants representing a range of urban, peri-urban and rural locations and a variety of authority roles such as site managers, rangers, club chairpersons and trail builders (see Table 2). Informants were based at publically funded leisure sites in multiple destinations across the South of England and all held at least one formally recognized role such as site manager, club chairperson, club committee member, or coach in either a voluntary or employed capacity, with many acting in several different roles. All were male, had previous mountain biking experience and were usually long standing participants in the sport. All were over 25 years of age. Consequently, the associated lifestyles and cultures and their user experiences often shaped their actions as 'user managers' of clubs, spaces and facilities (cf. King and Church 2017).

This second phase employed purposive theoretical sampling and participants were recruited through snowballing which enabled flexibility and dynamism in the relationship between the research aims, the data collected in the first phase and debates within the literature identified earlier in the paper around youth lifestyle sports, spaces and the conflicts and tensions that arise. Interviews were transcribed and subjected to thematic analysis using the coding framework developed as part of the first research phase. Respondents gave written consent for the recording of data and all participant names, roles and locations have been anonymized to protect participant confidentiality.

Findings

Youth in green spaces: conflict and transgression

Results from the first phase of the research indicated that youth mountain bikers use an assemblage of cycling spaces to perform their sport incorporating public, privately managed and informal spaces which were accessed both with and without authorization from landowners, sometimes resulting in conflicts linked to property rights. Participants chose sites for mountain biking based upon resource characteristics such as accessibility, property ownership, trail quality, cost, atmosphere and social scene. Most locations were constructed by participants as green or peri-urban, with the exception of those who

Table 2. Phase 2 research methods.

Participant	Role	Status (employed/volunteer)	Site
1	Site Manager	Employed	Single Site
	Club volunteer co-ordinator	Volunteer	
2	Multi site Manager	Employed	Multiple Sites
3	Club Secretary	Volunteer	Single Site
	Club Safety Officer	Volunteer	
4	Club Volunteer	Volunteer	Single Site
5	Site Ranger	Employed	Multiple Sites
6	Club volunteer	Voluntary	Multiple Sites
	Trail builder	Self employed	
	Sports Development Officer	Employed	
7	Club Youth Coach	Volunteer	Single Site
8	Club Chair person	Volunteer	Single Site
9	Multi site Manager	Employed	Multiple Sites

described using skate parks or took part in street riding near to their home environments in addition to riding in green spaces.

Young people expressed a positive attitude towards green spaces as a leisure resource that supports the lifestyle and ethos of their sport but were also clear that this did not mean they adopted traditional attitudes to the natural environment they associated with other users such as walkers or nature enthusiasts (King and Church 2013). Wooded areas were deemed the preferred environment for mountain biking affording the appropriate terrain, topography and shelter, yet the separation of these environments from everyday urban spaces was also an important feature, as demonstrated in the following examples:

> We say it's a bit of an escape really, like you can come here and relax. (Participant 20: Age 16)

> There's no-one telling you what to do, there's no-one for miles around. It's much more freer sort of thing ... that's part of the reason we're in the woods though is to get away from other people. (Participant 14: Age 18)

In managed green spaces such as designated bike parks or trails, where sites were mixed use or were easily accessible for wider public use, most participants valued the facilities this provided but two participants described how they sought to avoid encounters with other users or payment for entry instead preferring to carry out their activities unobserved.

> We've got no reason to go to the visitor centre, we come in down a back lane, it takes about ten minutes to get here cos another person we know from biking he told us about that back lane way. (Participant 19: Age 16)

> I start early enough so that we don't have to pay. (Participant 12: Age 16)

Despite the positive qualities of green spaces, most participants in this study reported restrictions in their ability to access the full range of spaces their local environment offered for performing their sport. Young people's use of green spaces can be perceived by others as both anti-social and spatially inappropriate. This is particularly apparent for young people who participate in non-traditional sports such as mountain biking where the nature of mobility and risk involved in these may conflict with the tranquility of these spaces (Ruff and Mellors 1993; Dougill and Stroh 2001). Consequently, approximately two-thirds of respondents described a threatened relationship in their use of them:

> There's quite a few jump spots round here, but when people say oh [the] scenery and countryside is so nice, but you find out at the end of the day it's all landowners who'd probably shoot you if you rode. (Participant 24: Age 18)

> We are always getting moaned at, it doesn't matter where we go someone has a problem with us for some reason. (Participant 14: Age 18)

Managers of green spaces also recognized the difficulties faced by young people in accessing green spaces for mountain biking. Three of these respondents described fragile relationships with neighbouring landowners and the difficulties they faced in negotiating between different stakeholder and user groups, particularly when concerning provision that offers the challenge and excitement that young people often seek.

Local people, they are mainly retired in their sixties and middle class people and they are more about preserving the park for their own benefit. So they are more concerned about are the flowers going to stay as opposed to are we going to build something that is going to get young people to use the park. (Manager 1)

Well I mean we have to be quite careful with our neighbours cos they are very wealthy people and very influential so we have to like bow our heads when they are around and keep the site ultra tidy and keep the music down and we have to make sure the road is kept swept and kept clean and we sort of we have to inform them if we have a race going on and we try and keep them onside the best we can. You know you have mountain bikers one side of the wood and other side is multimillionaires in their houses. (Manager 3)

The fragility of access to green spaces saw young people in this study form strong attachments to those sites which they were able to use unhindered. At managed mountain biking destinations where paths were clearly marked, several participants recounted experiences of defending what they considered to be their space and expressed frustration when the boundaries were breached by other users such as in the example below:

There's a forest track and I think it's just for bikes, like it's not for horses, it's not a bridleway, and everything in that area is especially for mountain bikers so we're like the top dog and there's people doing jumps and everyone's watching and a horse rider came up and she had a young girl on a smaller pony with her and we were going up and down and she goes and shouts at me, saying keep the noise down, and I was just like well you're not supposed to be here anyway it's not a bridleway. (Participant 40: Age 24)

Participants expressed feelings of frustration when they failed to exercise power and ownership in managed spaces. In addition to cycling itself, they sought out opportunities to design, shape and build within the terrain and saw this as an integral part of the sport which facilitated the progression and development of their skills. Six of the managers described opportunities for maintaining trails which were available to young people through organized 'dig days'. However, these were often co-ordinated through local cycle clubs or park management and involvement with formal structures was identified as problematic.

Keen cyclists even the road cyclists seem to have a passion for cycle clubs. Mountain bikers seem to be completely the opposite and they almost view a club as almost an infringement on their freedom. (Manager 9)

As a group there are always some who don't want to conform and don't want it formal they just want to turn up and ride and there will always be ones who can't engage within the same way and you can't get that sort of formal structure going. (Manager 2)

In addition, these activities rarely provided the opportunity to design or build new apparatus and therefore 28 out of 40 respondents identified either accessing informal spaces called secret spots or taking part in wild build[1] in locations that were sheltered from other users or managers and therefore less likely to be restricted.

If it's a secret place then it's loads better cos like places that are open to the public often have like safety and stuff but these ones can make it as rad [radical] as they like. (Participant 19: Age 16)

Near where I live, there's woods down the bottom and me and my mates build there all the time like pretty much most days, we've got these woods that no one has heard about. (Participant 16: Age 17)

Almost every manager in this study described examples of mountain bikers accessing areas and property beyond those which were sanctioned, for example, by straying from maintained pathways or creating new routes within existing mountain biking sites without the permission of management staff.

> We still get people that want desire lines they are called and we block them off with dead hedging and piles of branches. Two reasons for that is if you have cyclists going everywhere they want, whenever they want, then from our experience that will cause a negative impact on other users of the woods. (Manager 5)

A lack of opportunities for building and designing trails in ways which reflected the ethos of the youth sporting community and allowed participants independence from an organized club resulted in feelings of exclusion from decision making for a minority of participants in managed green spaces as demonstrated in the example below:

> Researcher: 'So do you think you get much say in what happens here?'
>
> Um not as much as I'd like, just put it like that. (Participant 24: Age 18)

The desire for ownership and participation in wild build without permission presents a challenge for managers of green spaces who seek to encourage mountain biking and participation by young people. The next section of the findings demonstrates how managers are often required to adjust their strategies to acknowledge the practices and preferences of youth users alongside those of other user groups.

Manager and user negotiations

Youth mountain bikers sought opportunities for autonomy and to contest normative management practices associated with supervised sites. Consequently, both managers and participants discussed tensions in their relationships with each other and conflicts over access to property. Conflicts between participants and managers or landowners usually occurred when wild build activities in secret spots were discovered and structures were removed or access prevented. The examples below show how wild build often breached health and safety regulations and managers were forced to remove anything that may cause injury.

> As soon as we know something is going on if we feel that it is a risk to the general public or to the people engaged in it we have to take some action as we have a duty of care and also criminal statute law. (Manager 2)

> When we first took over there were some people that would go off and build without permission but it's sort of made very clear now that it can potentially shut the site down so if anybody sees someone doing trail building which thankfully in the last three years nobody has. (Manager 3)

Lack of trail building experience was identified as a key problem from a management perspective. Young people had no training or expertise in trail building and managers identified modification to apparatus was often performed according to the trail builder's own skill level rather than enabling progression for a variety of riders. The account below demonstrates that for managed sites that have made a commitment to encouraging public access to facilities across a range of abilities this can cause significant problems.

The sort of people that want to get involved in building the trails want to build a lot of trail very quickly and then they can ride it the next day. So you know we obviously have standards that need to be upheld and to make sure the trail lasts a long time so that doesn't work well with that and also they will want to keep modifying the trail because they will be developing their cycling so neither of those things work well with the trails we are building about mass participation. (Manager 9)

For youth mountain bikers the actions of managers to curb their activities, such as demolishing jumps or prohibiting access, served as incentive to build more complex and ambitious projects.

The first woods we rode in we started making loads more stuff in them and then that got trashed, that got chainsawed up, and then we moved further in the forest to a more hidden place, built there, built loads more stuff, we started building north shore[2] and that all got chainsawed down as well. (Participant 22: Age 18)

Every time we built something someone would come along and knock them down so we'd start again and build them twice the size. (Participant 31: Age 22)

In other examples, however, young people engaged in informal negotiations with land-owners or managers to try and secure access to wild build. One respondent described how some jumps at his secret spot were knocked down because of safety fears and so he sought out the landowner in an attempt to gain permission to create something more permanent.

We went to the local council found out the name of the person who owned the land and knocked on her door basically, and she was just like it keeps you off the street, keeps you out of trouble so go for it, well this was when we were about 14. (Participant 31: Age 22)

Two further participants described a process of trial and error which occurred between managers and themselves where respondents learnt what was and was not acceptable to build or alter in particular locations by what was left for them to use and what was removed.

We've had our stuff cut down once. I think the problem is we cut down trees to make the northshore and I don't think they like that very much, and it's not that they don't mind us digging and stuff I think they prefer us doing that though. We don't cut down trees they're gonna harvest though we just cut down little ones. (Participant 11: Age 16)

It's kind of like an unsaid agreement between the rangers and the builders, and as long as the builders don't build anything that you can't roll over then it's ok, anything else gets flattened, it's kind of a weird relationship that's not really legitimate but it sort of works for both sides. (Participant 40: Age 24)

Three participants described accessing spaces by setting up their own membership clubs that unlike others was operated and governed by young people themselves which removed some of the barriers to traditional club-based participation. The respon-dent below described an agreement reached with landowners over a secret spot which used a participant run club to alleviate concerns about liability:

The only reason they can keep them [secret spot] is if they set up a proper membership club, and there's loads of signs up there saying if you're not a member you can't ride, and stuff. I think they get a lot of kids saying they hurt themselves ... so you can only go if you're a member or you've been invited. (Participant 28: Age 21)

For managers, engaging in dialogue with participants was considered a positive step and a dramatic shift from previous strategies of demolishing any wild build they uncovered. The respondent below described successful informal negotiations with young people that allowed the trail building to continue in a manner that suited the site, other users, and health and safety requirements.

> Initially our immediate reaction was to demolish everything and say we don't want this going on and we would rather this stopped and we would keep trashing it until you get the message and go away. That wasn't productive or helpful to anyone. We would now look at where the developments are going and whether it is appropriate for location and we have archaeology and SSSI's and occasional rare plants and local sensitivities. If you have just spent half a million pounds buying a lovely secluded property on the edge of the wood and someone is setting a two hundred member mountain biking site we have to be a little sensitive to that. So we consider whether it is appropriate area and whether we can manage it and then try and engage with the people that do it. (Manager 2)

In a further example the respondent below sought a dedicated site for young people and the provision of earth moving equipment and finances to support their participation in jump building and mountain biking.

> We engaged with the local group and said listen where you are riding it is a sensitive protective soil type and we don't want you there but we have got this site over the other side and we will put some money in and bring a digger. There is nothing commercial about it it's just a load of jumps in the middle of the wood with no car park or sign or anything so we had to try and find out who the kids were that rode in there and try and encourage them to build jumps in a certain way. (Manager 5)

In these examples, managers recognized the value of the involvement of young people in wild build and its potential contribution to wider agendas in health and social wellbeing rather than viewing young people's activities as transgressive. The quote below demonstrates the sense of responsibility felt by one manager to provide opportunities for these activities wherever possible despite the challenges they may bring.

> Some of these sites have got local youngsters going out and actually working in the woodlands, building and riding their bikes is a huge success and it's a management thing it really is and making sure they are not doing it in unsuitable areas or whatever … while you have got a large population of people you will get young people who want to replicate what they see on DVDs and YouTube and ultimately it is up to us to make sure there is somewhere they can do it that is suitable. (Manager 9)

Managers who recognized the potential for engaging young people embraced more informal approaches such as nurturing relationships with key individuals and adopting experimental or contextually specific approaches to encourage young people and continue their involvement alongside more conventional management approaches.

Discussion

Echoing the work of several youth theorists (White 1993; Owens 2001; Valentine 2004), participants in this study discussed the policing and surveillance of leisure activities, in this case mountain biking. Similar to the work of Robinson (2009), these findings suggest young people prefer to congregate in outdoor spaces because they are less likely to encounter surveillance or restrictions to their activities. Green spaces were experienced as spaces on the margin (Shields 1991), which were 'out of the town and tucked away' (Participant 24). In managed green spaces young people continue to encounter negativity in their use of them yet as others have also shown, young people in this study felt they were able to be absorbed by green spaces and could carry out much of their sport unobserved (cf. Bell, Ward Thompson, and Travlou 2003; Leyshon 2010).

As previous research on lifestyle sports has demonstrated, youth participation in mountain biking is characterized by a resistance to authority and opposition to normative ways of doing sport (Rinehart 2007; King and Church 2015). This paper has shown that through participation in nature sports, peripheral, counter hegemonic activities such as wild build may also occur. Sites which provided opportunities for appropriation and creative wild build activities were more highly valued than those provided through formal, managed or commodified environments. (Borden 2001; Rinehart and Grenfall 2002; Downs 2003; Woolley, Hazelwood, and Simkins 2011). These activities can result in contestation between site users and this testing of boundaries is often poorly understood by resource managers (Bell, Ward Thompson, and Travlou 2003). Managers in this research, however, showed a recognition of the value of these more complex activities to young people.

Youth mountain bikers and managers both felt that promoting a sense of community and ownership was crucial for successful management of mountain biking sites. Engaging local youth users in discussion facilitated a more productive approach to site management. Open communication between users and managers seems to remain a key method for ensuring the maximum use of the resource and for resolving conflict in management of sites for mountain biking. Managers of mountain biking locations, however, also viewed youth practices such as wild build and trail adaptation not simply as transgressive and anti-social but part of the negotiated process of managing green spaces where young people can be physically active through activities beyond the sport itself.

Strategies which required young people to engage with management through formal or organized club activities were least successful. Youth mountain bikers were resistant to joining official clubs which restricted managers abilities to monitor and control participation, and to involve young people in decision making at these sites. Instead, some managers adopted a more informal approach to negotiating with young people to maintain wild build spaces, limit young people's adaptation of managed formal trails and reach a compromise over the activities which occurred.

This research has demonstrated, that whilst not entirely problem free young people exercise significant agency in developing strategies to negotiate additional access to green spaces if required. In previous work, Gilchrist and Wheaton (2011) describe the actions of youth parkour participants to preserve and protect parkour spaces and in this study youth mountain bikers demonstrated the empowerment and resilience of youth lifestyle sport communities to overcome barriers to accessing leisure spaces. Youth mountain bikers were highly engaged in securing space for their sport and in seeking opportunities for participation. Rather than just rely on their hidden activities, some participants described attempts to negotiate with management staff and landowners, form their own clubs, or expose their activities to reduce the likelihood of losing the space entirely. Whilst many young mountain bikers experienced resistance to their activities they were often able to respond to these restrictions and create meaningful spaces for themselves. The emphasis on regular communication and negotiation between managers and young people as being at the core of managing conflict suggests the need to extend the approaches to managing recreational conflict beyond the more common responses identified by Watson et al. (2016) of zoning and education. The findings suggest that the successful management of these spaces requires not simply responding to different goals and values but also a recognition of the activities and views of young people that often include a desire for a sense of community and ownership linked to property and resources.

Conclusion and implications

There is limited research devoted to understanding the perceptions and experiences of young people who choose to access green spaces for leisure as it has been argued that the youth leisure experience has been largely understood through urbancentric approaches to research (Matthews et al. 2000; McCormack 2002; Leyshon 2008; 2010; Valentine et al. 2008). This study has sought to address this gap by exploring participation in a popular and growing lifestyle sport (i.e. mountain biking) by young people and their experiences of using green spaces.

Mountain biking is a lifestyle sport which offers an important means of being physically active in green spaces yet it is often portrayed in terms of its negative effects on other recreational users and ecology (White et al. 2006; Quinn and Chernoff 2010). It is underresearched in comparison to other lifestyle sports such as surfing, skateboarding, and parkour (Wheaton 2010). This paper has therefore sought to explore how young people experience green spaces through mountain biking and the resultant strategies for management.

Young people who participate in lifestyle sports such as mountain biking have been identified as presenting a distinct set of challenges to managers of green spaces (King and Church 2015) This research shows that whilst they were presented with complex issues, managers recognized the benefits of both mountain biking and the peripheral wild build activities which accompany youth mountain biking and discussed various strategies for seeking to ensure that these activities could be legitimized within the realms of the green space sites. In addition, the study showed the will of young people to be engaged in decision making at mountain biking sites if they are involved in ways which allows them autonomy outside of a formal club system.

The findings have revealed how conflict is experienced by managers and young people and indicate that the dominant approaches to understanding conflicts in the literature based on social values and goal interference (Church, Gilchrist, and Ravenscroft 2007) need to be broadened to take account of the characteristics of resource settings and property relations which often strongly influence the nature of conflicts involving young people. Conflict is likely to continue to be an important issue as demand for outdoor recreation continues to grow (Rowe 2012). Whilst previous research has identified education or zoning as effective strategies for conflict which is values based or related to goal interference (Watson et al. 2016), the conflicts between young people and managers considered in this paper were negotiated on a contextual basis and often informally between managers and active members of the local mountain biking community. Future research should focus on exploring the ways in which managers and groups of users informally and formally negotiate shared terms of use in green spaces.

As with the literature on conflicts in outdoor recreation generally, user perspectives tend to dominate in primary research and the views of managers are less well understood (Watson et al. 2016). This study has presented both user and manager perspectives on the use of green spaces by young people and in doing so has better understood the inter-actions between managers and user groups as a part of outdoor recreation research. This suggests future research should consider the role of research itself in connecting man-agers and user groups to discuss shared concerns.

Based on these conclusions, this study presents the following recommendations for managers seeking to encourage youth participation in mountain biking in green spaces:

- Seek to communicate with and engage the 'local' mountain biking community in site decision making.
- Avoid reliance on formal mountain biking clubs as a sole means of user group engage-ment as young people tend not to recognize these.
- Provide opportunities for young people to learn trail building and design skills in site specific settings.
- Avoid formal sanctioning or zoning of trail building activity but instead seek to identify committed individuals who may act to represent the community and help managers to maintain contact and negotiate more effectively with youth groups.

By taking actions linked to these recommendations the organizations and managers that provide green spaces for mountain biking will be managing any conflicts that arise and recognizing how young people wish to take part in lifestyle sports and hopefully encouraging physically, mentally and socially beneficial participation in nature sports.

Notes

1. Wild build refers to unauthorized trail building in secret locations in green spaces.
2. North shore refers to raised wooden apparatus such as ramps and ladders.

Disclosure statement

No potential conflict of interest was reported by the authors.

ORCID

Katherine King ⓘ http://orcid.org/0000-0002-9679-3142
Andrew Church ⓘ http://orcid.org/0000-0003-4863-8794

References

Beal, B., and L. Weidman. 2003. "Authenticity in the Skateboarding World." In *To the Extreme: Alternative Sports, Inside and out*, edited by R. E. Rinehart and S. Sydnor, 337–352. Albany: State University of New York Press.

Bell, S., C. Ward Thompson, and P. Travlou. 2003. "Contested Views of Freedom and Control: Children, Teenagers and Urban Fringe Woodlands in Central Scotland." *Urban Forestry and Urban Greening* 2: 87–100. doi:10.1078/1618-8667-00026.

Borden, I. 2001. *Skateboarding, Space and the City: Architecture and the Body*. Oxford: Berg.

Brown, D. 2013. "Young People, Anti-social Behaviour and Public Space: The Role of Community Wardens in Policing the 'ASBO Generation'." *Urban Studies* 50: 538–555. doi:10.1177/0042098012468899.

Brown, K. M. 2016. "The Role of Belonging and Affective Economies in Managing Outdoor Recreation: Mountain Biking and the Disengagement Tipping Point." *Journal of Outdoor Recreation and Tourism* 15: 35–46.

Bryman, A. 2015. *Social Research Methods*. 4th ed. Oxford: Oxford University Press.

Carothers, P., J. J. Vaske, and M. P. Donnelly. 2001. "Social Values Versus Interpersonal Conflict among Hikers and Mountain Bikers." *Leisure Sciences* 23: 47–61.

Cater, C. I. 2006. "Playing with Risk? Participant Perceptions of Risk and Management Implications in Adventure Tourism." *Tourism Management* 27: 317–325.

Cessford, G. 2003. "Perception and Reality of Conflict: Walkers and Mountain Bikes on the Queen Charlotte Track in New Zealand." *Journal for Nature Conservation* 11: 310–316.

Church, A., P. Gilchrist, and N. Ravenscroft. 2007. "Negotiating Recreational Access Under Asymmetrical Power Relations: The Case of Inland Waterways in England." *Society and Natural Resources* 20: 213–227.

Cooper, G. 2005. "Disconnected Children." *ECOS* 26: 26–31.

Creswell, J. W. 2003. *Research Design, Qualitative, Quantitative and Mixed Methods*. 2nd ed. Thousand Oaks, CA: Sage.

D'Antonio, A., C. Monz, N. Larson, and A. Rohman. 2016. "An Application of Recreation Resource Assessment Techniques to Inform Management Action in an Urban-proximate Natural Area." *Journal of Outdoor Recreation and Tourism* 14: 12–21.

DCMS. 2012. *Creating a Sporting Habit for Life: A New Youth Sport Strategy*. London: HMSO, Department for Culture, Media and Sport.

DH. 2010. *Healthy Lives, Healthy People*. London: HMSO, Department of Health.

Dougill, A. J., and M. Stroh. 2001. "Recreational Users of Lake District Bridleways: Conflict or Camaraderie?" *North West Geography* 1: 12–19.

Downs, B. 2003. "Small Bikes, Big Men." In *To the Extreme: Alternative Sports, Inside and out*, edited by R. E. Rinehart and S. Sydnor, 145–152. Albany: State University of New York Press.

Ewert, A. W., R. B. Dieser, and A. Voight. 1999. "Conflict and the Recreational Experience." In *Leisure Studies: Prospects for the Twenty-first Century*, edited by E. L. Jackson and T. L. Burton, 335–345. State College, PA: Venture.

Flick, U. 2005. *An Introduction to Qualitative Research*. London: Sage.

Gardsjord, H. S., M. S. Tveit, and H. Nordh. 2014. "Promoting Youth's Physical Activity Through Park Design: Linking Theory and Practice in a Public Health Perspective." *Landscape Research* 39: 70–81. doi:10.1080/01426397.2013.793764.

Gidlow, C. J., and N. J. Ellis. 2011. "Neighbourhood Green Space in Deprived Urban Communities: Issues and Barriers to Use." *Local Environment* 16: 989–1002.

Gilchrist, P., and B. Wheaton. 2011. "Lifestyle Sport, Public Policy and Youth Engagement: Examining the Emergences of Parkour." *International Journal of Sport Policy* 3: 109–131. doi:10.1080/19406940.2010.547866.

Gill, T. 2014. "The Benefits of Children's Engagement with Nature: A Systematic Literature Review." *Children, Youth and Environments* 24: 10–34.

Goretzki, J., A. Esser, and R. Claydon. 2008. *Increasing Participation in Sport: Research Debrief*. Report for Sport England. May 15.

Hallo, J. C., R. E. Manning, and P. A. Stokowski. 2009. "Understanding and Managing the Off-road Vehicle Experience: Indicators of Quality." *Managing Leisure* 14: 195–209.

Hardiman, N., and S. Burgin. 2013. "Mountain Biking: Downhill for the Environment or Chance to up a Gear?" *International Journal of Environmental Studies* 70: 976–986.

HHS. 2008. *Physical Activity Guidelines for Americans. US Department of Health and Human Services, Office of Disease Prevention and Health Promotion*. Washington, DC: HHS.

Hinds, J. 2011. "Woodland Adventure for Marginalized Adolescents: Environmental Attitudes, Identity and Competence." *Applied Environmental Education & Communication* 10: 228–237.

Holland, S., E. Renold, N. Ross, and A. Hillman. 2010. "Power, Agency and Participatory Agendas: A Critical Exploration of Young People's Engagement in Participative Qualitative Research." *Childhood: A Global Journal of Child Research* 17: 360–375.

Hollenhorst, S. J., M. A. Schuett, D. Olson, and D. Chavez. 1995. "An Examination of the Characteristics, Preferences, and Attitudes of Mountain Bike Users of the National Forests." *Journal of Park and Recreation Administration* 13: 41–51.

King, K., and A. Church. 2013. "We Don't Enjoy Nature Like That: Youth Identity and Lifestyle in the Countryside." *Journal of Rural Studies* 31: 67–76.

King, K., and A. Church. 2015. "Questioning Policy, Youth Participation and Lifestyle Sports." *Leisure Studies* 34 (3): 282–302.

King, K., and A. Church. 2017. "Lifestyle Sports Delivery and Sustainability: Clubs, Communities and User-managers." *International Journal of Sport Policy* 9 (1): 107–119.

Leberman, S., and P. Mason. 2000. "Local Planning for Recreation and Tourism: A Case Study of Mountain Biking From New Zealand's Manawatu Region." *Journal of Sustainable Tourism* 6: 97–115.

Lekies, K. S., G. Yost, and J. Rode. 2015. "Urban Youth's Experiences of Nature: Implications for Outdoor Adventure Recreation." *Journal of Outdoor Recreation and Tourism* 9: 1–10.

Leyshon, M. 2008. "The Betweeness of Being a Rural Youth: Inclusive and Exclusive Lifestyles." *Social and Cultural Geographies* 9: 1–26. doi:10.1080/14649360701789535.

Leyshon, M. 2010. "The Struggle to Belong: Young People on the Move in the Countryside." *Population Space and Place* 17: 304–325. doi:10.1002/psp.580.

Lincoln, Y. S., and E. G. Guba. 1985. *Naturalistic Inquiry*. London: Sage.

Lloyd, K., J. Burden, and J. Kiewa. 2008. "Young Girls and Urban Parks: Planning for Transition Through Adolescence." *Journal of Park and Recreation Administration* 26: 21–38.

Mason, J. 2002. *Qualitative Researching*. 2nd ed. London: Sage.

Mason, P., M. Augustyn, and A. Seakhoa-King. 2010. "Exploratory Study in Tourism: Designing an Initial, Qualitative Phase of Sequenced, Mixed Methods Research." *International Journal of Tourism Research* 12: 432–448. doi:10.1002/jtr.763.

Matthews, H., M. Limb, and M. Taylor. 2000. "The 'Street as Thirdspace'." In *Children's Geographies: Playing, Living, Learning*, edited by S. L. Holloway and G. Valentine, 54–68. London: Routledge.

Matthews, H., M. Taylor, K. Sherwood, F. Tucker, and M. Limb. 2000. "Growing-up in the Countryside: Children and the Rural Idyll." *Journal of Rural Studies* 16: 141–153.

McCormack, J. 2002. "Children's Understandings of Rurality: Exploring the Interrelationship Between Experience and Understanding." *Journal of Rural Studies* 18: 193–207.

Melo, R., and R. Gomes. 2017. "A Sociocultural Approach to Understanding the Development of Nature Sports." In *Sport Tourism: New Challenges in a Globalized World*, edited by R. Melo and C. Sobry, 47–76. Cambridge: Cambridge Scholars Publishing.

Milligan, C., and A. F. Bingley. 2007. "Restorative Places or Scary Spaces? The Impact of Woodland on the Mental Well-being of Young Adults." *Health and Place* 13: 799–811. doi:10.1016/j.healthplace.2007.01.005.

Monrad, M. 2013. "On a Scale of One to Five, Who Are You? Mixed Methods in Identity Research." *Acta Sociologica* 56: 347–360. doi:10.1177/0001699313481368.

Németh, J. 2006. "Conflict, Exclusion, Relocation: Skateboarding and Public Space." *Journal of Urban Design* 11: 297–318. doi:10.1080/13574800600888343.

Nichols, G. 2007. *Sport and Crime Reduction: The Role of Sports in Tackling Youth Crime*. London: Routledge.

Owens, P. E. 2001. "Recreation and Restrictions: Community Skateboard Parks in the United States." *Urban Geography* 22: 782–797.

Owens, P. E. 2002. "No Teens Allowed: The Exclusion of Adolescents from Public Spaces." *Landscape Journal* 21: 156–163.

Pickering, C., and S. Rossi. 2016. "Mountain Biking in Peri-Urban Parks: Social Factors Influencing Perceptions of Conflicts in Three Popular National Parks in Australia." *Journal of Outdoor Recreation and Tourism* 15: 71–81.

Quinn, M., and G. Chernoff. 2010. *Mountain Biking: A Review of the Ecological Effects. A Literature Review for Parks Canada*. Quebec: Parks Canada.

Rinehart, R. E. 2007. "The Performative Avant-garde and Action Sports: Vedic Philosophy in a Postmodern World." In *Philosophy, Risk, and Adventure Sports*, edited by M. McNamee, 118–137. Abingdon: Routledge.

Rinehart, R. E., and C. Grenfall. 2002. "BMX Spaces: Children's Grass Roots' Courses and Corporate-Sponsored Tracks." *Sociology of Sport Journal* 19: 302–314.

Roberts, K. 2006. *Leisure in Contemporary Society*. 2nd ed. Wallingford: CABI.

Robinson, C. 2009. "Nightscapes and Leisure Spaces: an Ethnographic Study of Young People's Use of Free Space." *Journal of Youth Studies* 12: 501–514. doi:10.1080/13676260903081657.

Rowe, N. 2012. *Review of the Research Evidence on Young People and Sport: What Does it Tell us About Their Underlying Attitudes and Interest in Sport and the Ingredients for Successful Programme Design*. London: Sport England Research.

Ruff, A. R., and O. Mellors. 1993. "The Mountain Bike-the Dream Machine?" *Landscape Research* 18: 104–109.

Sato, M., J. S. Jordan, and D. C. Funk. 2014. "The Role of Physically Active Leisure for Enhancing Quality of Life." *Leisure Sciences* 36: 293–313. doi:10/1080/01490400.2014.886912.

Shields, R. 1991. *Places on the Margin: Alternative Geographies of Modernity*. London: Routledge.

Shildrick, T., S. Blackman, and R. Macdonald. 2009. "Young People, Class and Place." *Journal of Youth Studies* 12: 457–465. doi:10.1080/13676260903114136.

Sport England. 2014. *The Challenge of Growing Youth Participation in Sport*. Youth Insights Pack. Henley Centre. Headlight Vision.

Sport England. 2016. *Once a Week Participation in Sport*. Active People Survey 9. October 2014–September 2015. London: Sport England.

Sport England, & Outdoor Industries Association. 2015. *A Study of Demography, Motivation, Participation and Provision in Outdoor Sport and Recreation in England*. London: Sport England, & Outdoor Industries Association.

Taylor, M. F., and U. Kahn. 2011. "Skate-Park Builds, Teenaphobia and the Adolescent Need for Hang-out Spaces: The Social Utility and Functionality of Urban Skate Parks." *Journal of Urban Design*, 489–510. doi:10.1080/13574809.2011.586142.

Thompson, A., L. Rehman, and M. Humbert. 2005. "Factors Influencing the Physically Active Leisures of Children and Youth: A Qualitative Study." *Leisure Sciences* 27: 421–438.

Tomlinson, A., N. Ravenscroft, B. Wheaton, and P. Gilchrist. 2005. *Lifestyle Sports & National Sport Policy: an Agenda for Research. Report to Sport England*. London: Sport England.

Valentine, G. 2004. *Public Space and the Culture of Childhood*. Aldershot: Ashgate.

Valentine, G., S. L. Holloway, C. Knell, and M. Jayne. 2008. "Drinking Places: Young People and Cultures of Alcohol Consumption in Rural Areas." *Journal of Rural Studies* 24: 28–40. doi:10.1016/j.jrurstud.2007.04.003.

Van Bottenburg, M., and L. Salome. 2010. "The Indoorisation of Outdoor Sports: An Exploration of the Rise of Lifestyle Sports in Artificial Settings." *Leisure Studies* 29: 143–160. doi:10.1080/02614360903261479.

Vaske, J. J., M. P. Donnelly, K. Wittmann, and S. Laidlaw. 1995. "Interpersonal Versus Social Values Conflict." *Leisure Sciences* 17: 205–222.

Watson, A. E., K. H. Cordell, R. Manning, and S. Martin. 2016. "The Evolution of Wilderness Social Science and Future Research to Protect Experiences, Resources and Societal Benefits." *Journal of Forestry* 114: 329–338.

Wheaton, B. 2010. "Introducing the Consumption and Representation of Lifestyle Sports." *Sport in Society* 13: 10571–10581.

White, R. 1993. "Youth and Conflict Over Urban Space." *Children's Environments* 10: 85–93.

White, D., M. Troy Waskey, G. P. Brodehl, and P. E. Foti. 2006. "A Comparative Study of Impacts of Mountain Bike Trails in Five Common Ecological Regions of the Southwestern U.S." *Journal of Park and Recreation Administration* 24: 21–41.

WHO. 2004. *Global Strategy on Diet, Physical Activity and Health*. Geneva: World Health Organization.

WHO. 2007. *Steps to Health: A European Framework to Promote Physical Activity for Health*. Copenhagen: World Health Organisation Regional Office for Europe.

WHO. 2010. *Global Recommendations on Physical Activity for Health*. Geneva: WHO. http://whqlibdoc. who.int/publications/2010/9789241599979_eng.pdf.

Wood, B. E. 2012. "Crafted Within Liminal Spaces: Young People's Everyday Politics." *Political Geography* 31: 337–346. doi:10.1016/j.polgeo.2012.05.003.

Woolley, H., T. Hazelwood, and I. Simkins. 2011. "Don't Skate Here: Exclusion of Skateboarders from Urban Civic Spaces in Three Northern Cities in England." *Journal of Urban Design* 16: 471–487. doi:10.1080/13574809.2011.585867.

Zajc, P., and N. Berzelak. 2016. "Riding Styles and Characteristics of Rides among Slovenian Mountain Bikers and Management Challenges." *Journal of Outdoor Recreation and Tourism* 11: 10–19. doi. org/10.1016/j.jort.2016.04.009.

'I don't want to die. That's not why I do it at all': multifaceted motivation, psychological health, and personal development in BASE jumping

John H. Kerr and Susan Houge Mackenzie ⓘ

ABSTRACT

This study explored a veteran female BASE jumper's experiences in relation to (a) participation phases, motivations and emotions; (b) risk perceptions and psychological management strategies; (c) psychological effects of accidents and fatalities on risk appraisals and her protective frame; and (d) psychological health and personal development benefits of extreme sport participation. Interview data revealed multifaceted motivations for BASE jumping that evolved over time. Emotion induction and pleasant psychological experiences associated with BASE jumping contributed to psychological health, well-being and personal development, while coping with negative experiences and dynamic risk perceptions fostered mental strength and resilience. Continued participation following negative experiences highlighted the importance of protective frames in facilitating positive extreme sport experiences. Findings suggested that BASE jumping motivations and experiences may be more complex and multifaceted than currently conceptualized, and that extreme sport has the potential to promote psychological health and personal development in ways that are often overlooked.

Introduction

There are few leisure pursuits that test mental and physical skills as acutely as extreme sport activities. Defined as 'recreational physical activity, which carries a risk of serious physical injury or even death' (Willig 2008, 691), extreme sports lie on the end of the adventurous leisure spectrum. Unlike traditional sports, extreme sports such as mountaineering, rock climbing, downhill mountain biking, whitewater kayaking, big wave surfing, skydiving, and BASE jumping, are less focused on defeating opponents and more focused on applying personal skills in diverse (often) natural environments to overcome mental and physical challenges.

A number of sociological and psychological accounts of extreme sport motivations have been proposed. These include thrill and sensation-seeking; hedonism; deviant personality structures; alexithymia; backlash against the alienated nature of modern society; the desire to belong to unique sub-cultures; and satisfying needs for status, social stratification, cultural capital, media recognition, and/or 'dramatic worldviews' (e.g. Barlow et al. 2015; Ferrel, Milovanovich, and Lyng 2001; Fletcher 2008; Giulianotti 2009; Laurendeau 2008; Lyng 2005; Self et al. 2006; Zuckerman 2007). As Celsi, Rose, and Leigh (1993, 2) note, 'high-risk sports have become a badge of our times.'

Nevertheless, extreme sport literature is in its infancy and the majority of this research has overlooked psychological health and personal development aspects. Furthermore, reductive quantitative research methods have dominated, and potentially limited, current understandings of extreme sport experiences. These issues have been repeatedly raised by Brymer and colleagues, as exemplified in a recent introductory chapter on the extreme sport experience (Brymer and Schweitzer 2017, 11)

> There is still only a vague understanding of the human dimension of [extreme sports]. This is unfortunate as, despite their popularity, there is still a negative perception about extreme sports participation. There is a pressing need for clarity. The dominant research perspective has focused on positivist theory-driven perspectives that attempt to match extreme sports against predetermined characteristics ... Other ways of knowing might reveal more nuanced perspectives of the human dimension of extreme sport participation.

Emerging research suggests that extreme sports may promote psychological health and personal development in a variety of ways, and that these benefits are fundamental to understanding dynamic motivations and extended participation (e.g. Brymer and Schweitzer 2013). However, as traditional theoretical and methodological approaches have not fully captured the lived extreme sport experience, interpretive paradigms and qualitative methodologies are needed to expand the extreme sport literature (e.g. Brymer 2010; Celsi et al.1993; Willig 2008). Furthermore, research that examines motivations and experiences across different participation phases (e.g. preparation, approach, active, post-activity; Brymer and Schweitzer 2017) can expand static explanations of extreme sport motivations and experiences to encompass more dynamic, ecologically relevant models.

The present case study addressed these gaps in the literature by examining the extreme sport experiences of a 33 year-old veteran female skydiver and BASE jumper who had completed over 800 skydives and 270 BASE jumps. Unique case studies are important when they challenge or extend previous research findings or theoretical viewpoints (e.g. Yin 2013). The participant's unique BASE jumping and, to a lesser degree, skydiving experiences warranted presentation as a case study for a number of reasons. In addition to providing an underrepresented female perspective on extreme sport motivations and experiences (Houge Mackenzie and Kerr 2013), this case study (a) challenged traditional extreme sport narratives; (b) provided unique insights across a range of participation phases; (c) extended current understandings of the psychological characteristics of extreme sport experiences, and (d) demonstrated how extreme sport participation may benefit psychological health and personal development in ways that are largely absent in the literature (e.g. Brymer 2010; Willig 2008).

Setting the scene: skydiving and BASE jumping

This paper explores participant experiences in two well-recognised extreme sports: skydiving and BASE jumping. While skydiving involves jumping and free falling from an airplane before deploying a parachute, BASE jumping involves jumping from four different types of objects: Buildings (skyscrapers), Antennas (towers) Spans (bridges) and Earth (cliffs). BASE jumpers rely on a single parachute or canopy, which gives them less time to complete required maneuvers or respond to emergencies than skydivers who have a reserve parachute. For example, at the annual bridge day BASE jumping festival in West Virginia, USA, BASE jumpers launch themselves from a bridge that is 876 feet high and have only seconds to deploy their canopies, adopt the correct body position, maintain their correct flight path in order to land safely. The bridge day festival is a legal one-day event, but often BASE jumping involves illicit risk-taking (Allman et al. 2009; Ferrel, Milovanovich, and Lyng 2001).

A relatively recent derivative of BASE jumping is wing suit BASE. Wing suit BASE involves BASE jumping while wearing a nylon 'squirrel' or 'bat' suit that slows the rate of descent, increases glide and manoeuverability, and allows jumpers to fly greater horizontal distances than traditional BASE jumpers at speeds of up to 160 kph. BASE jumpers often start out as skydivers and then progress to BASE jumping, with some going on to wing suit BASE. In all of these activities, the smallest error in judgment or equipment failure can result in serious injury or death. The media periodically report the latest deaths associated with skydiving and BASE jumping (e.g. Ellwand 2015; Morland 2015), and dedicated BASE jumping website BLiNC[1] reported 26 deaths in 2015 alone, many of which occurred during wing suit flights.

Given the small margin for error and high personal risks in skydiving and BASE jumping, understanding the experiences, motivations and benefits associated with these extreme sports may provide novel insights into the enigmatic relationships between extreme leisure pursuits, well-being, and personal development. For instance, stress levels have traditionally been conceptualized as having an inverse or 'U' shaped relationship with positive psychological outcomes and performance (e.g. Hardy 1996; Peifer et al. 2014). However, extreme sports represent an interesting psychological paradox insofar as some literature suggests that the high stress involved in extreme sports facilitates, or at least does not inhibit, positive psychological outcomes and well-being (e.g. Brymer and Schweitzer 2013; Monasterio et al. 2016). For example, despite differences in psychobiological stress reactivity amongst BASE jumpers, the vast majority of BASE jumpers display psychological resilience (i.e. 'The Right Stuff') in response to stress (Monasterio et al. 2016). The following section explores further findings and tensions in the literature related to extreme sport participation, with a focus on skydiving and BASE jumping studies.

Literature review: theoretical accounts of extreme sport participation

Risk, competence, and control accounts

In attempting to understand the behaviour of skydivers, BASE jumpers, and other high-risk leisure participants, researchers have often used the notion of 'edgework' put forward by Lyng (1990, 2005). According to Lyng, the edge is the boundary between juxtaposed conditions, such as chaos and order, safety and danger, sanity and insanity. Edgework involves individual risk-takers, such as skydivers, testing their ability and use of equipment while maintaining control and approaching the edge. Laurendeau (2006) conducted an ethnographic study of skydivers based on Lyng's edgework concept. Laurendeau was particularly interested in exploring how skydivers build and preserve beliefs that they can maintain control while working at the edge of safety. He concluded that skydivers have an 'illusion of control' that allows them to perceive hazardous conditions and dangerous environments (at the edge) as within their control (see also Celsi, Rose, and Leigh 1993).

Skydivers approach the edge in differing ways and to varying degrees. This is reflected in the ways they skydive and the manner in which they interpret their own experiences and those of other skydivers. For example, Laurendeau's (2006) interview data suggested that skydivers understand the physical requirements and technical demands of their leisure activity and relate these to their own abilities. Through personal experiences and discussions with veteran practitioners, they learn to identify important hazards. Over time, these experiences help them develop the technical skills and judgement to cope with unexpected events, which influences the type of skydiving they engage in. In other words, skydivers learn where or what 'the edge' is for them and how close they want to be to it. This allows them to maintain perceptions of control while learning to manage risks in a calculated way. These findings refute misconceptions that skydivers, and extreme sport participants more generally, are thrill-seeking 'adrenaline junkies' or that these individuals innately possess unique survival instincts (Brymer and Schweitzer 2013; Buckley 2012; Kerr and Houge Mackenzie 2012, 2014). The importance of maintaining perceptions of control is further evidenced by skydivers' tendency to attribute incidents (e.g. death of a fellow skydiver) to fate when they are caused by factors outside of the usual set of recognized hazards (e.g. pilot error, equipment failure, collisions; Laurendeau 2006).

Although emanating from psychology rather than sociology, the concept of phenomenological 'protective frames' from reversal theory (Apter 1982, 1992, 2001) is a model that overlaps with aspects of Lyng's edgework account. Reversal theory posits three cognitively-based, subjectively-determined protective frames that influence how a person experiences and interprets situations involving risk and possible danger. These frames are the 'confidence frame', the 'safety-zone frame' and the 'detachment frame'. The confidence frame is particularly important in high-risk activity contexts. In simple terms, it can be conceived of as a psychological bubble that envelops dangerous activities. Based on confidence in their own skills, previous experience, the skills of colleagues and, often, the use of advanced technical equipment, this protective frame allows participants to approach the 'dangerous edge' by decreasing their perception of the risks involved. For example, skydivers must have a sense of perceived control and personal security arising from familiarity and predictability of the situation, their equipment, and prevailing weather conditions, for their protective frame to be salient. This model has been used in extreme sport studies to explain how perceived changes in these variables may cause the protective frame to fail either temporarily or permanently (e.g. Apter and Batler 1997; Kerr 2007; Kerr and Houge Mackenzie 2012, 2014; Legrand and Apter 2004; Pain and Kerr 2004).

Motivational accounts

Qualitative psychological research on extreme sport motivations has identified a range of reasons for engaging in these activities, including: sensation- or thrill-seeking; experiencing 'rush'; goal achievement; social relationships; risk-taking; escape from boredom; pushing personal boundaries and overcoming fear; connecting with nature; pleasurable

kinaesthetic bodily sensations; positive transformation; transcendence of time; and mastering and improving skills and control (e.g. Allman et al. 2009; Apter and Batler 1997;
Brymer, Downey, and Gray 2009; Brymer and Oades 2009; Buckley 2012; Chirivella and
Martinez 1994; Kerr 1991; Kerr and Houge Mackenzie 2012, 2014; Rowland, Franken,
and Harrison 1986; Varley 2011; Willig 2008; Zuckerman 2007). Thus, research has identified multiple motives for extreme sport participation, which often differ in terms of
their relative importance for participants and may evolve over time. For example, although
excitement- or thrill-seeking was identified as important to many participants in Kerr and
Houge Mackenzie's (2012) study, it was not generally reported as a primary motive. In
addition, these participants reported motivational changes over time.

In an ethnographic study of skydivers, Celsi, Rose, and Leigh (1993) divided motives into
three groups: motives for initial involvement, motives for continued participation, and
transcendent motives. Initial motives were curiosity, thrill-seeking, social compliance
and a desire for adventure. Continuation motives were the desire to develop technical
skill for personal satisfaction and social status within the group; new challenges; achievement and mastery of skydiving skills; and developing an identity as a skydiver. Finally,
transcendent motives were concerned with individual heightened experience (e.g. flow,
peak experience), transcendent group camaraderie; and special communication with
shared experience and technical language (e.g. Csikszentmihalyi 2000; Lipscombe 1999;
Willig 2008). In short, skydiving motives were found to evolve from excitement and
thrill, through mastery and identity construction, to a sense of community and self-fulfil-
ment (Celsi, Rose, and Leigh 1993). These results support Lipscombe's (1999, p. 285) conclusion that: 'The initial attraction to skydiving, based on a perception of a variety of
experiential and non-experiential reasons, gradually shifts with increasing involvement
and competence to other experiential benefits which sustain participation.' Findings
from skydiving and BASE jumping studies suggest that motives evolve over time with
extended participation, which means that novices are likely to have different motives to
those of veterans, and that motivations are generally dynamic rather than static.

Psychological health and personal development accounts

Allman et al.'s (2009) study of BASE jumpers identified similar participation motives to
those discussed above (e.g. acquiring a new elite skill, gaining a sense of accomplishment,
experiencing a so-called adrenaline rush, maintaining control, overcoming fear, fostering a
sense of belonging), but also included personal or spiritual enlightenment. Allman et al.
concluded that BASE jumpers also took risks to become positively transformed. These
findings are congruent with Brymer and Oades' (2009) and Willig's (2008) investigations
in which extreme sport participants reported personal transformations that positively
influenced their personal growth and development. In contrast to popular perceptions
that extreme sport participants, and BASE jumpers in particular, do not experience fear
or anxiety, Brymer and Schweitzer (2013) reported how participants encountered unpleasant, intense fear and transformed these negative emotions into meaningful, constructive
experiences with well-being benefits. This process was illustrated in their participants'
narratives:

> The whole idea of 'no fear'- it's rubbish! ... Fear in adventure is a miserable, terrible, gut-
> wrenching experience. (BASE jumper, p. 480).

[I had] the feeling of well-being because [I] got into situations where [I was] frightened … the greatest fascination I had from it really was controlling the fear. (Solo climber, p. 482)

These findings are supported by emerging biopsychological accounts of emotional regulation and well-being. For instance, Kok and Fredrickson (2010) found that increased parasympathetic activation (i.e. vagal tone[2]) positively influences positive emotions and social connectedness, two important predictors of well-being. Their results are congruent with the 'broaden and build' theory of positive emotions (Fredrickson 2001), insofar as positive emotions and parasympathetic activation appear to have a reciprocal relationship. Kok and Fredrickson's research suggests that regular experiences of parasympathetic activation (such as those found in extreme sports) may increase habitual vagal tone and positive emotions, which supports overall well-being. This biopsychological explanation of emotional regulation may help account for seemingly paradoxical relationships between extreme sports, heighted arousal and stress (e.g. fear, anxiety), and psychological health and personal development outcomes.

While emerging research suggests that extreme sport participation has the potential to foster a range of psychological benefits, it is also important to examine literature that demonstrates how participation may lead to negative outcomes. For instance, the death or serious injury of fellow skydivers can negatively influence skydivers' motivational and emotional experiences and lead to poor mental health (Kerr 2007). Willig (2008) found that some participants not only described their extreme sports as addictive, but were also in danger of developing a dependency on their activities. Pain and Kerr (2004) provided an example of this type of dependency in their case study of a veteran high-risk sports participant (e.g. skydiving, rock climbing, driving high-speed cars), who had become dependent on the high arousal experiences facilitated by these activities. In one such incident he punctured both lungs, incurred serious brain damage, and broke his back, shoulder, and ribs. As a result, he spent two months in intensive care, including five weeks in a coma, followed by intensive rehabilitation. Despite these serious injuries, this individual expressed a strong need to continue participating in high-risk sports.

Study aims and research questions

The current study sought to expand the extreme sport literature by examining the experiences of a veteran female skydiver and BASE jumper throughout her career. In particular, the study explored motivations, risk perceptions, psychological management strategies, and psychological health and personal development aspects of participation. While the current study was designed to broadly explore the participant's extended experiences in BASE jumping and skydiving, the following research questions were used to guide the investigation:

(1) How are skydiving and BASE jumping experienced?
     (1a) What, if any, are the qualitative distinctions between these experiences?
(2) How are risks perceived in skydiving and BASE jumping, respectively?
     (2a) What, if any, are the psychological strategies used to manage these perceptions?
     (2b) Do protective frames (as conceptualized in reversal theory) influence these perceptions? If so, how?

(3) What are the motivations for skydiving and BASE jumping, respectively?

  (3a) Have these motivations changed over time or in relation to extended participation? If so, how?

(4) How has skydiving and BASE jumping, respectively, affected psychological well-being
  and/or personal development?

Method

Methodological approach

A post-positive interpretive approach guided the current study, which means that the
authors recognize the existence of multiple realities and the importance of exploring
diverse perspectives based on individual experiences to advance knowledge (Creswell
2012). In keeping with the interpretive approach, this study focused on the multiple meanings associated with participating in a specialized extreme leisure activity. Within the
broader interpretive paradigm, this study reflects a phenomenological philosophical orientation that seeks to understand the world through direct experiences (Myers 2008). In
order to understand experiences, phenomenological investigations explore the structure
of experiences from a first-person perspective, particularly in relation to specific objects
(Creswell 2012). This approach places the lived experience as the central study focus
and provides detailed descriptions of phenomena based on the structure and meaning
of an experience (e.g. Laverty 2003). Phenomenology has been increasingly used to
study extreme sport experiences and motivations (e.g. Brymer 2010; Brymer and Schweitzer 2013) and was appropriate for the current study as it explored the unique lived experiences of a veteran female skydiver and BASE jumper. Specifically, a theory of 'structural
phenomenology'[3] (i.e. reversal theory) was applied to understand the nature and
quality of her lived experiences, particularly in relation to experiences of motivation.

Case description

At the time of the interview, the participant, Mila (a pseudonym), was a 33 year-old female
skydiver and BASE jumper. Mila had begun skydiving at age 17 and spent 10 years as a
recreational skydiver before becoming a skydiving coach. After completing over 800 skydives, she joined friends on a European BASE jumping tour in which she completed her first
BASE jump. On her second BASE jump from a 30-meter high bridge, she broke her back.
Despite this setback and a second serious injury, Mila went on to complete 270 BASE
jumps and several wing suit BASE jumps.

  Mila's case study was initiated by serendipitous recruitment (Amis 2005). The second
author met Mila through an acquaintance at a skydiving event and learned of her
unique background in skydiving and BASE jumping. As the event did not involve BASE
jumping, there were very few BASE jumpers present and Mila was the sole female BASE
jumper in attendance. Given the very small number of highly experienced female BASE
jumpers globally, and Mila's unique motivational perspectives that contested traditional
theories of extreme sport motives and experiences, her case was deemed worthy of investigation as an in-depth case study (e.g. Yin 2013). Thus, after their serendipitous meeting,
the second author invited Mila to participate in an extended semi-structured interview

regarding her skydiving and BASE jumping experiences at a later date, to which she agreed.

Data collection

Prior to the interview, Mila was informed of the interview purpose, ethical research protocols, and assured that she could discontinue the interview at any time. The semi-structured interview was conducted face-to-face at a drop zone where Mila was participating in a sky-diving 'boogie'.[4] The interview included an exploration of Mila's: (1) skydiving and BASE jumping experiences, and potential subjective distinctions between these extreme sports; (2) risk perceptions associated with skydiving and BASE jumping, and the potential influence of management strategies and/or protective frames (as conceptualized in reversal theory) on these perceptions; (3) current and past motivations for skydiving and BASE jumping and potential links to long-term participation; and (4) emotional experiences during skydiving and BASE jumping, and their potential influence on psychological health and/or personal development. Example initial questions included: 'Can you tell me how you got involved in skydiving and BASE jumping?'; 'Can you explain how you feel before you BASE jump?'; 'When did you do your first BASE jump? Did that feel the same as your first skydive, or different?'; 'Can you talk me through how you felt: early that day [of your first BASE jump], when you went to do [the BASE jump], and through to after the jump?' Throughout the interview, open-ended probes were used to encourage Mila to elaborate on her perceptions and experiences. Example probes, included: 'Are you saying that [the experience is] more about accomplishing goals now than it used to be?'; 'Does that [experience] have to do with your surroundings or is it more of an internal thing?'; 'How did you feel when you went to do your first [BASE] jump after the accident?'. The interview was digitally recorded and lasted just over 70 min. The recording was later transcribed verbatim for analysis and interpretation.

Data analysis

Rather than judging the 'representativeness' of qualitative data in terms of objectivist criteria such as frequency or variability, the value of qualitative research is largely dependent on providing sufficient 'thick descriptions' of the researcher(s), data collection, and analysis procedures to establish trustworthiness (e.g. Denzin and Lincoln 2005). Data analysis began with the two authors independently reading the interview transcript several times to obtain an overall picture of Mila's skydiving and BASE jumping experiences. After holistically immersing themselves in the interview data, each author coded the data line-by-line and then grouped data into larger themes (Amis 2005; Brinkman 2013). Where relevant, the concept of psychological protective frames (i.e. reversal theory; Apter 1992, 2001) was applied as a theoretical coding tool for interview data. To minimize selective reporting and cognitive bias during data analysis, the authors employed the reflexive practices detailed below; referred to reversal theory literature and coding guidelines (e.g. O'Connell et al. 1991); and subjected analyses to external auditing. Upon completion of data analyses, a research assistant with no prior involvement or knowledge of the study audited the interview procedure and data interpretations. The research assistant's expertise in qualitative interview analyses and reversal theory allowed them to act as a 'critical friend' (Cresswell and Eklund 2007) and external data auditor (Denzin and Lincoln 2005). These methods were employed to reduce researcher bias and establish trustworthiness (Biddle et al. 2001).

Reflexive practices

Reflexivity is an important means of establishing trustworthiness and creating knowledge through qualitative research processes (D'Cruz, Gillingham, and Melendez 2007). Reflexivity involves 'continual internal dialogue and critical self-evaluation of researcher's positionality as well as active acknowledgement and explicit recognition that this position may affect the research process and outcome' (Berger 2015, 220). The authors reflected on their personal perspectives, beliefs, and experiences to cultivate awareness of how these elements could influence their analyses (Bradbury-Jones 2007), and employed the reflexive practices outlined above to minimize these influences (i.e. extended engagement, peer review, auditing; Ahern 1999; Bradbury-Jones 2007; Padgett 2008). For instance, when using a theoretical lens to interpret data, the authors focused on staying critically attentive to Mila's descriptions (i.e. of skydiving and BASE jumping experiences) while continuously cross-checking and comparing the meaning of her statements with theoretical explanations (Sparkes and Smith 2014).

Providing transparent descriptions of researcher backgrounds is another important reflexive practice that enhances the rigour of qualitative research (e.g. Padgett 2008). Both authors had a background in psychology, qualitative research, competitive sport, and adventure sport from predominantly Western cultural perspectives. One author was a former adventure guide, while the other was a former high-level athlete and coach. It is important to note that these personal and professional backgrounds and cultural values may have sensitized data analysis (e.g. in relation to risk perceptions, motivations, reversal theory constructs).

Results and discussion

The Results and Discussion sections are presented concurrently to improve readers' understanding of links between specific data and theory. Each subsection focuses on a key theme identified in data analysis, which is supported by pertinent verbatim interview statements and followed by discussion of the results in relation to the literature. The key themes are:

> Progressing from Skydiving to BASE jumping: Risk Perceptions and Management; Effect of Personal Accidents on Risk Appraisals and Protective Frame; Effect of Friends 'Gone In' on Risk Appraisals and Protective Frame; Evolving Motivations and Post-Activity Benefits; Connections to Nature and Well-Being; and Connections to Others and Well-Being.

Unless otherwise stated, the interview quotes in each subsection refer to distinct skydiving or BASE jumping events. Place names have been removed to protect participant confidentiality.

Progressing from skydiving to BASE jumping: risk perceptions and management

Like many novice skydivers and BASE jumpers, Mila recalled feeling nervous prior to her initial skydive and BASE jumps (Celsi, Rose, and Leigh 1993; Lipscombe 1999). However, she explained that this fear dissipated once she was in the air, 'Every time that I have jumped, I've been fine when my feet leave the ground or the plane. So, in free fall, everything is fine again.' Once Mila had mastered key skills through repeated skydiving experiences, the move from skydiving to BASE jumping was described as a natural progression,

> I think I had pretty much wanted to do it [BASE] ever since I got active in skydiving. But before, I didn't feel comfortable enough with my skills. I just wanted to get all the skills done that I thought that you need. ... It [skydiving] has helped me a lot in BASE jumping. I have the skills and the airtime in skydiving, so, some of the problems that you might have in BASE, I've already dealt with in skydiving.

Mila's progression from skydiving to BASE jumping appeared to result from confidence that her personal capabilities and knowledge were sufficient to meet this new challenge. In addition, repeated experiences of overcoming the fear involved in these extreme sports appeared to facilitate the development of psychological skills and coping mechanisms, which helped to build a protective frame. This supports findings by Brymer and Oades (2009), who found that despite (or possibly because of) fear and awareness of death as a possible outcome, extreme sport participants often reported powerful positive psychological experiences.

With regard to BASE jumping, Mila considered herself a conservative jumper. While she liked tracking (assuming a body position that allows horizontal movement in free fall) and thought she was good it, she had only undertaken two wing suit BASE jumps and had not tried advanced techniques, such as wing suit proximity flying (passing close to fixed objects or the ground at high speed). With no reserve canopy and less time to react if something went wrong, she clearly perceived that BASE jumping was riskier than skydiving and required a different mental focus.

> Skydiving is not so – the risk level is a lot smaller. So you're not that focused on it. And also in BASE, the thing that you're doing is really simple. Whereas in skydiving, you could have all kinds of things that you are trying to do, so that could take your mind off the actual moment of now because you have to think what happens next. ... [With BASE jumping] the gear only has one canopy in it. And then the altitudes are lower. And even if you jump high, you open low. You just have that one chance.

> In BASE, the tasks are simpler when everything goes right. But then when something goes wrong, you have to react really quickly. And for that, you need to have a calm state of mind. Yeah, that has happened to me a couple of times. Usually, I've been able to react quickly and efficiently. ... Probably one of the worst things that you can have on your canopy in BASE is to have a '180' [where] your canopy is turning towards the place that you were jumping from. Or even if I've been so far away that I couldn't have hit the cliff, you can always go into the forest or something.

Mila reported being aware of her skill level and consciously trying to operate within both her mental and physical capabilities throughout her jumping career. She also reported that her state of mind, particularly feeling calm, was critical to safe and successful jumping. This awareness was reflected in her description of an occasion when she was not in the required mental state for a difficult jump and subsequently landed in a forest: 'It was clearly too much for me ... my skill level was up to it, but my mind wasn't. I know that I could have really hurt myself.' These comments highlighted the importance of physical, technical and mental skills in risk perceptions and management as she progressed in her sport.

Effect of personal accidents on risk appraisals and protective frame

Mila was seriously injured in two accidents while BASE jumping. In the first, which occurred on her second BASE jump, she broke her back after the person manually deploying her parachute released it too early. Mila was lucky to survive what she anticipated would be an easy jump:

> I was jumping at a 30-meter [high] bridge in [name of country]. One guy was holding my para-chute to open my canopy when [I was] jumping to [wards] the water. He let go of the para-chute too early and my canopy didn't open. So I was jumping standing upright and then I turned on my side and when I was trying to turn myself back up again, I hit the water and broke my back – came up and then got picked in a boat. And trying to stand … It took me a while. I wasn't panicking or anything, but I was just a little in shock, I think, mixed-up, didn't know what to think. I didn't think that I had hurt myself. I thought I was okay. And I think everybody else was pretty [much] in shock too because they thought that I died when I went under the water.

It took eight months of rehabilitation for Mila's vertebrae to recover, the pain to cease, and for her to return to normal functioning. She spent much of this time reflecting on the accident. However, rather than feel angry with the person who had caused the accident, she felt that 'when you jump, you have to take the responsibility for the jump yourself'. In further probing, when asked if the accident had changed her feelings toward BASE jumping, Mila replied that despite altered perceptions of the risks involved, she was still motivated to continue participating:

> [The accident] changed my feelings in a way to [wards] BASE jumping. I had known that it's dangerous and I had known that you can get injured and I had known that you can die, but I hadn't really realized it. And now I really realized it that, yes, things can happen. I think it has just made the risk level really obvious. I prepare more and I've been conservative with the jumping. I always want to make sure that my skill level is up to the task.

When asked about her first jump after the accident and why she wanted to jump again, Mila responded:

> I knew all the time that I wanted to do it [BASE jump again], but I wasn't sure if I would be able to do it. Well, maybe it's a little too dramatic, but [thinking about] walking to my death or something. I don't know, it's just that it's a strong experience. You're doing something com-pletely pointless, jumping off a cliff, but it seems you're sort of climbing a mountain or some-thing. It seems a big thing that you've accomplished.

Risk-reward analysis is something that many extreme sport participants, including skydi-vers and BASE jumpers, engage in (Kerr and Houge Mackenzie 2012). This process is largely undertaken on an individual basis and is a crucial part of building a protective frame that allows participants to psychologically approach 'the dangerous edge' in extreme sports (Apter 1992). Mila's accident caused her to reappraise the risks involved in BASE jumping and, as a result, she became more intensely aware of and responsive to these risks. However, the resilience of her protective frame (Kerr 2007), was illustrated by statements describing her continued desire to master new challenges in BASE jumping and her perception that the risks involved remained manageable. As discussed in the next subsection, the resilience of her protective frame would be further tested by the deaths of friends while BASE jumping.

Effect of friends 'Gone in' on risk appraisals and protective frame

In the two years prior to the interview, Mila had lost four close friends and two acquaintances to BASE jumping accidents. In the BASE jumping community, this is referred to as 'gone in', in reference to a jumper who has gone into the ground or a rock wall. These incidents had significant psychological impacts on Mila and caused her to seriously question whether she would continue BASE jumping:

> Last spring, I almost quit because actually two of these [*deaths*] were freak accidents. There was nothing that they did that was wrong. It just happened. Well, it just shows that sometimes, you can do everything right and you're still gonna go in.

> Yeah, it definitely made me question the risk. It didn't actually affect the jumping itself, but it affected the preparation and the standing on the exit point when you're getting ready to jump. You should have the clear mind and then suddenly you get the thought of, 'What if I'm gonna die now? What if my gear is gonna fail? Is it worth it?'

> Now that I was jumping in [*name of country*] last summer, I didn't get that anymore. Obviously, I've dealt with the issue and it's not really there anymore. I think it's a little bit fatalistic; we're all going to die one day and thinking of this whole universe, I'm just a little piece of it. It's not the end of the world if I die BASE jumping. I mean, of course, I don't think that I'm going to die and I don't want to die. That's not why I do it at all. Somehow, it gives me some comfort that I know that I'm going to die someday anyway.

According to Celsi, Rose, and Leigh (1993), the acculturation of risk and the belief that sky-diving risk is psychologically manageable starts when people first engage in skydiving. Skydivers and BASE jumpers are informed by instructors and peers that human error and failure to effectively manage situations leads to death. Uncontrollable risk is seldom put forward as a reason for a fatality. When the cause of death cannot be attributed to human error or equipment failure, jumpers tend to ascribe what occurred in an incident to fate (Laurendeau 2006).

Mila's reports support and expand on these findings. She was psychologically affected, and nearly withdrew from BASE jumping, because two of her friends' deaths were 'freak accidents' that could not be attributed to mistakes during free fall. The nature of their deaths changed her perception of the risks involved in BASE jumping and negatively affected her mental state at the exit point prior to jumping. In time, Mila was able to psychologically cope with her friends' deaths and continue BASE jumping. One coping mechanism she employed to overcome this negative psychological experience was to become more fatalistic about mortality and the inevitability of death.

Mila's resilience and mental strength in response to these tragedies is notable given the contrasting reaction of an accomplished female skydiver 'Julie' (298 jumps; Kerr 2007) who suddenly withdrew from skydiving after a friend died in a similar, unexplained 'freak' sky-diving accident. That accident had a major impact on Julie's life in general. She became severely anxious and depressed, was unable to continue working, and contemplated suicide. Not all experiences in BASE jumping are positive and, in dealing with adversity, Mila cultivated psychological strength and personal development. These two contrasting cases demonstrate the pivotal role of psychological frames in fostering psychological health and well-being through extreme sport experiences, rather than negative psychological outcomes.

Protective frames may fail, either temporarily or permanently, if an extreme sport participant's subjective appraisal of the risks involved in her or his activity change (Kerr and Houge Mackenzie 2014). Mila's perception of BASE jumping risks, and her sense of control, changed as a result of her friends' unexplained deaths. However, unlike Julie whose protective frame was destroyed by a friend's death, Mila's robust protective frame allowed her to continue participating. This was illustrated by her statement: 'I think it's [now] more about trusting my skills, and trusting my mental abilities, and trusting my gear'. This comment suggested that she had an active, strong protective frame built around these three key elements.

Evolving motivations and post-Activity benefits

Mila's interview statements highlighted several motives for taking part in skydiving and BASE jumping, which evolved over time as she gained experience. These data supported previous findings with extreme sport participants (Celsi, Rose, and Leigh 1993; Kerr and Houge Mackenzie 2014) and expanded the literature on motivations and experiences across different extreme sport participation phases.

At the start of her skydiving career, Mila's enjoyment came from the excitement or 'rush' associated with jumping from the plane and her descent (Buckley 2012). As Mila reflected,

> I'm definitely in the group of people who enjoy fear and who seek ... that kind of experience. I think you really get a physical reward also. It's not just me knowing that I have this fear and how I overcame it, but it's also the [*physical*] feeling that it gives you.

For example, she reported feeling ecstatic on her first skydive when the canopy opened and her landing was easier than anticipated. However, over time, as Mila became accustomed to skydiving and progressed to BASE jumping, some of those initial 'rush' sensations and motivations dissipated: 'I don't think anyone would jump thousands of jumps just to jump out of the airplane. It's not that exciting; everything gets boring when you do it enough.' Over time, her enjoyment resulted from experiencing different locations and developing her BASE jumping skills:

> I think a lot of people, when they first start, that's how it's exciting because you keep jumping in different places all the time. Of course, with tracking skills, and you're jumping the same place, you can really [*tell*] if you've developed or not. No, it's about the skills too, but it has an impact on the experience if you jump in the same place or different places.

In response to questions about post-activity (i.e. post-BASE jump) experiences, Mila stated that, ' ... nowadays, it's just to clear the mind', and went on to describe positive, low arousal emotions resulting from BASE jumping:

> I don't really know why I have to do it. I know that there is no point really in doing it. I think it just makes me – it makes me relaxed and it makes me calmer after I've done it. So, I just enjoy the experience and I enjoy the way that I feel afterwards also.

Mila's interview statements indicate that, at this advanced stage of her extreme sport career, BASE jumping induces positive changes to her psychological state such as pleasant low arousal emotions (relaxed, calm) post-jump. Her descriptions corroborate and expand on findings that mastering new skills and feeling relaxed were important experiential aspects for an expert veteran male skydiver (Kerr and Houge Mackenzie 2014). That skydiver's motivation had also evolved over time as he continually endeavoured to develop expertise and master new challenges. When his efforts were successful, he reported feeling positive, calm, and relaxed post-activity (i.e. post-skydive).

Connections to nature and well-Being

Feeling connected to nature also played a surprisingly important role in Mila's BASE jumping experiences. As BASE jumping includes Buildings, Antennas, Spans, and Earth, it is not always nature-based. Rather, it is often associated with illicit social actions and deviance due to participants illegally accessing jump sites, such as buildings or statues (Ferrel, Milovanovich, and Lyng 2001; Self et al. 2006). Conversely, Mila preferred to jump in natural settings. She reported maximal enjoyment when jumping off cliffs or bridges in beautiful locations that allowed her to enjoy hiking to the jump site (preparation and approach phases) and to maintain quiet, calm, relaxed feelings in natural surround-ings after her jump (post-jump phase). Her motivation appeared strongly connected to special places in the natural world that facilitated positive BASE jumping experiences:

> I think nature is definitely a big thing in it and I'm sure that it's that for other people too. Maybe they just don't realize it. Maybe they don't talk about it. For me to come in from [*country name*] and then travel to these places to jump with mountains, which we don't have back at home, it makes me see it more than the people who are there all the time.

For Mila, connecting with nature was more pronounced and integral in BASE jumping than in skydiving:

> In BASE jumping, or at least in the kind of BASE jumping that I like to do, which is on the cliffs, of course you are in the nature all the time. Whereas in skydiving, you're at the drop zone at the airfield, which is usually nice too, but it's not beautiful, incredible in nature, as mountains are.

These reflections on the importance of the natural environment in extreme sports support Brymer and Gray's (2010) results. They found that veteran extreme sport participants developed an intimate and reciprocal relationship with nature, and eco-centric perspec-tives (i.e. viewing humanity as part of the natural environment), as a result of participation. Some participants also described spiritual benefits, such as developing a heightened respect for something greater than themselves. Mila echoed these sentiments when she commented on the psychological benefits of BASE jumping, 'It's a really nice feeling when you sort of feel a part of the universe'. These results are particularly noteworthy as, although BASE jumping entails greater objective risks than some other extreme sports such as skydiving, it was reported to more effectively foster connections to nature in this case. The heightened risks in BASE jumping either fostered, or at least did not detract from, Mila's ability to connect with the natural world.

Connections to others and well-Being

For extreme sport participants, a sense of camaraderie and connection to like-minded people with shared experiences may provide additional motivation and psychological benefits by promoting a sense of belonging (Celsi, Rose, and Leigh 1993; Deci and Ryan 2000; Lipscombe 1999; Stenseng, Forest, and Curran 2015). Interestingly, Mila identified the desire to feel autonomous and have solitary jumping experiences, while also expressing empathy and a sense of camaraderie with fellow skydivers and BASE jumpers. Self-determination theory (Deci and Ryan 2000) offers a well-developed explanation of how these seemingly contradictory motivations can be highly complementary, which Mila illustrated in her interview statements:

> I mean there was always a group of people that I hang out with, but I still might sometimes go and jump by myself. … Yeah, it's really just a personal thing – being by myself and experiencing the whole thing [*BASE jumping*].

> … by doing that [*landing in the forest*], I would have also hurt the community because it's a difficult place in a really famous BASE jumping place. And it's kind of new, so now if a lot of people hurt themselves there, it's bad for the place in general.

In addition, Mila's sense of community and connection to others became more pronounced when she began instructing student skydivers. This was a new challenge for Mila, who reported enjoying the responsibility and excitement associated with improving her skills as an instructor:

> Of course I enjoy it. Sometimes I feel excited if I've had a break [*from jumping*] or improving my skill level in something that I'm trying to learn like tracking. And at the moment, it would be improving my skills in instructing. … I think it's just nice to see how you can help people learn the skills that you need in skydiving. Of course, for the students, I feel a lot more responsibility.

Conclusion

The current study explored the experiences of a veteran female skydiver and BASE jumper throughout her career, including changes in motivations, risk perceptions, psychological management strategies, and psychological health and personal development benefits of participation. Much of the data addressed the research questions in an integrated, holistic manner, which illustrated how risk perceptions and psychological strategies (research question 2), motivations (research question 3), psychological well-being and personal development (research question 4) were entwined and profoundly influenced the overall lived experience of skydiving and BASE jumping (research question 1). In relation to research questions 1, 3 and 4, data revealed that Mila's skydiving and BASE jumping motivation was dynamic and multifaceted, and that she sought distinct benefits from these activities, particularly in relation to connecting with nature via BASE jumping. Her motives had evolved over time and included opportunities to: induce positive changes to her psychological state; feel heightened perceptions of control; master new skills; experience new natural locations; connect with nature; feel autonomous; enjoy solitude; and experience belonging through skydiving and BASE jumping communities. That Mila has multiple, evolving participation motives extends traditional theories of extreme sport participation (e.g. sensation- or thrill-seeking; Kerr 1991; Rowland, Franken, and Harrison 1986; Zuckerman 2007), and corroborates more contemporary understandings of skydiving and BASE jumping participation (Allman et al. 2009; Apter and Batler 1997; Celsi, Rose, and Leigh 1993; Lipscombe 1999; Willig 2008), and extreme sport participation in general (e.g. Brymer, Downey, and Gray 2009; Brymer and Oades 2009; Kerr and Houge Mackenzie 2012; Varley 2011).

In relation to research questions 1a, 2 and 4, the study revealed that BASE jumping was perceived to have higher risks than skydiving, which necessitated a range of unique psychological management strategies and fostered distinct experiences. These strategies included risk reappraisal and risk-reward analysis; cultivating a calm state of mind; adopting a more fatalistic perspective on death to combat feelings of low control in BASE jumping; and building a resilient protective frame through trust in technical skills, mental skills, and equipment. These strategies appeared to facilitate continued participation in BASE jumping despite negative experiences, and thereby promoted on-going psychological health and personal development opportunities. Mila reported psychological health and personal development outcomes across a number of hedonic and eudaimonic dimensions ranging from inducing positive psychological and emotional states (e.g. high arousal excitement and pleasant low arousal emotions); overcoming psychological challenges; successfully coping with grief and fear; promoting mindfulness and mental focus; opportunities for solitude and autonomy; connecting with nature; feelings of spirituality; and a sense of belonging and connection to others. As these outcomes have been identified as components of psychological well-being (e.g. Brymer and Schweitzer 2013; Deci and Ryan 2000; Fredrickson 2001), the current findings support and extend the literature linking extreme sport with a range of positive psychological outcomes. Furthermore, the results highlight the value of expanding extreme sport investigations beyond simplistic notions of risk or unidimensional motivation to encompass more holistic ways of conceptualizing these experiences.

Limitations, implications and future directions

It is important to note that these qualitative findings represent exploratory results from a unique case study and that they may not apply to larger skydiving or BASE jumping populations. Although the case study design precludes broad generalizations, it fundamentally questions traditional assumptions of extreme sport participation (e.g. Brymer and Schweitzer 2017) and provides a foundation for further investigations of extreme sport experiences and potential links to well-being. It also provides a female perspective on extreme sport experiences, which are traditionally underrepresented in the literature. Future research should investigate motivations, benefits and experiences in relation to risk perceptions and protective frames among a broader cross section of skydivers and BASE jumpers, and should strive to include a balance of male and female participants. Research could also examine how risk perceptions and protective frames developed in an extreme sport may influence other leisure experiences and/or change with participants' experience level (e.g. novice, intermediate, expert). A potentially fruitful area of investigation in relation to BASE jumping is exploring how recent developments in BASE jumping technologies (e.g. flight or wing suits) may influence participants' risk perceptions, protective frames and overall experiences. Researchers could further assess whether BASE jumping with wing suits yields different psychological benefits or drawbacks.

In addition to informing future research, these findings have important implications for practice. Traditional narratives and research accounts that portray extreme sports as strictly motivated by sensations-seeking and the desire to engage in socially illicit activities can prevent the development of more progressive public policies and health promotion strategies. In contrast, research that identifies important individual and social benefits of extreme sports can lead to increased mainstream acceptance and recognition of psychological health and personal development opportunities associated with extreme sports (e.g. Clough et al. 2016). From a business perspective, enhanced understanding of extreme sport experiences and motivations can also inform effective sport planning, managing and marketing strategies (e.g. Bennett, Henson, and Zhang 2003).

The authors recognize that even with the use of reflexive practices, their unique backgrounds and perspectives may have inherently privileged some results over others and that other researchers and practitioners may identify alternative interpretations. Notwithstanding, the novel findings of this case study expand on traditional narratives in the extreme sport literature, and may enhance future investigations of extreme sport experiences and motivations by providing a basis for working hypotheses, and means of facilitating learning and naturalistic generalization (e.g. Lincoln and Guba 1985; Skate 1995). In this way, it is hoped that the findings of this unique case study will extend current understandings of extreme sport participation by identifying dynamic multifaceted motivations, and by highlighting how these emerging leisure activities may foster psychological health, well-being and personal development.

Notes

1. www.blinc.magazine.com.
2. Vagal tone can be measured by changes in heart rate and breathing (e.g. Kok and Fredrickson 2010). The proposed 'vagal circuit of emotion' integrates brain function and the parasympathetic nervous system to account for the expression and regulation of emotion (Porges, Doussard-Roosevelt, and Maiti 1994).
3. Structural phenomenology has been defined as 'the search for pattern and structure in the way in which experience is interpreted.' (Apter 1981, 173).
4. This is the common term for a gathering of skydivers at a drop zone. Most drop zones have at least one official yearly boogie to celebrate local jumpers. These events range from small gatherings to hundreds of skydivers (see www.extremesports.about.com/od/skydiving/fl/TheHistoryoftheBoogieforfurtherinformation).

Disclosure statement

No potential conflict of interest was reported by the authors.

ORCID

Susan Houge Mackenzie ⓘ http://orcid.org/0000-0001-5660-6325

References

Ahern, K. 1999. "Ten Tips for Reflexive Bracketing." *Qualitative Health Research* 9: 407–411.

Allman, T. L., R. Mittelstaedt, B. Martin, and M. Goldenberg. 2009. "Exploring the Motivations of Base Jumpers: Extreme Sport Enthusiasts." *Journal of Sport & Tourism* 14: 229–247.

Amis, J. 2005. "Interviewing for Case Study Research." In *Qualitative Methods in Sport Studies*, edited by D. L. Andrews, D. S. Mason, and M. L. Silk, 104–138. Oxford, NY: Berg.

Apter, M. J. 1981. "The Possibility of a Structural Phenomenology: The Case of Reversal Theory." *Journal of Phenomenological Psychology* 12 (2): 173–187.

Apter, M. J. 1982. *The Experience of Motivation*. London, England: Academic Press.

Apter, M. J. 1992. *The Dangerous Edge*. New York, NY: Free Press.

Apter, M. J. 2001. *Motivational Styles in Everyday Life: A Guide to Reversal Theory*. Washington, D.C.: American Psychological Association.

Apter, M. J., and R. Batler. 1997. "Gratuitous Risk: A Study of Parachuting." In *Stress and Health: A Reversal Theory Perspective*, edited by S. Svebak and M. J. Apter, 119–129. Washington, DC: Taylor & Francis.

Barlow, M., T. Woodman, C. Chapman, M. Milton, D. Stone, T. Dodds, and B. Allen. 2015. "Who Takes Risks in High-Risk Sport? The Role of Alexithymia." *Journal of Sport and Exercise Psychology* 37 (1): 83–96.

Bennett, G., R. K. Henson, and J. Zhang. 2003. "Generation Y's Perceptions of the Action Sports Industry Segment." *Journal of Sport Management* 17 (2): 95–115.

Berger, R. 2015. "Now I see it, now I Don't: Researcher's Position and Reflexivity in Qualitative Research." *Qualitative Research* 15 (2): 219–234.

Biddle, S. J. H., D. Markland, D. Gilbourne, N. L. D. Chatzisarantis, and A. C. Sparkes. 2001. "Research Methods in Sport and Exercise Psychology: Quantitative and Qualitative Issues." *Journal of Sports Sciences* 19: 77–809.

Bradbury-Jones, C. 2007. "Enhancing Rigor in Qualitative Health Research: Exploring Subjectivity Through Peshkin's I's." *Journal of Advanced Nursing* 59: 290–298.

Brinkman, S. 2013. *Qualitative Interviewing*. Oxford, UK: Oxford University Press.

Brymer, E. 2010. "Risk Taking in Extreme Sports: A Phenomenological Perspective." *Annals of Leisure Research* 13 (1–2): 218–238.

Brymer, E., G. Downey, and T. Gray. 2009. "Extreme Sports as a Precursor to Environment Sustainability." *Journal of Sport and Tourism* 14: 193–204.

Brymer, E., and T. Gray. 2010. "Developing an Intimate 'Relationship' with Nature Through Extreme Sports Participation." *Leisure/Loisir* 34: 361–374.

Brymer, E., and L. G. Oades. 2009. "Extreme Sports: A Positive Transformation in Courage and Humility." *Journal of Humanistic Psychology* 49: 114–126.

Brymer, E., and R. Schweitzer. 2013. "Extreme Sports are Good for Your Health: a Phenomenological Understanding of Fear and Anxiety in Extreme Sport." *Journal of Health Psychology* 18 (4): 477–487.

Brymer, E., and R. Schweitzer. 2017. *Phenomenology and the Extreme Sport Experience*. New York: Taylor & Francis.

Buckley, R. C. 2012. "Rush as a key Motivation in Skilled Adventure Tourism: Resolving the Risk Recreation Paradox." *Tourism Management* 33: 961–970.

Celsi, R. L., R. L. Rose, and T. W. Leigh. 1993. "An Exploration of High-Risk Leisure Consumption Through Skydiving." *Journal of Consumer Research* 20: 1–23.

Chirivella, E. C., and L. M. Martinez. 1994. "The Sensation of Risk and Motivational Tendencies in Sports: An Empirical Study." *Personality and Individual Differences* 16: 777–786.

Clough, P., S. Houge Mackenzie, L. Mallabon, and E. Brymer. 2016. "Adventurous Physical Activity Environments: A Mainstream Intervention for Mental Health." *Sports Medicine* 46: 963–968. Advance online publication. http://www.ncbi.nlm.nih.gov/pubmed/26895993

Cresswell, S. L., and R. C. Eklund. 2007. "Athlete Burnout: A Longitudinal Qualitative Study." *The Sport Psychologist* 21: 1–20. doi:10.1123/tsp.21.1.1.

Creswell, J. W. 2012. *Qualitative Inquiry and Research Design: Choosing among Five Approaches.* Thousand Oaks, CA: Sage.

Csikszentmihalyi, M. 2000. *Beyond Boredom and Anxiety: Experiencing Flow in Work and Play.* 25th Anniversary Edition. San Francisco, CA: Jossey-Bass.

D'Cruz, H., P. Gillingham, and S. Melendez. 2007. "Reflexivity, its Meanings and Relevance for Social Work: A Critical Review of the Literature." *British Journal of Social Work* 37: 73–90.

Deci, E. L., and R. M. Ryan. 2000. "The 'What' and 'Why' of Goal Pursuits: Human Needs and the Self Determination of Behavior." *Psychological Inquiry* 11: 227–268.

Denzin, N. K., and Y. S. Lincoln (Eds.). 2005. *The Sage Handbook of Qualitative Research.* 3rd ed. Thousand Oaks, CA: Sage.

Ellwand, O. 2015, June 9. "Base Jump Kills Edmonton Man." *National Post*, p. A3.

Ferrel, J., D. Milovanovich, and S. Lyng. 2001. "Edgework, Media Practices and the Elongation of Meaning: A Theoretical Ethnography of the Bridge Day Event." *Theoretical Criminology* 5: 177–202.

Fletcher, R. 2008. "Living on the Edge: The Appeal of Risk Sports for the Professional Middle Class." *Sociology of Sport Journal* 25 (3): 310–330.

Fredrickson, B. L. 2001. "The Role of Positive Emotions in Positive Psychology: The Broaden-and-Build Theory of Positive Emotions." *American Psychologist* 56 (3): 218–226.

Giulianotti, R. 2009. "Risk and Sport: An Analysis of Sociological Theories and Research Agendas." *Sociology of Sport Journal* 26 (4): 540–556.

Hardy, L. 1996. "Testing the Predictions of the Cusp Catastrophe Model of Anxiety and Performance." *The Sport Psychologist* 10 (2): 140–156.

Houge Mackenzie, S., and J. H. Kerr. 2013. "Stress and Emotions at Work: An Adventure Tour Guide's Experiences." *Tourism Management* 36: 3–14.

Kerr, J. H. 1991. "Arousal-seeking in Risk Sport Participants." *Personality and Individual Differences* 12: 613–616.

Kerr, J. H. 2007. "Sudden Withdrawal From Skydiving: A Case Study Informed by Reversal Theory's Concept of Protective Frames." *Journal of Applied Sport Psychology* 19: 337–351.

Kerr, J. H., and S. Houge Mackenzie. 2012. "Multiple Motives for Participating in Adventure Sports." *Psychology of Sport and Exercise* 13: 649–657.

Kerr, J. H., and S. Houge Mackenzie. 2014. "Confidence Frames and the Mastery of new Challenges in the Motivation of an Expert Skydiver." *The Sport Psychologist* 28: 221–232.

Kok, B. E., and B. L. Fredrickson. 2010. "Upward Spirals of the Heart: Autonomic Flexibility, as Indexed by Vagal Tone, Reciprocally and Prospectively Predicts Positive Emotions and Social Connectedness." *Biological Psychology* 85 (3): 432–436.

Laurendeau, J. 2006. ""He Didn't go in Doing a Skydive": Sustaining the Illusion of Control in an Edgework Activity." *Sociological Perspectives* 49: 583–605.

Laurendeau, J. 2008. "'Gendered Risk Regimes': A Theoretical Consideration of Edgework and Gender." *Sociology of Sport Journal* 25 (3): 293–309.

Laverty, S. M. 2003. "Hermeneutic Phenomenology and Phenomenology: A Comparison of Historical and Methodological Considerations." *International Journal of Qualitative Methods* 2 (3): 21–35.

Legrand, F. D., and M. J. Apter. 2004. "Why do People Perform Thrilling Activities? A Study Based on Reversal Theory." *Psychological Reports* 94: 307–313.

Lincoln, Y. S., and E. G. Guba. 1985. *Naturalistic Inquiry.* Newberry Park, CA: Sage.

Lipscombe, N. 1999. "The Relevance of the Peak Experience to Continued Skydiving Participation: A Qualitative Approach to Assessing Motivations." *Leisure Studies* 18: 267‑288.

Lyng, S. 1990. "Edgework: A Social Psychological Analysis of Voluntary Risk Taking." *American Journal of Sociology* 95: 851–886.

Lyng, S. 2005. "Sociology at the Edge: Social Theory and Voluntary Risk Taking." In *Edgework: The Sociology of Risk-Taking*, edited by S. Lyng, 17–50. New York: Routledge.

Monasterio, E., O. Mei-Dan, A. C. Hackney, A. R. Lane, I. Zwir, S. Rozsa, and C. R. Cloninger. 2016. "Stress Reactivity and Personality in Extreme Sport Athletes: The Psychobiology of BASE Jumpers." *Physiology & Behavior* 167: 289–297.

Morland, P. 2015, May 19. "Dean Potter's Extreme Exploits Showed us the Beauty of Life on the Edge." *The Guardian*. http://www.theguardian.com.

Myers, M. D. 2008. *Qualitative Research in Business and Management*. Thousand Oaks, CA: Sage.

O'Connell, K. A., M. Potocky, M. R. Cook, and M. M. Gerkovich. 1991. *Metamotivational State Interview and Coding Schedule Instruction Manual*. Kansas City, MO: Midwest Research Institute.

Padgett, D. K. 2008. *Qualitative Methods in Social Work Research*. Thousand Oaks, CA: Sage.

Pain, M., and J. H. Kerr. 2004. "Extreme Risk Taker who Wants to Continue Taking Part in High Risk Sports After Serious Injury." *British Journal of Sports Medicine* 38: 337–339.

Peifer, C., A. Schulz, H. Schächinger, N. Baumann, and C. H. Antoni. 2014. "The Relation of Flow-Experience and Physiological Arousal Under Stress—Can u Shape it?" *Journal of Experimental Social Psychology* 53: 62–69.

Porges, S. W., J. A. Doussard-Roosevelt, and A. K. Maiti. 1994. "Vagal Tone and the Physiological Regulation of Emotion." *Monographs of the Society for Research in Child Development* 59 (2–3): 167–186.

Rowland, G. L., R. E. Franken, and K. Harrison. 1986. "Sensation Seeking and Participation in Sporting Activities." *International Journal of Sport Psychology* 8: 212–220.

Self, D. R., E. De Vries Henry, C. S. Findley, and E. Reilly. 2006. "Thrill Seeking: The Type T Personality and Extreme Sports." *International Journal of Sport Management and Marketing* 2 (1-2): 175–190.

Skate, R. E. 1995. *The art of Case Study Research*. Thousand Oaks, CA: Sage.

Sparkes, A. C., and B. Smith. 2014. *Qualitative Research Methods in Sport, Exercise and Health: From Process to Product*. London: Routledge.

Stenseng, F., J. Forest, and T. Curran. 2015. "Positive Emotions in Recreational Sport Activities: The Role of Passion and Belongingness." *Journal of Happiness Studies* 16 (5): 1117–1129. doi:http://dx.doi.org.ezproxy.otago.ac.nz/10.1007/s10902-014-9547-y.

Varley, P. J. 2011. "Sea Kayakers at the Margins: The Liminoid Character of Contemporary Adventures." *Leisure Studies* 30: 85–98.

Willig, C. 2008. "A Phenomenological Investigation of the Experience of Taking Part in Extreme Sport." *Journal of Health Psychology* 13: 690–702.

Yin, R. K. 2013. *Case Study Research: Design and Methods*. 5th ed. London, England: Sage.

Zuckerman, M. (Ed.). 2007. *Sensation Seeking and Risky Behavior*. Washington, DC: American Psychological Association.

Running away from the taskscape: ultramarathon as 'dark ecology'

Jim Cherrington, Jack Black and Nicholas Tiller

ABSTRACT

Drawing on reflections from a collaborative autoethnography, this article argues that ultramarathon running is defined by a 'dark' ecological sensibility [Morton, Timothy. 2007. *Ecology without Nature*. London: Harvard University Press; Morton, Timothy. 2010. *The Ecological Thought*. London: Harvard University Press; Morton, Timothy. 2016. *Dark Ecology: For a Logic of Future Coexistence*. New York: Columbia University Press], characterized by moments of pain, disgust, and the macabre. In contrast to existing accounts, we problematize the notion that runners 'use' nature for escape and/or competition, while questioning the aesthetic-causal relationships often evinced within these accounts. With specific reference to the discursive, embodied, spatial and temporal aspects of the sport, we explore the way in which participants begin to appreciate the immense power of nature, while being humbled by the fragile and unstable foundations of human experience. Accordingly this article contributes novel insights into the human-nature complex that seek to move beyond Romantic analyses towards a more sophisticated understanding of the relationships between (nature) sport, people and place.

Introduction

The relationship between humans and nature is one that is often framed through perspectives that consider 'nature' as a phenomenon that is battled with, in order to achieve some form of personal and/or sporting achievement. In such accounts nature is concieved as something to be 'tamed' by athletic prowess or by the heroic virtues of the intrepid explorer (see, for example Krein 2008; 2014). This is reflected in the case of extreme nature sports, whereby:

> the essential relationship between the natural world and the extreme athlete is to battle against or attempt to conquer or vanquish part of the natural world. In these accounts of extreme sports, the natural world has only anthropocentric worth, that is, it is recognized only for its use or value to humanity (Brymer and Gray 2009, 138).

By proving a 'value to humanity', nature becomes a tool through which an individual's 'true', 'authentic' or 'inner being' can be discovered and laid bare amidst the travails provided by nature (Arnould and Price 1993).

This perspective on nature is particularly evident in the discipline of obstacle running. Here, Weedon (2016) explains how much of the promotional material for the popular 'Spartan Race'[1] reinvents the Protestant work ethic while reinforcing the racial, gendered and classist exclusions that were typical of the nineteenth century wilderness movement. Notions of strong mindedness, personal suffering and bodily discipline can combine with Darwinist and Romantic notions of nature that preserve a Conservative vision of a past life, unfettered by 'overcivilization' (Weedon 2016), global immigration and progressive political change. In doing so:

> mud running is premised on an attitude to bodies in and of nature recuperated from the nineteenth century, through which the dynamic of reclaiming and breaking with the past characterizes the spirit of modernity, the renaissance of (interest in) physical culture, and the esprit de corps of the focal practice (Weedon 2016, 47).

Therefore, while maintaining 'a lingering cultural derivative of colonialist, imperialist and modernist thinking, and reflective of how mainstream-sport cultures often value the spirit of conquering in/as the athletic process' (Atkinson 2010a, 1262), obstacle sports, such as the Spartan Race, serve to reinforce the perspective that nature is something that can be 'sought' as a remedy for the 'degenerative effects of modern life' (Weedon 2016, 47).

In contrast, Morton (2007, 2010, 2016) undermines traditional conceptions of nature as something which was, at some point, before human intervention, thus challenging the belief that nature acts as a panacea for social problems. Instead, he proposes that nature has never been 'free' from disturbance and that if one is to understand the profound ecological impact that human beings have on their surroundings, then a far more nuanced approach is needed in which nature is 'concieved not as riefied nature "over there" outside the city or the factory gates, but "right here" (2007, 89). Important here, is the way in which humans orientate their relation to the 'symbiotic real' - 'an implosive whole in which entities [both human and non-human] are related in a non-total, ragged way' (2017, 1 [italics added]). This is particularly relevant to the study of nature sports, as we are interested in the various ways that nature is enacted, sensed and embodied in the movements of a runner, as well as the ways in which runners make sense of these movements in particular temporal, spatial and symbolic locations.

Taking the above into consideration, this paper will examine the relationship between nature and sport via the reflections of an ultramarathon runner.[2] Ultramarathon running is fast gaining popularity as an athletic competition and a means of personal accomplishment, the latter of which has exhibited the greatest mass appeal (Hashimoto et al. 2006). Although once considered a fringe sport, ultramarathon has seen a steady rise in popularity in the last 30 years (Hoffman, Ong, and Wang 2010), and is now a highly-competitive and often commercial pastime. Footraces are contested the world over in extreme and exotic environments. Most ultramarathons cover distances from 35 miles[3] (56 km) to 150 miles (240 km) in a single-stage, and up to 1600 miles (2500 km) in multi-stage events. Distances are often traversed solo and unaccompanied, but relay and/or team events are not uncommon.

In view of this discipline, we do not seek to criticize or denounce existing work on nature sports but to modify and extend it in order to encompass the discursive, embodied, spaced and timed aspects of nature sports and, therefore, explore how nature and the movements made in these environments, are thoroughly 'enmeshed' (Macnaghten and Urry 1998). To borrow a phrase from Latour (2004, 16), we wish to 'slow down' discussions regarding political ecology, in order to revisit the dichotomies of human and nature, subject and object, and consider how they are enacted by those who participate in ultra-marathon running.

Nature sports: examining the relationship between sport, nature and running

Drawing on the spatial triad developed by Lefebvre (1991), Hanold (2016) convincingly shows how scientific measurements of time and distance are priveleged by traditional cultures of distance running, which is evident in both the measures used to determine an athlete's success (minutes per mile/kilometer), and the experiential feedback that guides the pace and rhythm of their movement (heart rate, breathing, sweating). Similar findings are evidenced in studies concerned with the phenomenology of running; in which aspects geared towards measurable and linear standards of success, include: 'thermoregulation' (Hockey and Allen-Collinson 2016); 'aural attunement' (Allen-Collinson and Owton 2014); 'footwork' (Allen-Collinson 2011).

According to Hanold (2016), however, ultramarathon running has been noted for transforming and subverting dominant neo-liberal sensibilities, including those relating to linear movement. As a result, Hanold (2016) argues that, though not totally free of these tendencies, ultramarathon runners are able to destabilize the relationship between time and space by focussing on the distance moved as opposed to the time in which this distance is run. As a result, the athletes' movement is much more variable, shifting constantly between walking, scrambling and running. The by-products of this include both greater levels of interaction between runners, and increased support (both emotional and physical) for those who are struggling to complete the distance. In such instances, the experience of ultramarathon running is typified by 'extraordinary moments of elation for a million reasons, nearly none of which had anything to do with running quickly' (Hanold 2016, 216).

Expanding our understanding of running as beyond simply an activity that is completed to achieve a particular time, achievement or qualification, Atkinson (2010a, 1261) examined how the sport of 'fell-running crosses out dominant constructions of modernist sports forms'. Competing across 'mountains, elds, streams, hills, valleys and plains' (Atkinson 2010a, 1261), Atkinson (2010a, 1262) identified how:

> The rigours of running focus the mind on the present, and the body on the culturally uncooked nature of the space. When a run is stripped of urban contexts, and as the person is immersed in mud, wind, rain, grass, rock, sweat and occasionally blood, an almost Zen-like state may follow.

What was made explicit from Atkinson's (2010a, 1263) account was the 'communion with nature' that was expressed by fell runners. Both here, and in other work (Atkinson 2010a; 2010b; 2011; 2016), Atkinson (2010a) highlights how, alongside other sports, interactions between fellrunners and natural environments developed into various 'scapelands'. Following Lyotard (1989), Atkinson (2010a, 1253) details how 'Scapelands are … heterotopic encounters with physical space that produce an emancipating experiential awareness of impermanence, emptiness, unconscious remainder and missing presence'. Key to this process is the ability of the runners to find a balance between the physical challenges that the landscapes present, and their ability to manage psychologically with the omnipresence of fear, in a manner similar to that of the runners in Csikszentmihalyi, Latter, and Duranso's (2017)' study of 'flow'. It is in this state that athletes are able to experience a state of 'voluptuous panic' (Caillois 1967) which, through playful and childlike engagement with nature and the unpredictability of the terrain, can temporarily disrupt the rational, comfortable and lucid self, leading to profound moments of personal transformation. As Monbiot (2016, 98) elucidates:

> In these places we can leave our linearity and confinement behind, surrender to the unplanned and emergent world of nature, be surprised once more by joy, as unexpected encounters with great beasts … (almost all of which, despite our fears, are harmless to us) become possible again. We can rediscover those buried emotions that otherwise remain unexercised.

This feeling, writes Atkinson (2011, 11), is not goal-centred or outcome driven, but pursued for its own sake, sought for no other reason than the ability to temporarily relinquish one's self-consciousness and to abandon oneself 'in movement and flight'. Fell-running can thus be defined as a 'post-sport' (Pronger 1998) or 'anti-sport' (Atkinson 2009), in which modern sporting practices and institutions revolving around hierarchical competition and measurable outcomes are eschewed in favour of alternative states of being. Consequently, athletes can reflect critically on the complex relationships between nature, bodies and culture.

Nevertheless, while various 'post-sports' seek to escape the modernist entrapments that encase contemporary sports, in many instances, the act of running, whether middle, long, or ultra, is one in which 'physical space appears to figure prominently in the production of this social space and informs what it means to endure' (Hanold 2016, 181). Indeed, it is a sense of endurance that permeate accounts of running. For Howe (2016, 213), 'Running, like all physical activities, is a sensuous experience' and it is this sensuous experience which needs 'capturing', not as pure transcendence, but as something that is 'produced' in particular 'natural' spaces. Accordingly, Howe and Morris (2009, 309) argue that:

> middle-and long-distance running, unlike many other sports (including other types of performance running such as sprinting), is a spatially extensive practice involving multiple sites, spaces, and places and has a particularly close relationship with 'natural' spaces, both in terms of training and competition as evidenced in the disciplines of cross-country and fell running.

Detailing how running bodies and nature are co-produced through a range of corporeal schema inherent to the execution of a run, Howe and Morris (2009) draw on the work of Ingold (2000) to differentiate between two elements of running: 'dwelling', which refers to the ways in which human bodies are embedded in organic life; 'taskscapes', defined as 'any practical operation carried out by a skilled agent in an environment as part of his or her business of life' (Ingold 2000, 195). In applying these two notions, Howe and Morris (2009, 322) illustrate how athletes treat the landscape as both a gymnasium for physiological improvement and a 'shrine', which has spiritual, emotional and psychological connotations. Importantly, however, the treatment of these landscapes is paradoxical, in that the runners see them as both a source of physical enhancement and a place of worship (though these sentiments are dynamic and relational). Specifically, in case of the former, nature affords a particular set of opportunities for making the body faster, stronger and quicker. In the latter, it is experienced as having a particular role to play in rest and rehabilitation.

Together, both Atkinson (2010a, 2011) and Howe (2016; Howe and Morris 2009), draw attention to the notion that nature sports involve a communion with nature, rather than a battle to overcome or destroy it (Brymer and Gray 2010). This is also considered by Brymer and Gray (2009) who adopt the metaphor of a 'dance' to elucidate on the extent to which self-understandings are symbiotically changed with nature. With regard to participants of extreme nature sports, they detail how:

> The metaphor of 'dance' recognizes a dynamic, rhythmical, harmonious, fluid and responsive interplay between the extreme sport participant and nature. ... The dance metaphor embraces the holistic experience of extreme athletes within nature. Engaging in extreme sports (just like dance) is a transformational experience for some participants that taps into the emotional, spiritual and physical realms (Brymer and Gray 2009, 138).

What becomes apparent from these accounts is the extent to which the relationship between sport and nature remains tied to the notion that the sporting activity is itself a form of participation that is performed to either 'transcend' (Cidell 2014) or 'escape' modernity (Weedon 2016). Simultaneously, it is nature that presents a workable and 'task'-driven environment that can be used to help produce and train a sporting body (Bale 2004; Howe and Morris 2009; Allen-Collinson and Hockey 2010; Howe 2016). Unsurprisingly, therefore, running has been adopted as part of wider health and fitness initiatives as an activity that can be 'used' to help bolster government attempts to improve public health (Shipway and Holloway 2010).

While the reasons for running are various (Cidell 2014), we remain critical to an underlying functionality in the ways in which natural environments are 'used' by humans for particular purposes. We raise this issue on two important grounds. First, in much of the literature, there seems a tendency toward binary thinking in which nature is 'severed' from humanity (Morton 2017:13). In many of these accounts, 'either nothing is socially constructed, or everything is, and in both cases, "socially" means "by humans"' (2017:10). Indeed, while Brymer and Gray's (2009) 'dance' metaphor may ultimately continue the human versus nature separation – as nature is almost always considered the 'partner' – even 'post-sports', such as Parkour, are

> 'in the first instance[,] a political re-appropriation of commercial urban spaces. Buildings, parks, walkways, dumpsters, steps, and practically any edifice is viewed as an obstacle to be used for spiritual and physical development, and site for disrupting the order of technocapitalist space'. (Atkinson 2009, 183)

Secondly, in thinking about nature as the site of human intervention, these interpretations fall back on a patronizing vision in which nature is judged to be passively encountered; there to be used up and harvested for the purposes of human enjoyment. As a result, nature is reduced to an 'aesthetic judgement' (Urry 1992, 9), rather than a reasoned or principled one, in which we conveniently forget that our use, and over-use of nature can often have dark and disastrous consequences (i.e. disruption of habitats, pollution, etc.). Ecological thinking of this sort is problematic, according to Morton (2007, 98), as it 'offers the illusion of false intimacy that is belied by the immersed yet laid-back aesthetic distance it demands'. In other words, in treating nature as an object of beauty, humans create an artificial distance between 'them' and 'it', which results in the treatment of plants, animals and landscapes as ends rather than means. In the context of nature sports, we would add that such Romantic interpretations have the potential to legitimate long-standing inequality of access, because such inequalities are subsumed by the supposed healing qualities that nature is said to provide (Kay and Laberge 2004). Thus, it is important to remember that while nature sports can provide the opportunity for positive and meaningful interaction, they can also be the site of (further) regimentation, marginalization and oppression (Melo and Gomes 2017).

In view of these criticisms, we adopt a way of thinking that considers how natures and cultures might 'coalesce' (Cherrington and Gregory 2017). That is, how nature(s) both extend and reduce human capacities, and, more specifically, how ultramarathon running is constitutive of a particular type of nature experience that emerges through movement and dialogue (Folch-Serra 1990; Zimmermann and Saura 2017). In particular, we draw on Morton's (2007, 2016) notion of 'Dark Ecology' to illustrate how the subject of our narrative embraces a different type of ecological awareness that is less about an appreciation of the sublime than an openness towards the disgusting, inert and ruthless qualities of his surroundings. In what follows, we contend that this can have profound implications both within and outside of nature sport settings, as it offers a means of decentring Romantic portrayals of nature, while also encouraging more reponsible, caring and accountable attitudes towards the environment.

Methodology: collaborative (Analytic) autoethnography

The analysis that follows is the culmination of a collaborative autoethnography (Martinez and Andreatta 2015; Williams and Jauhari bin Zaini 2016), the purpose of which was to collectively examine the personal experiences of a colleague. Following a series of chance corridor conversations beginning October 2016, the first and third authors established a shared passion for nature sports and agreed to examine this phenomena further. An added impetus was the third author's existing interest in creative writing and critical reflection which he felt were forbidden in scientific publications. This led him to conclude that *real* science puts bias and subjectivity aside (Neuman 1994), and that creative writing, such as the type with which he was engaged in his spare time, was to be enjoyed as a form of 'release' rather than a legitimate mode of academic inquiry. Such experiences are not uncommon, and are reflected in other commentaries on authoethnography which indicate that, despite progressive attitudes towards qualitative research, traditional epistemological and ontological assumptions regarding validity, reliability and generalisability, continue to prevail (Sparkes 2000). However, having partially explored this method of writing in his own research on university basketball (Cherrington 2016), the first author encouraged the third author to bring his own experiences to bear on the cultural context of ultramarathon running.

Following initial discussions, the research followed the five-stage process for collaborative autoethnography outlined in the work of Chang, Ngunjiri, and Hernandez (2013), although in practice our roles and movement through each stage were more dynamic. Having formed our initial research partnership (stage 1) and agreed on our focus (stage 2), we held regular meetings to discuss the significance of the third author's existing reflections that extended back over a 6 year period. At this point, the researchers were engaged in a period of immersion, in which the first author became an active listener, absorbing the third author's stories while offering examples from his own experience to provoke further discussion. Our roles within the research and level of contribution to the personal narrative (stages 3 and 4), therefore, became more clearly delineated as the frequency of our meetings increased. More specifically, it was agreed that the third author's experience of ultramarathon running was integral to the study. Therefore, the first author would make only a partial contribution to the autobiographical data.

This intermediary period was significant for two reasons. Firstly, it enabled the third author to build confidence in the relevance and style of his storytelling, while receiving support and encouragement from two experienced qualitative researchers (first and second authors). During this time, conversations between the first and third authors became very informal, often relating to topics that did not have an immediate relevance to the research (e.g. work, family, or diet). This allowed the researchers to develop signifi-cant rapport which, we would argue, served to temporarily suspend our disciplinary alle-giances and sustain an emerging friendship (Cann and DeMeulenaere 2012). This became pertinent when deciding on the order with which the authors should be listed on the final paper (stage 5), as there were frank and honest discussions about the respective contri-butions, and the manner in which they should be rewarded. Secondly, and perhaps more importantly, by reading the autoethnographic accounts aloud, the first and second authors were able to add new layers of meaning and context to the existing story, which further enriched the ongoing analysis.

Following a period of immersion, the authors began to engage in a narrative thematic analysis (Smith 2016). This process allowed us to explore the layers of meaning that under-pin the third author's perception of reality and make sense of the social worlds around him. Our choice of narrative analysis was predicated on our belief that human beings are 'meaning makers who, in order to interpret, direct, and intelligibly communicate life, configure and constitute their experience and sense of who they are using narratives that the social and cultural world have passed down' (Smith 2016, 260).

The subsequent sections are a rich amalgam of different voices that represents our 'col-lective story' (Richardson 1990, 25), comprising all the meetings - formal and informal, email exchanges and phone conversations that have taken place over the course of 12 months between three people with a shared interest in nature sports. That being said, we are committed to the type of analytic autoethnography outlined by Anderson (2006) and believe, in agreement with Atkinson, Coffey, and Delamont (1999, 57) that autoethnographic work of this kind should not 'lose sight of the ethnographic imperative that we are seeking to understand'. That is, to shed light on 'the complex social worlds that we are only a part (but a part nonetheless)'. Therefore, the overall goal of our analysis, rep-resented in the commentary that follows, was to represent the dialectic between the subject and object of nature sport, while gaining complex insights into the 'nature-cul-tures' (Latour 1993) that transcend the stories themselves.

Running away from the taskscape

Although I've contested a number of races in recent years, Sahara was the last time I can remember being fully-immersed and committed to my training. The early appeal was that ultramarathon represented an unknown; a genuine unfathomable challenge that would test my physical and mental resolve. Having successfully finished the Marathon Des Sables (MDS), and others since, I now know that I am capable of extreme commitment and focus, with a strong mental and physical resilience. The sport of ultramarathon, therefore, became a sport of diminishing returns, and the problem was a question of my motivation.

For considerable time since, I contested races without any real enjoyment. There were moments of beauty, and fleeting elation, but marathons and ultramarathons became formulaic, following the route as a matter of course. The sport that once held so much mystery and intrigue had become stale and dull. Training was due process, for I knew that I could contest a marathon or an ultra, in the hills or on the fell, and drag my lazy feet kicking and screaming around the course in a respectable time. I also knew I could rely on my experience and resolve to bare the fatigue and finish a race that, for many, would be unreasonable without dedicated training. I was running for all the wrong reasons.

I would run through wonderful rolling hills, valleys, snow-capped mountains, green forests, and not enjoy nor appreciate them. Forest floors were reduced to mud and wet leaves and mountains became just another sharp, steep obstacle, littered with dangerous rocks. My lack of dedication had left me intrinsically focused, forcing me to dissociate from my surroundings, perhaps a necessary prerequisite to managing the fatigue. After many months of reflection, facilitated by this writing process, I finally understood that I needed to stop trying to recreate the experiences of my former races.

My journey into ultramarathon, the adventures in the mountains and in the desert, began with a simple desire; to push myself to perform to my potential, in any sport, with no expectations, and no boundaries. So, I decided to rekindle my love of exercise by running shorter races, curbing ultramarathon for a time, and instead focusing on expressing myself authentically and, more importantly, having a pleasurable experience. Finally, I am enjoying running again, because each session has a different focus and a short-term goal. I'm excited to see how far I can push myself.

This change in attitude was manifest in a recent footrace. I competed in a 16 mile trail race through the Derbyshire Peaks. It was a wonderful experience. For the first time in years I was fit and strong enough to enjoy the race; the scenery, the trails, the mountains and trees. The trail was short enough to avoid substantial pain or fatigue, but I was also well-conditioned, and I felt able to push my body without substantial restraint; my conditioning was no longer a boundary between me and a direct experience of the environment. I felt more connected to my surroundings this time.

Reading the race reports from this year's Ultra Machupichu and seeing the pictures of desolate desert and rolling snow-capped mountains, I feel thirsty once more. I could hike or trek the Machu Pichu trail, but for some reason that is relatively less appealing to me. It's important that I am able to run the trail, because running embodies freedom. It's more direct; more primal. Perhaps this is linked to an evolutionary vestigial trait? Does running in nature represent survival, or hunting? When I have good physical fitness, I feel like I can go anywhere and do anything. I have a basic confidence that I have the fitness and engine capacity to sustain the rigours of the environment, and be able to move with it, rather than being stifled by it. Ultimately, there is a conflict between running to push myself, but remaining fit enough to experience nature, directly, without barriers.

In the various dwellings encountered by the author, non-human actors, or 'actants' (Latour 1993) such as mountains, rocks, trails and deserts play a significant role in that they can reveal the frailty of human agency. This is especially pronounced in the passage regarding the changing significance of the author's surroundings, particularly when they suggest that 'the forest floor becomes nothing but mud and wet leaves and the mountains are reduced to steep obstacles, littered with dangerous rocks'. For Latour (1992), these instances of non-human intervention suggest that rocks and leaves, despite being designated as 'natural' phenomena, are as capable of causing human action as anything inherently 'human'. On numerous occasions throughout the author's narrative, he describes the pain that is induced by various non-human obstacles such as hillside trails. In these instances two things happen: first, the agency of the non-human is revealed; second, and, perhaps more significantly, his dependence on such intermediaries in daily life is temporarily exposed - suggesting, paradoxically, that nature is being both *done* and *undone* through the act of running.

Thus, to say that ultramarathon running represents an uncritical harmony with nature is to underplay the reflexive and lived qualities of these phenomena. Here, specific instances of shock, sadness or discomfort may encourage new body projects to be triggered (Crossley 2006), as opposed to the body's relationship with nature being thought of as static. For example, in the above narrative, the author's reflections continually oscillate between feelings of joy on the one hand, and sadness and confusion on the other. In the beginning, he is largely positive about his training and his motivations for competing; there is synergy between his expectations as a competitor (an enjoyable challenge) and his lived experience of each event (the joys of physical resilience). Consequently, he feels compelled to maintain an 'extreme commitment and focus'. However, shortly thereafter he goes on to suggest that certain body techniques (Mauss 1973) somehow become 'pointless' and 'dull' - that the sense of fatigue ingratiated by previous activities had now become 'unreasonable'.

The turning point in this process was his immersion in, and subsequent disenchantment with, the 'taskscape' (Ingold 1997) that emerges within these particular dwellings. Here, it would seem, nature had been *overtasked*, resulting in an inauthentic and impure experience. In one of our meetings, the author described the moment that he came to this realization. Having reached the top of the first hill during a race in the Peak District he stopped to talk to a fellow runner who was struggling with her fitness. He sat for a while as they spoke, sharing experiences of the race thus far, and regaling memories of past events. Having waved good bye to the runner he sat at the top of the hill for a while longer. At this point he began to do something that he would not normally have done. He observed the beautiful colours that surrounded him: the greens of the flora and fauna, and the oranges and purples of the heath. He was astounded by the size and beauty of the surrounding hills and took pleasure in the gentle breeze that was encircling his face, and for the first time in a long time he felt irreverence for nature. It was at this juncture, as he rose to his feet, that he decided to slow his pace and spend more time appreciating his environment, rather than striving to win. His sense of place, to paraphrase Brymer (2015) had been reconstituted from a unfamiliar landscape to one that was aligned with the human experience.

What the discussion herein reveals is exactly what Howe and Morris (2009, 325) concede, in that 'any one site or series of sites within the running taskscape could be differently co-produced at different times and in different places'. In addition, even when dwellings are constructed as taskscapes there remains the possibility for alternative interpretations to emerge. Ultramarathon runners engage with nature in ways that are very different from more orthodox sports, in that the body and the athlete must anticipate and react to the constantly changing environment (Hanold 2016). In so doing, they reveal the need for an expanded understanding of nature that moves away from simple causal explanations in favour of the kind of theorizing that understands nature as a complex virtuality (Thrift 2001). In our author's narrative there is a constant tension between deliberated embodied action (techne) and imagination and spiritedness (thumos) (Heywood 2006), and the more he moves towards the latter the more his activities threaten to disembed the taskscape. It is perhaps for this reason that the author enjoys running instead of hiking, as it requires a closer relationship with the landscape that is more 'direct' and 'primal', and therefore much easier to affect.

Interpassive escape

The beauty of a long, multi-stage race like the Marathon Des Sables (MDS) is that you can truly immerse yourself in the experience. This is true of any multi-stage race, but is compounded in the Sahara by the remote location and the solitude wrought by the arid desert. Under these conditions, my daily routine was quickly stripped to its bare essentials and I lost sight of the aesthetics that usually contrive to distract me from directly experiencing the world. Consequently, the challenge embodied something primal, in which the fabrications of common existence, e.g. money, power, work, relationships, ceased to harbour any significance. The tasks before me compelled a sense of urgency, and my day-to-day concerns were limited to how far I needed to travel, and what I was going to eat. Despite the physical and mental strain I endured, this liberation from civility was more of an escape than any holiday I'd experienced.

The MDS organisers are savvy to the sense of escapism afforded by the environment and the arduous task of traversing it. In preserving the ethos of freedom, runners are encouraged to leave their electronics (mobile devices, cameras, etc.) at home. Fortunately, most contestants preferred the relative isolation of the desert by forgoing their mobile phones, etc. I left mine at the hotel in Morocco, a few hundred miles north, and was delighted with my decision. Those who decided to retain their electronic connection with civilisation observed the site boundaries with respect by making calls to family and loved-ones on the perimeter, away from other competitors. This meant that I wasn't constantly reconnected with the daily existence from which I'd been temporarily emancipated.

When I am running I find myself continually searching for solitude. I am reminded of another, more recent, occasion when I was struck by a sudden sense of isolation. I was about halfway through a rugged and technical trail marathon staged in Yorkshire's Peak District. The ground was muddy; sliced and churned by hundreds of heavy, sodden trail shoes. I was one in a long line of runners trying to keep my footing among the mud and the rocks. I was surrounded by a sea of beautiful green hills, lightly-trodden pathways weaving in all directions into the distance, and the sky was mostly blue with pillows of bright white cloud. At the time, I was naïve as to why I wasn't enjoying the run (despite the aesthetic beauty), but reflected afterwards that it was because the race didn't feel organic; i.e. the process felt contrived and formulaic. I felt disconnected from the environment and restricted as a result.

After a time, we came to a fork in the path at which runners were directed in one direction if they were contesting the half-distance, down a valley to the left between some hills, and in another direction, into a vast clearing, if they were contesting the full marathon distance. I swayed right following the track, leaving the remaining field of runners in my wake. Within minutes I was alone, with only the tall grass, the mud and a handful of cows for company, and my mood lifted. Once I was alone, I felt able to acknowledge the temperate weather and the beautiful views overlooking the vast Peak District. I suddenly embodied a sense of adventure. There were no footsteps to follow here, no definitive path leading me to safety, no restrictions or ties, just endless green grass and a strew of cow shit. I felt free and, finally, this was my adventure.

In the Sahara, moments like these were laced with irony, because there was a wonderful sense of freedom afforded by the environment, but with an imposing sense of purgatory from all the sheer space, and the disconcerting notion that I could shift direction by just a few degrees, miss the checkpoint, and be lost to the desert. There are only a handful on environments on the planet where such a paradox would be possible.

A driving impulse here is the sense of isolation brought about by the author's spontaneous acts of subversion, in which the waymarked track laid out by the event organizers is rejected in favour of his own route. This is equivalent to the situationist notion of drifting, in which movement becomes less automated and is instead characterized as 'locomotion without a goal' (Plant 1992, 121), involving playful, imaginative interactions with the environment. Like the fell-running practices described by Atkinson (2010a, 2010b), ultra-marathons are encountered as a form of scapeland (Lyotard 1989), which 'produce an emancipating experiential awareness of impermanence, emptiness, unconscious remainder and missing presence' (Lyotard 1989, 6). These encounters act as the setting for a number of deviations, in which the runner's body is temporarily detached from the rigid hierarchies of interaction (i.e winning, recognition, reward) and movement (clearly delineated start and end point, performance judged by the clock), and is instead defined by moments of boundary transgression and 'socio-spatial inversion' (Laviolette 2011, 30).

What is significant, however, is that these perversions are predicated on the author's reflexive relationship with nature, and this is dependent on the practitioner being capable of understanding the ideologies controlling their geographical environment (i.e. a realist notion of nature and the manner in which nature is 'tasked') and the effects that these ideological arrangements have on the emotions and behaviour of its inhabitants; a tendency already established in the author's behaviour. Nonetheless, while they still carry an element of risk with regard to the sense of isolation and self-sufficiency that is experienced when negotiating unfamiliar territory, ultramarathon running requires an element of voluntary risk-taking (Stranger 2011) in that the activities that it comprises involve the increased likelihood of fear, anxiety and injury evident, for example, in the final paragraph of the narrative.

For the author, this is precisely the allure of such sports, which explains why he describes these moments as the 'embodiment of adventure'. Atkinson (2011), for instance, argues that running in treacherous and unfamiliar landscapes, as well as the forms of physical suffering that accompany these runs, can induce a sense of vertigo that delivers a momentary disruption in consciousness, inflicting 'a kind of voluptous panic on an otherwise lucid mind' (Caillois 1967, 23 cited in Atkinson [2011, 106]). He continues: 'in all cases, it is a question of surrendering to a kind of spasm, seizure, or shock that destroys reality with sovereign brusqueness' (Caillois 1967, 23 cited in Atkinson [2011, 106]). Lyng (1990) sees this as increasingly important given the predictable nature of contemporary life, in which institutionalized routines, alienation and hyper-commodification are commonplace.

One example where this manifests is in the author's discussion of the Marathon des Sables, in which he celebrates the (optional) removal of mobile phones, describing these as antithetical to the ethos of the event. According to Beal and Smith (2010), this reflects the marketing strategies of most major lifestyle sports corporations, in which the emancipatory potential of authentic, natural spaces is compromised by modern processes of rationalization and commodification. Therefore, the more natural and authentic the event is perceived to be, the more profit is likely to be made in its organization. Indeed, much of the promotional material surrounding Marathon des Sables draws on popular cultural tropes regarding the inherent virtues of the wilderness, in which runners are encouraged to explore their inner selves and contemplate the aesthetics of nature, free from the trappings of modern technology. It is in these instances that an inherent contradiction emerges regarding both the difficulty in maintaining the nature/culture binary and the contentions surrounding romantic notions of escape. That is, in succumbing to the allures of this ideological narrative, the runners are endorsing a 'demodernising impulse', indicating 'a resistance to modernization which is nevertheless at the same time a product of it' (Rosen 1993, 499).

We contend, therefore, that ultramarathon running can be analysed through the notion of 'interpassivity' (Žižek 1997, 111). This is defined as 'believing or enjoying through the other', in which individuals 'break out of the passive observer following a spectacle staged by others, not only to participate actively in the spectacle, but more and more to establish its very rules' (Žižek 1997, 111). This notion allows us to account for the tensions that exist between the de-legitimation and deconstruction of ideological versions of 'nature' conducted by human agents, as described in the first part of this analysis, and the re-reconstructed, re-appropriated (late-capitalist) narratives that appear in the promotion of the Marathon des Sables.

Indeed, according to Žižek (1997), ideologies – such as those surrounding nature (i.e. free from technology, isolated, authentic,) – stand in for impossible-real belief; an idealized but nonetheless believable 'thing' or notion. However, because we are enlightened beings we are also aware that these beliefs are partly constructed, that is to say, fabricated on behalf of the majority. It is for this reason that nature sports participants such as the author in this study choose to celebrate the virtues of nature and, therefore, participate in the perpetuation of ideological narratives, via a process of 'delegation'. This, in turn, acts as a defence mechanism that saves them from admitting what is real (i.e. that it is impossible to truly escape from the urban, technology, etc.). Such modes of existence are more widespread in modern societies, as the pace of life has accelerated and individuals are left searching for ways of decreasing their passivity, and increasing their activity, or rather projecting 'a *semblance* of incessant activity' (Van Oenen 2016, 8). The upshot of this is not one of indifference to, or detachment from, resistance, but rather a form of being which attempts to 'embed passivity within the interactive relation' (Van Oenen 2016, 15) and, therefore, experience life at a slower pace. This becomes increasingly important when we consider the arguments made in the following section, in which we explore the way in which ultramarathon running may encourage alternative, 'darker' readings of nature.

Ultra marathon as dark ecology

Just over seven hours into day four – the 52-mile stage which is sandwiched between a series of marathons – I am making good time but ultimately, my work rate will prove too high. The expanse of Saharan ground underfoot is flat and sandy, littered with rocks and dead trees, and flanked either side by an endless throng of red and yellow mountains and canyons. Yesterday we spent several hours traversing colossal, energy-sapping sand dunes; thick, dense sand clawing at the ankles, trying to pull you under with each and every step. My feet are swollen and bloody. My trainers are drowned in sand and they tear at the skin on my heels, but still I hold a tenacious pace. The midday sun is high in the sky and completely exposed, relentlessly radiating a raw naked heat which slowly boils my blood and cooks my brain. The hot, dry air gradually heats the electrolyte water in my bottle making it undrinkable, and forcing it down makes me nauseated. In about 30 min I'll be too dehydrated to stand.

I've been doing this now for many years. The pain that comes from an ultramarathon is different to the fatigue that manifests during standard exercise. There's the usual peripheral fatigue one feels in the legs, muscular pain and soreness, lethargy and tiredness; but in ultra-marathon there's an altogether more visceral experience; a deep guttural torment that manifests long after most have receded to the sanctuary of their living-rooms, an affliction that your body slowly rejects and fights with each passing mile. This extreme fatigue used to scare me, but I now recognize it as an old foe, not to be resented, but accepted as a welcome companion, because it's in these moments of fatigue and anguish and vulnerability, your soul stripped-bare, that you're given the chance to respond, endure, and learn your true self-worth.

I vividly recall an occasion, during the opening days of the race, when I ran into a large clearing that was speckled with dead plants and other foliage, and there, half immersed by the convections of sand, was a complete and undamaged camel skeleton. Its naked bones jutted from the ground, its curved ribcage picked-clean by the process of time. I was struck with the sudden and profound realisation that I really was in the desert.

There were hundreds of other contestants in this race, but there were substantial stretches of time and space when I saw nothing but miles of dry, flat, arid desert land. Quite often, between the various checkpoints, my only semblance of humanity manifested when another runner, several miles away, passed as a fleeting-spec in my peripheral vision. These were the moments I most valued during the race; traversing alone the desert plains that few before me had travelled as the sun slowly cooked my central nervous system, watched indifferently by colossal desert canyons that cared not for my presence, existence, or survival. My only company were the critters (beetles, scorpians and snakes) buried in the sand underfoot. I followed the generally-prescribed route, but from time-to-time I was compelled to take a somewhat drunken, swaying path on the landscape in the vain hope that I was, perhaps, the only person ever to have trodden this terrain. My footsteps crunched lightly on the ground as I moved, but were instantaneously lost to the vast emptiness. There was an overwhelming sense of the here and now, a mindfulness, that this step, in this place, at this time, would never be repeated.

This reflection contains many of the observations listed in other sections: the author's disenchantment with the taskscape; the intervening presence of non-humans (i.e. trainers, 'critters') and the overwhelming sense of (interpassive) escape brought on by running in the desert. At the same time, however, there is a distinct change in tone during this passage which suggests an altogether different relationship with nature. The author's words are sombre, the tone is bleak, and the movements being described seem laboured and painful. These are not the words of a person who feels harmony with nature (Brymer and Gray 2009), nor are they the words of someone who believes that these landscapes can be easily 'tasked' (Howe and Morris 2009). Furthermore, the transcendence, if any is experienced, is unlike that experienced by Atkinson's (2011, 2016) fell-runners. It is not joyful and uplifting but terrifying and ugly. Nature is not seen as a friend, but neither is it seen as an enemy, but rather a 'foe' that is hostile and unfriendly. In a word, nature is 'dark' (Morton 2007, 2010, 2016).

Morton's (2007, 104) dark ecology is a 'perverse, melancholy ethics that refuses to digest the object into an ideal form'. It is a mode of existence in which nature is treated as strange rather than familiar, and the individual is encouraged to question reified versions of nature in both their aesthetic and experiential forms. As Morton (2016, 125) explains:

> ecological awareness is dark, insofar as its essence is unspeakable. It is dark, insofar as illumination leads to a greater sense of entrapment. It is dark, because it compels us to recognise the melancholic wounds that make us up – the shocks and traumas and cataclysms that have made oxygen for our lungs to breathe, lungs out of swim bladders, and crushing, humiliating reason out of human domination on earth. But is it is also dark because it is weird.

For Žižek (2015), achieving such ecological awareness requires us to dispense with three orthodox perceptions. Firstly, we must learn to dispense with the notion that we are able to encounter a pure nature, untouched by human intervention. This becomes increasingly significant in the era of the anthropocene (Wark 2015), in which human activity is said to become a salient factor in geological change. This was evident, for instance, in the previous section when we described the way in which ultra-running landscapes can be constructed in rationally organized ways in the interests of capital accumulation. The number of people now inhabiting planet Earth, combined with our appetite for expansion and exploration, demonstrates the end of nature as an independent force. We are no longer, therefore, able to think of ourselves as a species that is influenced by larger forces - 'now we are those larger forces' (McKibben 2003, xiv).

Secondly, we must learn that human activity cannot be separated from nature's influence. 'Nature is not an abstract "'in itself'" but primarily the counterforce that we encounter in our labour' (Žižek 2015, 4), as per the manner in which non-humans intervene in the author's experience of a run. In this segment of narrative, we learn of the agency that is being exercised by the 'colossal, energy sapping sand dunes' and how the 'hot, dry air' heats the electrolytes in his water bottle to the point that it becomes undrinkable. In doing so, the various 'intermediaries' violently interrupt the 'semiotic flows' (Michael 2001, 116) between runner and the landscape, which make it difficult for the author to appreciate the sublime characteristics of nature. The level of pain induced by these obstacles is 'more visceral' than other forms of exercise, in that it permeates every ounce of his muscles, and in these moments the author begins to appreciate the immense power of nature as manifest through his bodily fatigue. This sense of awe is inherently perverse, as in realizing how deeply connected we are to nature, we both surrender ourselves to non-human objects while being humbled by the fragile and unstable nature of human experience (Morton 2016).

However, the most important feature of a dark ecological awareness, and the one that requires the biggest leap of faith, is to dispense with the fiction of a stable nature, disturbed by human intervention. Nature is already disturbed and out of joint, and needs to be recognized as such if we are to appreciate its profound effect(s) on human life (Wark 2015; Morton 2016). This is most evident in the author's recollection of the dead camel in the desert, in which the baron, savage and destructive qualities of nature are laid bare to his audience. At this moment, the author discovers the thing that he has been trying to avoid – death and decapitation, which is arguably more pointed given the author's professional background as a practitioner of health and wellbeing. Yet, despite this sense of melancholia, the author reaches the profound realization that he 'really was in the desert'. This further illustrates how dark ecological experiences such as those that are encouraged by ultramarathon running can stimulate a disruption in the aesthetic-causal notion of nature that can shock and disturb the participant in perverse yet positive ways. In addition, it requires the 'necessarily queer idea that we want to stay with a dying world' (Morton 2007, 185). In witnessing the skeleton remains of the camel, the author is encouraged to consider his own mortality while facing up to the realization that he is deeply implicated in this process of death and decay.

Conclusion

This article has sought to consider how nature and culture coalesce in the sport of ultramarathon running. Primarily, this aim was presented as a way of navigating the distinction between nature and culture, by exploring how such a distinction is dissolved in the ways in which a participant lost their sense of individuality as it merged with the natural surroundings.

Consequently, while nature sports can entail elements of 'nature mysticism' (Parry et al. 2007, 104), we were unconvinced by accounts that conceptualized nature's 'mysticism', and felt that the meaning of these transcendental practices extended beyond the 'unadulterated now' (Thorpe and Rinehart 2010, 4). Instead, one of the most important implications of nature's mysticism is that it is deeply tied to action and commitment. Accordingly, in view of both the literature and the author's narrative, the following experiences were identified.

First, in conjunction with other extreme nature sports, the author's accounts of ultramarathon running provided a clear interpretation of how the sport is closely related to nature and, in particular, the environments in which the sport takes place. Crucial here were the affordances (Ingold 2000) that allowed the author to engage practically with the lived environment, both constraining and accommodating his behaviour. The mountains, forests and valleys were perceived to be beautiful and picturesque, a relationship that was 'dialogical' (Folch-Serra 1990) in that the meanings attached to any given landscape were both 'anchored' and 'destabilized' as the author's body encountered them. Accordingly, rather than viewing nature as a taskscape, from which the 'task' of running in the quickest time possible could be achieved, for the author, an alternative account was presented, whereby the 'task' no longer mattered. Despite the long hours of training, the author was willing to permit a more 'direct' relationship with nature through which the unfamiliarity of the environment was directly appreciated. At the core of this experience was a partial merging with his surroundings, in which nature moved from being an 'other over there', to being fused with the self in the 'here and now' (Langer 1990).

Second, we identified a level of interpassivity in the author's experiences. That is, while the author lamented the routine trappings of everyday life in Western late-capitalist societies, in which technology, work and over-crowded cities are ubiquitous, and the negative connotations associated with his 'daily routine' and the sense of meaningless derived from modern 'fabrications' such as 'money, power, and work' prevailed, the sense of escape from these various 'contrivances' was reflected in the primal and immersive experience of ultramarathon running. Nevertheless, what emerged from such accounts was how these experiences centred on the extent to which the author's narrative paradoxically highlighted underlying contentions regarding the desire to use ultramarathon as a form of escapism. That is, while the sports were marketed as a form of escapism, such 'escape' and liberation was a constitutive feature of the sport's marketing. While these events were rationalized and marketed as 'escapist' pursuits, the author interpassively submitted to the illegitimacy of such hegemonic interpretations. Indeed, it was this sense of contradiction which underscored a 'darker' reading of nature.

Accordingly, in the penultimate section, we proposed that the author's experiences could be considered in accordance with Morton's 'dark ecology'. The profound effect of seeing the decayed remains of a dead camel – an affect that emphasized the author's realization that he was 'in the desert' – highlighted how 'nature' was no longer 'out there' and no longer an environment from which the task of running was simply completed. Instead, the binary between nature and culture, and between self and nature, had been dissolved through a sense of melancholia and the abject realization of nature's 'dark ecology'.

Certainly, the application of Morton's 'dark ecology' to the case of ultramarathon running is not an attempt to present nature as inherently exotic and mysterious, a perspective that, while acknowledging the 'threat' posed by nature, simply reinstates a privileged neocolonial, western-centric appreciation (Graulund 2006). Instead, Morton's (2007, 2010) perspective is one that promotes a form of ecological entanglement. Here, nature is not neutral, but rather, it is always defined, shaped and interpreted by the spaces in which it appears. Consequently, while Morton (2007, 2010, 2016) highlights that recent interpretations of nature have stressed the ecological impact of human beings, in contrast, he has emphasized the interdependence between humans and nature.

It is here that the experience of nature in ultramarathon running can be understood in accordance with Morton's notion of the 'mesh' (Morton 2010). Like a mesh, the concept of nature is both hard and delicate. Its premise is firmly held and staunchly defended, but can gradually unravel through reflexive embodied practice(s) such as those described in this paper. It is also a material that is characterized by a series of dense interconnections which are difficult to clearly delineate. Since the author is so embedded in this mesh, it is difficult to ascertain where nature ends and humanity begins. His feet become bloody from the sand in his shoes, the dunes swell his ankles, and the sun cooks his brain, resulting in nausea and panic, but as the human and non-human interact they become part of the same fabric. This merger carries with it a 'perilous sense of vulnerability' (Morton 2010, 25), but it is these moments that the runners crave. They thrive off a baroque sensibility in which the body is construed as a 'site of impurity and corruptibility, at once the locus of pleasure and suffering, of the most beautiful seductions and the basest deceptions' (Clark 2001, 18). As a consequence, ultramarathon running helps the author to realize nature for what it is – a disparate number of interconnected factors that never add up to a coherent whole.

Accordingly, we argue that such a realization is closely tied to notions of reflexivity and in the interdependence that locates such reflexivity as forged in/with nature. As noted above, it is through reflexivity that the concept of nature both exists, but also, unravels. For Atkinson (2010a, 1259), reflexivity 'is first achieved when one is literally forced to face the "essence" of one's self through rigorous movement and guided meditation'. As a form of 'knowing', reflexivity has been considered in relation to the way it is embodied (Burns 2003) so that individual actions are subject to interpretation.

Nevertheless, while remaining critical of these perspectives, we concur with Macnaghten and Urry (1998, 157 [italics added]) that 'notions of reflexivity need to be connected to people's sense of agency, that is, to their felt ability to structure or influence events through *their actions*'. Indeed, it is in accounting for these 'actions' that understandings of reflexivity can be ecologically reconfigured so that the relationship between nature, culture and human action(s) can be collectively considered. Moreover, it is by examining accounts of these actions that Morton's 'dark ecology' can be extended in the context of sport.

For instance, paradigmatically, Morton's (2013) work follows the 'object-oriented ontology' perspective (OOO). This approach asserts that 'The world is made of things that elude any other kind of knowing' (Wark 2017, 270) and that 'objects', whether these be real or fictional, human or non-human, are autonomous and exist beyond human interpretation. The obverse of an object means that no object is ever complete. By way of explanation, Wark (2017) highlights how Morton uses an example from Husserl to make sense of this withdrawal. By 'Holding a coin, one sees its face. But you can't see the other side of the coin *as the other side*. You can only flip it over and make it *this side*.' (Wark 2017, 272 [italics in original]).

While we remain open to Morton's 'dark ecology', and the benefits that it can have when studying nature and sport, we are also open to Ward's critique that the OOO approach 'continually represses … the labour or praxis via which a thing is known' (Wark 2017, 272). For Wark (2017), it is 'a mix of the human and inhuman' which provides a form of praxis that allows, in the first instance, for the 'object' – 'nature' – to be contemplated through action (Macnaghten and Urry 1998).

When applied to the current study, it is clear that such praxis forms an integral part of the author's understanding of 'nature' as some*thing* that is indelibly linked to the activity of ultramarathon running and which dissolves any nature and culture dichotomy. As noted by Wark (2017), this is not a simple reinsertion of the subject-object relationship, but rather, a consideration of the ways in which nature and society are interdependently conceived to the point that such distinctions can be upheld and dissolved through embodied actions that orientate individuals' perception of where nature begins and ends. It is these practices and actions (Macnaghten and Urry 1998) – processes of orientation (Black 2018) – that are performed through levels of praxis (taskscape/non-taskscape, interpassive and dark) and which serve to locate 'our' orientation to nature.

Notes

1. 'Spartan Race' is a franchised obstacle race, which began in the US.
2. Ultramarathons do not always take place in 'natural' environments. The actual criterion for classification is broad, and the substance of a given ultramarathon comprises absolute race distance, terrain, environmental conditions and challenge difficulty.
3. Throughout this paper we use imperial measures of distance. For those readers more familiar with the metric system, 1 mile is approximately equal to 1.7 kilometres.

Disclosure statement

No potential conflict of interest was reported by the authors.

References

Allen-Collinson, Jacquelyn. 2011. "Feminist Phenomenology and the Woman in the Running Body." *Sport, Ethics and Philosophy* 5 (3): 297–313.

Allen-Collinson, Jacquelyn, and John Hockey. 2010. "Feeling the Way: Notes Toward a Haptic Phenomenology of Distance Running and Scuba Diving." *International Review for the Sociology of Sport* 46 (3): 330–345.

Allen-Collinson, Jacquelyn, and Helen Owton. 2014. "Take a Deep Breath: Asthma, Sporting Embodiment, the Senses and 'Auditory Work'." *International Review for the Sociology of Sport* 49 (5): 592–608.

Anderson, Leon. 2006. "Analytic Autoethnography." *Journal of Contemporary Ethnography* 35 (4): 373–395.

Arnould, E. J., and L. L. Price. 1993. "River Magic: Extraordinary Experiences and the Extended Service Encounter." *Journal of Consumer Research* 20 (1): 24–45.

Atkinson, Michael. 2009. "Parkour, Anarcho- Environmentalism, and Poiesis." *Journal of Sport and Social Issues* 33 (2): 169–194.

Atkinson, Michael. 2010a. "Entering Scapeland: Yoga, Fell and Post-sport Physical Cultures." *Sport in Society* 13 (7-8): 1249–1267.

Atkinson, Michael. 2010b. "Fell Running in Post-Sport Territories." *Qualitative Research in Sport and Exercise* 2 (2): 109–132.

Atkinson, Michael. 2011. "Fell Running and Voluptous Panic." *American Journal of Play* 4 (1): 100–120.

Atkinson, Michael. 2016. "The Loneliness of the Fell Runner." In *Researching Embodied Sport: Exploring Movement Cultures*, edited by Ian Wellard, 47–63. London: Routledge.

Atkinson, Paul, Amanda Coffey, and Sara Delamont. 1999. "Ethnography – Post, Past, and Present." *Journal of Contemporary Ethnography* 28 (5): 460–471.

Bale, John. 2004. *Running Cultures: Racing in Time and Space*. London: Routledge.

Beal, Becky, and Maureen M. Smith. 2010. "Maverick's: Big-wave Surfing and the Dynamic of 'Nothing' and 'Something'." *Sport in Society* 13 (7): 1102–1116.

Black, Jack. 2018. "Reflexivity or Orientation? Collective Memories in the Australian, Canadian and New Zealand National Press." *Memory Studies*. doi:10.1177/1750698017749978.

Brymer, Eric. 2015. "Phenomenology of Extreme Sports in Natural Landscapes." In *Landscapes of Leisure*, edited by Sean Gammon, and Sam Elkington, 135–147. Basingstoke: Palgrave Macmillan.

Brymer, Eric, and Tonia Gray. 2009. "Dancing with Nature: Rhythm and Harmony in Extreme Sport Participation." *Journal of Adventure Education and Outdoor Learning* 9 (2): 135–149.

Brymer, Eric, and Tonia Gray. 2010. "Developing an Intimate 'Relationship' with Nature through Extreme Sports Participation." *Leisure/Loisir* 34 (4): 361–374.

Burns, Maree. 2003. "Interviewing: Embodied Communication." *Feminism and Psychology* 13 (2): 229–236.

Caillois, Roger. 1967. *Les jeux et les hommes. Le masque et le vertige*. Paris: Librairie Gallimard.

Cann, Colette N., and Eric J. DeMeulenaere. 2012. "Critical Co-Constructed Autoethnography." *Cultural Studies: Critical Methodologies* 12 (2): 146–158.

Chang, H., F. W. Ngunjiri, and K. C. Hernandez. 2013. *Collaborative Autoethnography*. Walnut Creek, CA: Left Coast Press.

Cherrington, Jim. 2016. "Basketball, Embodiment and the Everyday." In *Researching Embodied Sport: Exploring Movement Cultures*, edited by Ian Wellard, 101–117. London: Routledge.

Cherrington, James, and Maxine Gregory. 2017. "Where Nature and Culture Coalesce: The Social, Cultural and Political Impact of Outdoor Recreation in Sheffield." In *Lifestyle Sport and Public Policy*, edited by Daniel Turner, and Sandro Carnicelli, 100–116. London: Routledge.

Cidell, Julie. 2014. "Running Road Races as Transgressive Event Mobilities." *Social & Cultural Geography* 15 (5): 571–583.

Clark, N. 2001. "'Botanizing on the Asphalt'? The Complex Life of Cosmopolitan Bodies." In *Bodies of Nature*, edited by Phil Macnaghten, and John Urry, 12–33. London: Sage.

Crossley, Nick. 2006. *Reflexive Embodiment in Contemporary Societies*. Open University Press: Buckingham.

Csikszentmihalyi, Mihaly, Phillip Latter, and Christine Duranso. 2017. *Running Flow*. Champaign, IL: Human Kinetics.

Folch-Serra, M. 1990. "Place, Voice, Space – Bakhtin, Mikhail Dialogical Landscape." *Environment and Planning D-Society & Space* 8 (3): 255–274.

Graulund, Rune. 2006. "Travelling the Desert: Desert Travel Writing as Indicator Species." *Studies in Travel Writing* 10 (2): 141–159.

Hanold, Maylon. 2016. "Ultrarunning: Space, Place, and Social Experience." In *Endurance Running: A Socio-cultural Explanation*, edited by William Bridel, Pirkko Markula, and Jim Denison, 181–195. Abingdon: Routledge.

Hashimoto, M., N. Hagura, T. Kuriyama, and M. Nishiyamai. 2006. "Motivations and Psychological Characteristics of Japanese Ultra-marathon Runners Using Myers-Briggs Type Indicator." *Japanese Journal of Health and Human Ecology* 72 (1): 15–24.

Heywood, Ian. 2006. "Climbing Monsters: Excess and Restraint in Contemporary Rock Climbing." *Leisure Studies* 25 (4): 455–467.

Hockey, John, and Jacquelyn Allen-Collinson. 2016. "Digging in: The Sociological Phenomenology of 'Doing Endurance' in Distance-running." In *Endurance Running: A Socio-cultural Explanation*, edited by William Bridel, Pirkko Markula, and Jim Denison, 227–242. Abingdon: Routledge.

Hoffman, M., J. Ong, and G. Wang. 2010. "Historical Analysis of Participation in 161 km Ultramarathons in North America." *The International Journal of the History of Sport* 27 (11): 1877–1891.

Howe, David. P. 2016. "Hitting a Purple Patch: Building High Performance Runners at Runtleborough University." In *Endurance Running: A Socio-cultural Explanation*, edited by William Bridel, Pirkko Markula, and Jim Denison, 212–226. Abingdon: Routledge.

Howe, David. P., and Carol Morris. 2009. "An Exploration of the Co-production of Performance Running Bodies and Natures Within 'Running Taskscapes'." *Journal of Sport and Social Issues* 33 (3): 308–330.

Ingold, Tim. 1997. "Life Beyond the Edge of Nature? Or the Mirage of Society." In *The Mark of the Social*, edited by John D. Greenwood, 231–252. Lanham: Rowman & Littlefield.

Ingold, Tim. 2000. *The Perception of the Environment: Essays on Livelihood, Dwelling and Skill*. London: Routledge.

Kay, Joanne, and Suzanne Laberge. 2004. "Mandatory Equipment: Women in Adventure Racing." In *Understanding Lifestyle Sports: Consumption, Identity and Difference*, edited by Belinda Wheaton, 154–175. London: Routledge.

Krein, Kevin. 2008. "Sport, Nature and Worldmaking." *Sport Ethics and Philosophy* 2 (3): 285–301.

Krein, Kevin. 2014. "Nature Sports." *Journal of the Philosophy of Sport* 41 (2): 193–208.

Langer, Monika. 1990. "Merleau-Ponty and Deep Ecology." In *Ontology and Alterity in Merleau-Ponty*, edited by Gallen A. Johnson, and Michael B. Smith, 115–129. Evanston, IL: NorthWestern University Press.

Latour, Bruno. 1992. "Where are the Missing Masses? The Sociology of a Few Mundane Artifacts." In *Shaping Technology/Building Society: Studies in Sociotechnical Change*, edited by Wiebe E. Bijker, and John Law, 225–258. Cambridge, MA: MIT Press.

Latour, Bruno. 1993. *We Have Never Been Modern*. Cambridge, MA: Harvard University Press.

Latour, Bruno. 2004. *Politics of Nature: How to Bring the Sciences into Democracy*. London: Harvard University Press.

Laviolette, Patrick. 2011. *Extreme Landscapes of Leisure: Not a Hap-hazardous Sport*. Burlington, VT: Ashgate.

Lefebvre, Henri. 1991. *The Production of Space*. Oxford: Blackwell.

Lyng, Stephen. 1990. "Edgework: A Social Psychological Analysis of Voluntary Risk Taking." *American Journal of Sociology* 95 (4): 851–886.

Lyotard, Jean-Francois. 1989. "Scapeland." In *The Lyotard Reader*, edited by Andrew Benjamin, 212–219. Oxford: Blackwell.

Macnaghten, Phil, and John Urry. 1998. *Contested Natures*. London: Sage.

Martinez, A., and Maria Marta Andreatta. 2015. "'It's My Body and My Life': A Dialogued Collaborative Autoethnography." *Cultural Studies-Critical Methodologies* 15 (3): 224–232.

Mauss, Marcel. 1973. "Techniques of the Body." *Economy and Society* 2 (1): 70–88.

McKibben, Bill. 2003 [1990]. *The End of Nature: Humanity, Climate Change and the Natural World*. London: Bloomsbury Publishing.

Melo, Ricardo, and Rui Machado Gomes. 2017. "Nature Sports Participation: Understanding Demand, Practice Profile, Motivations and Constraints." *European Journal of Tourism Research* 16: 108–135.

Michael, M. 2001. "These Boots are Made for Walking ... Mundane Technology the Body and Human-Environment Relations." In *Bodies of Nature*, edited by Phil Macnaghten, and John Urry, 107–127. London: Sage.

Monbiot, George. 2016. *How did we get into this Mess?: Politics, Equality, Nature*. London; Brooklyn, NY: Verso.

Morton, Timothy. 2007. *Ecology without Nature*. London: Harvard University Press.

Morton, Timothy. 2010. *The Ecological Thought*. London: Harvard University Press.

Morton, Timothy. 2013. *Hyperobjects: Philosophy and Ecology after the End of the World*. Minneapolis: University of Minnesota Press.

Morton, Timothy. 2016. *Dark Ecology: For a Logic of Future Coexistence*. New York: Columbia University Press.

Morton, Timothy. 2017. *Humankind: Solidarity with Nonhuman People*. London: Verso.

Neuman, William. 1994. *Social Research Methods: Qualitative and Quantitative Approaches*. Needham Heights, MA: Allyn and Bacon.

Parry, Jim, Simon Robinson, Nick J. Watson, and Mark Nesti. 2007. *Sport and Spirituality: An Introduction*. London: Routledge.

Plant, Sadie. 1992. *The Most Radical Gesture: The Situationist International in a Postmodern age*. London: Routledge.

Pronger, Brian. 1998. "Post - Sport: Transgressing Boundaries in Physical Culture." In *Sport and Postmodern Times*, edited by Genevieve Rail, 277–301. Albany: State University of New York Press.

Richardson, Laurel. 1990. *Writing Strategies: Researching Diverse Audiences*. London: Sage.

Rosen, Paul. 1993. "The Social Construction of Mountain Bikes – Technology and Postmodernity in the Cycle Industry." *Social Studies of Science* 23 (3): 479–513.

Shipway, Richard, and Immy Holloway. 2010. "Running Free: Embracing a Healthy Lifestyle through Distance Running." *Perspectives in Public Health* 130 (6): 270–276.

Smith, B. 2016. "Narrative Analysis in Sport and Exercise: How Can it Be Done?" In *Routledge Handbook of Qualitative Research in Sport and Exercise*, edited by Brett Smith, and Andrew C. Sparkes, 260–274. London: Routledge.

Sparkes, Andrew C. 2000. "Autoethnography and Narratives of Self: Reflections on Criteria in Action." *Sociology of Sport Journal* 17: 21–43.

Stranger, Mark. 2011. *Surfing Life: Surface, Substructure and the Commodification of the Sublime*. Burlington, VT: Ashgate.

Thorpe, Holly, and Robert Rinehart. 2010. "Alternative Sport and Affect: Non-representational Theory Examined." *Sport in Society* 13 (7-8): 1268–1291.

Thrift, Nigel. 2001. "Still Life in Nearly Present Time: The Object of Nature." In *Bodies in Nature*, edited by Phil Macnaghten, and John Urry, 34–58. London: Sage.

Urry, John. 1992. "The Tourist Gaze and the Environment." *Theory Culture & Society* 9 (3): 1–26.

Van Oenen, Gijs. 2016. "Interpassivity Revisited: A Critical and Historical Reappraisal of Interpassive Phenomena." *International Journal of Zizek Studies* 2 (2): 1–16.

Wark, McKenzie. 2015. *Molecular Red: Theory for the Anthropocene*. London: Verso.

Wark, McKenzie. 2017. *General Intellects: Twenty-One Thinkers for the Twenty-First Century*. London: Verso.

Weedon, Gavin. 2016. "On the Entangled Origins of mud Running: 'Overcivilization', Physical Culture, and Overcoming Obstacles in the Spartan Race." In *Endurance Running: A Socio-cultural Explanation*, edited by William Bridel, Pirkko Markula, and Jim Denison, 35–49. Abingdon: Routledge.

Williams, J. Patrick, and Muhammad Kamal Jauhari bin Zaini. 2016. "Rude Boy Subculture, Critical Pedagogy, and the Collaborative Construction of an Analytic and Evocative Autoethnography." *Journal of Contemporary Ethnography* 45 (1): 34–59.

Zimmermann, Ana, and Soraia Saura. 2017. "Body, Environment and Adventure: Experience and Spatiality." *Sport, Ethics and Philosophy* 11 (2): 155–168.

Žižek, Slavoj. 1997. *The Plague of Fantasies*. London: Verso.

Žižek, Slavoj. 2015. "Ecology against Mother Nature: Slavoj Zizek on *Molecular Red*" *Verso Blog*, May 26. Accessed 18 July 2017. https://www.versobooks.com/blogs/2007-ecology-against-mother-nature-slavoj-zizek-on-molecular-red.

Index